RUSSIA'S
WESTERN BORDERLANDS,
1710-1870

RUSSIA'S WESTERN BORDERLANDS, 1710-1870

EDWARD C. THADEN

with the collaboration of

MARIANNA FORSTER THADEN

Princeton University Press
Princeton, New Jersey

Published by Princeton University Press, 41 William Street,
Princeton, New Jersey 08540
In the United Kingdom: Princeton University Press, Guildford,
Surrey

Library of Congress Cataloging in Publication Data will be
found on the last printed page of this book

ISBN-0-691-05420-7

This book has been composed in Linotron Caledonia and Bodoni

Clothbound editions of Princeton University Press Books
are printed on acid-free paper, and binding materials are
chosen for strength and durability

Printed in the United States of America by Princeton University Press
Princeton, New Jersey

CONTENTS

PREFACE

In a recent study of Russification in the Baltic provinces and Finland, four coauthors and I noted that the previous development of separate laws, customs, economies, institutions, and social structures among the Baltic Germans, Estonians, Finns, Latvians, and Swedes of this region ruled out the possibility of easy victories for Russification. Our principal concerns in this study were, however, the formulation and implementation of government policy and the responses of Finns, Estonians, Latvians, and Baltic Germans to Russification. We did not include in our study a systematic discussion of the responses to Russification of the Belorussians, Lithuanians, Poles, and Ukrainians of the former lands of the Polish-Lithuanian Commonwealth that Russia acquired between 1772 and 1815; nor did we examine in any detail the earlier history of the western borderlands of the Russian Empire. It is especially this earlier history, I believe, that helps us to understand why certain national and social groups succeeded to the extent they did in resisting Russificatory pressures during the years 1855-1914.

In this book I focus on two aspects of the history of the Baltic provinces, Belorussia, Congress Poland, Finland, Lithuania, and the Right-Bank Ukraine during the century and a half that preceded Russification: (1) the efforts of the Russian government to integrate these borderlands into the administrative-legal structure of the empire; and (2) the efforts of German, Polish, and Swedish elites to defend their traditional rights and privileges, to preserve the separate identity of their native provinces, and to isolate local society from the rest of the empire. The Russian government did not pursue its policy of administrative centralization consistently and resolutely. It had too high a regard for the local laws and institutions of these borderlands, and in them it continued to rely on coopted German, Polish, and Swedish elites to maintain social order. At the same time, the efforts of traditional borderland elites to resist centralizing pressures and to harness the forces of change locally for their own particular purposes unwittingly unleashed social and economic forces that favored the emergence of new native elites. By the 1860s a number of these new elites had become an important factor in the social, economic, and cultural life of the western borderlands.

vii

Both old and new elites operated within the traditional framework of institutions and political entities that no longer exist: namely, the *lantdag, Landtage,* Sejm, and *sejmiki* of the privileged estates of the Grand Duchy of Finland, the *Ritterschaften* of Estland, Kurland, and Livland, and the *szlachta* of the Polish-Lithuanian Commonwealth, Congress Poland, and the western *gubernii.* If we are to understand the persistence of particularism in this area, we must try to forget the political and national geography of the twentieth century and use an atlas published in Mitau (Jelgava), Wilno (Vil'na, Vilnius), Lwów (Lemberg, L'viv, L'vov), Witebsk (Vitebsk), or Åbo (Turku) in, let us say, 1795. I have, therefore, decided not to use place names transliterated from the Russian but those that would have been familiar to educated Germans, Poles, and Swedes living in these borderlands early in the nineteenth century. For the Belorussian, Estonian, Finnish, Latvian, Lithuanian, Russian, and Ukrainian forms of these place names, see the glossary at the end of this study. Dates are given according to the official Julian calendar of the Russian Empire (eleven days earlier than the Gregorian calendar in the eighteenth century and twelve in the nineteenth).

I begin in 1710, when Russia acquired Estland and Livland, and end in 1870, by which time Russia had definitely decided, in principle at least, on a policy of centralization and Russification in these borderlands. This policy was not applied immediately to Finland, but the Finns then failed to obtain the ironclad and constitutional guarantee of their autonomy they desired.

I will not discuss in detail two regions that might seem geographically and historically within the western borderlands of the empire: namely, Bessarabia and the Left-Bank Ukraine. Russia acquired Bessarabia in 1812, then recognizing the laws, customs, and autonomy of this borderland; however, Russian officials soon lost faith in the ability of the local Rumanian Boyars to manage their own affairs and abolished Bessarabian autonomy in 1828. In the Left-Bank Ukraine, Cossack rights and privileges steadily eroded following the defection of Mazepa to Charles XII in 1708, and by the early nineteenth century this area had been pretty much integrated into the social, economic, and political structure of the Russian empire. It should be pointed out, however, that the history of Russia's relations with privileged borderlands began in the Left-Bank Ukraine with the Treaty of Pereiaslav of 1654, more than a half century before Peter the Great annexed Estland and Livland in 1710.

Chicago, February 1984

ACKNOWLEDGMENTS

THE RESEARCH for this study was done in Finland, Germany, Poland, the Soviet Union, and the United States. Grants from the American Council of Learned Societies and the International Research and Exchanges Board supported my research at the Lenin, RSFSR Historical, and Saltykov-Shchedrin libraries, the Pushkinskii dom, and the Central State Historical Archives in Leningrad and Moscow. The Fulbright-Hays Program provided funding for further work at the Bremen, Göttingen, Helsinki, Marburg, and Warsaw university libraries, the Johann-Gottfried-Herder-Institut, the Finnish National Archives, and the District (Wojewódzkie) State Archive in Lublin, Poland. In Chicago the excellent collections of the University of Chicago and the University of Illinois were at my disposal. In Washington, D.C., I worked at the Library of Congress while a fellow at the Woodrow Wilson International Center for Scholars. It is a pleasure to thank the organizations that have supported and the staffs of the libraries and archives that have assisted me in pursuing my research.

James H. Billington, the director of the Wilson Center, Zdenek V. David, the Center's librarian, and Abbott Gleason, then secretary of the Kennan Institute for Advanced Russian Studies, opened for me the rich research and intellectual resources of the nation's capital. In June 1980 I made an oral presentation at the Wilson Center of my work-in-progress, at which time I greatly benefited from the viewpoints expressed by commentators Vlad Georgescu, then a fellow at the Center, and Orest Pelech, the Bibliographer for Russia and Eastern Europe, Princeton University.

The article I published in the *Journal of Baltic Studies* in 1981 ("Estland, Livland, and the Ukraine: Reflections on Eighteenth-Century Autonomy," 12: 311-17) has been incorporated into Chapter 1 with the permission of JBS editor Toivo U. Raun. On several occasions he has been helpful in answering questions concerning the demographic history of Estonia. W. Bruce Lincoln of Northern Illinois University made available to me his xerox copy of N. A. Miliutin's *Issledovaniia v Tsarstve Pol'skom po vysochaishemu poveleniiu*, an important source for studying Russian policy in Congress Poland during the 1860s. The constructive comments of John A. Armstrong have contributed much to the formulation of my concluding remarks. My

Acknowledgments

colleague John Kulczycki read the Polish chapters of this study and offered useful comments and criticism. Sandra Wearne of the UIC Computer Center has been of indispensable assistance to me and my collaborator in enabling us to use the university computer facilities for the production of this monograph.

My thanks also go to the competent and efficient staff of Princeton University Press, namely, to Gail Ullman for coordinating the publication of two manuscripts on the history of Russia's western borderlands; to Gretchen Oberfranc; and to Alice Calaprice for seeing this manuscript through the editorial process and the final stages of publication.

ABBREVIATIONS

BM   *Baltische Monatsschrift*, Riga, 1859-1913, vols. 1-76. The
            volumes for 1914-1915 and 1927-1931 are referred to
            by year of publication, not volume number. The BM
            was continued under the title *Baltische Monatshefte*
            between 1932 and 1939.

CHTENIIA   *Chteniia v imperatorskom obshchestve istorii i drev-
            nostei pri Moskovskom universitete*, 1846-1918, vols. 1-
            264.

DBL   *Deutschbaltisches biographisches Lexikon 1710-1960.*

PSZ   *Polnoe sobranie zakonov Rossiiskoi imperii*, 3 series (St.
            Petersburg: 2-oe Otdelenie Sobstvennoi ego Imperator-
            skogo Velichestva Kantseliarii, 1830-1916).

SIRIO   *Sbornik imperatorskogo istoricheskogo obshchestva*, St.
            Petersburg, 1867-1916, 148 vols.

LIST OF MAPS

PART I

THE EIGHTEENTH CENTURY

POLAND-LITHUANIA AND THE BALTIC PROVINCES IN 1773

━━━━━━━━━ Borders of Poland-Lithuania in 1772

  Territories annexed by Austria, Prussia, and Russia as a result of the First Partition of Poland

Between 1710 and 1815, the Russian Empire annexed western borderlands that, in 1815, accounted for about one-fifth of the land area and nearly 30 percent of the population of European Russia exclusive of the Caucasus. From the very beginning, Russian rulers and their officials wanted to bring this area closer to the rest of the empire, and under Catherine II and, again, under Nicholas I, a concerted effort was made to introduce Russian laws, institutions, and language. Yet, during the first century and a half of Russian rule, these borderlands retained their distinctive economic and social structures and networks of internal communication. Divided socially into estates resembling those of the old regime of central and western Europe (not the *sosloviia* of Muscovy and Imperial Russia), they were dominated by German, Polish, and Swedish elites. Until the 1860s, the Estonian, Finnish, Latvian, Lithuanian, Belorussian, Ukrainian, and even Polish nationality of the peasantry dominated by these elites was not a primary consideration. These borderlands had their own laws, customs, economies, institutions, and forms of social organization and were Catholic, Uniate, and Lutheran in religion. Culturally and socially, they remained a world apart from the rest of the empire.

The German, Polish, and Swedish estates of Russia's western borderlands held on to their special rights and privileges well into the nineteenth century. These rights and privileges were part of a political and social legacy inherited from the Polish-Lithuanian Commonwealth and Sweden. The Polish-Lithuanian Commonwealth was the classical land of the *liberum veto* and of the "Golden Freedom" of the nobility, or *szlachta*. Roman Catholicism and the Polish language and civilization united the *szlachta* in outlook, beliefs, and way of life throughout the vast lands of the Commonwealth that stretched from the Baltic to the Dnieper. This did not, however, prevent the pursuit of narrowly conceived local or personal interests at the expense of the central authority of the Crown. An indirect consequence of so-called

3

szlachta democracy was a degree of internal political chaos and weakness that made it increasingly difficult for the Polish king to conduct an effective foreign policy and to resist pressures to grant, at one time or another, special religious and political rights and privileges to the burghers of Danzig and Riga, the Ukrainian Cossacks, and the nobles of Ducal Prussia, Kurland, and Livland.

In the late sixteenth and early seventeenth centuries, Sweden, taking advantage of Polish internal weakness, conquered Estland and Livland. Initially, the Swedes allowed the German estates of these two provinces to retain the special rights and privileges they had enjoyed previously under Poland, the Teutonic Order, or the bishops of Riga, Ösel, and Dorpat. By the end of the seventeenth century, however, Sweden took measures to limit the extent of Baltic autonomy and to introduce Swedish norms, laws, and institutions. These measures only remained in effect briefly, for the historic duel between Charles XII of Sweden and Peter the Great soon provided the nobles and burghers of Livland and Estland an opportunity to shift their allegiance to Russia and to obtain from her formal confirmation of their special laws, institutions, German language, and Lutheran religion.

The wars Russia waged against Poland and Sweden between 1654 and 1815 contributed significantly to the consolidation of the special rights and privileges of elites in the western borderlands of the empire. As long as Poland and Sweden retained sufficient military power to contend for the control of these borderlands, Russia's position was not secure unless she could count on the cooperation of local native elites in newly annexed areas. To assure such cooperation, Russia allowed them to enjoy certain special rights and privileges as long as they remained loyal to the tsar and with the implied understanding that they would maintain locally a well-regulated society arranged into traditional social orders.

CHAPTER 1

ESTLAND AND LIVLAND:
TWO PRIVILEGED PROVINCES,
1710-1762

Estland and Livland, which had been depopulated and devastated by the famine of 1695-1697 and the Great Northern War, would seem to have had little more than 200,000 inhabitants at the time of their conquest by Peter the Great.[1] They occupied an area about the size of West Virginia, or six percent of the land area (that is, approximately 60,000 out of one million square kilometers) of the western borderlands acquired by Russia between 1710 and 1815. These two small provinces had close contacts with Germany and Scandinavia, and their local elites possessed the sort of military and administrative experience and skills that Peter I considered important for his own work of internal reform in Russia. Estland and Livland, then, represented for Peter a means of bringing Russia closer to the West, especially if their German townsmen and nobles could be convinced that it was in their interests to serve Russia.

The Baltic Germans' political and legal institutions and forms of

---

[1] There are no reliable demographic data for Estland and Livland at the beginning of the eighteenth century. Estonian historians estimate the pre-1695 population of Estland and of the Estonian northern half of Livland to have been in the neighborhood of 350,000 to 375,000 inhabitants, of which perhaps 60 to 70 percent perished between 1695 and 1721. (In addition, some 150,000 Latvians in the southern part of Livland seem to have experienced a similarly high fatality rate between 1695 and 1721.) See *Istoriia Estonskoi SSR*, ed. A. Vassar and G. Naan, 3 vols. (Tallinn: Estonskoe Gosudarstvennoe Izdatel'stvo, 1961-1974), 1: 434-35, 528-29; Herbert Ligi, "Chislennost' i razmeshchenie krest'ianskogo naseleniia v iuzhnoi Estonii v 1713-1816 gg.," in *Problemy istoricheskoi demografii SSSR: Sbornik statei*, ed. R. N. Pullat (Tallinn: Akademiia Nauk Estonskoi SSR, 1977), pp. 134-40; Herbert Ligi, "Talurahva arvu dunaamikast Eestimaal XVIII sajandi," in *Studia historica in honorem Hans Kruus*, ed. J. Kahk and A. Vassar (Tallinn: Eesti Teaduste Akadeemia Ajaloo Institut, 1971), pp. 223-52; Heldur Palli, "Historical Demography of Estonia in the 17th-18th Centuries and Computers," ibid., pp. 206, 211; Reinhard Wittram, *Baltische Geschichte 1180-1918: Die Ostseelande Livland, Estland, Kurland* (Munich: Oldenbourg, 1954), pp. 125-27, 143-44. Cf. V. M. Kabuzan, *Narodonaselenie Rossii v XVIII-pervoi polovine XIX veke* (Moscow: Akademiia Nauk SSSR, 1963), pp. 59, 63, 67, 68-69, 162.

social organization had evolved gradually since the Middle Ages. The municipal institutions of Reval (Tallinn) and Riga had their origins in the thirteenth century, while the first general diets of the vassals (that is, the future Baltic nobles) of the Teutonic Order and the bishops of the Livonian Confederation were held in the fourteenth century. The four separate *Ritterschaften* and the Diets (*Landtage*) of Estland, Livland, Ösel, and Kurland appeared in the sixteenth century with the triumph of Lutheranism in the Baltic provinces and the partition of the former Livonian Confederation between Sweden, Poland, and Denmark. Under Sweden in the seventeenth century, the Diets in Estland and Livland and on Ösel (or Saaremaa, an island belonging to Livland *guberniia*) became exclusively assemblies of the landowning nobility (except for the two delegates from Riga in the Livland Diet) as well as the highest administrative organ outside the cities and towns. In Estland the executive branch of the provincial administration was the Chancery of the Nobility (*Ritterschaftskanzlei*), and in Livland the Council of the Diet (*Landratskollegium*). In Livland, in particular, peasant, judicial, administrative, and police institutions were integrated into a legal-administrative system that extended downwards from the *Landratskollegium* through district high church wardens (*Oberkirchenvorsteher*) to the local church, police, and court institutions of the parish and peasant community.[2] This comprehensive police, court, and church network put the nobility in a good position to control the activities of Latvian and Estonian peasants and to oblige them to conform to patterns of economic, social, and political organization imposed on them from above.

During the last several decades of Swedish rule in Estland and Livland, an attempt was made to introduce Swedish laws, institutions, and social practices. This new policy seriously threatened the existing political and social order in these two provinces. Sweden was a well-governed state in which the peasants were free men with the right to participate in local self-government and to be represented in the *riksdag*. Not approving the total subordination of Latvian and Estonian serfs to the arbitrary power of German landowners, Swedish officials

[2] Oswald Schmidt, *Rechtsgeschichte Liv-, Est- und Curlands*, ed. E. von Rottbeck (1894; reprint ed., Hannover-Döhren: Hirschheydt, 1968), pp. 99-111, 157-62, 167-69, 187-89, 197-201; Alexander von Tobien, *Die Livländische Ritterschaft in ihrem Verhältnis zum Zarismus und russischen Nationalismus*, 2 vols. (Riga: G. Löffler, 1925; Berlin: Walter de Gruyter, 1930), 1: 4-9, 15-17, 460-70; Hasso von Wedel, *Die Estländische Ritterschaft vornehmlich zwischen 1710 und 1783: Das erste Jahrhundert russischer Herrschaft*, Osteuropäische Forschungen, no. 18 (Königsberg-Berlin: Ost-Europa Verlag, 1935), pp. 1-12, 65-66, 81-114, 154-72.

undertook to improve the legal position of these serfs, regulate their economic relations with the landowners, promote literacy among them, and involve them in rural self-government, though leaving the ultimate control of parish and other local institutions in the hands of the German nobles. During the 1680s and 1690s King Charles XI extended to Estland and Livland Swedish legislation requiring the reversion to the Crown of lands to which nobles could not prove legal ownership. This so-called *reduktion* took about one-third of the land from the nobles in Estland and five-sixths in Livland. The *reduktion* was resisted particularly energetically in Livland. In retaliation, the Swedish absolutist state undermined the foundations upon which the Livland *Landesstaat* rested by abolishing its principal administrative organ, the Council of the Diet, and the post of marshal of the nobility.[3]

On the whole, the privileged German strata of the population remained loyal to Sweden until Russia completed her conquest of Livland and Estland in 1710. In many ways, the two provinces had benefited from Swedish rule. The Swedes had organized local government, founded secondary schools and the first Dorpat University, protected and reformed the Lutheran Church, and improved the administration of justice in town and countryside. The Baltic towns had no particular quarrel with the Swedish king, and the conflict between nobles and king during the 1680s and 1690s was not as serious in Estland as in Livland. Even in Livland, Swedish absolutism became more accommodating toward the local nobility after the death of Charles XI in 1697 and the beginning of the Great Northern War in 1700.

Between 1710 and 1712 Estland and Livland rights and privileges were confirmed in capitulation agreements and letters of privilege issued to the corporations of the nobility and the upper strata of the German population in the towns. Russia guaranteed the rights of the Lutheran Church, returned to the landowners the land that had reverted to the Swedish Crown in the 1680s and 1690s, restored the *Landratskollegium* and the post of marshal of the nobility in Livland, confirmed German as the language of the courts and administration, and left local government and police and the administration of the courts and the church in the hands of town councils or of the Diets,

---

[3] Alvin Isberg, *Karl XI och den livländska adeln 1684-1685: Studier rörande det Karolinska envaldets införande i Livland* (Lund: Lindstedts Universitetsbokhandel, 1953), pp. 3-10, 285-94; Schmidt, *Rechtsgeschichte*, pp. 171-73, 184-91; Evald Uustalu, *The History of the Estonian People* (London: Boreas, 1952), pp. 79-91; Michael Roberts, *The Swedish Imperial Experience 1585-1721* (London-New York-Melbourne: Cambridge University Press, 1979), pp. 110-16.

councils of the nobility, and other autonomous bodies controlled by the *Ritterschaften*. Peter I, however, ignored German protests concerning the inclusion in these agreements of a conventional *clausula majestatis* and limited the granted rights and privileges to "the present government and times." The two provinces did not receive the higher court they had requested but were obliged to live with the subordination of their local courts to the higher authority of the Russian Justice College and Senate. Although the rights of the Lutheran Church were formally recognized by Russia, it lost the former position it had enjoyed in Swedish times of being the only officially sanctioned and tolerated church in Estland and Livland, for Article 10 of the Treaty of Nystad (1721) provided that Orthodox believers also had the right to practice their faith in the two provinces. Furthermore, on more than one occasion Peter acted arbitrarily and in disregard of local rights and privileges in his dealings with Estland and Livland between 1710 and 1725.[4]

Despite this occasional assertion of Russian sovereign rights in Estland and Livland, in the first half of the eighteenth century there was no question about the special position of these two provinces within the Russian Empire. It is interesting that Peter I granted Livland and Estland their privileged status at about the same time he began the dismantling of Ukrainian autonomy. Why did he follow such divergent policies in the Ukraine and the Baltic provinces? The mere fact of Mazepa's betrayal of Russia in 1708 is only part of the answer, which must also be sought in connection with Peter's work of internal reform.

The Petrine military, political, and social reforms profoundly affected the relationships of the Left-Bank Ukraine and of Livland and Estland to the rest of the empire. By the end of Peter's reign a large European-style, standing army had come into existence, the foundations of a modern bureaucracy had been laid, and the central state had undertaken to regulate in minute detail the activities of its subjects in the manner of the European *Polizeistaat* of the seventeenth and eighteenth centuries. Peter secularized and depersonalized the political authority in Russia and minimized the influence of the Or-

[4] Michael Haltzel, *Der Abbau der deutschen ständischen Selbstverwaltung in den Ostseeprovinzen Russlands 1855-1905*, Marburger Ostforschungen, no. 37 (Marburg: J. G. Herder-Institut, 1977), pp. 3-5; Schmidt, *Rechtsgeschichte*, pp. 237-41, 265-67; R. Staël von Holstein, "Zur Geschichte der livländischen Privilegien," BM 51 (1901): 1-4; Reinhard Wittram, *Peter I Czar und Kaiser: Zur Geschichte Peter des Grossen in seiner Zeit* (Göttingen: Vandenhoeck & Ruprecht, 1964), 2: 80-88; Ia. Ia. Zutis, *Ostzeiskii vopros v XVIII veke* (Riga: Knigoizdatel'stvo, 1946), pp. 59-62, 73, 80-81, 85-88.

thodox Church on state affairs. Henceforth, the "common good" and "general state interests" were to be promoted according to the precepts of good government and within the framework of institutions that Peter and his successors borrowed chiefly from Sweden and cameralists trained in the universities and bureaucracies of Germanic central Europe.[5]

One reason for the preferential treatment Peter I gave to Livland and Estland was the high opinion he had of their political institutions, which seemed to have much in common with the Swedish and German models he wished to imitate. The laws, church, courts, and local government of Estland and Livland had their origins in the Germanic Middle Ages and Reformation, and in the seventeenth century they were organized and reformed on Swedish lines. In reforming local government in the interior of the empire, not only Peter but also Catherine II found a good deal worth imitating in the existing courts and political institutions of Estland and Livland.[6] The privileged local Germans, to be sure, did their utmost to broadcast the virtues and advantages of a political and legal system that enabled them to control and run the affairs of the Baltic towns and countryside. On occasion, this local monopoly of political power was questioned by Polish, Swedish, and Russian rulers. In the face of such challenges to their rights and privileges, the Baltic German burghers and nobles usually managed to overcome internal differences within their diets and town councils; however, they not only defended the status quo with dogged tenacity but also frequently succeeded in responding realistically and resourcefully to changing conditions and circumstances.

The Left-Bank Ukrainians also had their Cossack and municipal institutions of self-government, which had been confirmed by both Russia and Poland. Repeated interventions of the Polish and Russian governments in local Ukrainian affairs during the seventeenth and eighteenth centuries prevented, however, the Ukrainians from developing regional institutions and diets capable of uniting the various elements of local society and dealing effectively with outside threats to the Ukrainians' autonomy and common interests. However much

---

[5] Wittram, *Peter I*, 2: 114-26; Claes Peterson, *Peter the Great's Administrative and Judicial Reforms: Swedish Antecedents and the Process of Reception*, Skrifter utgivna av Institutet för Rättshistorisk Forskning, series 1; Rättshistorisk Bibliotek, 29 (Stockholm: A.-B. Nordiska Bokhandeln, 1979), pp. 1-2, 4-11, 59-73, 89-90, 98-107, 133-39, 410-17.

[6] Zutis, *Ostzeiskii vopros*, pp. 88-90, 385-455; Wittram, *Peter I*, 2: 134-38, 150-59; Wittram, *Baltische Geschichte*, pp. 89-99; Roberts, *The Swedish Imperial Experience*, pp. 90-94.

the Ukrainian townsmen and Cossack *starshyna* were attached to their local institutions, Magdeburg law and the hetmanate had little attraction for an eighteenth-century Russia interested in building a well-planned and relatively sophisticated bureaucracy on the Swedish model. Russian policy toward the Ukraine vacillated, but from the beginning it was clear that frequent disorder and unrest in the Ukraine very much troubled the tsar and his advisers. For them Ukrainian privileges and rights had been graciously bestowed and could be revoked at any time.[7]

Russia's hunger for European expertise and scientific, technological, and professional knowledge was the second reason why the Baltic Germans were more successful than the Ukrainians in holding on to special rights and privileges. Wishing to develop the Russian economy and to build a modern army and rationally organized bureaucracy, Peter I and his successors needed educated and experienced officers, officials, technicians, and specialists familiar with the theory and practice of European government, warfare, technology, and economics. Although a new Russian service nobility identifying itself with Peter I's innovations then came into existence, throughout the eighteenth century there continued to be a chronic shortage of qualified individuals to carry out the Petrine work of reform. The Russian government, therefore, felt obliged to recruit educated and skilled non-Russians for service in the imperial army, navy, bureaucracy, and economy. In the eighteenth century Estland and Livland were the most important single source of such recruits, for here thousands of the local German nobles and burghers had the military, administrative, professional, and technical expertise Russia sought. Almost three-fifths of the Swedish army of Charles XII was commanded by officers from Livland and Estland; in the 1730s about one-fourth of the officers for a much larger Russian army consisted of Estlanders and Livlanders. The nobles from Estland and Livland generally preferred military to

[7] C. Bickford O'Brien, *Muscovy and the Ukraine: From the Pereiaslav Agreement to the Truce of Andrusovo, 1654-1667* (Berkeley and Los Angeles: University of California Press, 1963); O'Brien, "Russo-Polish Relations in the Second Half of the Seventeenth Century," in *American Contributions to the Seventeenth International Congress of Slavists* 3 (*History*, ed. Anna Cienciala; The Hague: Mouton, 1973): 53-61; Zenon E. Kohut, "The Abolition of Ukrainian Autonomy (1763-1786): A Case Study of the Integration of a Non-Russian Area into the Empire" (University of Pennsylvania Ph.D. dissertation, 1975), pp. 60-96, 204-5; P. V. Mykhailyna, *Mista Ukrainy v period feodalizmu* (Chernivtsi: Chernivets'kyi Derzhavnyi Universytet, 1971), pp. 107-9; Wladyslaw Serczyk, "The Commonwealth and the Cossacks in the First Quarter of the Seventeenth Century," *Harvard Ukrainian Studies* 2 (1978): 73-93; Orest Subtelny, "Mazepa, Peter I, and the Question of Treason," *Harvard Ukrainian Studies* 2 (1978): 181-82.

civil service, but a considerable number of them, often with higher juridical training from German universities or the first Dorpat University (which functioned intermittently between 1632 and 1710) were willing to avail themselves of opportunities to serve as officials in the interior of the empire. Other Livland and Estland recruits for civil service in Russia came from the so-called literati (*Literaten*), that is, university-trained Baltic pastors, doctors, jurists of non-noble origin. Together, Baltic German nobles and literati accounted for 355 of 2,867 (or one-eighth) of the high-ranking officials Erik Amburger mentioned in his study of the Russian bureaucracy between 1710 and 1917. More than two-thirds of these 355 high officials came from the four Baltic *Ritterschaften*. Baltic literati families, on the other hand, provided not only high civil servants for Russia but also physicians, pharmacists, scientists, educators, legal specialists, and Lutheran pastors for small, German-speaking settlements scattered across European Russia.[8]

In the seventeenth century, Ukrainians had also played an important role in transmitting European knowledge and culture to Russia. They then especially contributed to the development of Muscovite higher education and Orthodox theology because of their contacts with Polish civilization and the training many of them had received in Polish Catholic schools and academies and in their own secondary schools and Kievan Academy. In the eighteenth century, however, Russians wanted direct contacts with the secular culture of the West. Ukrainians continued to serve the tsar as religious advisers, scholars, and administrators, but they could not compete with the Baltic Germans as representatives of the Western world that official Russia wished to emulate.

A third reason for the special treatment accorded the Livlanders and Estlanders has already been mentioned in another context: Russia, in order to achieve her foreign-policy objectives in Europe, needed the support of privileged elites in the western borderlands of the empire. The Ukrainian Cossacks did not fit into this picture, for they tended to be unpredictable and to act in a manner that endangered the objectives of Russia's foreign policy. Mazepa's defection in 1708

[8] Wittram, *Baltische Geschichte*, pp. 91-92, 104, 197; Zutis, *Ostzeiskii vopros*, p. 182; Wilhelm Lenz, *Der baltische Literatenstand*, Wissenschaftliche Beiträge zur Geschichte und Landeskunde Ost-Mitteleuropas, no. 7 (Marburg, 1953), pp. 1-16; Erik Amburger, *Geschichte der Behördenorganisation Russlands von Peter dem Grossen bis 1917* (Leiden: E. J. Brill, 1966), p. 517; John A. Armstrong, "Mobilized Diaspora in Tsarist Russia: The Case of the Baltic Germans," in *Soviet Nationality Politics and Practices*, ed. J. R. Azrael (New York: Praeger, 1978), pp. 65-69, 75-82.

is but one illustration of this point. His successor, Pylyp Orlyk, continued the struggle against Russia for another generation, intriguing with Russia's enemies and disturbing the sleep of Russian leaders with rumors of an anti-Russian uprising of 60,000 Cossacks in the Ukraine.[9]

German-speaking elites, on the other hand, then helped to further the objectives of Russia's foreign policy. German, more than any other language, was the *lingua franca* of the Baltic region and Central Europe. German nobles and townsmen dominated a string of provinces beginning with Schleswig-Holstein in the southwest and extending to Mecklenburg, Brandenburg, Prussia, Kurland, Livland, and Estland toward the east and north. Sweden, Russia's principal opponent in the Great Northern War, had possessions in Germany and on the eastern shore of the Baltic and had established her presence in Poland. The war with Sweden brought Russian troops into Poland, Finland, Kurland, Estland, and northern Germany. As a result of the anti-Swedish coalition formed during the war, Russia came to be linked through marriage with the ruling houses of Kurland, Mecklenburg, Braunschweig-Wolfenbüttel, and Holstein, opening for Russia new opportunities to influence what happened in Poland and northern Germany. Only Estland, Livland, Ingria, and a small part of Finland were annexed during Peter's lifetime. Russia had every reason to treat the local privileged estates in this newly annexed area generously and to respect their traditional rights and privileges. It was essential for Russia to maintain and to further develop established Baltic commercial and financial connections with Germany and Western Europe. The satisfaction of the Baltic Germans in Estland and Livland was an assurance to other privileged elites in Kurland, Poland, Finland, Prussia, Mecklenburg, and Holstein that they had nothing to fear from Russia.[10]

A fourth and final reason for the divergent fates of Baltic and Ukrainian autonomy was that the Ukrainians lacked an effective lobby in St. Petersburg. The presence of Baltic and other Germans in high governmental posts facilitated the defense of Baltic autonomy throughout the Imperial period. The delegations of townsmen and nobles, who periodically took up residence in St. Petersburg to lobby for the special interests of the Baltic towns and nobility, were usually led by

[9] Orest Subtelny, "Great Power Politics in Eastern Europe and the Ukrainian Emigres, 1709-42," *Canadian-American Slavic Studies* 12 (1978): 136-53; Subtelny, *The Mazepists: Ukrainian Separatism in the Early Eighteenth Century* (Boulder: East European Monographs, 1981), pp. 59-171.

[10] Wittram, *Peter I*, 1: 323-54, 2: 150-59; Zutis, *Ostzeiskii vopros*, pp. 88-90, 385-455.

high-ranking town officials and marshals and counselors of the nobility whose official positions in the Baltic provinces automatically conferred on them high standing in the Russian Table of Ranks (for the counselors and marshals of the nobility, the fourth rank, which was equivalent to a major general in the army or real privy counselor in the civil service), aiding them to deal effectively with rank-conscious Russian officialdom. When the connections of their friends in the government failed to manipulate the patronage and personal clientele networks of the Russian capital to the benefit of the Baltic *Ritterschaften* and towns, bribery often did.[11] Russia's rulers, who were generally well disposed toward the Baltic Germans, customarily confirmed the special rights and privileges of the Baltic towns and *Ritterschaften* at the beginning of each new reign up to the ascension of Alexander III to the throne in 1881. But even under the last two emperors, when cosmopolitanism and the influence of the German element waned in the Russian capital, representatives of the *Ritterschaften* and of Baltic towns succeeded in preventing the total destruction of the special position of their provinces within the Russian Empire.

As long as Peter I lived, his firm hand limited what Baltic lobbyists could achieve. He almost had to turn to the local Germans, however, if he wished to retain in Estland and Livland what he considered the high level of Swedish bureaucratic efficiency. The Swedes had contributed significantly to the development of local institutions of self-government in these two provinces, but trained Swedish officials supervised the activities of the local Germans. Russia had neither the money nor the trained personnel to continue such supervision. The one way institutional continuity could be assured was, therefore, to have the Baltic Germans take over functions formerly performed by Swedes and to expand the scope of the activities of the local institutions of self-government. Even the offices of the Russian governors and governors-general in Riga and Reval soon came to be staffed almost exclusively by local German burghers and nobles. At the same time, the number of officials working for the administrative organs of the Estland and Livland corporations of the nobility steadily increased throughout the first part of the eighteenth century. In Livland twelve counselors of the nobility took turns advising the Russian governor-general for one month, in which capacity they were known as the

[11] Julius Eckardt, *Livland im achtzehnten Jahrhundert: Umrisse zu einer livländischen Geschichte* (Leipzig: Duncker & Humblot, 1876), pp. 288-97; Wedel, *Die Estländische Ritterschaft*, pp. 99-100; Zutis, *Ostzeiskii vopros*, pp. 110-14, 222-27, 318, 622-25; Erich Donnert, *Johann Georg Eisen (1717-1779): Ein Vorkämpfer der Bauernbefreiung in Russland* (Leipzig: Koehler & Amelang, 1978), pp. 151-55, 178.

resident counselors (*residierende Landräte*). These counselors were responsible not to the Russian government but to the Livland Diet, which also expanded the sphere of its activities after 1710. Because the Diet normally convened every third year, by the second part of the eighteenth century a smaller Deliberating Assembly of the Diet (*delibierender Adelskonvent*) met regularly in order to prepare items for the consideration of the Diet and to carry on its work in the period between its regular sessions.[12]

After Peter's death a succession of comparatively weak rulers provided the Germans of Estland and Livland with new opportunities to gain further concessions from Russia. During 1728 and 1729, a Financial Office (*Kamer-kontora*) for Livland and Estland Affairs and a separate College of Justice for Livland and Estland Affairs were established. Special organs to handle borderland affairs were no novelty in Russia, for both Muscovy and the Petrine empire experimented with a variety of *prikazy* and colleges to administer the borderlands during the seventeenth and eighteenth centuries. The *Kamer-kontora* and the Baltic College of Justice, however, were staffed by Germans and conducted their business and even customarily corresponded with branches of the central administration in German. Having a monopoly of expertise in all matters pertaining to Estland and Livland courts, law, taxes, finances, and peasant-landowner relations, the officers of the College and of the *Kamer-kontora* were in an excellent position to prepare papers and briefs reaching the Senate and other offices of the central government that were seldom prejudicial to Baltic interests.

The Baltic nobles continued to be in a strong position during the 1730s under Empress Anne, the former duchess of Kurland, who—on the basis of her own unhappy experience with Baltic nobles—was not well disposed toward privileged German corporations of the nobility. In the Ukraine her policies replaced the hetmanate with an administrative board dominated by Great Russians. The Estland and Livland estates gained no new privileges under Empress Anne and her favorite, Ernst Johann Biron, but they lost no privileges either and managed to consolidate their arbitrary powers over the Estonian and Latvian peasants. In this regard they were the beneficiaries of a general social policy that sacrificed the interests of the serfs almost

[12] Wedel, *Die estländische Ritterschaft*, pp. 79-81, 92-114, 125-30; Zutis, *Ostzeiskii vopros*, pp. 83-88; C. Rautenfeld, "Über den Ursprung und die Entwicklung des livländischen Adelskonvent," BM 65 (1908): 184-95.

everywhere in Russia for the sake of the interests of the state and of the landowning nobility.[13]

Estland and Livland privileges, at least those of the nobility, reached a high point during the reign of Empress Elizabeth between 1741 and 1761. To be sure, certain Germans who had played a prominent role under Empress Anne were removed from office or exiled, but other Germans continued to serve under Elizabeth; and the same pro-autonomy, pro-noble, and serf-owning mentality that then made possible the expansion of serfdom and restoration of the hetmanate in the Ukraine also permitted a handful of German nobles in Estland and Livland to gain for themselves additional power and influence at the expense of other social classes. Thus, during the reign of Elizabeth the Russian Senate consistently sided with the landowning nobles in their disputes with the peasantry, even going so far in 1744 as to declare that all Latvian- and Estonian-speaking persons who could not clearly document their status as free men were to be automatically classified as fugitive serfs. The compilation of new registers of the nobility (in 1743 in Estland and in 1747 in Livland) and the approval of revised regulations for the Estland and Livland Diets during the late 1750s limited Diet membership and officeholding in the institutions of the *Ritterschaften* to registered nobles in the possession of manors (*Rittergüter*). Previously, under the Poles and Swedes, other social groups still participated on a limited scale in the Diet. Now such participation was limited to two representatives from the city of Riga (who shared a single vote) and 127 families in Estland, 172 families in Livland, and 25 families on the island of Ösel enrolled in the respective registries of the three corporations of nobility.[14]

These families represented about two thousand men, women, and children, that is, they were but a small minority even among tens of thousands of Germans in eighteenth-century Estland and Livland. It was especially important for them to protect their monopoly of political and social power in the countryside against the social aspirations of German burghers in possession of manors and of other Germans who had acquired noble status through service in Russia. Now only individuals accepted by a three-fourths majority vote of the Diet could be added to the rolls of those who controlled church, courts, schools,

---

[13] Zutis, *Ostzeiskii vopros*, pp. 90-91, 96-97, 110-11, 124-25, 163-64, 223-25.

[14] Ibid., pp. 201-3, 215-17, 224-29, 232-53, 284; Wittram, *Baltische Geschichte*, pp. 135-37; Schmidt, *Rechtsgeschichte*, pp. 267-68, 279-81; *Istoriia Estonskoi SSR*, 1: 533. *Livländische Landtags-Ordnung* of 1759 is available in the edition published by A. W. Hupel in the *Nordische Miscellanen*, 7 (Riga: J. F. Hartknoch, 1783): 11-118.

local finances, government, and administration throughout the countryside of Estland and Livland.[15]

In the eighteenth century this powerful position of the three Baltic *Ritterschaften* gradually came under attack on several fronts. The nonregistered nobility as well as wealthy citizens of Riga who owned land naturally tried to break the monopoly held by a small number of registered nobles over local government, courts, and administration outside Riga and several other Baltic towns. And, changing attitudes toward Baltic privileges and social and economic order on the part of certain Russian officials and a segment of local German society began to call into question the political and social power of the *Ritterschaften*. Local critics of existing conditions in Estland and Livland usually had been either born or educated in Germany, where they became familiar with eighteenth-century cameralistic ideas on the responsibility of the state to promote the common welfare of a ruler's subjects through the systematic development of a country's natural and human resources and the efficient organization of its society and organs of administration and government. The most outspoken critics of Baltic social order emerged somewhat later—toward the end of the eighteenth century—but as early as the 1750s and 1760s Pastor Johann Georg Eisen and certain officials working for the Financial Office (*Kamer-kontora*) for Livland, Estland, and Finland Affairs advocated reforms to protect the Latvian and Estonian serfs from the arbitrary power of their landowners. Pastor Eisen even proposed that the peasants should own the land they cultivated, arguing that this was in the economic interest of both the state and the nobility.[16]

In 1761, when Landrat K. F. Schoultz von Ascheraden lobbied in St. Petersburg for the confirmation of Livland's rights and privileges, he was surprised to discover that the enemies of his native province in the Senate slightly outnumbered its friends. Livland still had powerful allies in the Russian capital, and by the end of 1762 Schoultz was able to obtain from Catherine II confirmation of Baltic rights and privileges.[17] The German-born empress, however, turned out to be no friend of the Baltic *Ritterschaften* and other privileged borderland elites.

[15] *Nordische Miscellanen*, 7: 43; Zutis, *Ostzeiskii vopros*, pp. 230-33.

[16] N. Wihksninsch, *Die Aufklärung und die Agrarfrage in Livland* (Riga: Verlag Walters und Rapa, 1933), pp. 163-76, 206-30; Zutis, *Ostzeiskii vopros*, pp. 334-37; Donnert, *Johann Georg Eisen*, pp. 23-101. On the German cameralists, the work Albion W. Small originally published in 1909 is still useful (reprint ed., New York: Bert Franklin, n.d.); Zutis, *Ostzeiskii vopros*, pp. 275-79, 282-84, 335.

[17] Staël von Holstein, "Zur Geschichte der livländischen Privilegien," p. 21.

In 1764 Catherine wrote to Prince Alexander Viazemskii, the newly appointed procuror-general of the Senate, that Little Russia, Livland, Finland, and Smolensk should be Russified (*obruset'*) "with the mildest means possible so that they would cease looking to the woods like wolves."[18] Catherine did not use the word "Russify" in the modern dictionary sense of forcibly making Russians out of non-Russians but in the eighteenth-century sense of making the borderlands conform to the laws and administrative norms of the Russian center. Smolensk and Little Russia (that is, the Left-Bank Ukraine) had been acquired from Poland in the seventeenth century, and the work of several generations of Russian officials had prepared the way for their incorporation into the political and social structure of Russia by the time Catherine ascended the throne. Here the task of the empress seemed to be little more than the elimination of a few last vestiges of local autonomy in these two provinces. The small part of Finland annexed by Russia from Sweden in 1721 and 1743 was not a major consideration. Livland and Estland were another matter. Catherine delayed somewhat in applying her centralizing policy to them, but during the last thirteen years of her reign they, too, lost their autonomy.

[18] SIRIO, 7 (1871): 348.

CHAPTER 2

CATHERINE II
AND BALTIC RIGHTS
AND PRIVILEGES

THE INTENTIONS and plans of Catherine II with regard to the western borderlands cannot be understood independently of the more general reform of society and government that she and her advisers envisaged for Russia. These intentions and plans must also be seen in a context of an expansionist military and foreign policy that annexed not only somewhat under a half million square kilometers of Polish-Lithuanian lands but also the Crimea and the littoral and steppes north of the Black Sea. During most of Catherine's reign, these heavily garrisoned borders and newly annexed areas were under the military and civil command of high-ranking army officers close to and trusted by the empress: Field Marshal P. A. Rumiantsev in the Left-Bank Ukraine, Field Marshal G. A. Potemkin in New Russia, General Z. G. Chernyshev in the part of Belorussia annexed from Poland in 1772, and General George Browne in the Baltic provinces.

Born in 1698 in County Limerick, Ireland, and a veteran of many Russian campaigns, General Browne served as governor-general of Livland after 1762 and of Livland and Estland after 1775 until the time of his death in 1792. A soldier, he dealt with the local Baltic Germans firmly and sometimes even highhandedly and capriciously; he did not tolerate open opposition to what he considered to be government policy. At the same time, because there was no developed Russian civilian bureaucratic apparatus in Riga to back up his authority, he had to depend on the cooperation of the local Germans employed by his own chancery, the Baltic municipalities, or the *Ritterschaften* to take care of the actual implementation of government policies. The new forms of legal, bureaucratic, and social order with which he and Catherine's government experimented during the 1780s and 1790s, therefore, were not likely to alter fundamentally customary Baltic patterns of thought and conduct and the structure of the local economy and society. Nor is it likely that Browne and Catherine really intended any basic restructuring of the existing social order in Estland

18

and Livland. Certainly, Browne did not, for he married into the Baltic nobility, owned land and serfs in the Baltic provinces, and came to be a matriculated member of the *Ritterschaften* in Estland, Livland, and Kurland.[1]

As a would-be enlightened absolutist ruler of the second part of the eighteenth century, Catherine II aimed at achieving uniformity, centralization, order, and rationality in law and government. Essentially, her political objectives did not differ greatly from those of the well-regulated *Polizeistaat* of Peter the Great: they both wanted hard-working, orderly, and obedient subjects stratified in a hierarchy of estates, and they considered the principal responsibility of a good ruler to be the successful conduct of military and diplomatic affairs and the promotion of the common good of his subjects. Unlike the pragmatic Peter, however, Catherine was a diligent student of political philosophy; she had carefully read the works of Montesquieu and other fashionable *philosophes* of the Enlightenment, and their influence is clearly reflected in her famous *Nakaz*, or *Instruction*, of 1767 to the Legislative Commission. She was perhaps even more indebted, as N. D. Chechulin and F. Taranovskii pointed out at the beginning of this century, to such eighteenth-century German cameralists as J. F. Bielfeld and J.H.G. Justi for her ideas. In any event, she used and modified their ideas for her own purposes, applying them to the special conditions of Russian history and society.[2]

The major administrative and social reforms of Catherine II were the Provincial Reform of 1775 and the Charters to the Nobility and Towns of 1785. It should also not be overlooked that Catherine was interested in doing something to improve the conditions among the Russian serfs. At the beginning of her reign, especially through projects of the newly founded Free Economic Society and the discussions of the Legislative Commission, Catherine tried to influence the no-

---

[1] *Histoire de la vie de George de Browne, Comte du Saint Empire, Gouverneur Général de Livonie et d'Estonie, Général en chef des armées de sa majesté l'impératrice de toutes les Russes, Chevalier des ordres de St. André, St. Alexandre Nevski et St. Wlodemir de Russie, de l'Aigle Blanc de Pologne, et de Ste. Anne de Holstein, seigneur héréditaire des terres de Smilten, Segewold, Palzmar et Galenhoff, etc., etc.* (Riga: I. F. Hartknoch, 1794); DBL, pp. 108-9.

[2] N. D. Chechulin, ed., *Nakaz Imperatritsy Ekateriny II, dannyi Kommissii o sochinenii proekta novogo ulozheniia*, Pamiatniki russkogo zakonodatel'stva 1649-1832 gg., izdavaemye Imperatorskoi Akademiei Nauk, no. 2 (St. Petersburg: Imperatorskaia Akademiia Nauk, 1907), pp. cxxix-cxl; F. Taranovskii, "Politicheskaia doktrina v Nakaze Imperatoritsy Ekateriny II," in *Sbornik statei po istorii prava posviashchennyi M. F. Vladimirskomu-Budanovu* (Kiev: S. V. Kul'zhenko, 1904), pp. 53-73, 76, 83-86; Zutis, *Ostzeiskii vopros*, pp. 288-97.

bles to accept minimal reforms that would protect some peasant rights according to law. She soon discovered, however, that few nobles were interested in altering the existing social and economic relationships in the Russian countryside.[3]

The discussions of the Legislative Commission between 1767 and 1769 are also an interesting reflection of how many Russians then viewed the western borderlands. At issue were the fears expressed by certain delegates to the Legislative Commission from the Ukraine, Estland, and Livland concerning the implications of the statement in Article 34 of Catherine's *Instruction* that equality of citizens consisted in their being "subject to the same laws." Russian delegates at the Legislative Commission sharply criticized these efforts to defend regional autonomy, scolding the delegates of the Baltic *Ritterschaften* and of the Ukrainian towns and *starshyna* for their preference of the antiquated, imprecise, and inadequate laws given to them by previous foreign kings to what Catherine proposed in her *Instruction*: uniform laws that would contribute to the glory and might of the entire empire and the general welfare of its citizens. Estland and Livland rights and privileges came under particularly heavy cross fire. One deputy, Egor Demidov of the town of Romanov, even questioned whether these rights and privileges had any firm foundation in history and legal precedent. Citing the authority of Lomonosov and Voltaire, he argued that the originals of the documents supporting these rights simply were not to be found. Artemii Shishkov, the deputy from the Financial Office for Livland, Estland, and Finland Affairs, joined Demidov in opposing separate Baltic laws and privileges, emphasizing that the area had been conquered by Russia, whose rulers were in no way bound to continue harmful and imprecise local laws that previous Swedish and Polish rulers had not been willing to confirm. Shishkov spelled out these ideas in some detail in a special memorandum he submitted to the Legislative Commission, which was entitled "A Voice Concerning the Necessity of Having in the Baltic *Gubernii* Laws Identical with the Laws of the Russian Empire."[4]

[3] Robert E. Jones, *The Emancipation of the Russian Nobility* (Princeton, N.J.: Princeton University Press, 1973), pp. 133-45, 147-53, 291; David M. Griffiths, "Catherine II: The Republican Empress," *Jahrbücher für Geschichte Osteuropas*, n.s. 21 (1973): 327-31.

[4] Paul Dukes, *Catherine the Great and the Russian Nobility: A Study Based on the Materials of the Legislative Commission of 1767* (Cambridge, England: At the University Press, 1967), pp. 153-56; SIRIO, 7: 330-31, 335-39, 348-49; Artemii Shishkov, "Golos o neobkhodimosti imet' odinakovye zakony pribaltiiskim guberniiam s zakonami Rossiiskoi Imperii," CHTENIIA, 4 (1867): 83-95.

In the 1760s, however, Russian intellectuals and nobles still were not sufficiently self-conscious and organized to work either together with or without the government on the Baltic, peasant, or any other pressing issue of the day. In the Baltic provinces, where the upper strata of privileged society were in close contact with Germany, it was different, for there social and provincial problems of general interest were discussed publicly by both the nobility and the *Literaten*. The latter, as well as many nobles and patricians, had studied at German universities, where, in the second part of the eighteenth century, they absorbed cameralistic or Enlightenment teachings concerning the dependence of the common good on improvement in the lot of the peasantry, the need to rationalize the utilization of each state's human resources, and the perfection of the organization and the functioning of its administrative apparatus.[5] Catherine II and the reform-minded minority in Baltic society had much in common, and, therefore, it is perhaps not surprising that such Baltic German advocates of the emancipation of the Estonian and Latvian serfs as Pastor Eisen, Heinrich Johann von Jannau, and Garlieb Merkel responded positively to Catherine's policies, praising her as an enlightened ruler interested in the welfare of all her subjects.[6]

Peasant reform also received support from officials in the Financial Office (*Kamer-kontora*) for Livland, Estland, and Finland Affairs. Beginning in the 1750s and continuing into Catherine's reign, these officials gathered detailed information concerning the collection of taxes (which were levied on peasant land only) and peasant-landowner relations in Estland and Livland. Especially noteworthy among such officials was one Andreas Johann Hoffmann, an expert on both Swedish and Baltic agrarian legislation and conditions. The first native-Russian official to undertake a thorough study of Baltic agrarian con-

[5] Wilhelm Lenz, *Der baltische Literatenstand*, Wissenschaftliche Beiträge zur Geschichte und Landeskunde Ost-Mitteleuropas, no. 7 (Marburg: Johann Gottfried Herder-Institut, 1953), pp. 1-19; Hubertus Neuschäffer, *Katharina II. und die baltischen Provinzen*, Beiträge zur baltischen Geschichte, no. 2 (Hannover: Hirschheydt, 1975), pp. 401-12; Wihksninsch, *Die Aufklärung*, pp. 163-76, 206-30; Zutis, *Ostzeiskii vopros*, pp. 275-79, 287-94, 334-54; Marc Raeff, "The Well-Ordered Police State and The Development of Modernity in Seventeenth- and Eighteenth-Century Europe: An Attempt at a Comparative Approach," *American Historical Review* 80 (1975): 1221-44.

[6] Wihksninsch, *Die Aufklärung*, pp. 206-30, 258-308; Zutis, *Ostzeiskii vopros*, pp. 561-66; Wittram, *Baltische Geschichte*, p. 157; H. J. Jannau, *Geschichte der Sklaverey, und Charakter der Bauern in Lief- und Ehstland: Ein Beytrag zur Verbesserung der Leibeigenschaft* (Riga: n.p., 1786), pp. 90-93, 133-70; Garlieb Merkel, *Die Letten, vorzüglich in Liefland, am Ende des philosophischen Jahrhunderts: Ein Beitrag zur Völker- und Menschenkunde* (Leipzig: Heinrich Graff, 1797), pp. 1-4, 292-325.

ditions was the same Artemii Shishkov who was to argue so forcefully against Livland and Estland special rights and privileges in Catherine II's Legislative Commission of 1767. Shishkov was a former army officer who knew German well and whom the Senate had assigned to the *Kamer-kontora* in 1755. Both he and Hoffmann were fiscal agents of the Russian state and were, therefore, above all concerned about increasing state revenues, but they also favored reforms based on seventeenth-century Swedish agrarian legislation that aimed at limiting the arbitrary power of local landowners over their serfs. Shishkov seems to have played a role in popularizing the notion that some sort of agrarian reform was necessary in Livland.[7]

In 1765 Livland Governor-General George Browne, acting on the instructions of Catherine, prevailed upon the Livland Diet to approve a fourteen-point program of peasant reform. Catherine familiarized herself with conditions in Estland and Livland during a one-month visit in these two provinces in the summer of 1764. Pastor Eisen had been officially presented to Catherine in the preceding year, and in 1764 she commissioned him to write an essay on peasant conditions in Livland. She also knew something about the views of supporters of reform in the Financial Office (*Kamer-kontora*) for Livland, Estland, and Finland Affairs and about the rules Livland *Landrat* Schoultz von Ascheraden had prepared for his own peasants on the basis of Swedish norms of the seventeenth century. Because of the existence of some public support in Estland and Livland for the improvement of the lot of the Estonian and Latvian peasants, Catherine apparently intended to have these two provinces serve as an example for the rest of the empire.[8] The discussions of the Legislative Commission two years later, however, made clear that the Russian nobles were still not prepared to accept peasant reform for the interior of the empire.

The fourteen-point program in Livland had been formulated by a minority within the Diet who believed that reforms initiated by the *Ritterschaft* would avoid Russian interference in their internal affairs. The program changed little; in it, the regulation of norms regarding peasant services was not spelled out in detail, but instead was left to the discretion of the landowners themselves.[9] The year 1765 was nevertheless an important landmark in the history of Baltic provinces,

---

[7] Zutis, *Ostzeiskii vopros*, pp. 275-79, 282-84; Zutis, *Politika tsarizma v Pribaltike v pervoi polovine XVIII v.* (Moscow: Gosudarstvennoe sotsial'no-ekonomicheskoe Izdatel'stvo, 1937), pp. 116-21.

[8] Donnert, *Johann Georg Eisen*, pp. 47-63; Neuschäffer, *Katharina II.*, pp. 389-412.

[9] Zutis, *Ostzeiskii vopros*, pp. 345-353; Georg Sacke, "Livländische Politik Katharinas II.," *Quellen und Forschungen zur baltischen Geschichte* 5 (1944): 32-33.

for the discussion of peasant and agrarian questions in the following decades helped to prepare local privileged society psychologically for the emancipation of the Estonian and Latvian serfs between 1816 and 1819.

The interior of the empire at the time had no organized elements comparable to the *Literaten* and the pro-reform minority in the Baltic Diets that were ready to enter into a dialogue with Catherine about peasant reform. Failing to find influential supporters for projects designed to improve the lot of the Russian serfs, she had to confine her work of social reform in the Russian provinces of the empire largely to the nobility and to the activities provided for in the Provincial Reform of 1775 and the two Charters to the Nobility and Towns of 1785.

The Provincial Reform and the Charters aimed to rationalize the organization and functioning of local government and to involve the provincial nobility and wealthier townsmen in administrative work and other socially useful activities. It was hoped that the increased involvement of nobles and more affluent townsmen in local affairs would help to overcome the chronic shortage of personnel that had until then made it so difficult to maintain order and promote economic, social, and cultural progress in Russia. Catherine's administrative reforms more than doubled the number of posts in the provincial administration between 1775 and 1795 and provided the general framework of *gubernii* and districts (*uezdy*) into which Russia was divided until the Revolution. The activities of both appointed and elected (by the nobility and wealthier townsmen) officials in each *guberniia* were, however, carefully regulated under the overall supervision of a governor, who was in his turn, subordinated to an all-powerful governor-general, or viceroy. Governors-general were usually in charge of two or three *gubernii* or of a major town, and they had access to the monarch and the right to participate in the Senate as ex-officio members while in St. Petersburg. The strong element of bureaucratic control, regulation, and supervision permeating the *guberniia* and town reforms of Catherine tended to weaken the attraction that service in elective posts might have otherwise had for wealthier townsmen and the provincial nobility.[10]

The Charter to the Nobility had offered Russian nobles corporate status and institutions, protection for their property and personal rights, and other privileges similar to those enjoyed by the nobility else-

[10] On the Provincial Reform of 1775 and the Charter to the Nobility, see Jones, *Emancipation*, pp. 210-43, 273-99.

where in Europe. If these new rights and privileges failed to achieve immediately the objectives envisaged by Catherine, they were welcomed by the Russian nobility.[11] This was not the case for the nobles of the western borderlands, who already had extensive rights and privileges and who had been relatively unhampered by the sort of bureaucratic regulation that accompanied both the Provincial Reform and the Charter to the Nobility.

From the beginning Catherine, who wanted uniform laws throughout the empire from Old Finland to Kamchatka, intended to extend her administrative and social reforms to the borderlands. Thus, she introduced the Provincial Reform of 1775 into Belorussia and Little Russia as early as 1778-1781. Her integration of Belorussia into the general political and social structure of the empire will be discussed in Chapter 3. The Left-Bank and southern Ukraine lie outside the purview of this study, but the importance of these two areas for Catherine II's overall borderland policy would seem to justify at least a few brief comments concerning them before examining what she did in the Baltic provinces.

In 1764, when Catherine wrote to Viazemskii about the need to "Russify" the borderlands, she also emphasized the need to abolish the Little Russian Hetmanate (which had been restored by Elizabeth in 1750) and to make every effort to see to it that the very title of hetman would be forgotten.[12] K. G. Razumovskii, the last hetman, was persuaded to resign. He was replaced by the Little Russian College, which consisted of four Russians and four Ukrainians and was presided over by Field Marshal P. A. Rumiantsev, who served simultaneously as Little Russia's governor-general and remained in charge of the Left-Bank Ukraine until his death in 1796. He had, then, some three decades to absorb the Cossacks into the regular Russian army, to transform the *starshyna* and higher-rank Cossack officers into hereditary nobles, and to subject lower-rank Cossacks and peasants to forms of taxation (for example, the poll tax was introduced in 1783) and to restrictions on the freedom of movement similar to those existing in the central Russian provinces of the empire. These changes were formalized by extending the 1775 Provincial Reform and the 1785 Charters to the Nobility and Towns to Little Russia and organizing the viceregency (*Namestnichestvo*) of Kiev, Chernigov, and Novgorod-Severskii under Rumiantsev in 1781.[13]

[11] Ibid., pp. 238-43.

[12] SIRIO, 7: 348.

[13] W. E. D. Allen, *The Ukraine: A History* (2nd ed.; New York: Russell & Russell, 1963), pp. 223-32; *Ocherki istorii SSSR. Period feodalizma: Rossiia vo vtoroi polovine*

Victories over Turkey and the Treaty of Kuchuk-Kainardzhi in 1774 gave Russia a foothold on the northern littoral of the Black Sea and enabled her to consolidate control over the politically and socially unstable region of the Zaporozhian Cossacks between the Bug and the Dnieper. In 1774 Catherine II appointed her favorite, G. A. Potemkin, as governor-general of New Russia, to which was added Azov in 1775 and the Crimea in 1784. In 1775, at the suggestion of Potemkin, the Zaporozhian Host was destroyed. The establishment of the viceregency of Ekaterinoslav in 1783 marked the introduction into this area of the 1775 Provincial Reform in a vast area under Potemkin's administration that extended from the Bug almost to the Volga.[14] Potemkin, like Rumiantsev, was a Russian administrator and empire builder who imposed Russian norms on important Ukrainian regions and opened new possibilities of economic and commercial development in them.[15] But the subsequent development of this area was achieved at a considerable human cost, being based on forms of peasant servitude and bureaucratic uniformity and regimentation that tended to retard the emergence of a modern Ukrainian society.

In Estland and Livland, on the other hand, the powerful position of German patricians in the towns and matriculated, landowning nobles in the countryside discouraged the sort of empire building and social and political engineering on the scale practiced by Rumiantsev and Potemkin. On the whole, the officials of Catherine II proceeded somewhat more cautiously and slowly in Estland and Livland than in the Ukraine. One reason for this was the good reputation enjoyed by Baltic institutions of the nobility and local government in eighteenth-century Russia; Catherine herself had assured that Livland and Est-

---

XVIII v., ed. A. I. Baranovich, B. B. Kafengauz et al. (Moscow: Akademiia Nauk, 1956), pp. 582-92; Amburger, *Geschichte*, pp. 373, 396-97.

[14] Amburger, *Geschichte*, pp. 373, 399-400; V. A. Golobutskii, *Zaporozhskoe kazachestvo* (Kiev: Gospolitizdat, 1957), pp. 417-23; Isabel de Madariaga, *Russia in the Age of Catherine the Great* (New Haven and London: Yale University Press, 1981), pp. 359-73.

[15] On the impetus given to economic, social, and cultural development in the Ukraine and New Russia by Catherine's reforms and the activities of Rumiantsev and Potemkin, see *Ocherki istorii SSSR . . . vo vtoroi polovine XVIII v.*, pp. 591-92; N. M. Druzhinin, "Prosveshchennyi absoliutizm v Rossii," in *Absoliutizm v Rossii (XVII-XVIII vv.): Sbornik statei k semidesiatiletiiu so dnia rozhdeniia i sorokapiatiletiiu nauchnoi i pedagogicheskoi deiatel'nosti B. B. Kafengauza*, ed. M. N. Druzhinin (Moscow: "Nauka," 1964), pp. 443-44; Hans Auerbach, *Die Besiedlung der Südukraine in den Jahren 1774-1787* (Wiesbaden: Otto Harrassowitz, 1965); Marc Raeff, "The Style of Russia's Imperial Policy and Prince G. A. Potemkin," in *Statesmen and Statecraft of the Modern West: Essays in Honor of Dwight E. Lee and H. Donaldson Jordan*, ed. G. N. Grob (Barre, Mass.: Barre Publishers, 1967), pp. 1-51.

land institutions and practices were studied in detail, and to a considerable extent her innovations in regard to the provinces and nobility were based on Baltic models.[16] Another consideration was the likelihood of organized resistance to her proposed reforms by the Estland and Livland nobility.

A first step was the placing of Estland under Governor-General Browne, whose authority had been limited to Livland between 1762 and 1775. After 1778, a number of measures to control and limit the activities of the *Kamer-kontora* and the Justice College for Livland, Estland, and Finland Affairs were introduced in order to prepare for the elimination of special organs in the central government dealing with Baltic affairs, thereby bringing the governor-general in Riga into direct contact with the Senate in St. Petersburg.[17] By 1779, Catherine had already formulated and communicated to representatives of the *Ritterschaften* her plans for extending the Provincial Reform of 1775 to Estland and Livland. As was anticipated, the local nobles stubbornly opposed these plans; however, alarming peasant disturbances among the Estonian and Latvian serfs during the late 1770s and early 1780s and Catherine's reopening of legal questions concerning titles to land held under feudal tenure made it difficult to organize effective resistance to the government's plan, especially in Livland, where about one-third of the estates were not held as allodia. Nevertheless, Catherine waited until July 3, 1783, before she extended the Provincial Reform of 1775 to Estland and Livland. Protests on the part of the *Ritterschaften* were scattered and not serious, perhaps because two months earlier, on May 3, 1783, she had converted to hereditary tenure all estates in Estland, Livland, the Ukraine, and Belorussia that until then had been held in feudal tenure. At about the same time, on May 29, Catherine introduced the poll tax in Estland and Livland. This violation of the traditional order of the provinces was not protested by the *Ritterschaften*. Here, of course, the main burden fell on the peasants, not the Estland and Livland landowners, while a major goal of Catherine's cameralistic fiscal policy was achieved: state revenues obtained from the two Baltic provinces were immediately increased by 50 percent.[18]

The absence of determined and sustained resistance to the intro-

[16] Zutis, *Ostzeiskii vopros*, pp. 387-450.

[17] Ibid., pp. 524-25; Amburger, *Geschichte*, p. 388.

[18] Zutis, *Ostzeiskii vopros*, pp. 491-543; *Istoriia Estonskoi SSR*, 1: 664-74; Friedrich Bienemann, *Die Statthalterschaft in Liv- und Estland (1783-1796): Ein Capitel aus der Regierungspraxis Katharinas II*. (Leipzig: Duncker & Humblot, 1886), pp. 49-51, 58-64, 128-32.

duction of the Russian Provincial Reform apparently persuaded Catherine to abandon her hesitation to complete the liquidation of Estland and Livland autonomy and special rights and privileges. In 1785 she extended to the two Baltic provinces the Charters to the Towns and to the Nobility, which were also promulgated for the rest of the empire that same year. Both charters dealt severe blows to the monopoly of political control exercised until then by a handful of German patricians and registered nobles in the Estland and Livland towns and countryside. Another blow came the following year, when the *Landratskollegium*, the organ of the German nobility that managed its affairs and defended its interests between the regular meetings of the Diet every third year, was abolished. Henceforth, the organs and offices of the Baltic nobility were patterned after and functioned according to norms prescribed for the empire as a whole. The Baltic nobles were still a privileged group, but now they were expected to carry on their activities under the watchful eyes of Russian bureaucrats.[19]

In the perspective of nineteenth-century national tensions and modernization, the reforms Catherine introduced in Estland and Livland between 1783 and 1785, especially if they had remained in effect after her death in 1796, would seem to have offered many advantages to the majority of Estonians, Latvians, and even Germans living in these two provinces. Accompanying these reforms, however, was the application locally of the Russian poll tax, which imposed additional burdens and constraints on the Estonian and Latvian peasants. On the other hand, reorganization of local courts under the Provincial Reform and their placement more directly under the supervision of agents of the governor-general and Senate resulted in the improvement of peasant prospects of obtaining justice in legal disputes with nobles. After 1764, peasants living on lands owned by the Crown (in 1758, 17 percent of estates in Livland but many fewer in Estland) were classified as state peasants, which meant that they could serve as assessors in the Lower *Rasprava*, a court for cases involving state peasants and consisting of four elected assessors and one appointed by the judge. State peasants also served as assessors in the Lower Land Court, a police organ on the *uezd* level that helped maintain order in the countryside and, after peasant disturbances in 1783-1784 and a senatorial inspection during the summer of 1784, became the first instance for examining peasant petitions alleging landowner vio-

---

[19] Zutis, *Ostzeiskii vopros*, pp. 533-35, 564-68, 581-87, 608-9; Sacke, "Livländische Politik Katharinas II.," *Quellen* 5: 45-49, 60-61.

lations of rules for the collection of the poll tax. During the social unrest of 1783-1784 caused by the introduction of the poll tax, serf assessors (or so-called *Rechtsfinder*) were even used by the Lower Land Courts, but such participation by serfs in the affairs of the Baltic countryside was neither encouraged nor did it continue in the following period of the Charter to the Nobility and of the French Revolution. Nevertheless, the peasants seemed to have had faith in the new police and judicial organs and brought to them disputes with nobles over labor-service norms and the collection of the poll tax. Latvian historian A. Altements has studied many such cases and concluded that the peasants were often able to obtain justice from Catherine's courts. This, of course, encouraged defiance of the authority of the local German landowners and perhaps an exaggerated faith on the part of Latvians and Estonians in the benevolence of the Russian authorities in St. Petersburg.[20]

At the time, Baltic nobles referred to the "judicial despotism" (*"richterlicher Despotismus"*) of the new courts. The judges, however, were still Germans and the language of the bureaucracy (except for the Department of Finance in the *guberniia* administrations) remained German, although Baltic schools were urged to help prepare their pupils for state service by teaching them Russian. There were, however, many new faces among those who served in the Baltic courts and bureaucracy. As before, noble status was a condition for occupying responsible positions, but now personal and hereditary noble status was determined by the Russian Table of Ranks and the Charter to the Nobility, not by the membership rolls of the *Ritterschaften* or by a three-fourths majority of the Estland and Livland Diets. The number of people working in the bureaucracy was increased, and Germans who had served in the Russian army or in the interior *gubernii* often replaced the old servants of the corporations of the nobility. These new men no longer viewed all matters from the narrow perspective of closed corporations of the nobility and ancient Baltic rights and privileges, and, where there was a conflict, they were expected to act according to the law of the empire, not according to local customary law.[21]

---

[20] Zutis, *Ostzeiskii vopros*, pp. 549-55, 565-66; John P. LeDonne, "The Judicial Reform of 1775 in Central Russia," *Jahrbücher für Geschichte Osteuropas*, n.s. 21 (1973): 32-35, 37-38; LeDonne, "The Provincial and Local Police under Catherine the Great, 1775-1796," *Canadian Slavic Studies* 4 (1970): 516-17, 520-22; Jones, *Emancipation*, pp. 224-31; A. Altements, "Vidzemes zemieku reformas jautājums 1795-97 g.," *Latvijas Vēstures Institūta Žurnāls* (1938, no. 1/5), pp. 36, 39, 40, 41-42 (cited in Zutis, *Ostzeiskii vopros*, p. 564).

[21] Julius Eckardt, *Bürgerthum und Büreaukratie* (Leipzig: Duncker & Humblot, 1870),

The introduction of the Charter to the Towns in Estland and Livland was also important. Catherine and her advisers especially wanted to develop more fully Riga's potential as a port and commercial center after the First Partition of Poland brought this city's hinterland—Latgale and the eastern part of Belorussia—into the Russian Empire. The trade monopoly of the German merchants and the restrictions imposed on handicrafts, industrial production, and marketing by the German guilds seemed to prevent Baltic towns from growing and serving the general economic and commercial needs of the empire. A number of measures were taken, even as early as the 1760s, to oblige the Baltic towns to permit competition from Russian merchants and to accept non-Germans into their guilds if they met all requirements for membership. In 1782, the tariff barrier separating Estland and Livland from the rest of Russia was abolished, and the introduction of the Provincial Reform and the Charter to the Towns in 1783 and 1785 completed the economic and administrative unification of the Baltic towns with the rest of the empire. During the decade that followed new Russian laws that defined burgher status in terms of property, taxes paid, and occupation permitted a larger number of Russians, Latvians, and Estonians to be accepted as full-fledged members of the organized citizenry of the Baltic towns. In Riga, with the old restraints removed, trade, commerce, and shipping perceptibly increased, and economically everyone seems to have benefited. However, social mobility accompanied prosperity. An expanded town population of varied and mixed origins did not always show deference and respect to former social superiors.[22] The extent of social change in Baltic towns between 1785 and 1796 should not, however, be exaggerated. Property-owning, wealthier Germans then retained control of government in all Baltic towns, traditional local laws were not abolished, and German remained the official language in which the business of town offices was conducted. If certain currents of social unrest and insubordination were perceptible in Riga, they were less so in other Baltic towns. Otto-Heinrich Elias has, for example, shown that in Reval (in 1782 a town of 10,653 inhabitants, or about half the size

p. 82; Sacke, "Livländische Politik Katharinas II.," *Quellen* 5: 35, 45-47, 66; Bienemann, *Die Statthalterschaft*, pp. 207-8; Zutis, *Ostzeiskii vopros*, pp. 445-46, 621; Iv. Tikhomirov, "Ekaterinskie reformy v Pribaltiiskom krae," *Vestnik Evropy* 242 (November 1877): 644-46.

[22] Zutis, *Ostzeiskii vopros*, pp. 588-609; Sacke, "Livländische Politik," pp. 49-65; Otto-Heinrich Elias, "Zur Lage der undeutschen Bevölkerung im Riga des 18. Jahrhunderts," *Jahrbücher für Geschichte Osteuropas*, n.s. 14 (1966): 481-84; Eckardt, *Bürgerthum und Büreaukratie*, pp. 65-68, 89; *Istoriia Estonskoi SSR*, 1: 674-75; Iu. R. Klokman, "Gorod v zakonodatel'stve russkogo absoliutizma vo vtoroi polovine XVII-XVIII vv.," in *Absoliutizm v Rossii*, pp. 336-38, 346-48, 352-54.

of Riga), resident Russians and Estonians were reluctant to assert the
political rights that had been granted to them by the Charter to the
Towns of 1785.[23] The Charter was in effect far too short a period, and
the guilds and German merchants and jurists were too influential to
permit any fundamental change in a social and political system that
discriminated against all so-called *Undeutsche*.

Judged by the goals and objectives Catherine II set for herself at
the beginning of her reign, her work of reform in Russia was a partial
success at best. The Russian nobility did not display the initiative,
maturity, and sense of responsibility that would have been required
to make Catherine's administrative and social reforms work. And, the
goal of a government and society run according to law was even more
illusory, especially as far as the common people were concerned.
Catherine's pro-noble social legislation of the 1780s left the peasantry
defenseless against illegal and harsh actions of masters and of officials
elected by the nobility or appointed by the state.[24]

In Estland and Livland, as elsewhere in the western borderlands,
Catherine II's administrative Russification seems to have been premature. She had failed to codify Russian law, and to the very end of
her reign she lacked a sufficient number of trained, dependable, and
responsible jurists and officials to assure the establishment of an acceptable legal and administrative order in the Great Russian center
of the empire. Was she, therefore, in a position to impose Russian
norms on the borderlands? In Estland and Livland, the pre-1783 legal-administrative order was, in certain respects, more satisfactory than
that of the Russian provinces. Catherine herself had found many features of the system of local self-government in Estland and Livland to
be worthy of imitation for the purposes of her own social and administrative legislation of the 1770s and 1780s. As was perhaps to be
expected, her reform was more successful in Estland and Livland than
elsewhere in the empire, for it was particularly in these two provinces
that nobles, intellectuals, and wealthier townsmen had been accustomed to playing an active role in public life.

Although it is possible that social and national justice was pro-

[23] Otto-Heinrich Elias, *Reval in der Reformpolitik Katharinas II.*, Quellen und Studien zur baltischen Geschichte, no. 3 (Bonn-Bad Godesberg: Verlag Wissenschaftliches
Archiv, 1978), pp. 118-39.

[24] Jones, *Emancipation*, pp. 290-99; Iv. Blinov, *Gubernatory: Istoriko-iuridicheskii
ocherk* (St. Petersburg: E. L. Pentkovskii, 1905), pp. 151-54; *Istoriia Pravitel'stvuiushchego senata za dvesti let 1711-1911 gg.* (St. Petersburg: Senatskaia Tipografiia,
1911), 3: 5-13; John P. LeDonne, "The Provincial Police under Catherine the Great,
1775-1796," *Canadian Slavic Studies* 4 (1970): 526-28.

moted, in one way or another, through the introduction of Catherine's Provincial Reform of 1775 and the Charter to the Towns of 1785, the improvement of life for the Estonians and Latvians would not seem to have had a very high priority for Catherine and her advisers. Of greater importance to them was certainly the maintenance of social stability and order. They, therefore, did not welcome the new defiant attitude and increased social unrest among Estonian and Latvian peasants and lower-class townsmen toward the end of the eighteenth and at the beginning of the nineteenth century. Government policy had contributed to producing this unrest, for the rapid introduction of the poll tax and the taking of measures to protect the rights of peasants and to remove certain obstacles to social mobility tended to disturb the equilibrium of a traditional society dominated by large landowners and wealthy townsmen. As Soviet historians have quite correctly pointed out, the introduction of Russian reforms in Estland and Livland had results unanticipated by Catherine and her advisers.[25]

Yet Paul I did not need to go to the extreme he did in 1796 in setting the Baltic provinces and the areas annexed from Poland after 1772 apart from the remainder of the empire as *gubernii* administered on "special foundations according to their rights and privileges."[26] Positive aspects of Catherine's Provincial Reform and of the Charter to the Towns could have been retained in the western borderlands without restoring institutions and rights that would subsequently prove to be a source of considerable inconvenience to Russian administrators.

[25] Zutis, *Ostzeiskii vopros*, pp. 616-20, 626-31; *Istoriia Estonskoi SSR*, 1: 669-81; *Istoriia Latviiskoi SSR*, ed. A. A. Drīzulis (2nd ed.; Riga: "Zinātne," 1971), pp. 111-12.

[26] M. V. Klochkov, *Ocherki pravitel'stvennoi deiatel'nosti vremeni Pavla I* (Petrograd: Senatskaia Tipografiia, 1916), p. 426. These privileges were restored in five separate *ukazy*: PSZ, no. 17,584 (28 Nov. 1796), no. 17,594 (Nov. 30), no. 17,634 (Dec. 12), no. 17,637 (Dec. 12), and no. 17,681 (Dec. 24).

CHAPTER 3

EASTERN BELORUSSIA, LITHUANIA, AND THE RIGHT-BANK UKRAINE

As a result of the three partitions of Poland between 1772 and 1795, Russia acquired 463,200 square kilometers of territory, populated (in 1795) by some 7.5 million Ukrainians, Belorussians, Lithuanians, Latvians, Poles, and Jews.[1] This Russian share of partitioned Poland can be conveniently divided into three areas: Eastern Belorussia, Lithuania, and the Right-Bank Ukraine. Catherine II introduced the Provincial Reform of 1775 and the Charters to the Nobility and Towns into all three of these newly acquired areas, but only in Eastern Belorussia, which was annexed in 1772, did her officials have sufficient time to experiment successfully with projects of administrative and social uniformity prior to Paul I's restoration of special rights and privileges in 1796.

Since the time of Peter I, however, Russian officials had had ample opportunity to involve themselves in the affairs of not only Lithuania and the Right-Bank Ukraine but also in those of Poland-Lithuania in general. The reasons for the extent of this involvement cannot be understood without at least a brief discussion of two subjects: (1) the consequences of Poland's confrontation with the Ukrainian Cossacks and of the partition of the Ukraine between Poland and Russia in the second part of the seventeenth century; and (2) the social structure and the political and constitutional crisis of the Polish-Lithuanian Commonwealth during the seventeenth and eighteenth centuries. This crisis and Polish efforts at social and constitutional reform (often with the consent or even support of Russia) continued throughout the period of the three partitions and into the first decades of the nineteenth century. After a discussion of these two subjects, we will turn to Russian policies in the annexed areas between 1772 and 1795.

The *szlachta* (nobility) was the political nation in Poland-Lithuania. Only members of the *szlachta* were full-fledged citizens in the Commonwealth. Only they could participate in dietine (*sejmik*) delibera-

---

[1] "Rozbiory Polski," *Mały słownik historii Polski* (Warsaw: Wiedza Powszechna, 1967), p. 310; Kabuzan, *Narodonaselenie Rossii v XVIII-pervoi polovine XIX v.*, pp. 161-63.

tions and elections; hold high office in the administration and church; own and inherit landed estates; be senators or deputies in the Sejm; elect the Polish king; and form armed confederations to defend the interests of the Commonwealth during an interregnum or another emergency, or to oppose illegal acts of the king. In the mid-eighteenth century, 99 percent of the *szlachta* was Roman Catholic in religion and Polish in nationality, whether by origin or assimilation. By then the *szlachta* saw the welfare of the Commonwealth in the teachings and institutions of the Roman Catholic Church and in the maintenance of the "Golden Freedom" of the nobility and of its "Sarmatian" way of life. All members of the *szlachta* were supposed to be equal and have the same political rights, but some 60 percent of the Polish nobility did not own land and, especially in the eastern palatinates, depended economically on powerful magnates who dominated politics and society in the Commonwealth.[2]

The Sarmatian way of life was, in the last analysis, a myth. It was based on the assumed descent of the *szlachta* from the inhabitants of ancient Sarmatia. Fashioned by an intellectual elite trained in the colleges and academies of the Jesuits and other orders of the Church in such centers as Cracow, Zamość, Wilno, Lwów, this myth gradually filtered down to the mass of the *szlachta*, which was scattered throughout the Commonwealth and accounted for about eight percent of the total population. Sarmatism undeniably helped to provide a basis for unity of belief and conviction in the Polish political nation; but it, as well as the pervasive influence of Jesuit education, tended to retard social and political development in Poland by fostering what has been called "Sarmatian and Catholic conformism."[3]

The *szlachta* of Eastern Belorussia, Lithuania, and the Right-Bank Ukraine proved to be difficult to accommodate to the Russian political and social order. Roughly 600,000 individuals (men, women, and children) living in these three areas considered themselves to be members of the nobility, whereas in 1795 there were only 150,000 nobles in all the Great Russian provinces of the empire.[4] In the first part of

[2] *History of Poland*, ed. A. Gieysztor, S. Kieniewicz et al. (Warsaw: PWN, 1968), pp. 262-66, 268-70, 297-301; Jörg K. Hoensch, *Sozialverfassung und politische Reform: Polen im vorrevolutionären Zeitalter* (Cologne-Vienna: Böhlau Verlag, 1973), pp. 50-86, 116-20.

[3] *History of Poland*, pp. 297-301.

[4] There are no reliable and exact statistics on the number of *szlachta* in this area at the end of the eighteenth century, but the elaborate calculations of Tadeusz Korzon concerning the size and distribution of the *szlachta* would seem to demonstrate that, as elsewhere in the Commonwealth, about eight percent of the population of these annexed territories consisted of would-be nobles: Korzon, *Wewnętrzne dzieje Polski za*

the nineteenth century, especially during the reign of Nicholas I, Russian officials undertook to reduce the size of the *szlachta*; but they had to proceed cautiously in Belorussia, Lithuania, and the Right-Bank Ukraine because here Polish noblemen had a monopoly of the experience and skills required to deal with the peasantry and problems of administrative and social order in accordance with local traditions and customary law. Even as late as the 1850s a majority of the Russian Empire's nobility still consisted of Poles.

The political institutions of the *szlachta's* Commonwealth functioned on both the provincial and national levels. On the provincial level, the *sejmiki* controlled organs of local self-government, taxation, and the nomination or appointment of officials and judges. They also formed an integral part of a complicated constitutional system that linked king, Sejm, or National Diet, and the local nobility. The Sejm consisted of a Chamber of Deputies and a Senate. The king, although elected by the nobility, was more than a mere figurehead, for he was supreme commander of the armed forces, could make alliances, and appointed the higher officials who sat in the Senate. The Chamber of Deputies, however, was a real center of political power in the Commonwealth, and in it matters of national policy were decided on the basis of instructions received by the deputies from their constituencies, i.e., the assembled nobility in each local *sejmik*. Since these constituencies generally opposed efforts of Polish kings to develop an effective central administration and to build a large standing army, Poland was militarily weak and her government decentralized and inadequate for the purposes of a major power in eighteenth-century Europe. Yet, until the mid-seventeenth century the Polish constitutional system functioned fairly well; but in the political confusion that followed the Khmel'nyts'kyi uprising of 1648 in the Ukraine and the Swedish invasion of 1655, abuse of the *liberum veto* and excessive and irresponsible exercise of the right to confederate led to political paralysis and repeated intervention by Russia and the other powers in the internal affairs of Poland.[5]

Stanisława Augusta (1764-1794): Badania historyczne ze stanowiska ekonomicznego i administracyjnego, 6 vols. (2nd ed.; Cracow-Warsaw: T. Paprocki, 1897-1898), 1: 87-154. On the nobility in the Great Russian provinces between 1744 and 1857, see Kabuzan, *Narodonaselenie*, p. 154; Kabuzan and S. M. Troitskii, "Izmeneniia v chislennosti, udel'noi vese i razmeshchenii dvorianstva v Rossii v 1782-1858 gg.," *Istoriia SSSR* (1971, nos. 4-5), pp. 153-69.

[5] Still to be consulted on the evolution and character of the Polish constitutional system is Stanisław Kutrzeba, *Historya ustroju Polski w zarysie*, 4 vols. (Lwów-Warsaw: Bernard Poloniecki, 1905-1920). See also *Historia państwa i prawa Polski*, vol. II: *Od połowy XV wieku do r. 1795*, ed. J. Bardach (4th ed.; Warsaw: PWN, 1971); Władysław

The Andruszów (Andrusovo) Truce of 1667 and the "Treaty of Eternal Peace" of 1686 were important turning points in Russo-Polish relations and marked the end of Poland's eastward expansion. Poland then ceded Smolensk to Russia and agreed to partition the Ukraine, retaining for herself the Right-Bank Ukraine but leaving the Left-Bank hetmanate and an enclave around Kiev in the hands of the Russians.[6] The four Right-Bank palatinates remaining in Poland (Bracław, Kiev, Podolia, and Volhynia) occupied an area of about 165,000 square kilometers and seem to have had a population in the neighborhood of three and a half million in 1795. More than three-fourths of the inhabitants of the Right-Bank palatinates were Ukrainians. The remainder of the population consisted mainly of Jews and Poles.[7]

During the fourteenth, fifteenth, and early sixteenth centuries, the palatinates of Bracław, Kiev, and Volhynia had been part of the Grand Duchy of Lithuania. During these centuries, their Orthodox Ukrainian inhabitants enjoyed such special rights as the official use locally of the Ruthenian language, their own laws (the Lithuanian Statute), and protection for their religious and other freedoms and privileges. The western Ukrainian lands acquired by Poland in the fourteenth and fifteenth centuries (that is, the Ruthenian and Podolian palatinates and the Chełm land) were not granted similar rights. In 1569, at the time of Lithuania's union with Poland, the palatinates of Bracław, Kiev, and Volhynia were transferred to Poland. Initially, the inhab-

Czapliński, "Das Problem der Einstimmigkeit im polnischen Sejm im 17. Jahrhundert," *Zeitschrift für Ostforschung* 28 (December 1979): 641-47.

[6] Zbigniew Wójcik, *Traktat andruszowski 1667 roku i jego geneza* (Warsaw: PWN, 1959); Bickford O'Brien, "Russo-Polish Relations in the Second Half of the Seventeenth Century," in *American Contributions to the Seventh International Congress of Slavists*, vol. 3: *History*, ed. Anna Cienciala (The Hague-Paris: Mouton, 1973), p. 63.

[7] Kabuzan, *Narodonaselenie*, p. 163; N. G. Krikun, "Naselenie Pravoberezhnoi Ukrainy v 1789 g.," in *Problemy istoricheskoi demografii SSSR*, ed. R. N. Pullat, pp. 92-103. There are also no reliable figures concerning the national composition of the population of this area at the time Russia annexed it. My estimates are based on Henryk Mościcki, *Dzieje porozbiorowe Litwy i Rusi 1772-1800* (Vilnius: J. Zawadzki, [1913]), pp. 23-24; and on the maps and statistical tables provided by P. N. Batiushkov, ed., *Atlas narodonaseleniia zapadnorusskogo kraia po ispovedovaniiam sostavlen pri Ministerstve vnutrennikh del v Kantseliarii zavedyvaiushchego ustroistvom Pravoslavnykh tserkvei zapadnykh gubernii* (St. Petersburg: n.p., 1864). Batiushkov tends to underestimate the number of Poles living in the western *gubernii*, but his tables and maps are based on the best data then available as compiled by Russian statisticians and ecclesiastical and government authorities. I have assumed that the basic national structure of the population changed relatively little during the pre-industrial period 1795-1863. It should be noted, however, that during this period the Jewish population of the western *gubernii*, especially in Eastern Belorussia, increased more rapidly than that of the other nationalities.

itants of these three palatinates were permitted to continue to use
Ruthenian as an official language and to retain the religious, political,
and legal rights they had enjoyed previously as part of the Grand
Duchy of Lithuania.[8] In the seventeenth century, however, the
Ukrainians of these palatinates gradually lost control of local society
and politics as the Roman Catholic Church increased its influence and
the political and economic power of the magnates and *szlachta* was
consolidated throughout the Polish-Lithuanian Commonwealth.

Important elements of Ukrainian society—especially among the
burghers, clergy, and Cossacks—stubbornly resisted the growing economic and political power of the Polish magnates and *szlachta* as well
as the allures of Polish secular and religious culture and civilization.
Orthodox brotherhoods and schools had flourished in the Right-Bank
Ukraine during the seventeenth century. In 1632 Kiev Metropolitan
Peter Mohyla organized a collegium, which, as the Kievan Academy,
was the first institution of higher education for the Orthodox Eastern
Slavs and which trained numerous Ukrainian nobles and clergy for
political and Church careers in the Commonwealth, the Ukraine, and
Russia. Although the Ukrainian aristocracy and a good part of the
middle gentry became Roman Catholic and Polish during the seventeenth century, simultaneously the Zaporozhian Cossacks emerged as
a nucleus of indigenous Ukrainian political and military power. Although Cossack leaders tended to be primarily concerned with their
own special rights and privileges, by the time of the Khmel'nyts'kyi
revolt in the mid-seventeenth century the periodic uprisings against
the Commonwealth organized in defense of Cossack rights and privileges had become associated with the grievances of other elements of
the Ukrainian population—the clergy, burghers, Orthodox petty nobles, and peasants. "Rus' consciousness and unity," as Frank Sysyn
has pointed out, was heightened during Khmel'nyts'kyi's revolt and
the "Ukrainian ethnic mass went through a phase of vertical integration." As short-lived as this phase was, it was not forgotten by Ukrainians. In the century that followed, Cossacks again and again joined

---

[8] Andrzej Kaminksi, "Polish-Lithuanian Commonwealth and Its Citizens: Was the
Commonwealth a Stepmother for Cossacks and Ruthenians?" in *Poland and Ukraine:
Past and Present*, ed. Peter J. Potichnyj (Edmonton-Toronto: The Canadian Institute
of Ukrainian Studies, 1980), pp. 36-37; Frank E. Sysyn, "Ukrainian-Polish Relations in
the Seventeenth Century: The Role of National Consciousness and National Conflict in
the Khmelnytsky Movement," in ibid., pp. 67-69; Jaroslav Pelenski, "The Incorporation of the Ukrainian Lands of Old Rus' into Crown Poland (1569): (Socio-Material
Interest and Ideology—A Reexamination)," in *American Contributions to the Seventh
International Congress of Slavists*, 3: 41-52.

forces with other elements of the population in opposing the existing social and political order of the Polish-Lithuanian Commonwealth.[9]

The peasants in the Right-Bank Ukraine represented a particular problem for the Commonwealth. Elsewhere within its borders, especially in ethnically Polish areas, the expansion of the lands of the *szlachta* and of the latifundia of the magnates was gradual, and peasant labor and other obligations owed to the landowners increased over an extended period of several generations; peasant uprisings occurred but were sporadic and did not seriously threaten the control that the Polish nobility exercised over the countryside. In the southeastern part of the Right-Bank Ukraine (that is, the southeastern regions of the palatinates of Bracław, Kiev, Volhynia, and also Podolia), on the other hand, the position of the Polish landowning nobility had been weakened by the Cossack wars of the seventeenth century, and disruptive Tatar raids continued into the eighteenth century. For some time the peasants in this border area were in a relatively strong economic position. Since local Polish landowners were interested in attracting and keeping new settlers on their lands, at the beginning of the eighteenth century money rents were common in this part of the Ukraine and peasant obligations to landowners were generally less onerous than was usually the case elsewhere in the Commonwealth. Within several decades, however, the economic position of a substantial portion of the Right-Bank Ukrainian peasants perceptibly worsened as the magnates and *szlachta* extended the corvée system and increased peasant obligations. Unwilling to accept the dominance of Polish Catholic landowners over their lives, tens of thousands of Right-Bank Ukrainians followed Zaporozhian and local leaders in destructive *haidamak* uprisings aimed at ending Polish rule and driving the *szlachta* and the Catholic Church from the Right-Bank Ukraine.[10]

Russia's rulers of the first part of the eighteenth century were self-proclaimed protectors of the Orthodox faith, the spiritual center of which in the Ukrainian lands was Kiev, which had belonged to Russia since 1667. Beginning with Peter the Great, the emperors and empresses of Russia had been the allies of August II and August III,

[9] Sysyn, "Ukrainian-Polish Relations," pp. 77-78; *Istoriia Ukrainskoi SSR*, ed. K. K. Dubina et al., 2 vols. (Kiev: "Naukova Dumka," 1969), 1: 186-206, 252-60, 335-44; Jaroslaw Pelenski, "The Haidamak Insurrections and the Old Regimes in Eastern Europe," in *The American and European Revolutions, 1776-1848: Sociopolitical and Ideological Aspects* (Iowa City: University of Iowa Press, 1980), pp. 228-47.

[10] Pelenski, "The *Haidamak* Insurrection," p. 234; V. A. Markina, *Krest'iane pravoberezhnoi Ukrainy konets XVII-60-e gody XVIII st.* (Kiev: Izdatel'stvo Kievskogo Universiteta, 1971), pp. 5-6, 21-25, 30-32, 59-78, 130-37, 157-74.

Poland's Saxon kings, and their supporters among the Polish *szlachta* and magnates. Russia frequently reminded the Poles of the religious rights to which Orthodox believers in the Commonwealth were entitled according to the terms of the "Eternal Peace" of 1686, but she was disinclined to take a strong stand on the so-called dissident question for fear of alienating the Poles and jeopardizing Russia's predominant position in Poland-Lithuania. Paradoxically, the Orthodox Church and the economic and social well-being of Belorussian and Ukrainian peasants reached a nadir in Poland at the very same time that Russian power and influence in that country was at its peak. Had it not been for Russia's willingness to use armed force to maintain social order in the Right-Bank Ukraine, it is highly unlikely that the Uniate and Catholic Churches and the Polish *szlachta* and magnates could have successfully defended themselves against the threat represented by a number of major Ukrainian uprisings during the eighteenth century. The revolt of Semen Palii between 1702 and 1704 and the devastating *haidamak* uprisings of 1734-1737, 1750, and 1768 were only suppressed thanks to Russian armed intervention. Poland, with an army of less than 20,000 soldiers, was no longer in a position to maintain social order in the Right-Bank Ukraine. In last analysis, in this troubled area it was above all the Russian army that enabled the Polish *szlachta* to complete the work of Polonizing the upper strata of the population, pacifying the peasantry, and keeping it within the fold of the Uniate Church.[11]

On the whole, the lower classes of the Right-Bank Ukraine—who were mainly priests, peasants, and townsmen—retained the Eastern Orthodox rite but were organized into Uniate parishes and dioceses. In union with the Roman Catholic Church, they lost almost all contact with the hierarchy of the Orthodox Church in the Left-Bank Ukraine and Russia. A few hundred thousand Ukrainian Orthodox believers and a small number of Orthodox churches and monasteries managed

---

[11] Pelenski, "The *Haidamak* Insurrection," pp. 238-42; Julian Janczak, "Der Palej-Aufstand von 1702 bis 1704 in der Ukraine und die Haltung der Rzeczpospolita zum Nordischen Krieg," in *Um die polnische Krone: Sachsen und Polen während des Nordischen Krieges 1700-1721*, ed. J. Kalisch and J. Gierowski (Berlin: Rutten & Loening, 1962), pp. 95-128; Z. E. Kohut, "Myths Old and New: The *Haidamak* Movement and the Koliivshchyna (1768) in Recent Historiography," *Harvard Ukrainian Studies* 1 (1977, no. 3): 359-78. There is no acceptable and detailed, scholarly study on Polish-Russian relations during the eighteenth century. A brief scholarly treatment is, however, provided in Hoensch's *Sozialverfassung und politische Reform*. Still useful for the facts of diplomatic history from a Russian point of view are the relevant volumes of S. M. Solov'ev's *Istoriia Rossii*, vols. 7-15 of the Soviet edition (Moscow: Sotsekizdat, 1959-1966).

to escape subordination to Rome and remained under the spiritual authority of Orthodoxy and the Metropolitan in Kiev. These Orthodox believers, monasteries, and churches, however, no longer possessed an organized church hierarchy to defend their interests within the Polish-Lithuanian Commonwealth. Only in the eastern part of Belorussia did the Uniates fail to take over the Orthodox Church hierarchy within the Commonwealth, but the Belorussian bishopric remained unoccupied for several decades at the end of the seventeenth and the beginning of the eighteenth centuries.[12]

Following the "Eternal Peace" of 1686, representatives of Orthodoxy in the Commonwealth and in Kiev and Pereiaslav complained repeatedly to the Russian government and Holy Synod about illegal Uniate seizures of Orthodox churches and monasteries and the persecution of Orthodox believers in the Right-Bank Ukraine, Belorussia, and Lithuania. In 1710 Peter I obliged August II of Poland-Lithuania to reaffirm the religious liberties promised Orthodox Christians in the "Eternal Peace"; and in 1720 the Polish king, again under pressure from his ally, Emperor Peter of Russia, confirmed Sil'vester Chetvertinskii as the Orthodox bishop of Belorussia. Sil'vester, who died in 1728, was followed by a succession of other Ukrainians (Arsenii Berlo [1728-1732], Iosif Volchanskii [1732-1742], Ieronim Volchanskii [1744-1754], and Georgii Konisskii [1755-1795]), all of whom had been educated at the Kievan Academy and who continued the efforts of Sil'vester to alert the Russian Holy Synod and government in St. Petersburg to the needs and problems of Orthodox Christians in the Commonwealth.[13] Until the time of Catherine II, however, the Russian government, although it again and again protested the violations of the rights of Orthodox believers in Poland, did not give the Ukrainian bishops of Belorussia and defenders of the cause of Orthodoxy in the Commonwealth the sort of support that they perhaps were entitled to expect from the rulers of the most powerful Slavic and Orthodox nation in Europe.

A reassessment of Russian official attitudes concerning the dissident

[12] Hoensch, *Sozialverfassung und politische Reform*, pp. 187-89; Albert M. Ammann, *Abriss der ostslawischen Kirchengeschichte* (Vienna: Verlag Herder, 1950), pp. 321-27, 422-23; P. N. Batiushkov, ed., *Belorussiia i Litva: Istoricheskaia sud'ba severozapadnogo kraia* (St. Petersburg: "Obshchestvennaia Pol'za," 1890), pp. 276-78, 294-96; Janusz Woliński, *Polska i kościół prawosławny: Zarys historyczny* (Lwów: Ossolineum, 1936), pp. 111-24.

[13] N. N. Bantysh-Kamenskii, *Istoricheskoe izvestie o voznikshei v Pol'she Unii* (2nd ed.; Vilnius: A. Syrkin, 1866), pp. 124-326; Batiushkov, *Belorussiia i Litva*, pp. 297-307; G. Ia. Kiprianovich, *Istoricheskii ocherk pravoslaviia, katolichestva i Unii v Belorussii i Litve* (2nd ed.; Vilnius: I. Bliumovich, 1899), pp. 127-32, 137-39, 188-90.

question in Poland began toward the end of Elizabeth's reign. In 1755 Russia obtained approval of the appointment of Georgii Konisskii, the former rector of the Kievan Academy, as Orthodox bishop of Belorussia. The Russian Senate then approved financial support of an Orthodox seminary and church construction in Belorussia as well as an annual salary of 500 rubles for Konisskii,[14] whose bishopric, it should be noted, still lay outside Russia in Poland-Lithuania. In 1757 Gervasii Lintsevskii, another learned Ukrainian educated at the Kievan Academy, became bishop of Pereiaslav and coadjutor of the Kievan Metropolitan. As bishop, Gervasii, no doubt with the knowledge of his superiors and Russian secular authorities, paid particular attention to the religious needs of Orthodox believers living to the south of Pereiaslav and in Poland on the right bank of the Dnieper. In 1761 he entrusted Mel'khisidek Znachko-Iavorskii, a third Kiev Academy graduate and Ukrainian defender of the religious rights of Right-Bank Orthodox believers, with the administration of all Orthodox churches subordinated to the authority of the Pereiaslav bishop and located in the Right-Bank Ukraine. Mel'khisidek, the archimandrite of the Motrenin Monastery in the Czehryń (Chigirin, Chyhyryn) region, soon became the focal point of Orthodox resistance to further encroachments of the Uniate Church and even of reconversion to Orthodoxy in an unstable border area contiguous to lands lying to the south and dominated by the Zaporozhian Cossacks.[15]

Catherine II's decision to combine defense of the rights of dissidents with more active intervention in Polish internal politics was an important factor in setting in motion a chain of events that led to the last great *haidamak* uprising in 1768 and the First Partition of Poland in 1772. Catherine was well informed about the dissident question from the very beginning of her reign. In 1762 Georgii Konisskii attended her coronation in Moscow, where he exhorted her in eloquent Biblical language not to abandon unfortunate fellow Orthodox believers who found themselves in "Egypt" far from "blessed Palestine" (apparently the Orthodox Russia of Catherine II). The Belorussian bishop then stayed away from his episcopal seat in Mohylew for several years. He remained in Russia, where he systematically collected

[14] Solov'ev, *Istoriia Russii*, 12: 492.
[15] P. N. Batiushkov, ed., *Podolia: Istoricheskoe opisanie* (St. Petersburg: "Obshchestvennaia Pol'za," 1891), pp. 183-90; Wladyslaw Serczyk, *Hajdamacy* (Cracow: Wydawnictwo Literackie, 1972), pp. 265-89; M. O. Koialovich, *Istoriia vossoedineniia zapadnorusskikh Uniatov starykh vremen* (St. Petersburg: Vtoroe Otdelenie Sobstvennoi E.I.V. Kantseliarii, 1873), pp. 11-89; M. Cecylia Łubieńska, *Sprawa dysydencka 1764-1766* (Cracow-Warsaw: W. L. Anczyc, 1911), pp. 73-82.

materials that documented illegal seizures of Orthodox churches and monasteries as well as other alleged Polish violations of the rights of Orthodox Christians living in the Commonwealth. In 1765 Catherine sent him to Warsaw with a guard of three Russian dragoons so that he could present his case to the Polish king and government. Mel'khisedek made trips to St. Petersburg and Warsaw during these same years to gain support for the rights of the Orthodox Church in the Right-Bank Ukraine. In the Ukraine, Bishop Gervasii worked together with both Mel'khisedek and Georgii Konisskii in promoting the interests of Orthodoxy. In 1765 Gervasii visited monasteries and parishes on the right bank of the Dnieper. This visitation, the first one in the Right-Bank Ukraine by an Orthodox bishop in more than fifty years, greatly encouraged the hopes of local Orthodox Christians in Poland for Russian assistance in defending their interests.[16]

In 1764 Stanisław August Poniatowski, Catherine's former lover, was elected king of Poland. Catherine made Russian support of him and of a moderate program of internal reform in Poland contingent upon recognition of equal political and religious rights for the dissidents within the Commonwealth. In 1767 and 1768 Russian Ambassador N. V. Repnin, after having failed to prevail by persuasion during the preceding three years, used force and intimidation to oblige Poland to accept a "perpetual peace" that guaranteed the rights and privileges of the dissidents and reduced Poland to the status of a protectorate of Russia, who became the guarantor of the constitution and of the territorial integrity of the Polish state. An almost immediate reaction to the treaty was the organization of the anti-Russian Confederation of Bar, which, centered in the southeastern Ukrainian part of the Commonwealth, helped spark the last major *haidamak* uprising, the violent *koliszczyna* of 1768. Turkey, feeling threatened by the consolidation of Russian power in Poland seemingly achieved by the "Perpetual Treaty," declared war against Russia in November of that same year. The diplomatic complications in Europe produced by the ensuing Russo-Turkish War of 1768-1774 resulted in the First Partition of Poland in 1772.[17]

Following the First Partition, Russia gradually reestablished her

---

[16] Bantysh-Kamenskii, *Istoricheskoe izvestie*, pp. 56, 312-26; Koialovich, *Istoriia vossoedineniia*, pp. 24-25; Łubieńska, *Sprawa*, pp. 48-60, 153-60; Solov'ev, *Istoriia Rossii*, 13: 129-30, 363-65, 449-50; 14: 243-45; Solov'ev, *Geschichte des Falles von Polen*, tr. J. Spörer (Gotha: E. F. Thienemann, 1865), pp. 33-35.

[17] On the diplomatic and military events associated with the First Partition, see Herbert H. Kaplan, *The First Partition of Poland* (New York and London: Columbia University Press, 1962).

position in Poland, which continued to be based on cooperation with Stanisław Poniatowski. Bishop Gervasii and Archimandrite Mel'khisedek, who were held responsible by certain high-ranking Russian officials for having contributed to bringing about the *kolisz-czyna*, were transferred to new posts in 1768.[18] For several years pressure on the Poles to grant religious equality to the dissidents was somewhat relaxed, and the integration of newly acquired Eastern Belorussia into the general administrative and social structure of the empire soon became a more immediate task for Russian officials.

Eastern Belorussia, occupying an area of about the size of Indiana (87,000 square kilometers),[19] extended from Livland in the northwest to the Russian Ukrainian province of Chernigov in the southeast. In 1772 this new Russian borderland had a population of 1.3 million, consisting of Belorussians, Latvians, Poles, Jews, and Russians. Its Latvian peasant population was concentrated in Polish Livonia to the northwest, or in *Inflanty*, which had a population of about 170,000. Outside *Inflanty* in the area acquired by Russia in 1772, approximately a million Belorussians accounted for almost 90 percent of the population. The remainder of the population of Eastern Belorussia and *Inflanty* was made up of Jews (ca. 50,000), Polish *szlachta* (ca. 80,000), and Great Russian Old Believers (ca. 40,000).[20]

In Eastern Belorussia, as in the southeastern part of the Right-Bank Ukraine, the position of the *szlachta* and of the Roman Catholic hierarchy was somewhat weaker than in the western Ukrainian and Belorussian lands. Although no military class comparable to the Cossacks emerged in Eastern Belorussia, the wars of the sixteenth and seventeenth centuries and peasant uprisings, on occasion with the support of the Ukrainian Cossacks, slowed the consolidation of the economic power of Polish landowners. In Eastern Belorussia the latter were also

[18] Koialovich, *Istoriia vossoedineniia*, pp. 89-104; Solov'ev, *Istoriia Rossii*, 14: 244-45, 247-48, 263-64.

[19] The figure usually given is 93,000 square kilometers, but see A. M. Karpachev and P. G. Kozlovskii, "Dinamika chislennosti naseleniia Belorussii vo vtoroi polovine XVII-XVIII v.," in *Ezhegodnik po agrarnoi istorii vostochnoi Evropy 1968 g.* (Leningrad: "Nauka," 1972), p. 84.

[20] For my 1772 estimates I have taken 80 percent of what the Batiushkov *Atlas* reports for Mohylew and Witebsk *gubernii* in 1863 (the population increased from 1.3 to 1.7 million between 1772 and 1863). The estimate of 80,000 *szlachta* is from Korzon, *Wewnętrzne dzieje Polski*, 1: 152; and Henryk Mościcki, *Dzieje porozbiorowe Litwy i Rusi 1772-1800*, p. 24. In the article cited in the preceding footnote, Karpachev and Kozlovskii ("Dinamika," pp. 89-94) provide a detailed commentary concerning some of the problems involved in estimating the population of Belorussia at the end of the eighteenth century.

obliged to adjust themselves to a local economy that resembled the Russian north-central region more than it did the grain-producing lands of the Vistula basin. The trade routes of Eastern Belorussia, which exported hemp, potash, vegetable oil, and forest products, led to Riga and the Ukraine via the Western Dvina and Dnieper rivers. Peasant holdings were considerably more important than the latifundia in producing for both the local and export markets; and, as in the southeastern part of the Right-Bank Ukraine, money rents, not the corvée, represented the most common form of peasant obligation to the landowners. Consequently, Eastern Belorussian peasants, although serfs and economically dependent on the landowning *szlachta*, would seem to have been in a better position to defend their own interests than was generally the case in other parts of the Commonwealth.[21] Perhaps this was one reason why about 30 percent of the Belorussian peasants (ca. 300,000) in this Polish-Lithuanian borderland succeeded in staying out of the Uniate Church, giving Russia an opportunity to pressure Poles into allowing a succession of Ukrainian bishops trained at Kiev to serve as the Orthodox bishops of Belorussia after 1720. The presence of these bishops in Mohylew as well as the occasional interest displayed by Russian rulers in defending the interests of the Orthodox Church in Poland must have reminded many Eastern Belorussians of certain common interests and of the historical and cultural background they shared with their Russian neighbors.

In the spring of 1772 Zakhar G. Chernyshev was appointed as the first Russian governor-general of Belorussia. He had been interested in Polish Livonia and Eastern Belorussia for some time, and as early as 1763 he had recommended the annexation of these areas. He then suggested that, once annexed, these two provinces could be more easily assimilated by Russia if they would be joined administratively to adjacent Great Russian *gubernii*. Accordingly, in 1772 Polish Livonia and the Połock region were united (in an enlarged Pskov *guberniia*) with the Great Russian districts of Pskov and Velikie Luki; but in 1776 Velikie Luki and Pskov were separated from the areas annexed from Poland, which then became the Belorussian *gubernii* of Połock and Mohylew. The Provincial Reform of 1775 was introduced into these two provinces in 1778, when Chernyshev received the new title of Viceroy of Belorussia.[22]

---

[21] *Istoriia Belorusskoi SSR*, ed. L. S. Abetsedarskii et al., 2 vols. (Minsk: Akademiia Nauk Belorusskoi SSR, 1961), 1: 120-34, 165-89, 200-5; V. I. Meleshko, *Ocherki agrarnoi istorii vostochnoi Belorussii (vtoraia polovina XVII-XVIII v.)* (Minsk: "Nauka i Tekhnika," 1975), pp. 3-39, 62-64, 217-20.

[22] U. L. Lehtonen, *Die polnischen Provinzen Russlands unter Katharina II. in den*

Between 1772 and 1778 Chernyshev and his assistants worked to prepare Belorussia for the introduction of the reform of provincial administration then being worked out for the empire as a whole. One of their first measures, and a very significant one at that, was the introduction of the Russian poll tax in 1773. From the very beginning Russian officials took over the higher offices in the provincial administration, which was organized as much as possible in conformity with the new institutions, administrative procedures, and social norms then being tested in nearby Tver', Novgorod, and Pskov *gubernii*, whose viceroy, the Baltic German Jakob Sievers, was one of the principal sources of ideas for Catherine II in matters relating to provincial reform. With the introduction in 1778 of Catherine II's Provincial Reform of 1775 into Belorussia, Russian courts, administration, laws, and language in the offices of the state bureaucracy largely replaced the hitherto dominant Polish legal administrative order in Połock and Mohylew *gubernii*. Local civil law (the Lithuanian Statute) continued, however, to remain in effect, Poles still controlled local government and courts, and their religious and property rights were respected.[23]

Indeed, Catherine II's social policies tended to perpetuate the special position of the Polish *szlachta* in local Belorussian society. An essential underlying assumption of both the 1775 Provincial Reform and the Charter to the Nobility was that the guarantee of certain rights and privileges for the nobility would encourage them to take an active part in public affairs and share with government officials the burden of administering and maintaining order in the empire's *uezdy* and *gubernii*. In the Połock and Mohylew regions this of course meant that Polish nobles would be the *guberniia* marshals of the nobility and that they would staff the Boards of Public Welfare and lower courts and administrative offices. The government, to be sure, exercised a greater degree of control and supervision over the activities of Mohylew and Połock nobles than they had known in the past, and it would seem that the imposition of Russian legal and bureaucratic norms did result in some improvement in the administration of justice and local

---

Jahren 1772-1782, tr. G. Schmidt (Berlin: Georg Reimer, 1907), pp. 234-37, 249; SIRIO, 51: 11; Amburger, *Geschichte der Behördenorganisation*, pp. 371, 393-94.

[23] Lehtonen, *Die polnischen Provinzen*, pp. 235-42, 247-48, 335-93, 422-23; B. E. Nol'de, *Ocherki russkogo gosudarstvennogo prava* (St. Petersburg: "Pravda," 1911), pp. 420-23; Jones, *Emancipation*, pp. 177-78, 214-17; Karl Ludwig Blum, *Ein russischer Staatsmann: Des Grafen Jakob Johann Sievers Denkwürdigkeiten zur Geschichte Russlands* (Leipzig-Heidelberg: C. F. Winter'sche Verlagsbuchhandlung, 1857-58), 1: 153-54; 2: 35-112; James A. Duran, "The Reform of Financial Administration in Russia during the Reign of Catherine II," *Canadian Slavic Studies* 4 (1970): 495.

affairs and in raising the educational and cultural level of local society.[24] But organized local society was largely Polish and Catholic, and its consolidation and reinforcement was one unanticipated result of the reforms of Catherine II in Belorussia.

At the same time, other aspects of Catherinean policy marked the beginning of the gradual Russification of the upper strata of the population in the areas acquired from Poland between 1772 and 1795. Her policy of granting settled state or confiscated lands in Belorussia to Russian favorites and high officials, for example, removed some 190,000 peasants from the control of Polish landowners.[25] This policy was continued by her successors, especially in the periods immediately following the 1830-1831 and 1863-1864 Polish insurrections. Her educational policy also remained and made state-supported education in the Russian language available to the nobles of these formerly Polish borderlands. Between 1789 and 1794 two *guberniia* four-class and five *uezd* two-class public schools were opened in towns of the Belorussian viceroyalty. The establishment of such schools throughout Russia had been projected in the Provincial Reform of 1775, and the Russian Statute of National Education of 1786 instructed governors to proceed with their construction.[26] Schools established in Russia during the reign of Catherine II represented, however, only a first, small step in the direction of establishing a national system of education for the privileged classes of the population. In Eastern Belorussia, Russian state schools found it difficult until the second quarter of the nineteenth century to compete with the well-established Polish schools of the Jesuits and other Roman Catholic orders.

The peasantry in Eastern Belorussia seems to have benefited very little from Catherine II's administrative Russification and introduction of Russian landowners into this borderland area. To be sure, its annexation by Russia opened new opportunities for enterprising peasants in marketing their products in the Left-Bank Ukraine, Great Russia, and the Baltic provinces. The strengthening of police and governmental authority may have been of some use to the Belorussian peasants in defending themselves against illegal and arbitrary acts by Polish landowners, but the reinforcement of the social and legal authority of Polish officials and nobles also made it more difficult for

---

[24] Lehtonen, *Die polnischen Provinzen*, pp. 297-302, 389-404.

[25] Ibid., pp. 505-12; Madariaga, *Russia*, pp. 554, 650 n. 26.

[26] Madariaga, *Russia*, pp. 495-99; *Istoriia Belorussii*, 1: 266-67; M. K. Kirillov, "Shkola i pedagogicheskaia mysl' v Belorussii," in *Ocherki istorii shkoly i pedagogicheskoi mysli narodov SSSR XVIII v.-pervaia polovina XIX v.*, ed. M. F. Shabaeva (Moscow: "Pedagogika," 1973), pp. 420-21.

local peasants to evade their obligations to both the state and land-owners. And Russian rule meant increased taxation and recruitment into the imperial army.[27]

Little was done to defend the religious rights of the Belorussian peasantry during the first decade of Russian rule. The annexation of Eastern Belorussia in 1772 brought Georgii Konisskii's Orthodox Belorussian episcopal seat in Mohylew within the borders of the Russian Empire. Throughout the remainder of the 1770s Konisskii worked in vain to obtain official approval for the mass conversion of Uniates to Orthodoxy. Catherine II probably hesitated to give such approval because she remembered that only a few years earlier a major *haidamak* uprising, the *koliszczyna* of 1768, had occurred. In addition, many practical problems were associated with bringing almost a million Uniates and Roman Catholics into the Russian Empire as a result of the First Partition of Poland. Until then the handful of Catholics living in Russia had been subject to the administrative authority of the Justice College for Livland, Estland, and Finland Affairs. At the time of the annexation of Eastern Belorussia, one of Catherine's first acts was to proclaim freedom of religion for her new subjects. By the end of 1772 she had approved a nine-point program for church administration in Belorussia that made the Catholics and Uniates in this province subject to the jurisdiction of the Baltic Justice College, and she had proposed the appointment of a single bishop for all the Catholics in Russia. Although the sanction of the Roman pontiff for the establishment of a Catholic bishopric for Russia had to be obtained sooner or later, Catherine acted promptly to subject the Roman Catholic clergy in Eastern Belorussia to the exclusive administrative authority of the Russian government. As early as November 1773 she named Stanisław Bohusz Siestrzencewicz as bishop of Mohylew. For nearly fifty years Siestrzencewicz was to cooperate with the Russian authorities in administering the affairs of the Roman Catholics and Uniates living in the Russian Empire, beginning with the nonpromulgation of the pope's brief *Dominus ac Redemptor* of 1773 that suppressed the Jesuit Order. Catherine chose to defy the pope with regard to the Jesuits because she and Belorussian Governor-General Chernyshev valued their skills and services as educators and wanted them to continue to maintain their network of schools in Belorussia. In 1782, again without consulting the pope, she elevated Siestrzencewicz to the position of archbishop of Mohylew. Two years later the pope, yielding to Russian

[27] Lehtonen, *Die polnischen Provinzen*, pp. 297-307; *Istoriia Belorusskoi SSR*, 1: 257-87.

pressure, finally confirmed Siestrzencewicz as the archbishop for the Catholics of the Russian Empire.[28]

Georgii Konisskii had to wait until 1780 for permission to act on the petitions of Eastern Belorussian Uniates to return to the Orthodox Church. Even after 1780 Konisskii was authorized to act only on petitions from vacant Uniate parishes (that is, parishes without priests). Parishes, however, could easily be declared vacant after their priest had been reunited individually with Orthodoxy, opening the possibility of legally accepting entire Uniate parishes into the Orthodox Church. During the 1780s Konisskii managed to reunite more than a hundred thousand Uniates with Orthodoxy. At the same time, he played a major role in arranging in 1783 the appointment of Viktor Sadkovskii (then the chaplain of the Russian embassy in Warsaw and once a pupil of Konisskii at the Kievan Academy and the prefect of the Mohylew Orthodox Seminary between 1758 and 1775) as archimandrite of the Orthodox monastery in Słuck. In 1785 he was made bishop of Pereiaslav and coadjutor of the Kievan Metropolitan. With these appointments Sadkovskii, in effect, became the bishop for Orthodox believers living in Poland, an office that had been envisaged in the treaty of 1768 between Russia and Poland. Although he resided in Słuck and became a Polish citizen, he remained under the religious authority of the Russian Holy Synod. Like Konisskii, he was a zealous defender of the interests of Orthodoxy in Poland-Lithuania.[29]

From the mid-1770s to the late 1780s Russia dominated what remained of Poland-Lithuania, a country of 520,000 square kilometers and 7.4 million inhabitants (in 1775). The Russian ambassador in Warsaw between 1772 and 1789 was Otto Magnus von Stackelberg, a Baltic German landowner from Estland who had studied at Leipzig

---

[28] Lehtonen, *Die polnischen Provinzen*, pp. 541-605; Ammann, *Abriss der ostslawischen Kirchengeschichte*, pp. 440-44; J. J. Zatko, "The Organization of the Catholic Church in Russia, 1772-1784," *Slavonic and East European Review* 43 (1965): 303-13. Both Lehtonen and Zatko give the number of Uniates and Catholics living in Eastern Belorussia and Latgale in 1772 as approximately 800,000 and 100,000, respectively. The number of Catholics would seem to have been greater, for there were 80,000 Polish *szlachta* in Mohylew and Witebsk *gubernii* and 170,000 people in Latgale, most of whom were Catholic Latvians. Furthermore, the mid-nineteenth-century population statistics contained in Batiushkov's *Atlas* indicate that 16 percent of the population of Mohylew and Witebsk *gubernii* consisted of Roman Catholics. In other words, there were probably something in the neighborhood of 200,000 Roman Catholics living in this area at the end of the eighteenth century.

[29] Koialovich, *Istoriia vossoedineniia zapadnorusskikh Uniatov*, pp. 121-34, 207-14, 226-27, 279-87; Batiushkov (ed.), *Belorussia i Litva*, pp. 308-9, 322-25; Korzon, *Wewnętrzne dzieje Polski za Stanisława Augusta*, 1: 203-15, 237-38.

University, traveled widely in Europe, and previously served as Russian minister in Madrid. In August 1772 Nikita Panin, Catherine II's principal foreign-affairs adviser, instructed Stackelberg to cooperate with his Prussian and Austrian colleagues in Warsaw in obtaining Sejm approval of the First Partition and to use fully the means at his disposal (mainly Russian money and troops) to manipulate the Polish political system in a manner that would ensure the continuation of the "perpetual peace" the Poles had made with Russia in 1768. But after 1775 the political status quo in Poland—including the elective monarchy, the republican form of government, and the *liberum veto* —was now guaranteed by not just Russia but by all three of the partitioning powers. This did not, however, hinder Russia from continuing to occupy a dominant position in Warsaw, for Stackelberg succeeded in using King Stanisław August Poniatowski and a newly established executive organ, the Permanent Council, for the purposes of Russian policy in Poland. Stanisław August himself referred to Stackelberg as a sort of Roman proconsul in Poland.[30]

Stackelberg's proconsulate helped stabilize Poland politically; and government by the Permanent Council represented, as E. Rostworowski has noted, "a step forward in comparison with the former anarchy and provided a school of administrative experience of great importance for the future."[31] The *liberum veto* then fell out of use, and the Poles practiced a degree of self-restraint unknown in the Polish Sejm for more than a century. Without the *liberum veto* it became possible to introduce a number of reforms during the 1770s and 1780s, including the reorganization and improvement of postal service, the police, and the administration of finances. Even more important was the creation in 1773 of the Commission of National Education, which laid the foundations for a national system of education in Poland based on sound pedagogical and administrative principles and financed with funds resulting from the abolition of the Jesuit Order in Poland-Lithuania. But Stanisław August and such reformers as Andrzej Zamoyski (a progressive landowner), Józef Wybicki (later an émigré patriot and author of the words for the future Polish national anthem, the *Ma-*

---

[30] DBL, p. 752; *History of Poland*, ed. Gieysztor and Kieniewicz, pp. 327-36; Solov'ev, *Geschichte des Falles von Polen*, pp. 147-54; Jerzy Łojek, "La politique de la Russie envers la Pologne pendant le premier partage de la Pologne d'après un document secret de la cour russe de 1772," *Canadian-American Slavic Studies* 8 (1974): 116-35; Daniel Stone, *Polish Politics and National Reform 1775-1788* (Boulder: East European Quarterly, 1976), pp. 9-13.

[31] "Tentative Reforms under Russia's Tutelage (1763-1788)," in *History of Poland*, p. 336.

zurka Dąbrowskiego), and Hugo Kołłątaj (the reformer of Cracow University and a notable publicist and political leader) suffered a major defeat in 1780 when the Sejm rejected the codification of Polish law they had prepared at the request of the Sejm of 1776. The so-called Zamoyski Code would have deprived the landless *szlachta* of political rights, regulated church-state relations, and protected certain legal rights of serfs and townsmen. Neither Stackelberg nor the clerical and magnate opposition in the Sejm was then willing to tolerate the changes in the Polish constitutional and social system contained in the Zamoyski Code. Its rejection indicated the limits of reform permitted under Stackelberg's proconsulate.[32]

A more fundamental reform of government and society in Poland obviously could only be undertaken if the Poles had full control over their own internal affairs. This they achieved during the Four-Year Sejm, 1788-1792, thanks to Russian involvement in another war with Turkey and thanks to a short-lived alliance with Prussia, a nation that was not in a position to dominate Poland to the extent Russia had prior to 1788. For four years the Sejm controlled the politics of a *szlachta* nation of some 700,000 individuals (out of a total population of nine million in 1791). The reform movement in the Sejm was supported by extensive journalistic discussions of the major problems of Polish society, including the freeing of the peasants and the extension of political rights to property-owning burghers. The leaders of the reform movement in Poland, the so-called Patriotic Party, were, however, also political realists prepared to compromise with the majority of their social peers that still clung to the "Golden Freedom" of the Polish nobility. Their compromise with this majority was embodied in the Constitution of May 3, 1791, which excluded the landless *szlachta* from the *sejmiki* (and Sejm), abolished the *liberum veto* as well as confederations and confederated Sejms, and provided for a ministerial form of government and for Poland's first systematized and centralized machinery of government. It also declared that the peasants were under the protection of the law, improved the legal position of burghers in Polish society, and entitled towns to send twenty-four plenipotentiaries with limited voting rights to the Sejm. There is little question that the Patriotic Party intended to proceed with further reforms as soon as circumstances permitted. Its intellectual leaders

[32] Ibid., pp. 331-37, 356-58; Stone, *Polish Politics and National Reform*, pp. 11-19, 26-28, 33-36; Jean Fabre, *Stanislas-Auguste Poniatowski et l'Europe des lumières* (Paris: "Les Belles Lettres," 1952), pp. 437-46, 458, 463-64; Ambroise Jobert, *La Commission d'Education Nationale en Pologne (1773-1794)* (Paris: Droz, 1941); Tadeusz Mizia, *O Komisji Educacji Narodowej* (Warsaw: PWN, 1972).

realized that Poland's future strength and prosperity depended to a large extent on including the burghers in the Polish political nation and on guaranteeing satisfactorily the personal, economic, and legal rights of some 6.5 million peasants, who accounted for more than 70 percent of the Commonwealth's population in 1791.[33]

A combination of Russian unwillingness to tolerate an independent Poland, Prussian territorial ambitions, and opposition within the *szlachta* to the Constitution of May 3 (especially, the Targowica Confederation of 1792) soon put an end to the Polish constitutional experiment. In the latter part of 1791 the success of Catherine II's diplomats in frustrating British plans for forming a coalition of powers to contain Russian expansionist designs on Turkish lands obliged Prussia to reassess the anti-Russian policy she had pursued in Poland since 1788. Peace with Turkey at the end of 1791 and the formation of the Targowica Confederation opened the way for renewed Russian military intervention in Polish affairs in May 1792. The Russians encountered relatively little military and political resistance in conquering Poland in 1792 and, together with the Prussians, in carrying out the Second Partition in 1793. The Poles, on the other hand, fought heroically during the Kościuszko insurrection of April-October 1794. The bitter and prolonged nature of Polish resistance in 1794 to the invading troops of Austria, Prussia, and Russia; the attention the Polish insurrectionists paid to the examples provided by the French and American revolutions; their relative success in mobilizing the Polish nation and economy for the purposes of the insurrection; and their promise of personal freedom and security of tenure to the Polish peasants all very much disturbed the partitioning powers. If the total partition of Poland had not been a foregone conclusion from the very beginning, now it no longer seemed prudent to allow even a Polish buffer state to continue to exist.[34]

---

[33] *History of Poland*, pp. 344, 359-76; Stone, *Polish Politics and National Reform*, pp. 76-83.

[34] *History of Poland*, pp. 377-92; Madariaga, *Russia*, pp. 427-51; Solov'ev, *Geschichte des Falles von Polen*, pp. 261-362; Jerzy Łojek, "Catherine II's Armed Intervention in Poland: Origins of the Political Decisions at the Russian Court in 1791 and 1792," *Canadian Slavic Studies* 4 (1970): 570-93; Łojek, "The International Crisis of 1791: Poland Between the Triple Alliance and Russia," *East Central Europe* 2 (1975): 1-63; Łojek, *Misja Debolego w Petersburgu w latach 1787-1792* (Wrocław: Ossolineum, 1962); idem, *Przed Konstytucje Trzeciego Maja* (Warsaw: Pax, 1977); idem, *Upadek Konstytucji 3 Maja* (Wrocław: Ossolineum, 1976); Robert H. Lord, *The Second Partition of Poland: A Study in Diplomatic History* (Cambridge: Harvard University Press, 1915); Lord, "The Third Partition of Poland," *Slavonic and East European Review* 3 (1925) : 481-98.

In the Second and Third Partitions of Poland, Russia acquired an additional area of 376,200 square kilometers (about the size of Montana), populated by some six million Belorussians, Jews, Lithuanians, Poles, and Ukrainians. The territory annexed in 1793 was organized into Bracław, Iziasław (that is, Eastern Volhynia), and Minsk *gubernii*, which were reorganized in 1795 at the time of the Third Partition into Podolia, Volhynia, Bracław, Minsk, Słonim, Wilno, and Kurland *gubernii*. From the outset the Russian authorities made it clear that the inhabitants of these provinces, although assured of their religious and property rights, were not to be granted autonomy or special rights and privileges similar to those enjoyed by Estland and Livland during the first part of the eighteenth century. Initially, however, the Polish and Kurland German court systems were to continue to function according to their own established procedures and according to the Lithuanian Statute and Kurland local law until Russian courts and laws could be introduced at some unspecified future date. Meanwhile, the Russian authorities proceeded to introduce the Provincial Reform of 1775 throughout the area that had been annexed from Poland.[35]

Catherine II's officials also worked to introduce changes in the organization of religious life in these provinces that had long-range effects on the majority of their Belorussian and Ukrainian inhabitants. During the 1780s Bishop Viktor Sadkovskii and Stackelberg, the Russian ambassador in Warsaw, were the principal defenders of the interests of the Orthodox Church in Poland-Lithuania. The Polish leaders of the Four-Year Sejm arrested Sadkovskii and kept him under guard in Warsaw or in prison between 1789 and 1792. Liberated by the Russians in June 1792, he was elevated to the position of archbishop of Minsk, Iziasław, and Bracław on April 13, 1793, shortly before the Polish Sejm, meeting in Grodno, confirmed the Second Partition of Poland. As early as December 1792 Catherine had emphasized, in her instructions to Jakob Sievers, the principal Russian negotiator at the Grodno Sejm, that something had to be done to

---

[35] PSZ, 1st ser., 23: 410-12, 417-19, 572-85, 641-44, 664-85, 691-92, 727-28, 844-46, 922-24, nos. 17,108, 17,112, 17,264, 17,300, 17,319, 17,323, 17,352, 17,354, 17,417, 17,418, 17,494, and 17,495, March 27 and April 23, 1793, October 30, 1794, January 27, April 15, May 1, July 5, and December 14, 1795, and August 8, 1796; ibid., 24: 228-30, 232-33, nos. 17,634 and 17,637, December 12, 1796; Nol'de, *Ocherki russkogo gosudarstvennogo prava*, pp. 423-27; Mościcki, *Dzieje porozbiorowe Litwy i Rusi 1772-1800*, pp. 405-6; Klochkov, *Ocherki pravitel'stvennoi deiatel'nosti vremeni Pavla I*, pp. 410-11; Amburger, *Geschichte der Behördenorganisation*, pp. 391, 398; "Rozbiory Polski," in *Mały słownik historii Polski*, p. 310; Karpachev and Kozlovskii, "Dinamika chislennosti naselenii Belorussii vo vtoroi polovine XVII-XVIII v.," in *Ezhegodnik po agrarnoi istorii vostochnoi Evropy 1968 g.*, pp. 83-84.

spare from religious oppression "lands and towns that had once belonged to Russia, populated and founded by her kinsmen (*edinoplemenniki*) and professing with us one faith."[36] Archbishop Viktor Sadkovski, however, did not immediately obtain permission from the Holy Synod to act on petitions for the conversion of entire Uniate parishes. Only after the Kościuszko insurrection had begun was he able, in a pastoral letter of May 1794, to appeal directly to the peasants and townsmen of Minsk, Iziasław, and Bracław *gubernii* to leave the Uniate Church and rejoin the church to which their ancestors had once belonged. The presence of victorious Russian armies and the chaos that reigned in Poland at that time no doubt assisted the work of reuniting the Uniates with Orthodoxy. Between 1794 and 1796 almost 1.7 million Uniates were separated from the Roman Catholic Church and brought directly under the authority of the Russian Orthodox hierarchy and Holy Synod.[37]

In the mid-1790s Archbishop Viktor won Uniates for the cause of Orthodoxy much more easily in the Right-Bank Ukraine than in Eastern Belorussia or Lithuania. Three-fourths of his new converts (1.3 million) came from the same southeastern corner of the Right-Bank where the *haidamak* revolts had taken place earlier in the eighteenth century. In Mohylew and Witebsk *gubernii*, 110,000 Uniates returned to Orthodoxy in addition to the conversions made by Georgii Konisskii in the 1780s. There were relatively few conversions in Volhynia, while in Minsk *guberniia* only 80,000 new converts were found for Orthodoxy out of a population of 870,000 in 1795. In Słonim and Wilno *gubernii*, which Russia acquired in the Third Partition of Poland, there is no record whatsoever of conversions to Orthodoxy.[38]

About half the population of the Lithuanian provinces acquired in the Second and Third Partitions was Roman Catholic in religion. Almost all Poles and Lithuanians of these provinces (roughly 40 percent of the total population of 2.5 million in 1795) belonged to the Catholic Church, as did 25 percent of the Belorussians. Somewhat more than a million Belorussians were the largest single ethnic group living in this area; they were generally either Catholics or Uniates and ac-

[36] Koialovich, *Istoriia vossoedineniia zapadnorusskikh Uniatov*, pp. 281-331, 350-53.

[37] Ibid., pp. 353-73; Bantysh-Kamenskii, *Istoricheskoe izvestie o voznikshei v Pol'she Unii*, pp. 349-51; P. N. Batiushkov (ed.), *Podoliia: Istoricheskoe opisanie* (St. Petersburg: "Obshchestvennaia Pol'za," 1891), pp. 208-12; Korzon, *Wewnętrzne dzieje Polski za Stanisława Augusta*, 1: 172-74, 205-11, 237-38; Mościcki, *Dzieje porozbiorowe Litwy i Rusi*, pp. 365-70.

[38] Korzon, *Wewnętrzne dzieje Polski*, 1: 237-38; Kabuzan, *Narodonaselenie Rossii*, p. 162.

counted for the majority of the 1.4 million Uniates remaining in the Russian Empire after the mass conversions to Orthodoxy of the mid-1790s.[39] The large Catholic population and the influence excercised by the Roman Catholic hierarchy over the Uniate Church in the Lithuanian provinces made their inhabitants more resistant to Russian political and cultural pressures than was the case for those of Eastern Belorussia and the Right-Bank Ukraine.

In the last analysis, Russia did not possess sufficient human and institutional resources to effect the rapid administrative, social, and legal integration of the areas annexed from Poland in 1793 and 1795. These areas were extraordinarily complex in their national, social, religious, and political structure and contained a population (in 1795) eight times larger than that of Estland and Livland and four times larger than that of Eastern Belorussia. Even in the Right-Bank Ukraine and in Eastern Belorussia, Russia found it convenient to work together with the Polish magnates, clergy, and landowning *szlachta* for the control of the local serfs. By the same token, privileged elements throughout Lithuania, Belorussia, and the Right-Bank Ukraine shared the aversion of the Russian authorities to the French Revolution and the new rights and freedoms Kościuszko promised Polish, Belorussian, Ukrainian, and Lithuanian peasants in 1794. After the suppression of the Kościuszko insurrection, thousands of Polish magnates, landed *szlachta*, and clergy hastened to the new *guberniia* centers to swear unconditional loyalty to Russia and to petition for permission to send delegations to St. Petersburg. Among other things, such delegations undertook to thank Catherine II for having saved them, as the Grodno *szlachta* phrased it, from the "yoke of the perfidious rebels." The Russian authorities not only accepted but encouraged such professions of loyalty to the empress following the Kościuszko insurrection and the Third Partition. At the same time, they reorganized the Roman Catholic bishoprics and placed all the Uniates remaining in the empire under an enlarged Połock Uniate archbishopric, both to exercise more effective bureaucratic supervision over their activities and to assure the continuation of these activities as an element of social order and stability in the newly annexed areas.[40]

---

[39] Edward Likowski, *Dzieje Kościoła unickiego na Litwie i Rusi*, 2 vols. (2nd ed.; Warsaw: Gebethner i Wolff, 1906), 2: 13. Our estimates concerning the religious and national composition of the population of the Lithuanian provinces have been made on the basis of statistics presented by Kabuzan (*Narodonaselenie*, p. 162) and by the *Atlas* edited by Batiushkov.

[40] Mościcki, *Dzieje porozbiorowe Litwy i Rusi*, pp. 371-85; D. A. Tolstoi, *Romanism in Russia: An Historical Survey*, tr. Mrs. M'Kibbin, 2 vols. (1874; reprint ed., New

As regards the 1.7 million Uniates who had been reunited with Orthodoxy, it was one thing to bring them under the formal authority of the hierarchy of the Russian Orthodox Church; another, to provide the teachers, schools, and educated and properly trained clergy to transform their parishes culturally and socially and to make them a useful and integral part of Orthodox Russia. In any event, the Russian government soon lost interest in further conversions to Orthodoxy. After Georgii Konisskii died in February 1795, the vigorous leadership for the conversion movement in Mohylew and Witebsk *gubernii* was lost. The disinclination of Catherine II's government to act resolutely to end the resistance of Polish landowners and Uniate priests in Minsk, Słonim, and Wilno *gubernii* to the conversion of additional parishes to Orthodoxy is indicated by its decision early in 1796 to transfer Archbishop Viktor Sadkovskii to Chernigov in the Left-Bank Ukraine.[41]

Paul I and Alexander I inherited from Catherine the problem of how to deal with the Polish borderlands of the empire. Catherine and her advisers had introduced these lands to the Provincial Reform of 1775, and they had intended to proceed rapidly with the elimination of the Lithuanian Statute and Polish courts. They did not, however, have at their disposal (and perhaps did not even understand the need for) the detailed, comparative studies of Polish and Russian law that would have helped them to avoid unnecessary and counterproductive conflicts between traditional Polish and newly introduced Russian administrative and legal practices. It was almost two generations later that Russian officials, after Russian laws had been codified and a sufficient number of legal specialists trained by university law faculties, the School of Jurisprudence (founded in 1835), and the Second Section of His Imperial Majesty's Own Chancery (established in 1826), that Russia was finally in a position to impose her legal norms and courts on the formerly Polish provinces in a fairly orderly manner. Even as late as the 1830s influential and well-informed Russian legal specialists questioned the wisdom of abolishing the Lithuanian Statute. Paul I's advisers seemed to have been aware of some of the problems and difficulties involved in introducing Russian legal order into the provinces annexed from Poland when they decided, in December 1796, to include Belorussia, Lithuania, and the Right-Bank Ukraine

---

York: AMS Press, 1971), 1: 336-37, 345, 364-69. The *ukazy* of 1793-1796 are listed in note 35 above. They clearly indicate the concern of the Russian government at the time about social order as well as its interest in having the support of the local *szlachta*, clergy, and property owners.

[41] Koailovich, *Istoriia vossoedineniia zapadnorusskikh Uniatov*, pp. 368-76.

among the provinces administered on "special foundations according to their rights and privileges."[42]

Paul I and Alexander I made a wager on the loyalty to Russia of the Polish magnates and landowning *szlachta*. This wager was reasonable. Even though many Poles fought for Napoleon, wealthier landowning Poles of the Commonwealth's former eastern borderlands had long had much in common with the Russians in their preservation of the society of the Old Regime in Poland and Russia. Poles and Russians also had certain common economic interests. The Prussian acquisition of the Upper Vistula in 1772 impeded the free export of Polish agricultural products via Baltic ports, obliging the Poles to develop new trade outlets via the Black Sea. This trade was facilitated by recent Russian conquests from Turkey, the making of the Dniester into a navigable waterway, and the building of canals connecting the Dnieper river basin with the basins of the western Dvina and Vistula. There was, then, apparently good reason for educated and landowning Poles to make available to Russia political, administrative, and other specialized skills and knowledge acquired in a changing Poland during the second part of the eighteenth century for the purposes of reforming and improving Russian society at the beginning of the nineteenth century.

In Part Two of this study the interaction of reform for the empire with borderland special rights and privileges will be discussed. Because the borderland Polish and German elites were often well informed about what was going on in England, France, and Germany and had experience with European-type institutions of self-government, they seemed well suited to assist Russia in accommodating herself to new forms of society, governmental organization, and economic production then evolving in central and western Europe. Their privileged provinces became a sort of laboratory in which to experiment with peasant, educational, and even political reform. As long as these provinces continued to be a laboratory for reform, their special rights and privileges were not seriously questioned; indeed, they were expanded and further developed with the annexation of Finland in 1809 and of Congress Poland in 1815.

[42] PSZ, 1st ser., 24: 229, no. 17,634, December 12, 1796; Klochkov, *Ocherki pravitel'stvennoi deiatel'nosti vremeni Pavla I*, pp. 410-11, 426-27.

PART II

POLISH, FINNISH, AND BALTIC AUTONOMY, 1796-1830

THE WORK of centralization in the western borderlands undertaken by Catherine II was largely suspended during the period beginning with the accession of Paul I and ending with the outbreak of the 1830 November insurrection in Poland. Baltic and Polish nobles enjoyed the favor of both Paul I and his son Alexander I, but factors other than the particular predilections of individual tsars would seem to explain what then happened in the western borderlands. For, it is clear that neither Paul nor Alexander intended to permit these borderlands to develop separately from the rest of the empire. Alexander I, for example, confirmed the rights and privileges of the Livland and Estland *Ritterschaften* but introduced the qualifying clause, "insofar as they are in agreement with the general decrees and laws of our state."[1] If Alexander and his father, Paul, were willing to allow the nobles of the western borderlands to deviate from norms observed elsewhere in the empire, this was done chiefly with strictly local affairs.

Favorable circumstances, however, served the interests of the privileged estates in the western borderlands. During the intermittent wars with France or Sweden from 1798 to 1815, it seemed prudent for Russia to cultivate as much good will as possible in the lands of partitioned Poland, the Baltic provinces, and Finland. The annexation of Finland in 1809 and Congress of Poland in 1815 added more than 450,000 square kilometers of land and four million inhabitants to the empire, increasing the land area of Russia's western borderlands by roughly three-fourths and their population by more than 40 percent. Congress Poland was granted a considerable degree of autonomy and a Constitutional Charter. The Grand Duchy of Finland, like Congress Poland, was governed separately from the rest of the empire, and

---

[1] Haltzel, *Der Abbau der deutschen ständischen Selbstverwaltung in den Ostseeprovinzen Russlands*, p. 5.

Alexander I specifically instructed the Russian ministers and Senate in St. Petersburg not to interfere in Finnish internal affairs. The Baltic German *Ritterschaften* in Estland, Livland, and Kurland, in contrast to the *szlachta* of Congress Poland and the estates of Finland, remained under the jurisdiction of officials in St. Petersburg; however, the addition of relatively advanced non-Russian provinces to the western borderlands seemed a guarantee that the empire would remain a multinational state ruled by cosmopolitan, landowning elites. Within this familiar and traditional Russian Empire, the historic rights and privileges of German nobles and townsmen seemed reasonably secure.

Various experiments with political and social reform early in the nineteenth century also played a role in the further development of the separate identity of the western borderlands. These experiments began with the reign of Paul I, who worked energetically during his short reign of four and one-third years to overcome what he considered the shortcomings of Russian government. Aiming at greater efficiency and economy in local government, he reduced the number of *gubernii* from fifty to forty-one and eliminated a number of governors-general and other posts in the courts and administrative offices of the provinces. He cut the cost of running local government by about 25 percent, and wherever he could he replaced elective local officials with officials appointed by the central government.[2]

The ministerial form of government introduced by Alexander I between 1802 and 1811 gave rise to many difficulties in administering the provinces. Although he tried, Alexander never succeeded in reforming local government, which remained under the nominal supervision of the Senate and still operated according to collegial principles of administration inherited from the eighteenth century. The newly created central ministries gradually extended their authority to the provinces, resulting in jurisdictional disputes with the collegially organized organs of the *gubernii* and considerable confusion in local government and administration. This confusion, as well as the inef-

[2] Klochkov, *Ocherki pravitel'stvennoi deiatel'nosti vremeni Pavla I*, pp. 144-50, 156-58, 224-26, 408-33; Blinov, *Gubernatory*, pp. 154-55. For recent views on Paul as a reformer and enlightened, absolutist ruler, see *Paul I: A Reassessment of His Life and Reign*, ed. Hugh Ragsdale, UCIS Series in Russian and East European Studies, no. 2 (Pittsburgh: University Center for International Studies, 1979); and Claus Scharf, "Staatsauffassung und Regierungsprogramm eines aufgeklärten Selbstherrschers: Die Instruktion des Grossfürsten Paul von 1788," in *Gedenkschrift Martin Göhring: Studien zur europäischen Geschichte*, ed. Ernst Schulin (Wiesbaden: Franz Steiner Verlag, 1968), pp. 91-106.

fectiveness of central control over local government, gave Polish, German, and Finnish political leaders in the borderlands many opportunities to defend their autonomy and special rights and privileges during the first quarter of the nineteenth century.[3]

One high-ranking Russian official, D. P. Troshchinskii (a member of the Permanent Council, minister of appanages from 1802 to 1806, and minister of justice from 1814 to 1817), advised Alexander not to allow the western borderlands to develop political and social institutions different from those of the rest of the empire.[4] Alexander did not heed Troshchinskii's advice, for he believed that Russia had much to learn from Finland, Poland, and the Baltic provinces. The free peasants of Finland, the emancipation of the peasants in the Duchy of Warsaw in 1807, the emancipation of the Estonian and Latvian peasants in the three Baltic provinces between 1816 and 1819, and the Polish Constitutional Charter of 1815 all seemed to offer examples that Russia, herself might follow.

Like his grandmother, Catherine, and father, Paul, Alexander had been educated in the school of eighteenth-century enlightenment and cameralism. Even during the period of Arakcheev and the Holy Alliance that followed 1815, Alexander never seemed to have tired of having his advisers prepare projects for the emancipation of the serfs and for the reorganization of government and provincial administration. Two well-known projects prepared during his reign are M. M. Speranskii's Plan of Government of 1809 and N. N. Novosil'tsev's Constitutional Charter of the Russian Empire of 1820. A third draft of Novosil'tsev's Charter was prepared as late as 1824. Simultaneously, Alexander experimented with plans for the reform of local government through the combining of a number of provinces under governors-general. Thus, in 1819 Pskov *guberniia* was united with Estland, Livland, and Kurland under Governor-General Marquis F. O. Paulucci; between 1823 and 1831 the Belorussian *gubernii* of Witebsk and Mohylew were combined with two Great Russian provinces, Smo-

---

[3] Blinov, *Gubernatory*, pp. 156-61; S. P. Pokrovskii, *Ministerskaia vlast' v Rossii: Istoriko-iuridicheskoe issledovanie* (Iaroslav: Tipografiia Gubernskogo Pravleniia, 1906), pp. 107-17; A. V. Predtechenskii, *Ocherki obshchestvenno-politicheskoi istorii Rossii v pervoi chetverti XIX veka* (Moscow-Leningrad: Akademiia Nauk SSSR, 1957), pp. 138-42, 395-406; D. P. Troshchinskii, "Zapiski Dmitriia Prokof'evicha Troshchinskogo o ministrakh," SIRIO, 3 (1868): 42-43, 98-101; George Yaney, *The Systematization of Russian Government: Social Evolution in the Domestic Administration of Imperial Russia 1711-1905* (Urbana-London-Chicago: University of Illinois Press, 1973), pp. 206-7, 331-32; David Christian, "The 'Senatorial Party' and the Theory of Collegial Government, 1801-1803," *Russian Review* 38 (1979): 298-322.

[4] Troshchinskii, "Zapiska," pp. 100-109, 150-58.

lensk and Kaluga, under Governor-General N. N. Khovanskii; and between 1819 and 1827 Riazan', Tula, Tambov, and Orel became the constituent parts of a single *general-gubernatorstvo* under the administration of A. D. Balashev, the former minister of police.[5]

Alexander I's more ambitious plans for the social and political reform of Russia produced few concrete results, but the policies that he and his father pursued in the western borderlands fared better. Prior to 1796, common political institutions, serfdom, and the poll tax provided a common political, social, and fiscal framework within which the Baltic provinces and the annexed Polish areas could have been brought closer to the rest of the empire. In 1825 these provinces not only enjoyed a special status based on ancient rights and privileges, but two new autonomous provinces, Finland and Congress Poland, had been added to the empire. These two new provinces differed even more markedly from the Russian provinces in legal, political, and social structure than did Belorussia, Lithuania, the Right-Bank Ukraine, and the Baltic provinces.

[5] Predtechenskii, *Ocherki*, pp. 63-178, 235-67, 367-406; Allen McConnell, *Tsar Alexander I: Paternalistic Reformer* (New York: Thomas Y. Crowell Co., 1970), pp. 3-10, 24, 39-41, 145-55; George V. Vernadsky, *La charte constitutionnelle de l'Empire russe de l'an 1820* (Paris: Librairie du Recueil Sirey, 1933); Amburger, *Geschichte der Behördenorganisation*, p. 389.

CHAPTER 4

THE POLISH PROVINCES

AT THE BEGINNING of the nineteenth century Russians were still inclined to view the "territories annexed from Poland" (*oblasti ot Pol'shi prisoediennye*), as they were officially designated, as Polish provinces. In the second part of the eighteenth century the historian N. N. Bantysh-Kamenskii and such Orthodox religious figures as Konisskii, Sadkovskii, and Mel'khisidek had pointed to the trials and tribulations of Belorussian and Ukrainian Uniates and Orthodox believers in the Polish-Lithuanian Commonwealth; and Catherine II had rhetorically hailed the reunion of these allegedly oppressed Christians with their Russian kinsmen. Early in the nineteenth century the historian Karamzin and certain Russian officials serving in the western borderlands warned about the dangers Polish national ambitions posed for the Russian state. On the whole, however, upper-class Russians did not pay much attention to such warnings. The Polish provinces then had much the same importance for Russia that Estland and Livland had had for Peter I almost a century earlier. Members of the Polish *szlachta* did not possess the military skills of the Estland and Livland nobles, but they had been trained in the arts of political and social reform in the last years of the Polish-Lithuanian Commonwealth and under the constitutional regime of the Duchy of Warsaw. Such Poles as Adam Czartoryski, Sewerin Potocki, Stanisław Staszic, and Ksawery Drucki-Lubecki served Russia well under Alexander I. Poles were also important for Russia in the context of European diplomacy. Between 1804 and 1815, Russia was at war with one country or another—Persia, France, Turkey, or Sweden. These wars enabled Russia to annex or retain such strategically important areas as Georgia, part of Azerbaidzhan and Armenia, Bessarabia, Finland, and, finally, additional Polish territory, but Russian control over these areas was not secure as long as she could not count on the cooperation of the local native elites in the annexed areas. Polish elites were encouraged to cooperate by the presence in the Russian government of Prince Adam Czartoryski, deputy foreign minister between 1802 and 1806, a Russian senator, and the curator of the Wilno School Region.

The personal friendship of Alexander I and Czartoryski encouraged many Poles to dream of the resurrection of Poland under the auspices of Russia. During the first years of Alexander's reign, Czartoryski not only occupied many important official positions but was also a member of the "unofficial committee," a group of four "young friends" who provided Alexander I much of the inspiration for his initial social and administrative reforms. Alexander seemed particularly inclined to make a restored Poland the cornerstone of his European policy when he visited the Czartoryski family estate at Pulawy in Austrian Poland in 1805. Alexander refused, however, to pursue the anti-Prussian policy recommended by Czartoryski, and in 1806 the latter resigned as acting foreign minister shortly before Russia entered into a military alliance with Prussia. Polish enthusiasm for Russia then understandably cooled, and for a number of years the majority of Polish leaders identified the cause of Poland with the fortunes of Napoleon Bonaparte, who, in 1807 and 1809, rewarded the Poles for loyalty to France by carving the Duchy of Warsaw out of territories populated by Poles that had formerly belonged to Prussia and Austria. Nevertheless, some Poles, especially magnates with large estates in Russian Poland, had their doubts about Napoleon's ultimate victory in Europe.

Czartoryski, for example, still served as a Russian senator and as curator of the Wilno School Region, and he continued to correspond with Alexander about the restoration of Poland. M. K. Ogiński, another wealthy Polish magnate, proposed to Alexander in 1811 the creation of an autonomous Grand Duchy of Lithuania in personal union with Russia and with its own army, laws, and institutions.[1] None of the plans presented to Alexander on the eve of Napoleon's invasion of Russia in 1812 were accepted, but the mere fact that Poles were willing to make such proposals suggested the compatibility of Russian and Polish interests and the possibility of Russia's using the Poles to extend the empire's borders to the west. But some concessions had to be made to the socially and economically dominant Polish element

[1] The best discussion of the influence European diplomacy had on Alexander I's Polish policy is provided by William L. Blackwell, "Alexander I and Poland: The Foundations of His Polish Policy and Its Repercussions on Russia, 1801-1825" (Princeton University Ph.D. dissertation, 1959), pp. 27-45, 62-117. See also A. J. Czartoryski, *Mémoires du Prince Adam Czartoryski et correspondance avec l'Empereur Alexandre 1er*, 2 vols. (Paris: Librairie Plon, 1887), 1: 350-51, 371-73; 2: 272-78; Michał Kleofas Ogiński, *Mémoires de Michel Ogiński sur la Pologne et les Polonais depuis 1788 jusqu'à la fin de 1815*, 4 vols. (Paris: Ponthieu, 1826-1827), 2: 323-25, 375-89; 3: 47-70, 94-97, 110-21, 219-43; Patricia K. Grimsted, *The Foreign Ministers of Alexander I: Political Attitudes and the Conduct of Russian Diplomacy, 1821-1825* (Berkeley-Los Angeles: University of California Press, 1969), pp. 104-50.

The Polish Provinces

CONGRESS POLAND AND THE NINE WESTERN GUBERNII IN 1843

in the western borderlands if it was to be convinced that its interests were really compatible with those of Russia.

Alexander I, however, had to be more cautious in granting concessions to privileged elites of partitioned Poland than Peter I had been in dealing with Estland and Livland almost a century earlier. In 1710 the several thousand German nobles and town patricians who dominated Estland and Livland, two small provinces of 60,000 square kilometers in an area with little more than two hundred thousand inhabitants, were scarcely in a position to threaten the vital interests of Russia, even if they had wanted to do so. The numerous Polish *szlachta* scattered throughout Russia's "Polish" provinces at the beginning of the nineteenth century were another matter. They represented not only the socially mobile and dominant elements in an area of almost 500,000 square kilometers and populated by some eight million Belorussians, Ukrainians, Lithuanians, Poles, and Jews, but they were also closely linked with millions of other Poles in the contiguous, ethnically Polish provinces of Austria and Prussia and, between 1807 and 1815, of the Duchy of Warsaw.[2]

The large Belorussian and Lithuanian provinces that Paul I had created disappeared in 1802. With certain modifications, the area annexed from Poland was again broken down into the smaller *gubernii* of the time of Catherine II: Podolia, Volhynia, Minsk, Grodno, Wilno, Kiev, Witebsk, and Mohylew, with a separate district of Białystock formed out of the Polish territory Napoleon took from Prussia in 1807. Paul I's restoration of special rights and privileges in 1796 applied particularly to Podolia, Volhynia, Minsk, Grodno, and Wilno *gubernii* and the Białystock *oblast'*. Kiev, Mohylew, and Witebsk, on the other hand, were generally treated (with the major exception of educational affairs) as "Russian" *gubernii*, despite the Polish *szlachta*'s leading position in local affairs. Furthermore, throughout the lands annexed from Poland, governors-general, civil and military governors, boards of public welfare, *guberniia* financial and treasury offices still represented the authority of St. Petersburg on the basis of Catherine II's Provincial Reform of 1775.[3]

Paul I's restoration of rights and privileges in the Polish borderlands applied especially to the activities of district dietines (*sejmiki*). In the Polish-Lithuanian Commonwealth, the meetings of these dietines, which played an important role in local administration and the selection of judges and other officials, were often characterized by considerable chaos and disorder. The Second and Third Partitions of Poland had prevented much-needed reform of the political structure of Poland, especially as embodied in the Constitution of May 3, 1791, from being carried out. The disappearance of Polish state authority, its brief replacement by Catherine II's Russian provincial institutions, and then Paul I's partial restoration of Polish institutions further delayed the reform of local government in Russia's "Polish" provinces.

Russian officials disliked the frequent disorders within the dietines, the lifetime tenure of elected officials, and the Polish practice of permitting all members of the numerous *szlachta* to participate in the discussion of local affairs. In this respect, they did not greatly differ from many reform-minded Poles, who had tried to eliminate these same abuses and practices during the latter part of the eighteenth

[2] On some of the problems and uncertainties involved in estimating the size and composition of the population in the areas annexed by Russia from Poland, see footnotes 1, 4, and 7 to Chapter 3 of this study.

[3] Bohdan Winiarksi, *Les institutions politiques en Pologne au XIXe siècle* (Paris: Picart, 1924), pp. 35-36, 135-37; Klochkov, *Ocherki pravitel'stvennoi deiatel'nosti vremeni Pavla I*, pp. 115-16, 426-27.

century. In 1802 the dietines of the "Polish" provinces were instructed to elect their judges and marshals of the nobility for three years and in all cases to present two candidates for confirmation in accordance with the Provincial Reform of 1775. In 1804 the government limited participation in the dietines to nobles who owned estates, earned at least 150 rubles annually, or held an appropriate civil or military rank. These measures did not put an end to the disorders in the dietines; in 1809 the government announced that nobles responsible for such disorders would lose their right to participate in local self-government and that governors would be removed from office if they failed to act resolutely in dealing with serious cases of disorder in the dietines.[4]

The government also tried to regulate its relations with the Roman Catholic and Uniate churches. St. Petersburg officialdom, learning how difficult it was to provide converts to Orthodoxy with church books and priests, and witnessing the social unrest and disorders accompanying mass conversion to Orthodoxy, now discouraged the activities of proselytizing Orthodox clergy in Lithuania, Belorussia, and the Right-Bank Ukraine, leaving well over a million unconverted Uniates under the spiritual authority of Rome.[5] Until 1797 Catholic and Uniate affairs were administered by the Justice College for Livland, Estland, and Finland Affairs. In that year a separate department for Roman Catholic affairs was created within the Justice College, from which it was separated in 1798 and placed under the Catholic metropolitan of Mohylew, Stanisław Bohusz Siestrzencewicz. In 1801 this department became the Roman Catholic Ecclesiastical College. In 1805 a Uniate department was established within the College, headed by Herakly Lissowski, the Uniate archbishop of Połock.[6] The establishment of a separate agency for Uniate affairs meant, despite its continued subordination to the Roman Catholic hierarchy, a form of official recognition of the special position of the Uniates within the empire. It was perhaps more than coincidental that the man who

---

[4] Nol'de, *Ocherki*, pp. 429-33; Winiarski, *Les institutions politiques en Pologne*, pp. 135-37, 139-43; Russia, Pravitel'stvuiushchii Senat, *Istoriia Pravitel'stvuiushchego senata za dvesti let 1711-1911 gg.*, 5 vols. (St. Petersburg: Senatskaia Tipografiia, 1911), 4: 362-63; Stanisław Kutrzeba, *Historya ustroju Polski w zarysie*, 3: 195-96; A. Romanovich-Slavatinskii, *Dvorianstvo v. Rossii ot nachala XVIII veka do otmeny krepostnogo prava* (St. Petersburg: Tipografiia Ministerstva Vnutrennikh Del, 1879), pp. 483-87.

[5] Koialovich, *Istoriia vossoedineniia zapadnorusskikh Uniatov*, pp. 366-70, 380-84, 392-400; Wasyl Lenchyk, *The Eastern Catholic Church and Czar Nicholas I* (Rome-New York: Ukrainian Catholic University Press, 1966), p. 20.

[6] Amburger, *Geschichte der Behördenorganisation*, pp. 182-84; Ammann, *Abriss der ostslawischen Kirchengeschichte*, pp. 458, 468-74.

subsequently did more than anyone else to reunite the remaining Uniates of the "Polish" provinces with Orthodoxy, Iosif Semasako, was an assessor in the Uniate Department of the Roman Catholic Ecclesiastical College in St. Petersburg.

The government's measures to regulate Roman Catholic, Uniate, and *szlachta* affairs, however, obviously fell far short of totally integrating the "Polish" provinces into the political and social structure of the empire. Russia continued to rely on Poles to run local government, the courts, and schools in this area. Only military, police, and the highest civil officials were Russians, while lower administrative positions and even a number of the civil governors were Poles. Although the Third Department of the Russian Senate became the highest court of appeals for Lithuania, Volhynia, and Podolia, local courts remained Polish in language and form and, with the exception of certain areas of criminal law, tried cases in accordance with Polish law and precedents.[7] But it was above all with regard to education that the Russian authorities allowed the local Poles freedom of action.

Alexander I's educational reform of 1802 was influenced by the advice of two Poles, Czartoryski and Count Seweryn Potocki, and was based to a considerable extent on the experience of the Polish Commission of National Education. Administration of the system of national education established in 1802 was decentralized among six school regions with headquarters in Dorpat, Kazan, Kharkov, Moscow, St. Petersburg, and Wilno. However, a modicum of central direction for this educational system was provided by a curator for each educational region who resided in St. Petersburg. Two of these curators were Poles: Czartoryski (Wilno) and Potocki (Kharkov).[8]

Nationalistic Russian historians of education writing around 1900

---

[7] *Istoriia Pravitel'stvuiushchego senata*, 3: 282-87; Winiarski, *Les institutions politiques*, pp. 137, 139-41; Szymon Askenazy, *Rosya-Polska 1815-1830* (Lwów: H. Altenberg, 1907), pp. 118-19.

[8] *Ocherki istorii shkoly i pedagogicheskoi mysli narodov SSSR*, pp. 197-206; S. V. Rozhdestvenskii (ed.), *Istoricheskii obzor deiatel'nosti Ministerstva narodnogo prosveshcheniia 1802-1902* (St. Petersburg: Gosudarstvennaia Tipografiia, 1902), pp. 80-89, 151-54; Daniel Beauvois, "Les écoles polonaises de l'Empire russe: Aspects du centralisme administratif de l'Université de Vilna (1803-1831)," in VIIe Congrès International des Slavistes, *Communications de la délégation française* (Paris: Institut d'Etudes Slaves, 1973), pp. 35-38; Beauvois, *Lumières et société en Europe de l'Est: L'Université de Vilna et les écoles polonaises de l'Empire russe (1804-1832)*, 2 vols. (Lille: Atelier Reproduction des Thèses Université de Lille III, 1977), 1: 21-43; Stefan Truchim, *Współpraca polski-rosyjska nad organizacją szkolnictwa rosyjskiego w początkach XIX wieku* (Łódź: Ossolineum, 1969), pp. 38-39, 44-49, 51-52, 62-67, 81, 89-90, 123-24, 138-39.

often criticized Alexander I for allowing Poles to play a major role in the organization of education in Russia.[9] These critics usually failed to note, however, that eighteenth-century Russia had failed to produce forms of public financing and local support for education and to develop educational institutions capable of preparing nobles and others psychologically and professionally for service in a modernized Russian army, society, and bureaucracy. Catherine II had made some efforts to organize a national system of education during the 1780s and 1790s, but these modest efforts did not contribute significantly to supplying the increased number of trained personnel and educated nobles needed to translate into reality the provisions of the Provincial Reform of 1775 and the Charter to the Nobility of 1785. The empire's western borderlands, on the other hand, had a developed network of educational institutions and their nobles displayed a degree of public support for education that put them at least a generation ahead of the rest of the empire. This was especially the case for the active element among the nobility of the Wilno School Region, who had been involved in work of the Polish Commission of National Education since the 1770s. In 1809 there were more students in gymnasia and *uezd* secondary schools of the Wilno School Region than in all the gymnasia and *uezd* schools of the empire's four Russian school regions.[10] The introduction of Russian schools and language into this borderland would only have discouraged the participation of local privileged society in the promotion of education as well as its cooperation with the government in maintaining social order and in endeavoring to raise the cultural level of local society. Even Catherine II did not undertake the systematic Russification of the schools of the western borderlands; after all, the eighteenth-century *Polizeistaat* was based on a partnership between the state and the nobility, which in this area was Polish.

The Wilno School Region was completely Polish in terms of its pupils, its textbooks, its language of instruction, its rector and council of professors who administered its affairs in Wilno, and its curator, Czartoryski, who represented its interests in St. Petersburg. Educational policy decisions were generally made in Wilno, for Czartoryski was too busy as assistant or acting foreign minister between 1802 and 1806 and as a member of the Russian Senate after 1805 to devote a

---

[9] See, for example, the introductory discussions and the editorial comments by O. Kryzhanovskii in the four volumes of documents he edited concerning education in the former Polish provinces at the beginning of the nineteenth century, *Sbornik materialov dlia istorii prosveshcheniia v Rossii izvlechennykh iz arkhiva Ministerstva narodnogo prosveshcheniia* (St. Petersburg: "Obshchestvennaia Pol'za," 1893-1902), 4 vols.

[10] Beauvois, *Lumières et société*, 2: 690-91.

substantial amount of his time to the affairs of the Wilno School Region. But he wholeheartedly supported the use of schools as a means of disseminating Polish civilization and of raising the cultural level of the dominant Polish minority in Belorussia, Lithuania, and the Right-Bank Ukraine. In so doing, Czartoryski and other Poles involved in the educational work of the Wilno School Region were not necessarily engaged in some kind of Polish national conspiracy against Russia. Indeed, their correspondence at the time indicates that they were primarily concerned about education and that they believed that the advancement of Polish civilization in this area was not incompatible with the interests of the Russian Empire.[11]

Some Russian officials, however, opposed the strengthening of Polish influence in this area from the very beginning. As early as 1801, the civil governor of Volhynia and the military governor of Podolia expressed their concern about the republican and anti-monarchial ideas to be found in the textbooks used in the Polish schools of their respective provinces. Podolian Military Governor Andreas von Rosenberg, a Baltic German, then proposed the local adoption of textbooks approved for the empire's Russian schools.[12] This proposal led to the first thorough study by an agency of the central government, namely, the Commission for the Establishment of Schools, of problems connected with Polish schools in the Right-Bank Ukraine. The Commission confirmed the critical judgment of the Volhynian and Podolian governors concerning the textbooks used in Polish schools, especially finding fault with ancient-history books that associated autocracy with the suppression of freedom and the republican form of government in ancient Greece with eloquence, wisdom, and nobility of the soul. Although the members of the commission were aware of the Germanization of education in the Austrian and Prussian parts of partitioned Poland, they did not recommend the Russification of the schools of Lithuania, Belorussia, and the Right-Bank Ukraine. Their report emphasized, however, that the annexed Polish territory had to be brought into a "close union with Russia" by introducing translated Russian textbooks into Polish schools and teaching in them a certain number of courses in Russian.[13]

[11] One illustration of this point is the correspondence of Hugo Kołłątaj with Tadeusz Czacki: *X. Hugona Kołłątaja korrespondencya listowna z Tadeuszem Czackim* (Cracow: W Drukarni Uniwersyteckiej, 1844-1845), 4 vols.

[12] Letter of I. A. Kuris to P. S. Svistunov, March 12, 1801, and Journal of the Commission for the Establishment of Schools, May 31, 1801, *Sbornik materialov dlia istorii prosveshcheniia v Rossii*, vol. 1, nos. 43 and 51, cols. 192-93, 371-75; DBL, p. 650.

[13] Journal of the Commission for the Establishment of Schools, *Sbornik materialov*, vol. 1, no. 53, cols. 378-79, 383-86, 391-96.

The Commission's report was never acted upon. Czartoryski then enjoyed the respect and confidence of Alexander I and of P. V. Zavadovskii, the first minister of education (1802-1810) and a Polonophile who had attended Polish Jesuit schools in his youth.[14] Even more important, the creation of the Ministry of Education in 1802 and the subordination of all schools in Belorussia, Lithuania, and the Right-Bank Ukraine, including even the "Russian" *gubernii* of Witebsk, Mohylew, and Kiev, to Polish educational administrators at the University of Wilno soon gave an entirely different direction to the administration of education in this area. Russian governors-general, governors, and officials attached to boards of public welfare and other local organs of the *guberniia* administration were no longer responsible for the direct supervision of education in the Wilno School Region and, therefore, now found it more difficult to curtail the activities of more zealous Polish school officials. The most successful of such Polish officials was Tadeusz Czacki, the school inspector for Volhynia, Podolia, and Kiev. Czacki even managed to gain Minister of Education Zavadovskii's support in preventing a Russian university from being established at Kiev in 1804-1805; in 1809, he founded the famous lyceum at Krzemieniec (Kremenets), the "Volhynian Athens" which educated, on the soil of the Right-Bank Ukraine, an entire *szlachta* generation in the spirit of Polish national tradition and civilization.[15] Only when he tried to have a Polish, not a Russian, gymnasium established in Kiev did Czacki run into concerted opposition by local Russian officials, who were appalled at the thought of a Polish secondary school in a city of such great importance in the history of Orthodox Russia. When the new gymnasium opened its doors in 1812, it was a Russian institution. And in 1818, all schools in the city of Kiev were separated from Wilno and transferred to the Kharkov School Region, in which the language of instruction was Russian.[16]

This insistence on Russian-language instruction in Kiev did not, however, result from any overall reassessment of Russian policy toward the Poles. On the contrary, it was especially at the Congress of Vienna and in the years immediately preceding and following it that Alexander openly identified himself with Czartoryski's ideas on the

[14] Beauvois, *Lumières et société*, 1: 26, 32-43.

[15] Kryzhanovskii, "Vvedenie," *Sbornik materialov*, 3: xlviii-xlix, lxxiii-lxxiv, lxxix-lxxxi, cxiii, cxxi-cxxii; X. *Hugona Kołłątaja korrespondencya listowna z T. Czackim*, 2: 355-58; 3: 121-24; 4: 246; Beauvois, "Les écoles polonaises de l'Empire russe," pp. 41-42, 47; "Liceum Krzemienieckie," *Mały słownik historii polski*, p. 168.

[16] Kryzhanovskii, "Vvedenie," *Sbornik materialov*, 3: xlix-li; letter of P. P. Pankrat'ev to P. V. Zavadovskii, April 5, 1805, ibid., no. 269, pp. 38-88; Beauvois, "Les écoles polonaises de l'Empire russe," pp. 47-48.

regeneration of Poland as an autonomous, constitutional kingdom united
with Russia by common interests and the same ruler, even going so
far as to suggest to the Poles that at least part of Lithuania might be
added to the Polish kingdom at some future date. He acted so generously in part for tactical reasons, since the identification of Russia
as Poland's benefactor served as an argument for extending Russia's
frontiers to the west and incorporating Polish territories acquired earlier by Prussia and Austria. This expansionist policy was opposed by
many of his own advisers and the majority of the powers at the Congress of Vienna, but, although not entirely successful, it did bring
into the empire another three million inhabitants and 127,000 square
kilometers of Polish territory.[17]

A Polish kingdom within Russia also offered Alexander an opportunity to experiment with "constitutional" projects. His interest
in such projects reached a high point during the period 1815-1820,
and it is certainly more than coincidental that the author of the Constitutional Charter for the Russian Empire of 1820 was Alexander's
commissioner in Warsaw, N. N. Novosil'tsev. For Alexander, the word
"constitution" in no way implied the willingness on his part to surren-
der any of his autocratic powers; it connoted, instead, a means
of enabling himself to act more effectively in promoting what he considered the welfare of his subjects on the basis of a rationalized
administrative structure and a detailed description of the functions
and activities of the principal branches of the government.[18] Alexander remained a Russian autocrat, and his not infrequent use of the
word "constitution" signified no break with the *Polizeistaat* mentality
of his predecessors.

The one "constitutional" document Alexander I actually approved,
promulgated, and even tried to put into effect was the Polish Constitutional Charter of 1815. Given that the Poles of the Congress
Kingdom had already received a constitution from Napoleon in 1807
and that Alexander wished to win their favor, they could hardly be
denied a constitution in 1815. Under Napoleon, the serfs had been

---

[17] Askenazy, *Rosya-Polska 1815-1830*, pp. 63-65, 78; Grimsted, *The Foreign Ministers of Alexander I*, pp. 221-24; *The Cambridge History of Poland*, ed. W. F. Redda-
way et al., 2 vols. (1941-1950; reprint ed., New York: Octagon Books, 1971), 2: 257-
75.

[18] One of the first writers to make this point was E. N. Berendts, "Proekty reformy
Senata v tsarstvovaniia Aleksandra I i Nikolaia I," in *Istoriia Pravitel'stvuiushchego
senata za dvesti let 1711-1911 gg.*, 3: 12, 127-36. For more recent comments on the
"constitutionalism" of Alexander I, see Marc Raeff, *Michael Speransky: Statesman of
Imperial Russia 1772-1839* (The Hague: Martinus Nijhoff, 1957), pp. 29-46.

emancipated; the principle of the equality of all citizens before the law was established through the introduction of the French Code Napoleon; and an elected Sejm (60 percent by the *szlachta's* dietines and 40 percent by communal assemblies) and an appointed Senate were organized to assist the king, a Council of Ministers, and a State Council in running the affairs of the Duchy of Warsaw. This small Polish state had been a vassal of France, and its government could do very little without the approval of the French resident in Warsaw and the commander of the French occupation troops; and serf emancipation and equality before the law meant very little as long as the Duchy's peasant majority did not own the land they cultivated and remained economically dependent upon the landowning *szlachta*. But the Napoleonic legislation, which resumed the work of social and political reform interrupted by the partitions, won favor among many Poles. If nothing else, Poland had gained a constitution that regulated her government and the lives of her citizens according to principles of law and administration widely accepted by reformers on the Continent.[19]

The Polish Constitutional Charter of 1815 was drafted by a mixed group of prominent Polish and Russian officials, including Czartoryski and Novosil'tsev. It confirmed the principle of equality before the law and the personal liberty of the peasants; it guaranteed such basic rights as the freedom of religion and of the press, freedom from arbitrary arrest, and the sanctity of private property; but it also placed the executive and legislative powers in the hands of the Russian autocrat in his alternate role as the king of Poland. To be sure, legislative power was shared with the Sejm, which consisted of an appointed Senate and a Lower Chamber whose members were elected by the landowning *szlachta* and the more prosperous or successful members of the middle class and professions. The Russian king had the right to convoke, dissolve, and adjourn the Sejm and to confirm or reject its enactments.[20] All orders and decrees of the king or viceroy were,

[19] Kutrzeba, *Historya ustroju Polski w zarysie*, 3: 37-74; Winiarski, *Les institutions politiques en Pologne*, pp. 55-70; *History of Poland*, ed. A. Gieysztor, S. Kieniewicz et al., pp. 410-18; S. A. Blejwas, "The Origins and Practice of 'Organic Work' in Poland," *Polish Review* 15 (1970): 28-29; Barbara Szacka, *Stanisław Staszic* (Warsaw: PWN, 1966), pp. 167-71; Stefan Kieniewicz, *The Emancipation of the Polish Peasantry* (Chicago: University of Chicago Press, 1969), pp. 44-57.

[20] The French and Polish versions of the original Charter can be found in *Dziennik praw*, 71 vols. (Warsaw: W Drukarni Rządowej, 1815-1871), 1 (1815): 1-123. These texts, together with a Russian translation, were republished in *Konstitutsionnaia khartiia 1815 goda i nekotorye drugie akty byvshego Tsarstva Pol'skogo (1814-1881)*, Biblioteka Okrain Rossii, no. 5 (St. Petersburg: A. S. Suvorin, 1907).

however, supposed to be countersigned by an appropriate minister to verify that they were not contrary to the constitution and the laws of Poland.[21] Article 76 of the Charter provided for the post of a Polish minister state secretary who resided in St. Petersburg, where he served as a representative of Polish interests and as an intermediary between the emperor and the Russian authorities in Congress Poland.

For the Russian Empire, and even for much of continental Europe of that time, the Polish Constitutional Charter was a remarkable document. Initially, a large part of educated Polish society seems to have considered it to be an acceptable foundation upon which to build an autonomous Poland within the Russian Empire. Alexander I indicated his high opinion of the Polish Constitutional Charter in a famous speech before the Warsaw Sejm in 1818, when he expressed the hope that the "salutary influence" of the principles of the Polish "liberal institutions" could be extended, "with the help of God," to "all the countries entrusted to my care by Providence."[22] At the end of the speech, Alexander expressed his satisfaction with the Poles and the desire to carry out his plans for extending the programs designed to benefit them.[23] Poles then generally interpreted these words to mean that he intended to do what he had more than once hinted at since 1815: unify Lithuania with Congress Poland.

Even at the very beginning of Russian rule in Poland, many Poles had doubts about the true intentions of Alexander. An early disappointment was Alexander's decision not to name Czartoryski as the first viceroy (that is, the official who presided over the government whenever the Polish king was absent from Congress Poland). Instead, he appointed General Józef Zajączek, an elderly veteran of the Napoleonic wars who was willing to carry out Russian orders. Alexander made his own brother, Grand Duke Konstantin Pavlovich, commander-in-chief of the Polish army and sent Novosil'tsev to Poland as a special and all-powerful Russian commissioner (a post not provided for in the Constitutional Charter) with the right to sit on the State Council and with access to all organs of the government. Konstantin soon claimed extra-constitutional power with regard to military affairs, and he almost immediately clashed with Minister of War M. Wielhorski, who refused to take and countersign orders given by Konstantin without following the prescribed constitutional procedures. Em-

---

[21] Articles 47 and 68 of the Charter, *Konstitutsionnaia khartiia 1815 goda*, pp. 69, 72.

[22] N. K. Shil'der, *Imperator Aleksandr Pervyi: Ego zhizn' i tsarstvovanie*, 4 vols. (2nd ed.; St. Petersburg: A. S. Suvorin, 1905), 4: 86.

[23] Ibid., p. 88.

peror Alexander's support of his brother and acceptance of Wielhorski's resignation in early 1816 greatly disturbed Czartoryski and many other Poles, who felt that the Constitutional Charter was no longer inviolable and was even in jeopardy. Czartoryski, who was a member of the Administrative Council and the kingdom's Senate, soon ceased his participation in the government of the Congress Kingdom and turned his attention almost exclusively to his duties as curator of the Wilno School Region.[24]

Despite these efforts to keep the Polish constitutional experiment under close Russian supervision, many Russians felt that Alexander gave too much latitude to the Poles. His advisers usually disapproved of his Polish policy, and his brother Konstantin counseled him to return to Catherine II's policy of the full integration of the areas annexed from Poland into the general system of provincial administration established in 1775. Alexander resisted these pressures. In 1818, for example, in the text of the speech he intended to deliver before the Warsaw Sejm, he insisted on retaining his words of praise for Polish liberal institutions and the hint of more favors for the Poles, even though Count I. A. Capo d'Istrias had warned him that Russians would be offended and that Poles living in the provinces adjacent to Congress Poland would misinterpret his words.[25] Capo d'Istrias was quite correct in predicting a negative Russian response to Alexander's Warsaw speech: radicals and liberals were infuriated by the suggestion that Poland was more advanced than Russia, and Russians of all shadings of opinion opposed the joining of any part of the western provinces with the Congress Kingdom. In 1819 the historian N. M. Karamzin reminded Alexander that the western provinces had belonged to Russia in the past and had again become a legal Russian possession at the time of Catherine II, and cautioned him that the restoration of Poland would mean the ruin of Russia, "for our sons will stain Polish soil with their blood and again take Praga by storm."[26]

[24] Angela T. Pienkos, "Grand Duke Constantine: A Study in Early Nineteenth-Century Russo-Polish Relations, 1815-1831" (University of Wisconsin, Madison, Ph.D. dissertation, 1971), pp. 57-64; Tadeusz Łepkowski, *Warszawa w Powstaniu Listopadowym* (Warsaw: Wiedza Powszechna, 1965), pp. 22-26.

[25] Shil'der, *Imperator Aleksandr I*, 4: 84; Predtechenskii, *Ocherki*, p. 375; Pienkos, "Grand Duke Constantine," pp. 43-45.

[26] N. M. Karamzin, "Mnenie russkogo grazhdanina," in *Neidannye sochineniia i perepiska Nikolaia Mikhailovicha Karamzina* (St. Petersburg: N. Tiblen, 1862), pp. 5-7; N. P. Meshcherskii, "Iz bumag N. M. Karamzina, khraniashchikhsia v gosudarstvennom arkhive," *Starina i novizna* 2 (1898): 5-8, 17-19; R. Vydrin, "Natsional'nyi vopros v russkom obshchestvennom dvizhenii," *Golos minuvshego* 1 (January 1915): 105-12; Shil'der, *Imperator Aleksandr I*, 4: 92-96; Blackwell, "Alexander I and Poland," pp. 143-77.

Essentially, Alexander's policy in Poland was a delicate balancing act. On the one hand, he ignored the advice of his Russian critics and kept open the option of a conciliatory policy in Poland; on the other, he, as a Russian autocrat, overlooked Polish sensitivities in approving repressive or precautionary measures in response to signs of political opposition in the Sejm, and to reports concerning secret societies and nationalistic revolutionary sentiment among the Polish youth. Censorship was introduced in 1819, and arrests were made in the early twenties. In 1823 nationalistic ferment among Wilno students led to an investigation conducted by Novosil'tsev, who soon replaced Czartoryski as the curator of the Wilno School Region.[27] Also in 1823 the Belorussian *gubernii* of Witebsk and Mohylew were combined with the Great Russian *gubernii* of Smolensk and Kaluga in a new *general-gubernatorstvo* under N. N. Khovanskii. And in 1824 the schools of Mohylew and Witebsk *gubernii* were separated from Wilno and transferred to the jurisdiction of the St. Petersburg School Region because of complaints made by Governor-General Khovanskii about the poor Russian instruction and the anti-Russian spirit prevalent in the Catholic-dominated Polish schools of the Belorussian provinces.[28]

When the Second Sejm of the Congress Kingdom met in 1820, Alexander warned the Poles that their constitutional regime could only be justified and preserved through their own moderation and prudence. The meeting of the Third Sejm was delayed until measures could be taken to assure the absence of political opposition to government policy. When this Sejm finally met in 1825, the restrained behavior of the Poles very much pleased Alexander. In the period between the Second and Third Sejms, he had on occasion considered the possibility of abolishing the Charter of 1815. He did so, however, in the general context of preparing a constitutional charter for the empire as a whole; immediate action along these lines was unlikely as long as the succession crisis and the question of compensation for his brother Konstantin remained unsettled. In 1823 Konstantin secretly gave his pledge to abdicate. Alexander declined to satisfy fully his brother's demands for compensation; but he publicly kept open to the very end of his reign (for example, in his last appearance before the Sejm in 1825) the possibility of the unification of Congress Poland with Lithuania under the authority of Konstantin. He apparently did so in the hope of weakening political opposition and winning friends among the Poles, who had become increasingly disenchanted with

[27] Rozhdestvenskii, *Obzor deiatel'nosti Ministerstva narodnogo prosveshcheniia*, pp. 152-54.

[28] I. P. Kornilov, "Vvedenie," *Sbornik materialov dlia istorii prosveshcheniia v Rossii*, 2: xci-xcii; Beauvois, "Les écoles polonaises de l'Empire russe," p. 29.

Russia as a result of the repressive police, censorship, and educational policies pursued by Konstantin and Novosil'tsev in both Congress Poland and Lithuania throughout the period 1820-1825.[29]

Polish-Russian relations continued to worsen during the first five years of Nicholas I's reign. Unlike his brother Alexander, Nicholas was no Polonophile: he instinctively distrusted Poles and was particularly adamant about putting an end to what he considered irresponsible talk about the reunion of Congress Poland with Lithuania. He described Lithuania as a "Russian province" that could not be returned to Poland because this would "infringe upon the territorial integrity of the empire."[30] Nicholas also did not like the Polish colors and composition of the Lithuanian Army Corps, which Konstantin had commanded since 1817 in addition to his military responsibilities in the Congress Kingdom. In order to discourage Poles from seeing in Konstantin's dual command a symbol of unity of Lithuania and Congress Poland, Nicholas assigned Polish officers to service in the interior of the empire and Russian soldiers and officers to the Lithuanian Corps. Nicholas also replaced with Russians a number of the Polish civil governors and other high officials in the western *gubernii*. In 1828 he approved plans for reuniting the remaining Uniates in these *gubernii* with the Russian Orthodox Church. With regard to Congress Poland, Nicholas was particularly concerned about the activities of a small group of Polish revolutionaries who had close relations with the Russian Decembrists. The Poles, in their turn, strongly disapproved of Nicholas's decision to create by decree a mixed Polish-Russian Commission of Investigation, which the Poles considered to be unconstitutional. They won, however, a small victory when Nicholas agreed, in 1827, to have eight accused revolutionaries tried in Poland, not in Russia, by a special Sejm tribunal. In 1828 three defendants were found innocent, while the others were sentenced to three years or less of imprisonment, not for high treason but for having belonged to a secret society. The Poles were once again outraged when Nicholas ordered a second trial for the leader of the group, Seweryn Krzyżanowski, who happened to have been born in the Ukraine. In the second trial Krzyżanowski was sentenced to hard labor in Siberia, where he went mad and died in 1839.[31]

[29] Frank W. Thackeray, *Antecedents of Revolution: Alexander I and the Polish Kingdom, 1815-1825* (Boulder: East European Monographs, 1980), pp. 79-131, 178 n. 44; Askenazy, *Rosya-Polska 1815-1830*, pp. 90-107.

[30] Letter of Nicholas I to Konstantin Pavlovich, November 5 and 24, 1827, "Imperator Nikolai I i Pol'sha v 1825-1831 gg.," ed. N. K. Shil'der, *Russkaia starina* 101 (1900): 299, 302.

[31] Askenazy, *Rosya-Polska 1815-1830*, pp. 107-14, 122-24; Pienkos, "Grand Duke

In 1830 Poles in the Congress Kingdom and the western *gubernii* still retained either a good measure of autonomy or at least important rights and privileges. Hundreds of thousands of Poles made up the dominant social, economic, and political element in the western *gubernii*, and Polish was the language of the schools, courts, and local administration. On the whole, Russian society and officialdom still tended to consider this area Polish. In 1824 even a Polonophobe like Novosil'tsev opposed transferring the schools of Mohylew and Witebsk *gubernii* to the St. Petersburg School Region, arguing that the youth of the Belorussian provinces were much closer to that of Wilno than to the youth of Russia by virtue of its origins, social usages, and language.[32] Obviously, for Novosil'tsev the Wilno School Region, his bureaucratic empire, was more important than the nationality of Belorussian peasants. In addition, he clearly shared many of the social attitudes and preconceptions of his upper-class, landowning peers in Russia and elsewhere.

In the Congress Kingdom, both the peasants and the *szlachta* were Polish. If the Russians occasionally violated the Constitutional Charter, they nevertheless respected the kingdom's special status within the empire. Beginning around 1820, Grand Duke Konstantin Pavlovich gradually changed his attitude toward the Poles and became the most influential advocate among high-placed Russians of a conciliatory policy in Congress Poland. In 1829 Nicholas I followed his advice by coming to Warsaw to be crowned king of Poland and swearing to uphold the Polish Constitutional Charter.[33] But this gesture did not greatly impress Polish leaders; they were no longer the divided magnates and Russia's dependent clients of the eighteenth century. Intensive efforts at internal political reform, the partitions, the flourishing of Polish scholarship at the Universities of Warsaw and Wilno, the work of civic and national education throughout the Russian part of the lands of partitioned Poland, the beginnings of a modern textile industry in Łódź, the expansion of mining and metallurgy in Congress Poland encouraged by the policies of Mining Department Head Stanisław Staszic and Finance Minister Ksawery Drucki-Lubecki, and the emergence of Warsaw as the unquestioned urban center of the

---

Constantine Pavlovich," pp. 149-54; R. F. Leslie, *Polish Politics and the Revolution of 1830* (1956; reprint ed., Westport, Conn.: Greenwood Press, 1969), p. 114.

[32] Beauvois, "Les écoles polonaises de l'Empire russe," p. 49; E. Orlovskii, *Sud'by pravoslaviia v sviazi s istorieiu Latinstva i Unii v Grodnenskoi gubernii v XIX stoletii (1794-1900)* (Grodno: Gubernskaia Tipografiia, 1903), pp. 51-52.

[33] Askenazy, *Rosya-Polska*, pp. 113-14; Pienkos, "Grand-Duke Constantine," pp. 105-6, 131-32, 149-61.

western borderlands (the third city in the empire with a population of more than 130,000)—all combined to produce a degree of unity and cohesiveness among educated Poles that they had tended to lack previously. The process Tadeusz Łepkowski has described as the "birth of a modern nation"[34] was well under way.

For early nineteenth-century Poles, however, the Polish nation encompassed not only Congress Poland and adjacent, formerly Polish territories in Austria and Prussia (that is, more or less the post-1945 Poland Łepkowski has in mind) but also Lithuania, Belorussia, and the Right-Bank Ukraine. In the decades preceding the insurrection of 1830-1831, the numerous *szlachta* of these eastern provinces of the former Polish-Lithuanian Commonwealth still formed an integral part of the Polish nation. Warsaw, if for no more than its intellectual and artistic life and the opportunities for employment it offered, was their capital as much as that of the Poles of the Congress Kingdom. The University of Wilno, the Polish world's leading center of scholarship and learning between 1802 and 1830, coordinated a Polish system of education in an area three times the size of Congress Poland; it brought the educated elite among the *szlachta* and selected Ukrainians, Belorussians, and Lithuanians intended for service in the Uniate or Roman Catholic clergy into contact with European Enlightenment and Romanticism. Adam Mickiewicz, perhaps Poland's greatest romantic and patriotic poet, studied at Wilno; Joachim Lelewel, the founder of modern Polish romantic and patriotic historiography and a future leader of the Polish emigration, taught there. Noteworthy figures not of Polish origin who studied at Wilno included Motiejus Valančius, a future Lithuanian national hero and bishop of Samogitia, and the Ukrainian or Belorussian Uniates Iosif Semashko, Vasilii Luzhinskii, and Antonii Zubko, who helped Nicholas I during the 1830s to reunite the Uniates with Orthodoxy.

As early as the 1820s a number of influential Russians had become aware of growing Polish dissatisfaction with Russian rule. The crux of the matter was that the educated segment of Polish society had greatly changed its outlook on the world and its expectations for the future; Russian autocracy had not. This parting of ways was particularly serious in a borderland of some 600,000 square kilometers in which the *szlachta* dominated local society politically, economically, and cultur-

---

[34] T. Łepkowski, *Polska-narodziny nowoczesnego narodu 1764-1870* (Warsaw: PWN, 1970). For a detailed, recent discussion of the social and economic development of the Congress Kingdom between 1815 and 1830, see L. A. Obushenkova, *Korolevstvo Pol'skoe v 1815-1830 gg.: Ekonomicheskoe i sotsial'noe razvitie* (Moscow: "Nauka," 1979).

ally. A basic reassessment of Russian policy in this borderland was almost unavoidable, even without the Polish insurrection in 1830-1831.

This reassessment of Russian borderland policy applied especially to Lithuania, Belorussia, the Right-Bank Ukraine, and Congress Poland, but only partially to the Baltic provinces, and not at all to the Grand Duchy of Finland acquired by Russia in 1809. The case of Finland is important. It illustrates that throughout the first part of the nineteenth century Russia still preferred to rely on coopted, non-Russian elites to run local government and society in the western borderlands as long as these elites remained loyal to the tsar and managed to maintain a well-ordered traditional society, and as long as they could keep under control peasant unrest in the countryside and intellectual and revolutionary ferment among the academic youth and townsmen.

Finland, then, was an exemplary borderland for Russia. Here a handful of conservative Swedish-speaking aristocrats and officials firmly and effectively guided a well-ordered Finnish society and administration on the basis of Swedish laws, institutions, and parochial self-government. New ideas were not likely to take root immediately in Finland and upset her social equilibrium. She was a sparsely populated country (about one million inhabitants in 1811 in an area of 371,481 square kilometers) on the periphery of Europe, with no major urban centers; her two largest cities in 1810 were Åbo with 10,224 inhabitants, and Helsingfors with 4,065. In this quiet backwater of the empire and of Europe, so different from the "Polish" provinces, Finnish autonomy was born and matured almost unnoticed by nearby St. Petersburg officialdom which at the very same time had begun to experiment with measures to Russify the western *gubernii* and Congress Poland.

CHAPTER 5

THE GRAND DUCHY OF FINLAND

Prior to 1808 Finland had been a Swedish province. The overwhelming majority of her inhabitants (85 percent in the early nineteenth century), however, spoke Finnish, not Swedish. Even the
dominant Swedish minority in Finland was separated physically from
Sweden by the Gulf of Bothnia and had its own local self-interests to
defend. On occasion, therefore, influential Swedish-speaking leaders

FINLAND AND THE BALTIC PROVINCES, 1812 — 1917

in Finland criticized or even resisted policies decided upon in the Swedish capital. But the structure of Finland's government and society was basically the same as Sweden's, and Finland was ruled from Stockholm by a Swedish king and *riksdag*, to which all four Finnish Estates (nobles, clergy, townsmen, and peasants) sent their representatives. There was no separate Finnish Diet, and the Finnish nobility had no special institutions that enabled it to control local society in the manner of the Baltic nobility or the Polish *szlachta*. The Finnish peasants were free and participated in the running of local community affairs. At the same time, the Finnish (and Swedish) peasants were less dependent economically on the nobility than was the case elsewhere in the Baltic region and eastern Europe, for the *reduktion* of estates carried out in the Swedish Empire during the reign of Charles XI prevented the nobles from completely dominating the rural economy in Finland. A large proportion of the peasants could read, largely because of the measures taken by the Swedish state in Sweden, Finland, and the Baltic provinces to teach children from the lower classes in each parish how to read in preparation of their confirmation as members of the official Lutheran Church.[1]

Finnish autonomy, and even the existence of a Finnish nation, can be considered an incidental byproduct of wars between Sweden and Russia during the eighteenth and at the beginning of the nineteenth centuries. In four wars with Russia, Sweden only held her own in one, the war of 1789-1790; on three occasions almost all of Finland was occupied by the Russian army. On the whole, Russia did not pay very much attention to the Finnish problem during the eighteenth century; nor did Russia have particularly aggressive designs on Finland, considering the repeated Swedish provocations and the preponderance of Russian power in the Baltic region. As a result of the Treaty of Nystad (1721), Russia, in order to make St. Petersburg less vulnerable to attack from the northwest, annexed a small area of southeastern Finland consisting of Viborg and a part of Finnish Karelia. Although this area was brought into the empire at the same time as Estland and Livland, its inhabitants received no guarantees of their

---

[1] Eino Jutikkala (with Kauko Perinen), *A History of Finland*, tr. Paul Sjöblom (London: Thames and Hudson, 1962), pp. 57-58, 95-99, 106-10, 114-23. It should be noted that there was no organized system of universal elementary education in eighteenth-century Sweden. The Swedish government did, however, endeavor to regulate and encourage education on the parish level. On such efforts in eighteenth-century Finland, see Gösta Cavonius, *Folkskollärarnas föregångare i Finland: Klockare och sockenskolmästare under Frihetstiden*, Bidrag utgivna af Finska Vetenskaps-Societen, no. 90 (Helsinki: Centraltryckeri, 1943).

ancient rights and privileges other than the right to retain the religion of their ancestors. However, because of the apparent unimportance of the area and inattention to detail after the death of Peter I, Russian officials erroneously assumed that the Treaty of Nystad assured the inhabitants of Viborg and Karelia rights similar to those of Estland and Livland. Consequently, the administration of this area was soon separated from that of the internal Russian provinces; it was placed in the hands of Baltic Germans and under the jurisdiction of what became known in the 1730s as the Financial Office (*Kamer-kontora*) for Livland, Estland, and Finland Affairs, and of the Justice College for Livland, Estland, and Finland Affairs. When so-called Russian "Old Finland" was enlarged in the Treaty of Åbo (1743) by another slice of territory from southeastern Swedish Finland, the special laws and rights of the inhabitants of the newly annexed area were guaranteed. In newly formed Viborg *guberniia*, which united the territories annexed in 1721 and 1743, a Russian governor presided over the local administration and the official language was Russian, but financial and judicial affairs were administered separately by the *Kamer-kontora* and the Justice College for Livland, Estland, and Finland Affairs. Since higher financial and judicial officials continued to be Baltic Germans, much of the business in the new *guberniia* was conducted in German, while Swedish, the language of lower officials, was also recognized. Swedish laws and customs were generally respected, though the local Swedes were much less successful in defending the autonomy of Viborg *guberniia* than the German elites had been in Estland and Livland. Nevertheless, enough historical continuity was maintained to avoid absorption into Russia and to keep alive hopes for the eventual reunion of Viborg with the rest of Finland.[2]

During the eighteenth century many members of the Swedo-Finnish officer and official class lost patience with Sweden's repeated involvement of Finland in unsuccessful wars with Russia. These wars demonstrated the instability and irresponsibility of those who ruled in Stockholm as well as Sweden's inability to defend Finland. Russian diplomats and officials were well aware of Finnish dissatisfaction with Sweden. Thus, while at war with Sweden between 1741 and 1743, Russia offered to support the Finns if they tried to separate themselves from Sweden. This offer accomplished little at the time, but somewhat more than forty years later Colonel G. M. Sprengtporten, a Finnish nobleman, reopened the subject of a Russian-supported au-

[2] Jutikkala, *A History of Finland*, pp. 125-83; Lehtonen, *Die polnischen Provinzen Russlands*, pp. 202-7.

tonomous Finland, and in 1786 he left Finland and entered Russian state service. Sprengtporten's views were shared by at least some of 113 officers of the so-called Anjala League who, in 1788, criticized the foreign policy of Sweden, especially the unnecessary war Gustav III had just provoked against Russia. A similar trend to assert Finnish distinctiveness from Sweden was discernible in intellectual circles at the University of Åbo, where Professor Henrik Gabriel Porthan laid the foundations for the critical study of Finnish history, language, and folklore and directed the attention of young Swedo-Finns to the popular culture and the language that separated the majority of Finland's inhabitants from the rest of Sweden.[3]

In 1808 Sprengtporten and other former members of the Anjala League were presented with a unique opportunity to work for an autonomous Finland within the framework of the Russian Empire. Russia had invaded Finland early in 1808 as an ally of Napoleonic France; Sweden was forced to break with England and adhere to the continental system; and in March Russia announced the annexation of Finland. At the beginning of this war Sprengtporten revived his plan for an autonomous Finland, proposing the early convocation of a Finnish Diet in order to organize the affairs of the new Finland. Although the convocation of this Diet was delayed for about a year, from the very beginning Alexander seems to have believed that the Finns— especially their officials and military leaders—had to be convinced that their rights, customs, and traditions would be respected and that their own personal and national interests would be served if they cooperated with Russia. Such cooperation seemed essential because of Russia's precarious position in the Baltic area and Europe. Napoleon's intentions were uncertain, Finnish peasants conducted guerrilla warfare against the Russian army in northern Finland, Turkey prepared to renew hostilities against Russia, and a Swedish war of revenge and Anglo-Swedish invasions of Finland were very much feared. The meeting with Napoleon in Erfurt during September 1808 made Alexander all the more uneasy about Napoleon's intentions. An added complication became apparent at this meeting: a likely war between Austria and France, whom Russia was supposed to assist. After Alexander returned to St. Petersburg from Erfurt, he assured a Finnish deputation that a Diet would be convened. He accepted the recommendation made by Sprengtporten to place Finnish affairs directly

[3] M. M. Borodkin, *Istoriia Finliandii: Vremia Elizavety Petrovny* (St. Petersburg: Gosudarstvennaia Tipografiia, 1910), pp. 160-70, 282-85; Jutikkala, *A History of Finland*, pp. 147-50, 159-71, 176-77; Peter Scheibert, *Volk und Staat in Finnland in der ersten Hälfte des vorigen Jahrhunderts* (Breslau: P. Plischke, 1941), pp. 3-10, 22-24.

under the emperor, keeping them out of the hands of the Russian ministers and Senate in St. Petersburg. In so doing, he rejected the advice of Minister of War A. A. Arakcheev.[4]

On November 19 (December 1), 1808, Sprengtporten was appointed governor-general of Finland. As one Soviet-Karelian historian has pointed out, Alexander I, in siding with Sprengtporten against Arakcheev on the question of Finnish autonomy, made Sprengtporten the only governor in Russia who was not subordinated to the Imperial Senate but only to the emperor himself.[5] From this time on Alexander insisted that the Russian ministries and Senate were not to interfere in Finnish affairs, which were to be dealt with separately from the administration of the rest of the empire. His principal adviser on both Finnish and internal Russian affairs was then M. M. Speranskii, who quickly familiarized himself with the broad outlines of Finland's history, law, and administrative organization. Thanks to Speranskii's assistance, Alexander was well informed about Finnish conditions and expectations when he appeared, in 1809, before the assembled Finnish Estates in Borgå, the only meeting of the Finnish Diet until Alexander II finally reconvened it in 1863. At Borgå Alexander I confirmed the rights and privileges the Finns had enjoyed under Swedish rule and granted them a degree of self-rule and autonomy that Sweden had never permitted. Alexander, however, following Speranskii's advice, did not confirm the Swedish legislation and statutes upon which the Finns hoped to base their autonomy: namely, the Form of Government of 1772 and the Union and Security Act of 1789. In other words, Finland's autonomy and special rights were based on the emperor's generosity and magnanimity, not on a formal recognition and confirmation of fundamental Finnish laws.[6]

[4] I. I. Käiväräinen (Kiaiviariainen), *Mezhdurnarodnye otnosheniia na severe Evropy v nachale XIX veka i prisoedinenie Finliandii k Rossii v 1809 godu* (Petrozavodsk: Karel'skoe Knizhnoe Izdatel'stvo, 1965), pp. 36-41, 146-53, 172-93, 211-25: Päiviö Tommila, *La Finlande dans la politique européenne en 1809-1815*, Studia Historica, no. 3 (Helsinki: Suomen Historiallinen Seura, 1962), pp. 19-22; "Proekt nakaza finliandskomu general-gubernatoru 14 sentiabria 1809 g.," *Sbornik istoricheskikh materialov izvlechennykh iz arkhiva Sobstvennoi ego Imperatorskogo Velichestva Kantseliarii*, ed. N. Dubrovin (St. Petersburg: Gosudarstvennaia Tipografiia, 1890), p. 298; Peter Scheibert, "Die Anfange der finnischen Staatswerdung unter Alexander I," *Jahrbücher für Geschichte Osteuropas*, o.s. 4 (1939): 375-88.

[5] Käiväräinen, *Mezhdunarodnye otnosheniia*, p. 219

[6] M. M. Borodkin, *Istoriia Finliandii: Vremia Imperatora Aleksandra I* (St. Petersburg: Gosudarstvennaia Tipografiia, 1909), pp. 221-23, 235-50; Osmo Jussila, *Suomen perustuslait venäläisten ja suomalaisten tulkintojen mukaan 1808-1863*, Historiallisia Tutkimuksia Julkaissut, no. 77 (Helsinki: Suomen Historiallinen Seura, 1969), pp. 18-21, 73-92, 129-34.

At the time, Finland could only be a secondary consideration for Speranskii, who was concentrating his energies on preparing a general plan for the reorganization of government and society in Russia. His work with Finnish affairs did, however, provide him with firsthand information concerning the former province of Sweden in which the peasants were free and local legal, administrative, and social institutions were, in Speranskii's own opinion, superior to those of Russia.[7] In the spring and early summer of 1809 Alexander I promised at Borgå that Finland's existing laws and institutions would be respected; he also announced that a Government Council, consisting exclusively of inhabitants of Finland, would be established to organize and coordinate the administration of Finland's internal police, religious, financial, economic, and judicial affairs. This council and a Commission for Finnish Affairs in St. Petersburg to assist Speranskii began to function in the early fall of 1809. The initial task of both the Council and the Commission was to organize a viable autonomous administrative system inside Finland and to establish orderly lines of communication with St. Petersburg. Relations with Russia were a particularly sensitive topic for the Finnish leaders, who wished to minimize Russian interference in their internal affairs without appearing to be ungrateful for what Alexander I had done for them.[8]

Finnish political leaders had to rely mainly on their own tact, perseverance, and expertise in their efforts to improve Finland's position within the Russian Empire. Their efforts were given a degree of continuity they would not otherwise have had by the fortunate circumstance that one man, Robert Henrik Rehbinder, served for thirty years as the principal liaison between the Russian emperor in St. Petersburg and the governor-general and the Finnish civil government in Helsingfors. Rehbinder was slightly more than thirty years old in 1809 when he became Speranskii's assistant in the Commission for Finnish Affairs. He was a worldly, well-educated nobleman who had been a

[7] Keijo Korhonen, *Suomen asian komitea: Suomen korkeimman hallinnon järjestelyt ja toteuttaminen vuosina 1811-1826*, Historiallisia Tutkimuksia, no. 65 (Helsinki: Suomen Historiallinen Seura, 1963), pp. 17-20; O. Jussila, "Finnland in der Gesetzkodifikation zur Zeit Nikolajs I," *Jahrbücher für Geschichte Osteuropas*, n.s. 20 (1972): 26; P. Scheibert, "Eine Denkschrift Speranskijs zur Reform des Russischen Reiches aus dem Jahre 1811," *Forschungen zur osteuropäischen Geschichte* 7 (1959): 26-40.

[8] Korhonen, *Suomen asian komitea*, pp. 36-41; *Finlands Senat för och nu* (Stockholm: K. B. Boström, 1903), pp. 5-10; *Åttioariga minnen: Deklarationer, proklamationer, kungörelser och andra officiella publikationer utfördade i Finland under kriget 1808-1809* (Helsinki: G. W. Edlunds Förlag, 1890), pp. 129-31; Borodkin, *Istoriia Finliandii: Vremia Imperatora Aleksandra I*, pp. 320-21; Amburger, *Geschichte der Behördenorganisation Russlands*, pp. 175-76, 435-37.

kammarjunkare at the Swedish court and a lawyer in Åbo before coming to St. Petersburg in the fall of 1808 as a member of an official Finnish delegation sent to meet with Alexander I. As Speranskii's Finnish assistant and, then, as secretary of the Committee for Finnish Affairs, Rehbinder soon became an extraordinarily well-informed and skilled defender of Finnish interests in the Russian capital.[9] The important initial battle to reform the original Commission for Finnish Affairs was won not by Rehbinder, however, but by a more mature Swedish courtier, statesman, diplomat, and military commander, Gustav Mauritz Armfelt, who, in the spring of 1811, swore an oath of allegiance to Russia.

Armfelt was among a number of high-ranking, Finnish-born, Swedish officials and officers who then left Sweden in order to return to their estates in Finland and to participate in the organization of a new, autonomous Finnish government within the framework of the Russian Empire. He was summoned to St. Petersburg in the spring of 1811 mainly because of the prominent role he had played as a Swedish diplomat, general, and statesman in opposing Napoleonic France. At a time of growing tension between France and Russia, Armfelt was potentially useful to the Russians as a diplomat who could help to establish contacts between England, Russia, and Sweden with a view to neutralizing Sweden or even winning her as an ally in the event of war with France.[10] At the same time, Armfelt's talents as an administrator were very much needed to provide direction and leadership for Finnish affairs in the Russian capital.

On October 26 (December 8), 1811, a new Committee for Finnish Affairs was organized with Armfelt as chairman, Rehbinder attached to it as a state secretary, and three additional Finnish members. Speranskii himself had come to recognize that the old Commission over which he had presided lacked both the knowledge and authority to put Finnish affairs in order; and, apparently wishing to be relieved of the Finnish responsibilities that had been assigned to him, proposed replacing the Commission with a committee that would be chaired by a state secretary and include two Russian members and two Finnish members. The actual committee, formed in October 1811, was based not on Speranskii's proposal, to which the Finns had objected, but on one submitted by Armfelt in May which provided that all members of the committee had to be citizens of Finland. Armfelt's committee

[9] Borodkin, *Istoriia . . . Aleksandra I*, pp. 465-68; Bernhard Estlander, *Elva årtionden ur Finlands historia*, 5 vols. (Helsinki: Söderström, 1929-1930), 1: 101.
[10] Tommila, *La Finlande dans la politique européenne*, pp. 201-37.

was to prepare all legislation pertaining to the civil administration of Finland for presentation to the emperor. As chairman of the Committee for Finnish Affairs, Armfelt took an active part in completing the organization of Finland's internal administration. Up to the time of his death in 1814, a number of new economic, medical, postal, and other specialized sections were added to the Government Council, the central organ of Finland's system of local self-government. In 1816 the Government Council was renamed, then becoming the Finnish Senate.[11] Two other accomplishments of Armfelt's were the creation of a small but separate Finnish army and the reunion of Viborg *guberniia* with Finland. He originally saw the organization of Finnish army units as a means of demonstrating Finnish gratitude toward Alexander at the time of Napoleon's invasion of Russia, but these units were not formed in time to be of any use to the Russian army in 1812. This gesture did, however, help obtain Russian approval for the formation of special Finnish army and naval units in which a few thousand Finnish officers and enlisted men continued to serve throughout the nineteenth century. Although separate Finnish army units did fight for Russia in Poland during the winter of 1830-1831, they were usually not called upon to participate in Russia's wars. In the Crimean War it was the Russian army and navy, not the Finns themselves, that defended Finland against the possible English invasion.[12] Until the twentieth century, Finns were not recruited into the Russian army, and even then this was for but a brief period preceding the Revolution of 1905.

In 1808, even before the conquest of Finland had been completed, Sprengtporten had proposed the reunion of Viborg with Finland. During the following years, Finns reminded the Russians on several occasions of the importance they attached to this subject, but the matter was not pursued energetically until Armfelt arrived in St. Petersburg in the spring of 1811. Alexander's decision in December 1811 to return Viborg to Finland was a major concession. He made it mainly because of a perceived need for Swedish and Finnish friendship on the eve of

[11] Borodkin, *Istoriia . . . Aleksandra I*, pp. 301-9, 319-39; Korhonen, *Suomen asian komitea*, pp. 41-48, 97-124, 153-55, 161-64, 229-32; Carl von Bonsdorff, *Gustav Mauritz Armfelt: Levnadsskildring*, 4 vols., Skrifter utgivna av Svenska Litteratursällskapet i Finland, nos. 212, 223, 231, 245 (Helsinki: Mercators Tryckeri, 1930-1934), 3: 40-43, 101-5, 111-21, 171-99, 271-75, 293-345; 4: 86-97. Hans Hirn, *Gustav Fredric Stjernvall 1767-1815: En Tidsskildring*, Skrifter utgivna av Svenska Litteratursällskapet, Finland, no. 232 (Helsinki: Mercators Tryckeri, 1931), pp. 271-304, 704-11.

[12] Borodkin, *Istoriia . . . Aleksandra I*, pp. 421-55; Borodkin, *Istoriia Finliandii: Vremia Imperatora Nikolaia I* (St. Petersburg: Gosudarstvennaia Tipografiia, 1915), pp. 68-107, 627-70; Bonsdorff, *Gustav Mauritz Armfelt*, 3: 293-345.

what seemed an imminent war with France; Viborg *guberniia* was, moreover, a difficult and troublesome province to administer because of the badly coordinated and confusing coexistence there of Swedish and Russian legal and administrative norms and practices. Once Viborg was reunited with Finland, Armfelt inherited this administrative nightmare. At the same time, he and his associates faced sensitive problems involving the conflicting interests of a number of Finnish peasants with Russian nobles who had been granted land in Viborg *guberniia* during the eighteenth century. These various problems were, however, dealt with realistically, and within a few years a viable administrative and legal order was organized that provided a firm basis for a reunited Finland.[13]

Alexander I's Finnish policies, especially his decision to unite Viborg with Finland, almost inevitably made enemies for the Finns in Russia. During the period of Napoleon's invasion and the following war of liberation, xenophobia grew in Russia, and many non-Russians in the army, at court, and in the civil service were viewed with considerable suspicion. Armfelt was but one of many foreigners favored by Alexander I, but he perhaps found himself in a stronger position than many others because of his role in bringing about the fall of the unpopular Speranskii and in contributing to the success of Russian diplomatic negotiations with Sweden in 1812. Finns then in Russian service realized that the two to three thousand educated officials and officers who ran Finland's government, church, and society had to replace their emotional attachment to a Swedish fatherland with a new patriotic identification with the Grand Duchy of Finland, whose ruler was the Russian emperor. Finns had to become inwardly convinced that the fate of their country was inextricably linked to that of Russia, and Russians had to be persuaded that the Finns were loyal subjects. Finnish leaders, therefore, then introduced measures to teach the Finnish youth and officials the Russian language and to increase trade and establish closer economic relations with Russia.[14]

In the spring of 1812 Alexander I announced that Helsingfors was going to be Finland's new capital; in 1819 both the Senate and the

[13] Borodkin, *Istoriia . . . Aleksandra I*, pp. 351-90.

[14] Bonsdorff, *Gustav Mauritz Armfelt*, 3: 217-24, 236-51, 282-92, 480-505; Hirn, *Gustav Fredric Stjernvall*, pp. 238-44; Tommila, *La Finlande dans la politique européenne*, pp. 44-46, 51-53, 230-36, 280-85, 308-10, 375-77, 400-401, 408-11, 417-19, 439-40; Korhonen, *Suomen asian kometea*, pp. 187-214; Carl von Bonsdorff, *Opinioner och stämningar i Finland 1808-1814*, Skrifter utgivna av Svenska Litteratursällskapet i Finland, no. 141 (Helsinki: Tidnings- och Tryckeri-Aktiebolagets Tryckeri, 1918), pp. 224-36.

residence and offices of the Russian governor-general were moved from Åbo to Helsingfors. Finnish leaders, who wanted to disassociate Finland as much as possible from pro-Swedish Åbo, had proposed this relocation of Finland's government 150 kilometers to the southeast on the Gulf of Finland and in closer proximity to Russia and St. Petersburg. Helsingfors, then a small town with fewer than 5,000 inhabitants consisting chiefly of fishermen and handworkers, had burned almost completely to the ground in 1808. The planning of a new Helsingfors was entrusted to Johan Albert Ehrenström, a personal friend of Armfelt. Ehrenström was another Finnish nobleman who had returned to his native land after many years in the service of the Swedish king. In 1816 Ehrenström was joined by the talented German-born architect Carl Ludwig Engel, who built the impressive Senate and university buildings flanking the Senate Square in Helsingfors. Dominating and standing above that same square still stands the imposing Lutheran Nikolai Church, whose construction was begun by Engel before he died in 1840. By then Ehrenström and Engel had transformed the old Helsingfors into perhaps the most aesthetically pleasing provincial capital of the entire Russian Empire. With 16,592 inhabitants in 1841, it had surpassed Åbo in population (13,145); it had also assumed undisputed intellectual leadership in Finland following the devastating fire of 1827 in Åbo and the relocating of Finland's almost 200-year-old university in Helsingfors in 1828.[15]

Yet, Helsingfors remained for some time a small town that was clearly overshadowed on the Gulf of Finland by its neighbor 300 kilometers to the southeast, St. Petersburg. As a large and important metropolitan center, St. Petersburg exercised a powerful force of attraction on thousands of Finns who sought jobs and professional opportunities not always available in the small urban settlements of Finland. In the first part of the nineteenth century, emigrants from the central and eastern parts of Finland (Kuopio, Viborg, St. Michel, and the eastern part of Nyland) moved eastward in greater numbers to St. Petersburg than southward or westward to Helsingfors. Finns also lived in other parts of Russia. Some two to three thousand Finns, for example, served as officers in the Russian army or navy during the nineteenth century. More than any other single Finnish group, they became intimately familiar with conditions in the interior of Russia and provided that essential link between the empire and the Grand

---

[15] Bonsdorff, *Gustav Mauritz Armfelt*, 3: 217-24; Borodkin, *Istoriia . . . Aleksandra I*, pp. 546-49; Borodkin, *Istoriia . . . Nikolaia I*, pp. 408-503; Estlander, *Elva årtionden*, 1: 120-24; *Entsyklopedicheskii slovar'*, 8: 292-93; 35a: 917.

Duchy that Armfelt and others had considered so important during the first years of Russian rule in Finland.[16]

This interest of Armfelt and his closest associates in cultivating cordial relations with Russia in no way deterred them from resisting all attempts of ministers and other high-placed officials in St. Petersburg to interfere in Finnish internal affairs. The Finns could usually count on Emperor Alexander's support in resisting such interference, but during the first decade of Russian rule it was often difficult to separate Finnish from Russian affairs, especially in dealing with tariffs, the monetary system, taxation, and other financial matters. In 1816 Alexander I, in approving the new name of Senate for the former Finnish Government Council, reconfirmed Finland's special status in the empire; and in 1819 the Russian Senate ordered all Russian officials to refer business related to Finland to the Committee for Finnish Affairs. After this, interference by Russian officials in Finnish affairs gradually discontinued. But Finnish officials still felt uneasy about the absence of a clear constitutional definition of Finnish rights and privileges. Therefore, after 1815 they made every effort to obtain for Finland a Diet that would meet at regular intervals, as well as explicit and written constitutional guarantees of Finnish rights similar to those granted by Alexander to the Poles and by the king of France and certain other European rulers to their subjects. After some vacillation during the period that Novosil'tsev's constitutional project received serious consideration, Alexander decided not to give Finland a written constitution and not to reconvene the Finnish Diet.[17] Without a regular Diet and without more precise assurances of Finnish autonomy than those given by Alexander I at Borgå in 1809, Finland's special status in the empire necessarily had to depend to a large extent on the emperor's good will and the importance he then attached to having the voluntary cooperation of the Finnish Estates at a time of international tension and crisis for Russia. But the administrative separation of Finland, if continued, was bound to become institutionalized and sanctioned by the passage of time.

As defined by Alexander I and his advisers, Finland's new autonomous status permitted only one Russian official, the governor-general, to interfere in Finnish internal affairs. The governor-general, who was considered the tsar's personal representative in Finland, presided over the Finnish Senate. He was in a very good position to control the

[16] Sune Jungar, *Finländare i Ryssland: Utflyttningen till Ryssland 1809-1917* (Turku: Åbo Akademi, 1971), pp. 33-39, 46-48, 56-61, 81-83, 115-21.

[17] Korhonen, *Suomen asian komitea*, pp. 229-32, 278-81, 297-328; Borodkin, *Istoriia . . . Aleksandra I*, pp. 339-49, 465-528.

internal administration of Finland, had he had the desire and approval of the tsar to do so and had he had the detailed knowledge of Finnish affairs that this would have required. Fortunately for Finland, prior to the 1890s no Russian governor-general ever seriously undertook to make use of the extensive powers of his office to limit the extent of Finnish autonomy. Sprengtporten, the only Finnish-born governor-general, and M. B. Barclay de Tolly held office too briefly to have had much of an impact on Finnish-Russian relations. General Fabian Steinheil, like Barclay de Tolly a Baltic German, was governor-general between 1810 and 1823. A Finlandophile who spoke Swedish fluently, Steinheil occasionally became angry when Finnish leaders in the Senate and the Committee for Finnish Affairs in St. Petersburg made appointments or important decisions without bothering to consult him. However, he was neither a very strong personality nor an effective administrator and could usually be persuaded to accept ideas and proposals presented to him by the Finns.[18] His immediate successor, General A. A. Zakrevskii, was not so accommodating.

Before coming to Finland Zakrevskii had fought in the war of liberation against Napoleon and, between 1815 and 1823, he had been an adjutant general attached to the General Staff in St. Petersburg. As a soldier, an energetic, competent, and ambitious administrator, and the first Russian to occupy the office of governor-general in Helsingfors, Zakrevskii quickly asserted his rights as the highest executive authority in Finland. Under Steinheil the Committee for Finnish Affairs had corresponded directly with departments of the Senate and with governors (*landshövdingar*) of Finland's provinces, and the Finnish Senate had paid very little attention to the governor-general in its administration of local affairs. Zakrevskii pointed out, quite correctly, that the Committee for Finnish Affairs never had been intended to function as an executive organ and that the Senate was to work under the immediate supervision and control of the governor-general.[19]

[18] Korhonen, *Suomen asian komitea*, pp. 103-5; Amburger, *Geschichte der Behördenorganisation*, p. 438; C. von Bonsdorff, *Staatsmän och dignitärer: Interiörer ur ämbetsmannavärlden i Finland vid ryska tidens början*, Skrifter utgivna av Svenska Litteratursällskapet i Finland, no. 159 (Helsinki: Tidnings- och Tryckeri-Aktienbologets Tryckeri, 1921), pp. 57-74, 141-44, 305-7, 420-21, 541-45, 577-88; E. N. Berendts, *Lektsii po administrativnomu pravu Velikogo Kniazhestva Finliandii*, vol. 2: *Glavnye organy upravlenii v Finliandii* (St. Petersburg: R. Golike: A. Vil'borg, 1903), pp. 173-204.

[19] Korhonen, *Suomen asian komitea*, pp. 373-97; Jussila, *Suomen perustuslait*, pp. 92-95, 147-50; Alexis A. Lillja, *Arsenjij Andrejevitj Zakrevskij* (Helsinki: Mercators Tryckeri, 1948), pp. 74-88, 141-62; Borodkin, *Istoriia . . . Aleksandra I*, pp. 556-62;

In 1826 Zakrevskii obtained the full support of Nicholas I for his position. The Committee for Finnish Affairs was replaced by a new State Secretariat for Finnish Affairs, which had no legislative or advisory functions but was to serve only as the emperor's chancery for Finnish affairs. But all matters pertaining to Finland originating either in the Russian central government or in the Senate or in the chancery of the governor-general in Helsingfors were to be channeled through the State Secretariat in St. Petersburg, and the internal administration of Finland remained separate from that of the empire. Unless specifically asked to do so, State Secretary for Finnish Affairs Rehbinder did not have the right to comment officially concerning matters sent to the State Secretariat.[20]

Zakrevskii's victory over Rehbinder was, however, more apparent than real. Zakrevskii did not know Swedish, the language in which the Senate administered the internal affairs of Finland. Furthermore, during his last three years as Finnish governor-general he resided in St. Petersburg and was seldom in Helsingfors, having taken on in 1828 a second time-consuming post as Russian minister of the interior. In the Russian capital, Rehbinder, who was elevated to the position of minister state secretary in 1834, no longer occupied the powerful position he had under Alexander I. However, as an intelligent and skilled courtier, he continued to exercise considerable influence because of his good personal relations with Nicholas I, Minister of the Interior Zakrevskii, and Prince A. S. Menshikov, the naval minister and Zakrevskii's successor as Finnish governor-general between 1831 and 1855.[21] Menshikov, the principal representative of Russian imperial authority in Finland, served simultaneously in the naval ministry and resided in St. Petersburg, which meant that he had to deal with the fourteen senators who administered Finland internally through subordinates and intermediaries. It is therefore perhaps not surprising that the internal administrative, social, and economic changes that took place in Finland during these years provided the firm foundation

---

"Bumagi grafa Andreia Andreevicha Zakrevskogo," ed. N. Dubrovin, SIRIO, 73 (1890): viii-ix; "Vsepoddanneishaia zapiska grafa A. Zakrevskogo," February 2, 1826, ibid., 78 (1891): 467-79.

[20] Lillja, *Zakrevskij*, pp. 217-19, 235-37; Korhonen, *Suomen asian komitea*, pp. 397-416; Jussila, *Suomen perustuslait*, pp. 147-50; Borodkin, *Istoriia . . . Nikolaia I*, pp. 505-14; Hans Hirn, *Alexander Armfelt*, 2 vols., Skrifter utgivna av Svenska Litteratursällskapet in Finland, nos. 267, 315 (Helsinki: Merkators Tryckeri, 1938-1948), 1: 170-77; 2: 9-15.

[21] Borodkin, *Istoriia . . . Nikolaia I*, pp. 505-11; Berendts, *Lektsii*, p. 35.

upon which the wide degree of autonomy Finland enjoyed in the second part of the nineteenth century could be built.

One reason these changes in Finnish society and government could take place almost unnoticed by St. Petersburg was the caution, conservatism, and tenacity of the officials in charge of the Senate in Helsingfors and the State Secretariat in St. Petersburg. Not only did they defend Finland's interests in St. Petersburg and manage her internal affairs in a responsible and realistic manner, but they also kept a lid on any social and intellectual ferment in Finland likely to disturb the Russians. Thus in 1821 and 1822, when Åbo University docent Adolf Ivar Arwidsson, in articles published in Sweden and Finland, criticized the Finns for their servility toward Russia and inability to build a nation on the basis of its constitution and the nationality of its Finnish-speaking majority, Finnish political leaders cooperated with the Russian authorities in closing Arwidsson's newspaper, the *Åbo Morgonblad*, which he had been permitted to publish for nine months. They dismissed him and his sympathizers from the faculty of the university, and forced him into Swedish exile by denying him all possibility of professional employment in Finland. Later in the 1820s, Finnish leaders saw to it that Finnish censorship practices conformed with the new and more rigorous norms introduced by Nicholas I by establishing censorship offices in Åbo, Viborg, Vasa, and Uleåborg under the general supervision of the Finnish Senate. In a country with no major urban centers and only three hundred students and a handful of professors in a single university, such eager and prompt compliance with Russian wishes and strict censorship helped to nip in the bud any premature birth of liberal ideas and agitation for a free press.[22] Reassuringly for the Russia of Nicholas I, Finland remained quiet and almost unaffected by the ferment and troubling events then taking place in western Europe and the empire's own Polish provinces.

Across the Gulf of Finland and to the south lay the Baltic provinces, another well-ordered world arranged into traditional estates of Old Europe. The German town patricians and *Ritterschaften* of Estland, Livland, and Kurland were every bit as eager as Finnish leaders to keep order locally and to demonstrate their loyalty to Russia. They also shared the Finns' determination to retain special rights and privileges and to minimize Russian interference in local affairs; however, they had entered the empire almost a century earlier than the Finns,

---

[22] Borodkin, *Istoriia . . . Aleksandra I*, pp. 544, 575-77; Berendts, *Lektsii*, pp. 215-16; Estlander, *Elva årtionden*, 1: 128-33.

and by the beginning of the nineteenth century they had been subjected to the influence of the central authorities of St. Petersburg to
an extent that Finland never experienced, even at the height of so-
called Russification at the beginning of the twentieth century. Unlike
the Finns, the Baltic Germans had serious internal social and economic problems associated with the resentments of former serfs
emancipated without land. The manner in which these serfs were
emancipated is an important part of the story of how the privileged
German estates were able to hold on to their special rights and privileges and to follow their own particularistic and individual path of
development during the first three decades of the nineteenth century.

CHAPTER 6

LIVLAND, ESTLAND, AND KURLAND

IN THE FIRST PART of the eighteenth century the German nobles and townsmen of Estland and Livland had played a unique role as officers and officials in Russian service and as intermediaries between Russia and the German-speaking part of central Europe. Their importance for Russia diminished as she expanded to the Black Sea and into Poland and Finland during the second part of the eighteenth and at the beginning of the nineteenth centuries. They lost their privileged position within the empire during the last thirteen years of the reign of Catherine II. Even though Paul I and Alexander I eventually restored their special rights and privileges, as was pointed out in the introductory discussion for Part Two, this was done with a qualifying clause that suggested possible future changes in the status of these two provinces within the empire.

The position of Estland and Livland was somewhat strengthened by the Third Partition of Poland in 1795, which brought the 27,000 square kilometers and some 400,000 inhabitants of Kurland into the Russian Empire as well. Paul I's restoration of privileges in 1796 thus included Kurland, whose institutions and social and political practices had differed in some respects from those of Estland and Livland because of its membership in the Polish-Lithuanian Commonwealth for more than two centuries. As a vassal state of Poland, Kurland had had her own duke, Diet, internal administration, Lutheran Church, German official language, and privileged nobility. Before 1795 the Poles and officials of the duke had prevented the Kurland *Ritterschaft* from fully developing institutions of self-government comparable to those of the Livlanders and Estlanders to the north. The Kurland nobles did, however, form an important new executive and administrative organ after 1795 to replace the officials of their former duke. This was the *Ritterschaftskomité*, a committee made up of ten district marshals elected by the nobility and presided over by the *Landesbevollmäch-tigter*, a figure who combined the functions of the resident counselor and the marshal of the nobility in Livland.[1] The Diet in Kurland, it

[1] Alexander V. Berkis, *The History of the Duchy of Courland (1561-1795)* (Towson,

should be noted, was a representative body whose deputies were elected in parish assemblies by the matriculated nobility, whereas all members of the Estland, Livland, and Ösel *Ritterschaften* had the responsibility of taking part in the deliberations of their respective Diets.[2]

Kurland continued to differ in many ways from the other two Baltic provinces throughout the nineteenth century, although the large German-speaking minority of all three provinces (some 125,000 individuals in a total population for the three provinces of 1.6 million in mid-century) became increasingly aware of its common heritage and identity. Livland, which was about equal in area to the other Baltic provinces combined, usually played the leading role. It contained not only Riga, the largest metropolitan center in the area and the seat of the Russian governor-general, but also Dorpat University, where young people from all three provinces came into contact with the main currents of German idealism, romanticism, and nationalism. The major battles with Russian officials over Baltic privileges and peasant and institutional reforms were fought in Livland. The success of the Livlanders during the first part of the century in gaining greater influence over the affairs of the countryside and in lessening their dependence on the central government usually also benefited the Kurlanders and Estlanders. This created another common bond, that of shared self-interest, but the three provinces never coordinated their lobbying in St. Petersburg very effectively and in many ways remained divided by narrowly provincial views and loyalties.[3]

The decision in 1801 to put the Russian military governor in Riga in charge of the civil administration of all three Baltic provinces was an important landmark in the history of Baltic Germans during the nineteenth century. Alexander I and his advisers experimented with a variety of administrative arrangements in this part of the empire. Between 1810 and 1818, for example, they separated Estland from Kurland and Livland, but in 1819 all three provinces were reunited under Governor-General Filippo Paulucci. Between 1823 and 1829 Pskov was brought together with the three Baltic provinces in an enlarged *general-gubernatorstvo* administered by Paulucci in Riga.[4] The association of Pskov with the three Baltic provinces was but an

---

Maryland: P. M. Harrod, 1969), pp. 6-11, 44-49; Michael H. Haltzel, "The Reaction of the Baltic Germans to Russification during the Nineteenth Century" (Harvard University Ph.D. dissertation, 1971), p. 17; Hamilkar Fölkersahm, *Das alte Kurland: Eine kulturhistorische Skizze* (Rostock: C. Hinstorff, 1925).

[2] Haltzel, *Der Abbau der deutschen ständischen Selbstverwaltung*, pp. 6-7.

[3] Ibid., pp. 24-25, 40-43, 48-50, 159-60.

[4] Amburger, *Geschichte der Behördenorganisation*, p. 389.

episode that left no lasting traces. The administrative unification of Livland, Kurland, and Estland under a Russian governor-general in Riga, on the other hand, tended to emphasize what these three provinces had in common: the Lutheran religion, similarly structured social and political institutions, and the German language, law, and culture of their privileged elites.

In the first part of the nineteenth century and until the mid-1860s, Russian officials used the term *ostzeiskie gubernii* in referring to the Baltic provinces and their affairs. The adjective *ostzeiskii* comes from the German word *Ostsee*, that is, "Baltic." This particular neologism, presumably dating from the first decade of the nineteenth century and now archaic in Russian, illustrates the then-prevalent view among Russian officials that the Baltic provinces were a self-contained and Germanic world where Russian norms were not always applicable.[5] They saw the Baltic provinces in this light partly because of Russia's experience during the eighteenth century in dealing with them and their privileged townsmen and *Ritterschaften*. In the nineteenth century new social, economic, and cultural changes set into motion forces that accelerated the formation of Estonian and Latvian national elites and the internal development of Baltic economy and society. These changes reinforced local particularism and the separate identity of the three Baltic provinces within the Russian Empire.

In the early nineteenth century the consolidation of the special position of the three Baltic provinces within the empire rested on three pillars: (1) Russian recognition of their rights and privileges, (2) the emancipation of the Estonian and Latvian serfs under conditions determined in large part by the Baltic German landowners, and (3) educational reforms that provided primary education in Latvian and Estonian for the peasant population and high-quality secondary and higher education and professional training in German for the nobility, German *Literaten*, and propertied townsmen, and for a few socially mobile Estonians and Latvians.

Alexander I confirmed the rights and privileges of Estland, Livland, and Riga as early as September 15, 1801.[6] At the same time, however,

---

[5] The earliest use of the term *ostzeiskie gubernii* that I have been able to find is in a Senate report of November 9, 1807, PSZ, 1st ser., 29: 1324-25, no. 22,691, November 19, 1807. This term was used with increasing frequency until the 1850s, when it was gradually replaced by a more idiomatically Russian geographical designation: the *Pribaltiiskie gubernii*. See M. N. Kharuzin (ed.), *Ukazatel' khronologicheskii i sistematicheskii zakonov dlia Pribalitiiskikh gubernii s 1704 g. po 1888 g.* (Tallinn: Estliandskaia Gubernskaia Tipografiia, 1888), pp. 43-124.

[6] PSZ, 1st ser., 26: 787, 791-92, nos. 20,010, 20,014, September 15, 1801; Haltzel, *Der Abbau der deutschen ständischen Selbstverwaltung*, p. 6.

as has already been noted, the Russian government implicitly reserved for itself the right to modify the relationship of these provinces to the empire should any of their rights and privileges come into conflict with Russia's "general decrees and laws." No written agreement assured Baltic autonomy in the manner that the Constitutional Charter guaranteed Congress Poland's rights and freedoms between 1815 and 1830; nor was the internal administration of the Baltic provinces ever formally separated from that of the rest of the empire, for they had been under the direct authority of the central colleges and ministries in St. Petersburg from the very beginning of Russian rule. Powerful governors-general (for example, George Browne in the eighteenth century and Filippo Paulucci and A. A. Suvorov in the nineteenth century), however, usually could be counted on to discourage excessive interference by St. Petersburg officials in the domestic affairs of the Baltic provinces.

D. P. Troshchinskii, an enemy of Baltic privileges, once complained that the Russian authorities could not act directly in what concerned the affairs of the Baltic towns and countryside but only in cooperation with and through the Baltic Germans' town councils and the institutions of self-government controlled by the four corporations of the nobility.[7] What Troshchinskii referred to applied particularly to the institutions of the *Ritterschaft* in Livland, where the powerful influence of the twelve members of the Council of the Diet (*Landratskollegium*) was not only felt by the Diet and higher courts but also extended downward to district (*Kreis*) organs of the nobility and to the individual peasant. This was done through the participation of the counselors of the nobility (*Landräte*) in the administration of an elaborate parish infrastructure organized to provide, however inadequately, for such basic needs of society as law and order, religion, education, postal, police, and welfare services, the supervision of recruitment, and the maintenance of roads, bridges, and public buildings.[8] Russian formal confirmation of Livland rights and privileges no doubt helped to preserve this institutional infrastructure. The mere fact of confirmation, however, did not necessarily prevent the Russian authorities from modifying or reforming it and depriving the twelve counselors of the nobility of the powerful influence they had over the

---

[7] Troshchinskii, "Zapiska," SIRIO, 3: 106-7, 151-53.

[8] Nol'de, *Ocherki*, pp. 403-6; Tobien, *Die Livländische Ritterschaft*, 1: 460-65; Haltzel, "The Reaction of the Baltic Germans to Russification during the Nineteenth Century," pp. 13-19; Georg Hermann Schlingensiepen, *Der Strukturwandel des baltischen Adels in der Zeit vor dem Ersten Weltkrieg*, Wissenschaftliche Beiträge zur Geschichte und Landeskunde Ost-Mitteleuropas, no. 41 (Marburg/Lahn: n.p., 1959), pp. 12-27.

everyday affairs and internal social and economic development of Livland. This was, above all, what not only the Livland *Landräte* and *Landmarschall* but also Riga patricians and the political leaders of the other three Baltic *Ritterschaften* wanted to avoid.

At the beginning of the nineteenth century the first serious challenge to the local power of the Riga patricians and the leadership of the Livland *Ritterschaft* came from within the Baltic German society, not from the Russian government. In Riga, Paul I's restoration of borderland privileges in 1796 had greatly strengthened the position of the town council and the boards of elders of the merchants' and artisans' guilds. New elements that had been brought into these two guilds by Catherine II's Charter to the Towns of 1785 resented their own political impotence vis-à-vis the town council and the guilds' two boards of elders. In 1802 the merchants' guild voted 185 to 78 in favor of reintroducing in Riga Catherine II's Charter to the Towns of 1785. The Riga town council and the elders of the two guilds eventually managed to arrange majority support in the guilds for retention of the old system of town government. Opposition remained strong, however, and two successive Russian governors-general, S. F. Golitsyn and F. W. Buxhoeveden, commented negatively about the tactics and objectives of the Riga town council and of the elders of the two guilds. Clearly, had the Russian government wanted to, it could have made use of the political crisis and turmoil in Riga to increase the central government's influence over that town's administration and internal affairs. The committee Alexander I appointed in 1803 to review Riga's town statutes was, however, composed of a majority of local Germans from the town councils and the elders of the two guilds who favored retention of the old system. As was to be expected, the committee's final report did not go beyond recommending certain minor improvements in Riga's administration. In approving this report Alexander I noted that any basic reform of town government in Riga would have to await the completion of work on the new town statute for the entire empire.[9] To be sure, the question of town reform for Riga was reopened in the 1840s and after the Crimean War, but work on a new town statute for the empire was only completed in 1870 and introduced in Riga in 1877.

In 1803 the government also neglected to act on a unique opportunity to increase its influence over the affairs of the Livland country-

[9] Iu. F. Samarin, *Sochineniia*, vols. 1-10, 12 published (Moscow: A. I. Mamontov, 1877-1911), 7: 508-21; Julius Eckardt, *Bürgerthum und Büreaukratie*, pp. 119-37, 141-47.

side. At that time Fredrich von Sivers-Rantzen, a former marshal of the nobility and the senior and most influential counselor of the nobility in the Livland *Landratskollegium*, energetically worked in both Livland and St. Petersburg for a program of agricultural reform that would give the peasants some protection against the arbitrary power of landowning nobles. Sivers' enemies in the Livland Diet disliked him for various reasons: some felt that he threatened their interests as masters of serfs; others disapproved of his manipulation of good personal relations with Emperor Alexander I and of his powerful position in the *Landratskollegium* to pressure the Diet to accept his ideas on peasant reform; and a Livland elder statesman and former confidant of Catherine II, Jakob Johann Sievers, argued that the reforms Sivers-Rantzen was trying to force on the Diet were unsatisfactory because they gave inadequate attention to the plight of landless farm laborers. To stop Sivers a number of his opponents were even prepared to propose in 1803 to the Diet the abolition of the *Landratskollegium* and the restoration in Livland of the institution of local government that had been in effect elsewhere in Russia since 1775. However, Governor-General Golitsyn was informed prior to the meeting of the Diet through Minister of the Interior V. P. Kochubei that Emperor Alexander considered it unnecessary for the Diet to concern itself with this question. Whether or not the introduction of the empire's institution into Livland was preferable to retention of the "existing order" could only be determined by the government after careful study and "with mature respect for all the circumstances."[10] "Thus," the Slavophile Iurii F. Samarin commented ironically more than 70 years later, "we ourselves rejected the unification of the region with the [Russian] state."[11]

The administrative unification of the Baltic provinces with the rest of the empire did not have a very high priority in St. Petersburg at the beginning of the reign of Alexander I. The experience of the eighteenth century had taught that Russia needed schools, trained officials, good laws, rationally organized institutions, and productive peasants before she could proceed with the introduction of her reforms into all of the empire's borderlands. These were all questions to which Alexander and his "young friends" then paid particular attention. The political infighting of various factions of the Livland Diet and Riga guilds had very little interest for them. Baltic problems were

[10] Samarin, *Sochineniia*, 10: 76-90, 262-63; Blum, *Ein russischer Staatsmann: Des Grafen Jakob Johann Sievers Denkwürdigkeiten*, 4: 565-79.
[11] Samarin, *Sochineniia*, 10: 80.

to be dealt with by the autocrat's own advisers working together with the leaders of local society—such as wealthy Riga merchants and a counselor of the nobility like Sivers-Rantzen, who was well known in government circles as a peasant reformer, as the former Livland marshal of the nobility, and as successful lobbyist for the restoration of Baltic rights and privileges in the mid-1790s.

Only in 1818 did a high-placed official serving Alexander I, namely, Filippo Paulucci, launch a sustained and direct attack against the "existing order" in the Baltic provinces. Until then, wars with Napoleon, Turkey, and Sweden and the discussion of peasant reform in Livland, Estland, and Kurland tended to push into the background any questions pertaining to the relationship of the privileged provinces with the rest of the empire.

Paulucci, an effervescent and willful Italian who had been a popular and successful general before becoming governor-general of Livland and Kurland in 1812, had gotten along splendidly with the Baltic nobility during his first six years in office. After 1818 he had a number of disputes with the Livland *Ritterschaft* about the appointment of secretaries to the five district courts and the nine *Ordnungsgerichte* (a police institution similar to the Lower Land Courts in Catherine II's Provincial Reform of 1775), the administration and maintenance of postal services, judicial reform, and the election of the marshal of the nobility. These put an end to the friendly relations that had existed between the nobles and Paulucci during his first six years in office.[12]

Two considerations seem to have motivated Paulucci's attacks on Livland privileges between 1818 and 1823. First of all, the Livland marshal of the nobility during this five-year period was Friedrich von Loewis of Menar, a fellow general and personal rival in the Napoleonic wars. It would seem more than coincidental that Paulucci's relations with the Livland *Ritterschaft* improved immediately once Loewis of Menar resigned as marshal of the nobility in 1823.[13] Secondly, Paulucci seemed determined to consolidate his position as the tsar's chief representative in the empire's Baltic *general-gubernatorstvo*, which was enlarged to include Estland in 1819. Indeed, he dealt just as peremptorily with the central ministries and the Committee of Ministers in St. Petersburg as he did with the Livland nobility in defending what he considered the prerogatives of his office. As gov-

[12] R. Staël von Holstein, "Die Gefährdung der Landesrechte durch den Marques Paulucci," BM 51 (1901): 242-58.

[13] Ibid., pp. 242-43, 246-48, 378-83; [Alexander Buchholtz], *Deutsch-protestantische Kämpfe in den Baltischen Provinzen Russlands* (Leipzig: Duncker & Humblot, 1888), pp. 102-3.

ernor-general he possessed personal power, authority, and access to the ruler that put him on the same level in the Russian governmental hierarchy as the tsar's ministers. During the reign of Alexander I the ministers and Committee of Ministers in St. Petersburg had more difficulties with Paulucci than perhaps with any other governor. As often as not, Alexander sided with Paulucci. Thus, when the Committee of Ministers reproached Paulucci in 1819 for not carrying out the orders of the minister of finance concerning a fairly minor matter, Alexander I, while admitting that the Baltic governor-general had been careless, gently scolded the minister of finance for not having showed more respect for "My Governor-General."[14]

The highhanded manner in which Paulucci dealt with the *Landratskollegium* and other offices and organs of the nobility around 1820 greatly alarmed the Livland *Ritterschaft*. Marshal of the Nobility Loewis of Menar appealed directly to Alexander I and the minister of interior, accusing Paulucci of having violated Livland rights and privileges that had been confirmed by all Russian rulers since Peter I. The emperor and the Committee of Ministers wavered uncertainly between upholding the authority of the tsar's own personal representative in Riga and preventing this same representative from taking actions that unnecessarily disturbed the local nobles and possibly violated rights and privileges guaranteed by the Russian sovereign himself. In last analysis, Alexander and his advisers did not try to impose their will on either Paulucci or the Livland *Ritterschaft*. The validity of the *Landratskollegium*'s position in regard to the administration of local postal and police affairs was affirmed and the unique features of the office of the Livland *Landmarschall*, as distinguished from the office of marshal of the nobility in the Russian *gubernii*, was recognized. But also recognized was the right of the representative of Russian state power in Riga, Paulucci, to remove *Ordnungsgericht* secretaries whom he considered unfit for office and to demand from the Diet two *Landmarschall* candidates, not just one, for confirmation when elections for this office were held every three years. In other words, a compromise was reached. Because this compromise was justified in terms of Baltic, not Russian, precedents, it represented at least a modest victory for the defenders of Livland rights and privileges.[15]

Paulucci, it should be emphasized, was by no means the pioneer of

[14] Russia, Komitet ministrov, *Istoricheskii obzor deiatel'nosti Komiteta ministrov*, ed. S. M. Seredonin, 4 vols. (St. Petersburg: Gosudarstvennaia Tipografiia, 1902), 1: 93-109.

[15] Ibid., pp. 290-95; Staël von Holstein, "Die Gefährdung der Landesrechte," pp. 246-70, 355-94.

administrative Russification in the Baltic provinces. Although he insisted on the governor-general's right to have his say about important appointments and the administration of local affairs, he never attacked the substance of Baltic special rights and privileges. Apart from the five years Loewis of Menar served as marshal of the nobility, Paulucci lived on good terms with the Baltic nobles. On more than one occasion he, as the energetic and influential administrative head of the Baltic *general-gubernatorstvo* in Riga, proved to be extremely helpful in enabling the local nobles to minimize the interference of St. Petersburg officials in the organization of a local school system and in the working out of the details of Baltic peasant reform. Control over these two areas of activity put the local German elites in a good position to determine the direction and character of social and economic change in the Baltic provinces during the nineteenth century.

St. Petersburg officials had sporadically interfered in Baltic peasant affairs since the time of Catherine II. Organized elements in the Baltic provinces, as has already been pointed out, were at least willing to discuss emancipation, which was not the case in the interior of the empire. In the Livland Diet, agrarian reform was discussed as early as the 1760s, and serfdom was criticized in the name of *Aufklärung* in such notable works as Johann Georg Eisen's *Eines Livländischen Patrioten Beschreibung der Leibeigenschaft* (1764), Heinrich Johann von Jannau's *Geschichte der Sklaverey und Charakter der Bauern in Lief- und Ehstland* (1786), and Garlieb Merkel's *Die Letten* (1797). The Baltic nobles met criticism of the existing agrarian order by considering and even accepting certain aspects of reform, but without sacrificing the social and economic control they exercised over the Estonian and Latvian peasants.

In Livland and Estland the debate over peasant reform in the assemblies of the nobility that finally led to the emancipation of the Estonian and Latvian serfs began in the 1790s. In Livland this debate commenced as early as 1792. Peasant unrest and the constant danger of Russian interference in local peasant affairs were an important consideration in both provinces, especially in Estland. Here, a report of 1795 concerning Catherine II's displeasure about the arbitrary treatment of Estonian peasants prompted Marshal of the Nobility Alexander Salza to propose to the Estland nobles measures to protect the rights of the peasants and regulate their obligations according to inventories, or *Wackenbücher*, that had been compiled by the Swedes during the seventeenth century.[16] At about the same

---

[16] Tobien, *Die Agrargesetzgebung Livlands im 19. Jahrhundert*, 2 vols. (Berlin: Puttkammer & Mühlbrecht, 1899; Riga: G. Löffler, 1911), 1: 111-21, 293; Zutis, *Ostzeiskii vopros*, pp. 615, 623-24.

time, the marshal of the nobility in Livland, Sivers-Rantzen, pressed for a more far-reaching reform that called for a regulation of peasant obligations on the basis of *Wackenbücher* compiled according to pre-scribed procedures and under the supervision of appointed and elected *Ritterschaft* officials. Paul I favored action on the reform proposals of the Estland and Livland Diets but delayed action on them because of his reservations about the wisdom of restricting peasant reform to one small part of the empire. Alexander I had no such reservations and welcomed the initiative of the Baltic nobility, apparently hoping that Russian nobles would soon follow its example in moving in the direc-tion of serf emancipation. Only the serfs of Livland and Estland, how-ever, were emancipated with the approval of the Russian government during the reign of Alexander I.[17]

Initially, the Russian government closely followed and even influ-enced the discussion of emancipation in the Baltic Diets, especially in Livland. An indication of the government's interest in having a voice in the shaping of Baltic peasant reform was the establishment in 1803 of a St. Petersburg Committee for the Investigation of Livland Affairs, chaired by Minister of the Interior Kochubei and made up of four Russians and two Livland counselors of the nobility.[18]

It is unlikely that the Livland and Estland Diets would have acted as quickly as they did between 1802 and 1804 in approving peasant reforms had it not been for pressure from the Russian government. Especially important was the Livland statute of 1804 that regulated the obligations of the Estonian and Latvian serfs and assured lease-holders, with certain exceptions, a hereditary right to cultivate their holdings. Similar statutes were approved for Estland in 1802 and 1804, but they protected peasant rights even less satisfactorily than did the 1804 law for Livland. Furthermore, only in Livland were four Re-gional Inspection (*Revizionnye*) Commissions established (in Riga, Wenden, Pernau, and Dorpat) to collect and verify data concerning peasant obligations and landholding on the basis of which new and more reliable *Wackenbücher* could be compiled.[19]

After 1804 the influence of the Russian government on the discus-sion of peasant reform in the Baltic provinces declined. How and why it did can perhaps be best illustrated by briefly commenting on what

---

[17] Tobien, *Agrargesetzgebung*, 1: 114-33, 154-205; *Istoriia Estonskoi SSR*, 1: 688-92; Samarin, *Sochineniia*, 10: 64-78.

[18] Samarin, *Sochineniia*, 10: 115-28.

[19] Juhan Kahk, *Krest'ianskoe dvizhenie i krest'ianskii vopros v Estonii v kontse XVIII i v pervoi chetverti XIX veka* (Tallinn: Akademiia Nauk Estonskoi SSR, 1962), pp. 171-216; *Istoriia Estonskoi SSR*, 1: 689-97. For the text of the 1804 statute on Livland peasants, see PSZ, 1st ser., 28: 100-37, no. 21,162.

happened in the four Livland Inspection Commissions. Each commission consisted of a Russian chairman who spoke German and six members elected by the local district (*Kreis*) nobility and approved by the tsar. The high church warden (*Oberkirchenvorsteher*) of each district, who was always one of the twelve Livland counselors of the nobility, was attached to each commission in an advisory capacity. Inasmuch as the Russian chairman of these commissions had little firsthand knowledge about local conditions, he tended to accept the advice of the Germans with whom he worked. With the exception of Sivers-Rantzen in Wenden, the high church warden attached to each commission usually did not take a position different from that of the two counselors of the nobility on the St. Petersburg Committee for the Investigation of Livland Affairs. Only the chairman of the Riga Commission during the brief period 1805-1806 was well enough informed about Livland agrarian questions to act independently of his German colleagues. In regard to Sivers-Rantzen, he was no longer able to play a leading role in local politics because his pro-peasant orientation and cooperation with the central government had discredited him in the eyes of his social peers. After 1803-1804 the *Landratskollegium* was clearly in the hands of Sivers' opponents.[20]

The one commission chairman who had studied systematically the entire history of Livland agrarian legislation and conducted thorough personal investigations on the spot of the actual living conditions of the peasants was A. I. Arsen'ev, the chairman of the Riga Inspection Commission during 1805-1806. A former colonel in the Russian army, Arsen'ev then served simultaneously as assistant minister of appanages; he was a sober, competent, and extraordinarily conscientious official. He quickly became somewhat of an expert on Livland peasant questions and soon made a number of valid criticisms of the 1804 reform, urging its modification so that the plight of landless agrarian workers in Livland could be alleviated. Being neither tactful nor politically adept, Arsen'ev alienated too many people in both St. Petersburg and Livland to remain chairman of the Riga Commission very long, and he was dismissed in 1806.[21] It should be noted that his superior in the Ministry of Appanages was Troshchinskii,[22] and it was no doubt because of Arsen'ev that Troshchinskii was so well informed about Livland. The latter, however, never occupied an office that enabled him to influence Russian Baltic policy; it is not certain that

[20] Samarin, *Sochineniia*, 10: 110-20, 127-69, 203-14, 293-313, 345-46, 352-53, 364-65, 376-377; Tobien, *Die Agrargesetzgebung*, 1: 111-14, 158-60, 166-67, 198; *Istoriia Estonskoi SSR*, 1: 703-5.

[21] Samarin, *Sochineniia*, 10: 227-84; Tobien, *Agrargesetzgebung*, 1: 218-20.

[22] Amburger, *Geschichte der Behördenorganisation*, p. 107.

Alexander ever even read Troshchinskii's famous memorandum on the ministerial form of government and the inconveniences it caused for Russian policy in the Baltic provinces and elsewhere in the western borderlands.

Between 1809 and 1819 Russian interference in the remaining details of Baltic peasant reform was reduced to a minimum. In 1809 the government allowed the four District Inspection Commissions, whose work had been badly coordinated, to be replaced by a single so-called Land-Survey (*Mezhevaia*) Commission, which was to finish uncompleted work and to verify all the *Wackenbücher* that had been prepared up to that time. This new commission was located in Walk and consisted of eight Livland nobles and not a single Russian—with the exception of a land surveyor attached to the committee. In the beginning all verified *Wackenbücher* were to be sent to St. Petersburg for approval, but these *Wackenbücher* were actually inspected by young Livlanders working for a newly created subcommittee (the so-called *Konferentsiia*) of the main St. Petersburg Committee chaired by the minister of the interior. The main committee had less and less to do and met less and less frequently. Work on the reform was suspended altogether during 1812, and in 1813 the subcommittee was moved to Riga at the request of Governor-General Paulucci, who now became the chairman of a Riga section of the St. Petersburg Committee. Paulucci, who was advised by two senior counselors of the nobility who had served many years on the St. Petersburg Committee, seemed to have been only interested in bringing about the emancipation of the Baltic serfs as soon as possible, and he consistently defended the point of view of Baltic landowners in order to attain that end. Emancipation came first in Estland and Kurland in 1816 and 1817; neither province could afford to ignore prolonged reform discussions in Livland, and both of them were under heavy pressure from Alexander I and Paulucci to emancipate their serfs.[23] And once emancipation took place in two of the three Baltic provinces, Paulucci exerted himself all the more energetically to overcome the last hesitations of the Livland nobles, whose serfs were finally liberated in 1819 without land and, in certain respects, with less satisfactory protection for their rights than the Livland peasants had received in 1804.[24]

---

[23] *Istoriia Estonskoi SSR*, 1: 705, 714-15; H. Strods, "Proekt latyshskikh krest'ian ob otmene krepostnogo prava i barshchiny v kazennykh imeniiakh Kurliandskoi gubernii (1810 g.)," *Ezhegodnik po agrarnoi istorii vostochnoi Evropy 1968 g.* (Leningrad: "Nauka," 1972), pp. 213-23; Wittram, *Baltische Geschichte*, pp. 159-60; Samarin, *Sochineniia*, 10: 352-77, 399-406.

[24] Samarin, *Sochineniia*, 10: 396-97, 406-7; Tobien, *Die Agrargesetzgebung*, 1: 349-50; Hamilcar Baron Foelkersahm, *Die Entwicklung der Agrarverfassung Livlands und*

The laws that defined the terms of emancipation in the three Baltic provinces were extraordinarily complicated and cannot be discussed in detail here. In Livland the peasants lost the hereditary right to the use of land they had acquired in 1804. Instead, they were offered the possibility of entering voluntarily into contracts with the landowners to work or lease land—a somewhat perverse application of Adam Smith's liberal economics to the Baltic region. In all three Baltic provinces, the economic power of the landowners placed the peasants at a distinct disadvantage in negotiating contracts, and the high level of corvée proved to be very deleterious to peasant interests. Personal freedom was also a mixed blessing, for the landowner no longer had the legal and moral responsibility of taking care of the peasants in times of need, crop failure, and famine. Social mobility continued to be limited for some time: even after the initial transitional period, a peasant could only move freely within his native province if he obtained permission from his local noble estate owner and peasant community officials, who customarily demanded evidence that he had taken care of all his local obligations.[25] Furthermore, the peasant police and court institutions organized as a result of legislation approved for the three Baltic provinces between 1802 and 1819 also gave the corporations of the nobility new functions and new opportunities to interfere in the affairs of the local peasantry. This was particularly the case in Livland, where peasant self-government was subordinated to a comprehensive police and court network coordinated by the *Landratskollegium*'s twelve counselors of the nobility and controlled locally on the levels of the individual manor and parish (*Kirchspiel*) by the nobility.[26]

At the same time, the laws that emancipated the Estonian and Latvian serfs provided an institutional and legal framework within which certain enterprising nobles and peasants (especially after they acquired the right to own land in the mid-nineteenth century) were able to modernize the society and agricultural economy of the Baltic provinces, whose economic and social progress compared very favorably with that of other areas of the Russian Empire throughout the nine-

Kurlands und die Umwälzung der Agrarverhältnisse in der Republik Lettland, Greifswalder Staatswissenschaftliche Abhandlungen, no. 21 (Greifswald: L. Bamberg, 1923), pp. 31-32.

[25] PSZ, 1st ser., 33: 670-727, no. 26,278, May 29, 1816; ibid., 34: 529-743, no. 27,024, August 25, 1817; ibid., 36: 114, 542-734, no. 27,735, March 26, 1819; Wittram, *Baltische Geschichte*, pp. 159-61; Tobien, *Die Agrargesetzgebung*, 1: 439-40; *Istoriia Estonskoi SSR*, 1: 716-18; J. Kahk, *Die Krise der feudalen Landwirtschaft in Estland (Das zweite Viertel des 19. Jahrhunderts)* (Tallinn: "Eesti Raamat," 1969), pp. 134-37.

[26] *Istoriia Estonskoi SSR*, 1: 719-21. On the Livland system of corporate government, see Schlingensiepen, *Der Strukturwandel des baltischen Adels*, pp. 12-27, 39-44.

teenth century. Baltic emancipation, it should be noted, provided Estonian and Latvian peasants with opportunities for local self-government and elementary education that existed for few other peasants in Russia at that time. The Baltic peasant became a member of a rural community that elected its own officers; he was called upon to help organize and support rural elementary schools and to participate in the administration of local affairs. The placing of responsibilities in the hands of peasants was a very significant step in the development of Estonian and Latvian public attitudes. Concerning the Latvians, Andrejs Plakans has written:

> As never before, issues could be discussed, answers to local problems experimented with, and the techniques of local government learned by individuals who had never before had such opportunities. Since local governmental problems tended to be similar over large regions of the provinces, and were confronted in roughly similar forms by each new generation of the peasantry, traditions of expertise could be built up.[27]

Such expertise was communicated in Estonian and Latvian, giving the two peasant tongues a new meaning in the eyes of the inhabitants of the Baltic countryside.

The emancipation of the Estonian and Latvian serfs between 1816 and 1819 also gave impetus to the development of rural elementary education in the three Baltic provinces. Since the Reformation, a limited amount of instruction, especially in reading and learning the catechism, had been given by church sextons (usually Estonians or Latvians) under the general direction of the Lutheran pastors. During the time of Swedish rule, peasant education was brought under the overall supervision of the high church warden, and textbooks were translated into Estonian and Latvian. Throughout the seventeenth and eighteenth centuries neither the Swedish nor the Russian governments regarded the peasant school in the Baltic provinces as a state institution but left its support to the local communities and *Ritterschaften*. Since local support was minimal, there were few organized peasant schools, and a good part of the actual instruction was given by mothers to their children at home and under indirect, general supervision by the church sextons and their pastors.[28] The discussion

---

[27] Andrejs Plakans, "The Latvians," in *Russification in the Baltic Provinces and Finland, 1855-1914*, ed. E. C. Thaden (Princeton: Princeton University Press, 1981), p. 217.

[28] Arthur von Villebois, "Die Landvolksschulen," in *Baltische Bürgerkunde: Versuch einer gemeinverständlichen Darstellung der Grundlagen des politischen und sozialen*

of peasant reform and emancipation early in the nineteenth century suggested to many a need for expansion of the rudimentary and inadequate school system. At first the School Commission of the University of Dorpat, which was established in 1802 and represented the authority of the newly created Ministry of Education in the Baltic provinces, tried to establish its influence over all levels of Baltic education, but it only succeeded in keeping the University of Dorpat and state-supported secondary schools out of the hands of the nobility. Meanwhile, the Livland *Ritterschaft* lobbied in St. Petersburg and persuaded Alexander I and his advisers that the supervision and control of education for Estonian and Latvian peasants should remain under the supervision of Baltic pastors and nobles. The statute of March 26, 1819, for Livland elementary schools formally recognized the special rights and authority of the Lutheran High Consistory and the Diet and their subordinate organs in all matters pertaining to rural elementary education in Livland. In Estland the nobles were less adamant in their opposition to state participation in elementary education, hoping that such possible participation would be accompanied by financial support. When it turned out that it was not, they also requested, in 1824, that schools for the peasants in Estland be left under the exclusive authority of the nobility and the clergy. This request was supported by Paulucci and approved in St. Petersburg. The Kurland nobility and clergy even had to be prodded into accepting responsibility for educating their former Latvian serfs, which they reluctantly did in April of 1827.[29]

During the first decades of the nineteenth century the Russian government, as S. V. Rozhdestvenskii observed in 1902 in his official history of the Ministry of Education, "was altogether eliminated from

---

Lebens in den Ostseeprovinzen Russlands (Riga: G. Löffler, 1908), pp. 241-42; A. Iu. Elango, "Shkola i pedagogicheskaia mysl' v Estonii," in *Ocherki istorii shkoly i pedagogicheskoi mysli narodov SSSR*, p. 480.

[29] Elango, "Shkola i pedagogicheskaia mysl' v Estonii," in *Ocherki*, pp. 480-82; R. M. Mikel'son, "Shkola i pedagogicheskaia mysl' v Latvii," ibid., pp. 469-71; S. V. Rozhdestvenskii, *Istoricheskii obzor deiatel'nosti Ministerstva narodnogo prosveshcheniia 1802-1902*, pp. 89-96, 157-58; Woldemar von Bock, "Notizen aus dem Gebiet der livländischen Landvolksschule," in *Livländische Beiträge: Zur Verbreitung gründlicher Kunde von der protestantischen Landeskirche und dem deutschen Landesstaate in den Ostseeprovinzen Russlands, von ihrem guten Rechte und von ihrem Kampf um Gewissensfreiheit*, 3 vols. (Berlin: Stilke & van Muyden, 1867-1868; Leipzig: Duncker & Humblot, 1869-1871), vol. 1, Heft 2, Beilage B, pp. 115-127; Helmut Speer, *Das Bauernschulwesen im Gouvernement Estland von Ende des achtzehnten Jahrhunderts bis zur Russifizierung* (Tartu: J. G. Krüger, 1936), pp. 53-88, 96-132.

the business of elementary popular education in the Baltic region."[30] The Russian government, however, was on the horns of a dilemma: in the Baltic provinces it either had to leave popular education in the hands of the local nobles and pastors or not develop it at all. Inasmuch as the Russian educational authorities, because of the shortage of teachers and inadequate funding and public support, could do so little in the Russian center of the empire during the first part of the nineteenth century to promote popular education, how could they exert any significant influence on elementary rural education in an area where the peasants were Estonian and Latvian and the nobility and clergy were German, and where the level of literacy compared with that of western Europe, not Russia?[31] An ambitious administrator like Governor-General Paulucci saw this point. Interested in results, he used his considerable influence to discourage interference by St. Petersburg bureaucrats in the organization of a separate system of elementary education for peasants under the control and supervision of the German nobility and clergy.

The Russian government also had relatively little influence on secondary and higher education in the Baltic provinces. Secondary schools had existed in Baltic towns since the thirteenth and fourteenth centuries, and a number of new schools were founded by the Swedish government during the seventeenth century, including the first University of Dorpat. This network of schools was expanded under the decentralized educational system introduced in Russia in 1802, which the Poles of Lithuania, Belorussia, and the Right-Bank Ukraine had so profoundly influenced and found so convenient for their purposes. The first three curators of the Dorpat School Region during the period 1802-1835 were Friedrich Maximilian Klinger, a famous poet of the German *Sturm und Drang*, and the Baltic Germans Karl von Lieven (minister of education between 1828 and 1833) and Karl Magnus von der Pahlen (the Baltic governor-general between 1830 and 1845). These curators worked closely with such outstanding rectors as the French-born natural scientist Georg Friedrich Parrot and the German-born historian Gustav Ewers in attracting to Dorpat first-rate academic talent from Germany and in making it one of the leading universities of

[30] Rozhdestvenskii, *Istoricheskii obzor*, p. 158.

[31] Toivo U. Raun, "The Development of Estonian Literacy in the 18th and 19th Centuries," *Journal of Baltic Studies* 10 (1979): 115-26; Andrejs Plakans, "The Spread of Literacy among Latvians," unpublished paper presented at the Sixth Conference on Baltic Studies, May 1978; V. I. Charnoluskii, "Nachal'noe obrazovanie v pervoi polovine XIX stoletiia," in *Istoriia Rossii v XIX veke*, 9 vols. (St. Petersburg: A. I. Granat, n.d.), 4: 74, 87-88, 97-100, 105-11, 122-23.

Russia and northern Europe. As was the case for Wilno University, the professors at Dorpat initially trained teachers for secondary schools and administered their instructional programs. These schools had high standards, and provided, until they were Russified in the 1880s, the nobility, the *Literaten*, affluent or ambitious German townsmen, and a small number of socially mobile Estonians and Latvians with a basic education in German.[32]

In a word, Russian officialdom was then in no position to prevent German nobles, pastors, and educational administrators from using the schoolroom to develop local particularism and to instill attitudes and values in the minds of young people likely to draw them culturally and psychologically to Germany rather than to Russia. Among the first high-ranking Russian officials to see the dangers of a purely German system of education in the Baltic provinces was S. S. Uvarov, Lieven's successor and minister of education from 1833 to 1849. Uvarov's efforts to overcome the "provincial spirit" in these schools and to reform them so that they would contribute to bringing the Baltic provinces closer to the rest of the empire will be discussed in Part Three of this study. Baltic social and economic problems and tensions, to be sure, gave Uvarov and other centralizing St. Petersburg officials opportunities for intervention that did not exist in the Grand Duchy of Finland. Like Finland, however, the Baltic provinces enjoyed the support of powerful governors-general and benefited from the connections and diplomatic skill of their representatives in St. Petersburg. As a result, throughout the first two-thirds of the nineteenth century both Finland and the Baltic provinces continued to evolve socially and culturally under the umbrella of special rights and privileges and in isolation from the rest of the empire.

Finns and Baltic Germans combined particularism with loyalty to the tsar and empire, which contributed to their success in preserving so long their autonomy and special rights and privileges. In 1830-1831, on the other hand, the Polish *szlachta* and many members of the Roman Catholic clergy of Lithuania, Belorussia, Congress Poland, and the Right-Bank Ukraine dramatically demonstrated their hostility to Russia by rejecting the authority of the tsar. In this vast borderland inherited from Poland, however, an old-regime and undergoverned country such as Russia still had to depend on the services of the local

---

[32] Haltzel, *Der Abbau der deutschen ständischen Selbstverwaltung*, pp. 15-16; Tobien, *Die Livländische Ritterschaft*, 1: 276-81, 308-18; E. V. Petukhov, *Imperatorskii iure'evskii, byvshii derptskii universitet za sto let ego sushchestvovaniia (1802-1902)*, 2 vols. (Tartu: K. Mattisen, 1902; St. Petersburg: Senatskaia Tipografiia, 1906), 1: 198-207.

nobility and clergy to maintain order, recruit soldiers for the army, collect taxes, and, generally, carry out, to one extent or another, policies decided upon in St. Petersburg. When these policies threatened or affected adversely the interests of the local *szlachta* and clergy (for example, the Russification of education and administration, the regulation of peasant-landowner relations, and the improvement of the position of the Orthodox Church in this region), Russian officials soon encountered some difficulties. They learned it was not easy for an old-regime *Polizeistaat* to reshape, in the image of Nicholas I's Orthodox and autocratic Russia, a multinational peasant society dominated by Polish and Roman Catholic civilization and controlled and run locally by the Polish *szlachta* and clergy.

PART III

CENTRALIZATION
AND DECENTRALIZATION,
1830-1870

Even before the Polish insurrection of 1830-1831, Nicholas I dropped Alexander I's experiments with constitutionalism and decentralization of government in Russia. Instead, he concentrated on the gradual improvement of government and society and on bringing matters of vital interest under the immediate and direct supervision of his own most trusted agents, who usually worked in either sections of His Imperial Majesty's Own Chancery or certain key ministries. Quite aware of the shortcomings of local government in Russia, Nicholas I sought to achieve some degree of influence and control over local affairs by establishing a network of gendarmes throughout the empire, by creating an agency (the Fifth Section of His Majesty's Own Chancery, which later became the Ministry of State Domains) to protect and promote the interests of the state peasants, and by placing the *guberniia* administration directly under the control of the governors and the Ministry of the Interior. At the same time, such other branches of the central government as the Ministries of Education, Justice, and Finance also increased the number of their agents and inspectors in the provinces. The number of educated and competent officials working in the provinces, although still insufficient to meet the basic needs of local society, was expanded considerably during the first part of the nineteenth century.[1]

Nicholas I's bureaucratic centralism provided the Russian provinces with neither adequate police, cultural, and social services nor an ef-

[1] S. Frederick Starr, *Decentralization and Self-Government in Russia 1830-1870* (Princeton: Princeton University Press, 1972), pp. 33-34, 47-48; Daniel T. Orlovsky, *The Limits of Reform: The Ministry of Internal Affairs in Imperial Russia* (Cambridge: Harvard University Press, 1981), pp. 17-51; N. V. Vavardinov, *Istoriia Ministerstva vnutrennikh del*, 3 pts., 8 knigi (St. Petersburg: V Tipografii Ministerstva Vnutrennikh Del, 1858-1862), pt. 3, bk. 2, pp. 275-85; bk. 3, pp. 227-28; Hans-Joachim Torke, "Das russische Beamtentum in der ersten Hälfte des 19. Jahrhunderts," *Forschungen zur osteuropäischen Geschichte* 12 (1967): 133-73; Yaney, *The Systematization of Russian Government*, pp. 164-68, 205-7, 212-29, 322-27.

ficient and effective local administration. Throughout Nicholas's reign Russia continued to be undergoverned as well as socially and economically backward. In the 1850s and early 1860s defeat in the Crimean War and widespread awareness of the many deficiencies of Russian society and government influenced educated Russians and their officials to proceed with the emancipation of the Russian serfs and to consider a number of other reforms. These included the decentralization of government and the devolution of certain social and economic functions to the local authorities and society. The pendulum swung back in the direction of bureaucratic centralism following the second Polish insurrection and the revolutionary agitation and social unrest in Russia of the early 1860s. However, before the advocates of stricter and more rigorous controls over society fully routed their opponents in government, zemstvos and institutions of peasant self-administration had been created in order to encourage the local nobility and peasants to involve themselves in activities that promoted social, cultural, and economic progress in the provinces.[2] In the 1860s Russian zemstvos and peasant institutions were not extended to the western borderlands, but here, too, the general empire-wide discussion of decentralization and reform of local government then helped to relax centralizing pressures. This gave local German, Polish, and Swedish leaders, who opposed the introduction of the Russian reforms of the sixties into their respective areas, an opportunity to propose their own projects for judicial, municipal, educational, and peasant reforms. The consideration, approval, and implementation of reforms designed specifically for the western borderlands revitalized their local forms of legal-administrative order and of socioeconomic organization, in this way setting these borderlands apart from the rest of the empire.

The reform projects in Congress Poland, the Baltic provinces, and Finland of the 1860s were based on their own local experience and activities in the spheres of education, codification of laws, and municipal, peasant, and economic affairs. Nicholas I's centralizing officials tried to influence, as well as reform, the internal life of the western borderlands, but usually with minimal results. As had been the case for their predecessors, they did not have the financial resources and sufficient agents with expertise and knowledge of local languages and traditions to assure them success in this endeavor. Furthermore, such governors-general as A. S. Menshikov in Finland, I. F. Paskev-

[2] S. Frederick Starr, *Decentralization and Self-Government in Russia*, pp. 1-5, 44-58, 182-83, 289-91, 325-47; Orlovsky, *The Limits of Reform*, pp. 58-84.

ich in Congress Poland, and Karl Magnus von der Pahlen and A. A. Suvorov in the Baltic provinces frequently questioned the wisdom of policies formulated in the ministries and chanceries of St. Petersburg. Bureaucratic centralism meant very little in borderlands where the tsar's more or less permanent and all-powerful personal representatives—namely, his governors-general—were inclined to rely on their own judgment of what was needed locally rather than on the judgment of high officials in the capital. The tsar usually acted as an arbitrator of disputes among his governors-general and ministers rather than as the decisive coordinator of a general plan of bureaucratic centralization for the entire empire. As a result, the leaders of borderland society usually found one way or another to defend traditional practices and institutions and to discourage agents of the central government from interfering in local affairs.

In the long run, especially after the return to bureaucratic centralism in the mid-1860s, the ministries and the other organs of the central government prevailed over both the governors-general and the privileged elites in the western borderlands. The centralizing policies that applied to Congress Poland, the western *gubernii*, and the Baltic provinces in the 1860s and to Finland somewhat later were formulated to a considerable extent by agents of the central government who had come during the reign of Nicholas I and were experts in such matters as the codification of local laws and peasant, municipal, educational, and religious affairs. Many of these agents were young men who had received a thorough education either in Russian universities or at such elite schools as the School of Jurisprudence in St. Petersburg and the Tsarskoe Selo Lyceum. They included such figures as P. N. Batiushkov, who had served as vice curator of the Wilno School Region in the early fifties and who later became the Ministry of the Interior's leading authority on religious and nationality questions in the western *gubernii*; Iu. F. Samarin, who had researched the historical background of urban problems and conflicts in Riga for the Ministry of the Interior during the 1840s, worked under both Governors-General E. A. Golovin and D. G. Bibikov, and achieved reknown under Alexander II as a peasant reformer, Russifier in Poland, and the most effective of all Russian polemicists against the special rights and privileges of the Baltic Germans; I. S. Aksakov, who had acquired firsthand knowledge of the Russian provinces, including the Ukraine, on various assignments for the Ministry of the Interior and the Imperial Geographic Society during the 1840s and 1850s and who, in the newspapers he published during the 1860s and 1880s, aggressively defended Russian national interests in the western borderlands; Count D. A. Tolstoi, who had studied the history of Roman Catholicism in Russia for the Main Administration for Ecclesiastical Affairs of the Foreign Confessions of the Ministry of the Interior during the late 1840s, published a famous anti-Catholic book on the same subject in 1864, shortly after the Polish uprising of 1863, and inaugurated a policy of Russifying all Polish schools as minister of education between 1866 and 1880; and P. A. Valuev, who served in the Baltic provinces in the forties and early fifties and pursued, as minister of the interior in the sixties, a firm but moderate policy in regard to the Baltic Germans.

Nicholas I's efforts to expand the activities of his bureaucracy in the provinces did not alter fundamentally the structure of society in the western borderlands or their relationship to the rest of the empire. Yet these efforts were important for the future, for the men who attempted to carry out a policy of Russification in the western borderlands during the second part of the nineteenth century had been trained in the school of Nicholas I. It was there that they gained the art of dealing with the extraordinarily complicated legal, religious, political, economic, and social conditions of this important and large borderland area conquered for Russia by the soldiers of Peter I, Catherine II, and Alexander I.

CHAPTER 7

THE WESTERN *GUBERNII*

UNLIKE FINLAND and Congress Poland, the western *gubernii* did not enjoy an autonomous position in the empire prior to 1830. Despite Paul I's assurances of 1796 to the contrary, the all-Russian institutions created by Catherine II's Provincial Reform of 1775 were gradually reintroduced at the beginning of the nineteenth century in the Right-Bank Ukraine, Belorussia, and Lithuania. Teachers, judges, lawyers, officials, and churchmen in these provinces, therefore, operated under the general supervision and control of Russian governors and governors-general and of the central ministries and sections of His Imperial Majesty's Own Chancery. Until 1830, however, the courts, schools, churches, and lower administrative offices in this area remained the special preserve of the Polish *szlachta*. Here central supervision and control were not very effective, especially in a school system staffed by Polish teachers and administered by Polish professors at the University of Wilno.

Before the Warsaw insurrection of November 1830, Russians had viewed Polish constitutionalism with suspicion and opposed Polish aspirations in the western *gubernii*, but a Polish question as such hardly existed for them. The difficulties experienced by Russia during the insurrection of 1830-1831 and foreign support for the Polish rebels completely changed the attitudes of Russia toward Poles. Now Russians began to see in the unresolved Polish question a threat to the very existence of the Russian state. This feeling was by no means confined to conservative publicists. Even the great Pushkin, who had once sympathized with the Decembrists, defended Russia's suppression of the Polish revolt in 1831 and argued that either Russia or Poland had to perish in the duel over the historical heritage of the Grand Duchy of Lithuania and in the struggle for supremacy in the Slavic world. Such views were common in the Russia of the 1830s, and the official historians M. P. Pogodin and N. G. Ustrialov popularized them in articles published in literary historical journals and in textbooks used in Russian secondary schools and universities.[1]

---

[1] Władysław Bortnowski, *Powstanie listopadowe w oczach Rosjan*, Uniwersytet Łódzki,

121

Nicholas I, of course, did not need Pushkin, Pogodin, and Ustrialov to tell him that the Grand Duchy of Lithuania was an ancient Russian possession or that Russian state interests in the western borderlands had to be defended. Indeed, he had cautiously begun to defend these interests before the Poles revolted in 1830, and earlier that year he had warned the Poles in the last meeting of the Sejm in Congress Poland that they needed to use the rights that had been granted to them "with wise moderation."[2] Their disregard of this advice served as justification for Nicholas's abolition of many Polish rights and privileges and for a program integrating the Polish borderlands into the general legal and administrative structure of the empire.

In 1840 Nicholas I ordered that the terms "Belorussia" and "Lithuania" were no longer to be used officially in referring to the western *gubernii*. After the abolition of the Białystok district in 1842 and the creation of Kowno *guberniia* in 1843, there were nine such *gubernii*: Grodno, Kiev, Kowno, Minsk, Mohylew, Podolia, Volhynia, Wilno, and Witebsk. Podolia and Volhynia were subordinated to the military governor of Kiev; Minsk, Grodno, and Kowno to the military governor of Wilno. Witebsk and Mohylew were combined with Smolensk in a single *general-gubernatorstvo*, which was abolished in 1856. Smolensk, which Russia acquired prior to the First Partition of Poland, was not considered as one of the nine western *gubernii*.[3]

For the coordination of Russian policy in the western *gubernii*, a so-called Western Committee was organized and attached to the Committee of Ministers on September 16, 1831.[4] The projects examined by the Western Committee originated above all the chanceries of the men who were among Nicholas I's most trusted representatives in the Western *gubernii*: such governors and governors-general as Prince N. N. Khovanskii in the Witebsk, Mohylew, Minsk, and Smolensk *gubernatorstvo* (1823-1836); M. N. Murav'ev in Mohylew and Grodno *gubernii* (1828-1835); and General-Governor D. G. Bibikov in the southwestern *gubernii* of Kiev, Podolia, and Volhynia (1837-1852). Khovanskii, as we have already seen, was instrumental

---

Prace Instytutu Historycznego, no. 10 (Warsaw: Wykonanno w Zakładzie Graficznim Politechniki Warszawskiej, 1964), pp. 23, 128-211; Wacław Lednicki, *Pouchkine et la Pologne: A propos de la trilogie antipolonaise de Pouchkine* (Paris: Leroux, 1928), pp. 23-28, 63-96, 101, 113, 129-31, 146-55, 191; J. L. Black, "M. P. Pogodin: A Russian Nationalist Historian and the 'Problem' of Poland," *Canadian Review of Studies in Nationalism* 1 (1973): 61-63, 67-68.

[2] N. Reinke, *Ocherk zakonodatel'stva Tsarstva Pol'skogo (1807-1881 g.)* (St. Petersburg: Senatskaia Tipografiia, 1902), p. 64.

[3] Amburger, *Geschichte der Behördenorganisation*, pp. 390-99.

[4] Russia, Komitet ministrov, *Istoricheskii obzor deiatel'nosti Komiteta ministrov*, 2: 54-58.

in separating Mohylew and Witebsk *gubernii* from the Polish Wilno School Region as early as 1824. During the Polish insurrection of 1830-1831 he persuaded the central government to act promptly in bringing the legal system of Mohylew and Witebsk *gubernii* into conformity with that of the Great Russian provinces of the empire. Even before the suppression of the Polish insurrection had been completed, *ukazy* of January 1 and February 6, 1831, abolished the Lithuanian Statute and introduced Russian courts and laws in Mohylew and Witebsk *gubernii*.[5] Elsewhere in the western *gubernii* the Lithuanian Statute remained in effect until 1840.

Russian administrators in both the capital and the western *gubernii* agreed that the Polish *szlachta* had to be curtailed and eliminated as much as possible from positions of influence over local government and society. The estates of *szlachta* involved in the uprising were of course confiscated, and tens of thousands of Poles forced to settle in other parts of the empire. The petty *szlachta* received special attention, for their instability and lack of property made them, in the words of an *ukaz* of October 19, 1831, "most susceptible to insurrection and to criminal activities against legal authority."[6] The *ukaz* of October 19 reclassified petty *szlachta* who owned little or no land or who could not document their noble ancestry satisfactorily as either *odnodvortsy* (a category of state peasant) if they lived in the countryside or as burghers if they were townsmen. These new *odnodvortsy* and burghers, unlike the majority of the *szlachta* who were certified as hereditary *dvoriane*, were subject to a special tax of one to three rubles and to recruitment into the Russian army (but for fifteen instead of the usual twenty-five years that applied to state peasants, serfs, and burghers elsewhere in the empire).[7] They were not, however, immediately deprived of all claim to the title of nobility, although in 1847 they were specifically forbidden to own land populated by serfs; only in 1857 were they completely absorbed into the ranks of the state peasants and townsmen.[8] In this manner the Russian government substantially reduced the size of the Polish nobility in the western *gubernii*, for

[5] Amburger, *Geschichte der Behördenorganisation*, pp. 195-96, 391; A. E. Nol'de, *Ocherki po istorii kodifikatsii mestnykh grazhdanskikh zakonov pri grafe Speranskim*, vol. 1: *Popytka kodifikatsii litovsko-pol'skogo prava* (St. Petersburg: Senatskaia Tipografiia, 1906), p. 237; PSZ, 2nd ser., 6: 1,171, nos. 4,233 and 4,369, January 1 and February 18, 1831.

[6] PSZ, 2nd ser., 6: 135, no. 4,869, October 19, 1831; Korzon, *Wewnętrzne dzieje Polski*, 1: 138-149; Winiarski, *Les institutions politiques en Pologne*, pp. 151-53.

[7] PSZ, 2nd ser., 6: 134-38, no. 4,869, October 19, 1831.

[8] PSZ, 2nd ser., 22: 84-85, no. 20,845, January 23, 1847; ibid., 32: 553-54, no. 32,000, June 17, 1857; N. N. Ulashchik, *Predposylki krest'ianskoi reformy 1861 g. v zapadnoi Belorussii* (Moscow: "Nauka," 1965), p. 96.

about 40 percent of the former *szlachta* in this area were then classified as *odnodvortsy* or burghers.[9] Nonetheless, in 1858 the majority
of the nobles in the Russian Empire (377,627 out of a total of 611,973)
still lived in the nine western *gubernii*. Only a handful of Russian
landowning nobles had been introduced into this area; the overwhelming majority of almost 400,000 nobles consisted of Poles, who
continued to be the masters of millions of Lithuanian, Belorussian,
and Ukrainian serfs (for example, 95 percent of the landowners in
Wilno *guberniia* were Poles; 94 percent in Minsk *guberniia*; and 82
percent in Kiev *guberniia*).[10] Twenty-five years of anti-*szlachta* policy
in the western *gubernii* obviously had not broken the back of Polish
social and economic power.

In 1831 governors and governors-general in the western *gubernii*
received instructions to fill administrative positions on the provincial
and district levels as much as possible with natives of other *gubernii*,
whereas officials of local origin were to be used preferably for service
elsewhere in the empire. In 1855 these same instructions were reaffirmed, and in the intervening period of twenty-four years the government continued its efforts to bring Russian officials into the area
and to oblige officials of Polish origin to begin their civil service careers in the Russian interior of the empire. Nicholas I's notions of
state service were also extended to the local elected offices of the
nobility in the western *gubernii*, for after 1835 only nobles with ten
years of civil or military service were allowed to be presented for
election to such posts.[11] Although these measures did contribute to
the Russification of the western *gubernii*, at the end of Nicholas's
reign their officials were still predominantly Poles. In 1855 Lithuanian
Metropolitan Iosif Semashko complained that 723 of 866 senior officials in Grodno and Wilno *gubernii* were Catholic, and he warned
against the dangers of the "Latin-Polish party's" activities in Belorussia.[12]

Catholic Poles retained important positions in the administration of
the western *gubernii* for obvious reasons. Even if trained and com-

---

[9] The estimate of 40 percent is based on figures compiled by Korzon for seven of the
nine western *gubernii* (*Wewnętrzne dzieje Polski*, 1: 110). For three of these seven
gubernii, Korzon's figures are for the period of the forties; for the other four they apply
to 1857 and 1858.

[10] A. P. Korelin, *Dvorianstvo v poreformennoi Rossii 1861-1904 gg.: Sostav, chislennost', korporativnaia organizatsiia* (Moscow: "Nauka," 1979), pp. 40, 45; *Sprava po
voprosu o vosstanovlenii sobranii i vyborov dvorianstva v deviati zapadnykh guberniiakh* (n.p., n.d.), 3: 6-7.

[11] *Istoricheskii obzor deiatel'nosti Komiteta ministrov*, vol. 2, pt. 2, pp. 279-80.

[12] *Istoricheskii obzor*, p. 277.

petent Russian officials had been available for service in this borderland, they would have been obliged to work within an unfamiliar
framework of Polish laws, customs, and institutions until these could
be eventually replaced by a new Russian social and legal-administrative order. The abolition in 1831 of the Lithuanian Statute in Mohylew and Witebsk *gubernii* was a first step in this direction. Another
step was made in 1835, when Magdeburg law in Kiev was replaced
by Russian municipal law and institutions. Here the initiative came
from Governor-General V. V. Levashov, who had found Kiev's special
laws, town and court institutions, and colorful religious parades to be
a constant source of unnecessary irritation and complications in the
relations of Kiev's inhabitants with the Russian government.[13] Levashov's successor, D. G. Bibikov, shared his dislike of the special laws
and legal institutions of the western *gubernii*.

When Bibikov became governor-general in 1837, the so-called
Western Code, or the codification of laws for the western *gubernii*,
was in its last stages of preparation. When the Second Section of His
Imperial Majesty's Own Chancery was established in 1826, materials
on local law collected previously by *guberniia* codification committees
were transferred to it. Serious work on the Western Code began in
1830, when Ignacy Danilowicz, a specialist in Lithuanian law who had
once taught at the University of Wilno, was attached to the Second
Section. Under Danilowicz's direction, laws in effect in the western
gubernii were systematically studied, codified, and prepared for publication. Bibikov, however, opposed publication of the Western Code,
arguing that only uniformity in law and court procedures could unite
Russia's inhabitants and that retention of special laws would only keep
alive a separatist spirit in the area and perpetuate a Polish legal system alien to the majority of its inhabitants. Several memoranda prepared by Bibikov were considered in the Western Committee and the
Second Section during 1839 and 1840. Second Section Head D. N.
Bludov rejected Bibikov's rather political approach to legal problems
of the former Polish provinces, pointing out that much chaos and
confusion would result unless due consideration was given to existing
legal practices and customs in the area. He did not find any particular
danger to the vital interests of the empire in the Western Code that
Danilowicz had so painstakingly prepared. Nicholas I, however, sided

[13] A. E. Nol'de, *Ocherki po istorii kodifikatskii*, pp. 274-83; V. Iu. Shul'gin, "Iugo-
zapadnyi krai pod upravleniem D. G. Bibikova," *Drevniaia i novaia Rossiia*, vol. 5
(1879), no. 2, pp. 116-17.

with Bibikov, and on June 25, 1840, the Lithuanian Statute was abolished throughout the western *gubernii*.[14]

The introduction of Russian courts and laws into the nine western *gubernii* lessened the dependence of the government on officials of local origin. The public affairs of these *gubernii*, however, still could not be administered without the assistance of the local Poles. Therefore, a new generation of local officials of Polish origin had to be educated in Russian state schools, where they were not only to master the Russian language but also gain respect for Russian culture and national tradition and become loyal subjects of the Russian tsar.

But first the Polish educational system centered at Wilno had to be destroyed. As early as April 1831 the Ministry of Education instructed the curator of the Belorussian School Region to begin closing schools controlled by the Roman Catholic clergy and to take measures to insure that all instruction in state institutions be conducted in the Russian language, for the purpose of public education in this area was to bring "the local inhabitants closer to native (*prirodnye*) Russians."[15] On May 1, 1832, Wilno University was closed and the Wilno School Region was dissolved. Minsk, Wilno, and Grodno *gubernii* and the Białystok district became part of the Belorussian School Region, while Podolia and Volhynia were temporarily assigned to the Kharkov School Region. In December 1832 Podolia and Volhynia, together with Kiev and Chernigov *gubernii*, became part of the new Kiev School Region. The "Volhynian Athens," that is, the Lyceum at Krzemieniec and its library and financial resources, were assigned to the new Russian St. Vladimir University in Kiev, which opened its doors on July 15, 1833.[16] An important purpose of this new university was, in the words of Minister of Education S. S. Uvarov, "to unite the Polish youth with the Russians in Kiev."[17] Until the 1860s a majority of the students attending St. Vladimir University came from Polish-*szlachta* families of Belorussia, Lithuania, and the Right-Bank Ukraine.[18]

The educational measures taken in the western *gubernii* during the thirties and forties were part of a general policy of the central government to assert its direct control over education in these provinces. The University Statute of 1804 had granted Russian universities au-

---

[14] Nol'de, *Ocherki po istorii kodifikatsii*, pp. 49-68, 86-119, 230-38, 244-50; Shul'gin, "Iugo-zapadnyi krai," pp. 117-18.

[15] Rozhdestvenskii, *Istoricheskii obzor*, p. 212.

[16] Ibid., p. 298; Winiarksi, *Les institutions politiques en Pologne*, p. 156.

[17] Rozhdestvenskii, *Istoricheskii obzor*, p. 298.

[18] Jan Tabiś, *Polacy na Uniwersytecie Kijowskim 1834-1863* (Cracow: Wydawnictwo Literackie, 1974), pp. 34-47.

tonomy and had entrusted their councils with the administration of the lower schools in each educational region. Between 1804 and 1835 the curators of the six school regions resided in St. Petersburg. It was, of course, this decentralization of education in Russia that had permitted the flourishing of Polish schools throughout the Right-Bank Ukraine, Lithuania, and Belorussia during the period 1804-1830. This system had obvious disadvantages from the standpoint of administrative efficiency, for, as it was then argued, university professors had neither the time nor the experience required to administer the educational programs of the schools subordinated to their respective universities.[19] Statutes of June 25 and 26, 1835, deprived the university councils of their supervisory powers over lower schools, moved the curators to the administrative centers of their respective school regions, limited university autonomy, and subordinated all gymnasia, district and parish schools, and other local educational institutions to the control and supervision of the curators, that is, the regional representatives of the Ministry of Education in St. Petersburg.[20]

About the same time Uvarov reorganized the administration of the empire's schools, Szymon Konarski, an emissary of Young Poland, crossed the Russian frontier. Up to the time of his arrest in May 1838, Konarski traveled throughout the Right-Bank Ukraine, Lithuania, Belorussia, and even as far as St. Petersburg, involving some 3,000 Polish *szlachta*, students, teachers, and clergy in the conspiratorial activities of his Society of the Polish People (*Stowarzyszenie Ludu Polskiego*). By 1840 Konarski had been executed, several hundred of his followers imprisoned, Kiev University briefly closed, many Polish students expelled, and the Wilno Medical-Surgical Academy abolished altogether. Because a large proportion of the Polish students at Kiev University had joined Konarski's society, some Russian officials recommended closing this university permanently. Nicholas I did not follow this advice; but the Konarski affair had made clear that it would not be easy for Uvarov to carry out his self-imposed task of reeducating the Polish youth of Belorussia, Lithuania, and the Right-Bank Ukraine.[21]

[19] Rozhdestvenskii, *Istoricheskii obzor*, p. 238.

[20] Ibid., pp. 238-45; *Ocherki istorii shkoly i pedagogicheskoi mysli narodov SSSR*, pp. 210-11.

[21] On Konarski, see the biographical sketch by Stefan Kieniewicz in *Polski słownik biograficzny* (Wrocław: Ossolineum, 1935-), 13: 477-79; Orest Pelech, "Toward a Historical Sociology of the Ukrainian Ideologues in the Russian Empire of the 1830's and 1840's" (Princeton University Ph.D. dissertation, 1976), pp. 113-14; Alina Barszczewska, *Szymon Konarski* (Warsaw: "Wiedza Powszechna," 1976), pp. 140-238.

In both the Belorussian and Kiev School Regions instruction in Polish was gradually discontinued during the 1830s, and measures were taken to curtail the teaching of the Polish language in secondary schools.[22] These schools, however, enrolled too small a proportion of *szlachta* children to have had much prospect of transforming this Polish social class into loyal supporters of autocracy and Russian national culture. In the nine western *gubernii* around 600 students attended the University of Kiev in mid-century, while several hundred others from this area studied in Moscow and St. Petersburg; their seventeen gymnasia and thirty-three district schools enrolled fewer than 10,000 students. In other words, from 1832 to 1855 it is quite possible that tens of thousands of young Polish nobles (non-nobles accounted for less than 20 percent of the students in secondary and higher schools) learned Russian well; but they were only a handful of individuals among nearly a million Poles (in 1863) living in this region. Young Poles continued to be educated in Polish at home, and the Russian authorities even failed to eliminate the teaching of Polish in state schools. Women's education was a special problem, for the Ministry of Education's inability to provide adequate educational facilities for the daughters of the *szlachta* made it seem unwise to abolish private schools for women in which instruction was given in Polish. And in state schools for men a large proportion of the teachers were still Roman Catholic Poles. When Emperor Nikolai Pavlovich called this fact to Uvarov's attention in 1849, the minister defended the continued use of Poles in the schools of the western *gubernii* by noting that they often were more effective than Russians in teaching patriotism and loyalty to Russia. These Poles, Uvarov argued, had the advantage of understanding the family life and milieu from which their pupils came.[23]

Furthermore, the establishment of the Russian schools in the western *gubernii* sometimes produced results unanticipated by St. Petersburg officialdom. The teaching of folklore, ethnography, and romantic nationalism and history at the Universities of Kharkov and Kiev, for example, profoundly influenced a handful of Russian and Ukrainian students who helped to give birth to the Ukrainian national movement. Poles, on the other hand, often learned Russian well in state schools and in the universities of the empire but were more impressed by the revolutionary ideas of Russian student radicals than by

[22] Rozhdestvenskii, *Istoricheskii obzor*, pp. 303-4; Winiarski, *Les institutions politiques en Pologne*, pp. 155-56; Kutrzeba, *Historya ustroju Polski*, 3: 214-15.

[23] Rozhdestvenskii, *Istoricheskii obzor*, pp. 308-10; *Istoricheskii obzor deiatel'nosti Komiteta ministrov*, vol. 2, pt. 2, pp. 254-56; V. Ia. Shul'gin, "Iugo-zapadnyi krai pod upravleniem D. G. Bibikova," *Drevniaia i novaia Rossiia*, vol. 5 (1879), no. 2, pp. 126-29.

official ideology of Uvarov's educational establishment. Fluent in Russian and moving freely within the borders of the empire, educated young Poles easily came into contact with the Russian revolutionary movement. They established a communications network that assured a steady flow of information and new ideas among Polish students and nationalist leaders located in St. Petersburg, Moscow, Kiev, Warsaw, and Wilno. Contact with such Russian revolutionary intellectuals as N. G. Chernyshevskii, A. I. Herzen, and N. A. Serno-Solov'evich certainly contributed to radicalize the Polish opposition movement. Poles who had lived in the interior of Russia played a major role in the Polish insurrection of 1863-1864.[24]

The relative failure of Uvarov's educational policy in the western *gubernii* illustrates some of the dilemmas of Russian borderland policy during the 1830s and 1840s. In Russia social and political order was maintained on a foundation of the nobility's economic power, familiarity with local conditions, and cooperation with the government within the general framework provided by serfdom. In the western *gubernii* the greater part of the population consisted of Orthodox or Uniate Belorussian or Ukrainian serfs or state peasants, while the nobles were mainly Poles whose willingness to cooperate with the government was not always certain. It was, therefore, not surprising that the government would make some effort to win for itself the support of the Belorussian and Ukrainian peasantry as a sort of counterpoise to the predominant economic and social order of the *szlachta* in the western *gubernii*.

Russia's old-regime bureaucrats, however, always found administrative reforms easier to introduce than social ones. In their efforts to establish a closer relationship between the government and the Belorussian and Ukrainian majority of the population in the western *gubernii*, they, therefore, began not with peasant reform but with the reorganization of the central organs in St. Petersburg that administered the affairs of the Orthodox Church and of the empire's foreign confessions. In Volume I of the Digest of Laws compiled during the early 1830s, the Orthodox Church was defined as the "dominant faith" of the Russian Empire.[25] The chief procurator of the Holy Synod be-

---

[24] Tabiś, *Polacy na Uniwersytecie Kijowskim*, pp. 63-140; A. F. Smirnov, *Vosstanie 1863 goda v Litve i Belorussii* (Moscow: Akademiia Nauk, 1963), pp. 141-57.

[25] David W. Edwards, "Orthodoxy During the Reign of Tsar Nicholas I: A Study in Church-State Relations" (Kansas State University Ph.D. dissertation, 1967), pp. 172-76; F. V. Blagovidov, *Ober-prokurory Sviateishego sinoda XVIII i v pervoi polovine XIX stoletiia* (Kazan: Imperatorksii Universitet, 1899), pp. 400-13; *Svod zakonov Rossiiskoi Imperii*, 32 vols. (St. Petersburg: Gosudarstvennaia Tipografiia, 1832), 1: i, nos. 40-46.

tween 1836 and 1855, N. A. Protasov, once described the official church as a "marvelous source" of "pure Christian morality for future generations" that united the "Russian Orthodox people in its unlimited devotion to a Throne consecrated by Faith."[26] Protasov, a civilian and former army general, deprived this church of the "Russian Orthodox people" of almost all spiritual independence, subordinating it to the bureaucratic supervision and control of his own personal chancery. Non-Orthodox religions in Russia—except for the various forms of Old Believerism, which Nicholas I persecuted as an impermissible deviation from Orthodoxy[27]—were tolerated but subjected to regulation and supervision by the Main Administration for the Ecclesiastical Affairs of the Foreign Confessions, which was transferred from the jurisdiction of the Ministry of Education to that of the Ministry of the Interior in 1832.[28]

In 1827 Iosif Semashko, an assessor in the Uniate Department of the Roman Catholic College in St. Petersburg, which was subordinated to the Main Administration for the Ecclesiastical Affairs of the Foreign Confessions, submitted to the Russian authorities the first of a number of memoranda outlining how the remaining Belorussian and Ukrainian Uniates could be reunited with Orthodoxy. Semashko had worked in the St. Petersburg Roman Catholic College since 1822. Born in a Ukrainian village and the son of a Uniate priest, he had received a Polish education at the University of Wilno, where he had been taught by teachers trained in eighteenth-century Enlightenment Austria to be critical of the papacy and aspects of Roman Catholicism. In St. Petersburg Semashko prepared a Russian version of the written proceedings of the Uniate Department for his colleagues, who spoke Polish among themselves. Semashko himself always spoke Russian with an accent, but the Russian Orthodox setting of the capital had a different effect on him than on his colleagues, for his study of Russian and European works on Roman Catholicism, Orthodoxy, and the Uniate Church eventually persuaded him to work for the reunion of the Uniates with the Russian Orthodox Church.[29] His betrayal of the Uniate cause was an unexpected and welcome windfall for Nicholas I and

[26] Russia, Sviateishii sinod, *Izvlecheniia iz otcheta ober-prokurora Sviateishego sino da za 1845 god* (St. Petersburg: Sinodnaia Tipografiia, 1846), p. 110.

[27] Russia, Ministerstvo vnutrennikh del, *Ministerstvo vnutrennikh del: Istoricheskii ocherk* (St. Petersburg: Tipografiia Ministerstva Vnutrennikh Del, 1901), p. 93.

[28] *Ministerstvo vnutrennikh del*, p. 87.

[29] Iosif Semashko's background and role in reuniting the Uniates with Orthodoxy are described in detail in *Zapiski Iosifa Mitropolita Litovskogo*, 4 vols. (St. Petersburg: Imperatorskaia Akademiia Nauk, 1883). See also Daniel Beauvois, "Les lumières au carrefour de l'Orthodoxie et du Catholicism: Le cas des Uniates de l'Empire russe au début du XIXe siècle," *Cahiers du monde russe et soviétique* 19 (1978): 423-41.

the officials of the Main Administration for the Ecclesiastical Affairs of the Foreign Confessions. Semashko, after five years' work in the Uniate Department of the Roman Catholic College, had the intimate knowledge and expertise about Uniate affairs needed by Russian officialdom to effect an orderly reunion of the Uniates with Orthodoxy.

Nicholas I approved Semashko's program for the reunion of the Uniates with Orthodoxy at the end of 1827. In the spring of 1828 Roman Catholic influence over the administration of Uniate affairs was reduced to a minimum by creating an independent Greek Uniate Ecclesiastical College in St. Petersburg and by eliminating two of four Uniate bishoprics. At the same time, the Uniate Church's Basilian Order and the education of Uniate priests were subordinated directly to the new Uniate Ecclesiastical College in St. Petersburg. After 1828 the Russian government gradually assigned churchmen sympathetic to Orthodoxy to the St. Petersburg College and appointed appropriate auxiliary bishops in the Lithuanian and Belorussian dioceses. The remaining two Uniate bishops loyal to Rome, it is important to note, were old men, the first of whom died in 1833. As a result, Semashko then became Uniate bishop of Lithuania.[30]

The involvement of a number of Polish monks and priests in the 1830-1831 uprising provided the Russian government with a convenient pretext to close and confiscate the funds and property of Roman Catholic and Uniate monasteries; to arrest, imprison, or deport monks and priests; to close many Roman Catholic or Uniate schools; and to reaffirm laws regulating mixed marriages and forbidding the conversion of Orthodox believers to other religions. The Basilian Order was particularly affected. In 1832 it was subjected to detailed regulations and even more rigorous control than before by the St. Petersburg Uniate College. By 1835 two-thirds of its monasteries had been closed. And as the Basilian Order, which had long been the source of moral strength for the Uniate Church, rapidly declined, Semashko and the officials of the Uniate College and of the Ministry of the Interior proceeded with the complete Russification of the schools and seminaries that prepared Uniate priests for their calling; they also purged Uniate institutions and religious services of all Roman Catholic elements that had been introduced since the end of the sixteenth century.[31]

---

[30] PSZ, 2nd ser., 3: 457-59, no. 1,977, April 22, 1828; Lenchyk, *The Eastern Catholic Church and Czar Nicholas I*, pp. 39-45; Semashko, *Zapiski*, 1: 45, 53-54; V. Moroshkin, "Vossoedinenie Unii," *Vestnik Evropy*, April, 1872, no. 3, pp. 588-90; Edwards, "Orthodoxy," p. 264.

[31] Lenchyk, *The Eastern Orthodox Church*, pp. 45-64; Edwards, "Orthodoxy," p. 266; Winiarski, *Les institutions politiques en Pologne*, pp. 162-63; Ammann, *Abriss*, pp. 504-15.

Until 1837 D. N. Bludov, a very circumspect and prudent administrator, coordinated the government's policy toward the Uniates. Between 1828 and 1832 he was director of the Main Administration for the Ecclesiastical Affairs of the Foreign Confessions, and in 1832 he became minister of the interior. At first the government proceeded cautiously and did not reveal its intention of reuniting the Uniates with Orthodoxy. After 1835, however, all doubt was removed about the government's plans for the Uniates; in that year supervision of their schools was transferred from the Ministry of the Interior to the Commission on Ecclesiastical Schools, which operated under the control of the Russian Holy Synod. In 1837 the Greco-Uniate Ecclesiastical College was placed directly under Protasov, the chief procurator of the Holy Synod. After the death of Jozafat Bulhak in 1838, Semashko circulated petitions among Uniate priests and monks calling for the reunion of their church with Russian Orthodoxy. All three Uniate bishops and more than thirteen hundred priests and monks signed these petitions. On March 17, 1839, the reunion with Orthodoxy of some two million Uniates living in the nine western *gubernii* was proclaimed.[32]

Uniate resistance to reunion with Orthodoxy was sporadic, ineffective, and difficult to coordinate. The neutralization and weakening of the Basilian Order in the 1830s and the placement of Russian loyalists in control of the Uniate College in St. Petersburg and of the Uniate hierarchy frustrated Uniate attempts to prevent the takeover of their church by the agents of Bludov, Semashko, and Protasov. Recalcitrant priests and monks were threatened with reassignment, arrest, confinement in monasteries, or even corporal punishment. Soldiers were used against peasant villages in which organized resistance to the reunion occurred. Extreme measures, however, were probably the exception rather than the rule. In all, the reorganization of the hierarchy and the careful and gradual reform of the Uniate liturgical books and divine services do not seem to have had a profound effect on the Belorussians and Ukrainians who were reunited with Orthodoxy in 1839.[33]

[32] Edwards, "Orthodoxy," pp. 267-68; Lenchyk, *The Eastern Orthodox Church*, pp. 40, 43-44, 78-112; *Ministerstvo vnutrennikh del: Istoricheskii ocherk*, pp. 89-91.

[33] The methods and means actually used by the Russian authorities to reunite Belorussian and Ukrainian parishes with Orthodoxy have not been satisfactorily studied on the basis of a systematic examination of materials in Russian and/or Soviet archives. But the fragmentary evidence collected by Roman Catholic and Uniate historians clearly indicates that a good measure of force and coercion was used in dealing with the minority of peasants and priests who persisted in resisting reunion with Orthodoxy. On

It is questionable whether the reunion appreciably altered the relationship of these peasants to Russia. After all, there was no reason to doubt their loyalty to begin with. True, they were no longer jurisdictionally under the pope and the Polish Catholic hierarchy, but before 1839 the influence of Polish Catholicism on popular attitudes and behavior in the Belorussian and Ukrainian village seems to have been a superficial one. And could the Russian state really rely on the poorly educated and impoverished local priests, so recently cajoled or forced back into the Orthodox Church, to serve as persuasive and enthusiastic intermediaries between Great Russian *chinovniki* and Ukrainian and Belorussian peasants? At the same time, the government was not able to finance an ambitious program of church maintenance and construction and of elementary and religious education in the western *gubernii*. The Catholic landowning *szlachta* was understandably not interested in underwriting the cost of such a program, and St. Petersburg officialdom soon discovered how futile it was to try to oblige Polish landowners to build, repair, and maintain Orthodox churches and schools for their Belorussian and Ukrainian serfs.[34]

But could not the Russian government have gained the confidence of these peasants by promoting their well-being and defending their rights vis-à-vis the Polish Catholic *szlachta*? The most outspoken advocate of such a policy was Kiev Governor-General D. G. Bibikov, who again and again emphasized the importance of protecting "peasants of Greco-Russian faith" from the "cruel persecution" of Polish landowners.[35] Concrete measures to defend the interests of "peasants of Greco-Russian faith" were proposed as early as 1835, and again in 1839, by P. D. Kiselev, who became minister of state domains in 1837. In 1835 Kiselev suggested that the interests of the government in the western *gubernii* could be furthered by introducing regulations to govern peasant-landlord relations on estates confiscated from Polish *szlachta* involved in the uprising of 1830-1831. In 1839 he recommended extending a system of similar regulations to all state-owned land in the western *gubernii* and enforcing corrected inventories of the obligations and of the distribution of land among the local state

---

the scattered resistance that did occur, see Lenchyk, *Eastern Catholic Church*, pp. 67-73, 92-105, 119-31; Ammann, *Abriss*, pp. 511-13; Edward Likowski, *Dzieje kościoła unickiego na Litwie i Rusi*, 2: 116-29. Cf. Semashko, *Zapiski*, 1: 115-19, 128-40; 2: 87-88; 3: 413, 420, 422, 423.

[34] *Istoricheskii obzor deiatel'nosti Komiteta ministrov*, vol. 2, pt. 1, pp. 273-76.

[35] V. I. Semevskii, *Krest'ianskii vopros v Rossii v XVIII i pervoi polovine XIX veka*, 2 vols. (St. Petersburg: "Obshchestvennaia Pol'za," 1888), 2: 483-89; Shul'gin, "Iugo-zapadnyi krai pod upravleniem D. G. Bibikova," pp. 10-11, 92-98.

peasants. On state lands in the former Polish-Lithuanian Common-wealth, these inventories had been known as *lustracje* (the plural form in Polish; in the singular, *lustracja*; in Russian, *liustratsiia* and *liu-stratsii*). Prior to Nicholas I's approval of Kiselev's new project, state lands in the former Polish provinces had been administered by mem-bers of the Polish *szlachta*, who controlled the local officials and in-stitutions of the state peasants and received labor services from the peasants on a given estate according to norms fixed by a *lustracja*. The *lustracje*, however, were generally inaccurate and interpreted by the local Polish leaseholders in a manner detrimental to the peasants, which gave rise to considerable social unrest. Kiselev hoped to im-prove the lot of the local state peasants by establishing new *lustracja* norms, by gradually converting peasant compulsory labor services to money payments (*obrok*) based on land surveys and careful investi-gations of local conditions, and by replacing *szlachta* leaseholders with officials who worked under the supervision of the Ministry of State Domains.[36]

Kiselev's *lustracja* reform did somewhat improve the situation of state peasants in the western *gubernii*. By defining peasant obligations more satisfactorily, surveying the extent of land allotted to the peas-ants, gradually replacing compulsory labor with money payments, and partly freeing the state peasants from the control of the local Polish nobility, his ministry undeniably made at least a modest contribution to the economic and social development of peasants living on state-owned land in Belorussia, Lithuania, and the Right-Bank Ukraine.[37] But the Ministry of State Domains hardly acted any more effectively in the western *gubernii* than it did elsewhere in the empire. Bureau-cratic regulation of state-peasant affairs, compulsion, corruption, and inefficiency on the part of many officials, the modest scale of the re-forms which never called into question the legitimacy of subordinating the welfare of serfs and state peasants to the economic interests of landowners and of the Ministry of State Domains—these affairs caused

[36] A. P. Zablotskii-Desiatovskii, *Graf P. D. Kiselev i ego vremia*, 4 vols. (St. Peters-burg: M. M. Stasiulevich, 1882), 4: 147; N. M. Druzhinin, *Gosudarstvennye krest'iane i reforma P. D. Kiseleva*, 2 vols. (Moscow-Leningrad: Akademiia Nauk, 1946-1958), 1: 588-603; Russia, Ministerstvo gosudarstvennykh imushchestv, *Istoricheskoe obozrenie piatidesiatiletnei deiatel'nosti Ministerstva gosudarstvennykh imushchestv 1837-1887*, 5 vols. (St. Petersburg: Iablonskii i Perott, Ia. I. Liberman, V. Bezobrazov, etc., 1888), pt. 2, sec. 2, pp. 111-30; T. A. Koniukhova, *Gosudarstvennaia derevnia Litvy i reforma P. D. Kiseleva* (Moscow: Izdatel'stvo Moskovskogo Universiteta, 1975), p. 144-209; V. I. Neupokoev, *Krest'ianskii vopros v Litve vo vtoroi treti XIX veka* (Moscow: "Nauka," 1976), pp. 84-141.

[37] Druzhinin, *Gosudarstvennye krest'iane*, 2: 418, 436-39.

general dissatisfaction and often serious social unrest among Russian state peasants. One special problem was the lack of trustworthy and trained personnel available to work for the Ministry of State Domains in the provinces. Between 1838 and 1842 it opened forty-seven *guberniia* boards (*palaty*) and 280 district, 1,308 township, and 5,860 village administrations to carry out its policies in the countryside. The ministry was in a position to staff only its own central administration and some of its provincial boards with competent personnel. Otherwise, it had to rely on local nobles, clerks, intellectuals, and peasants to administer state-peasant affairs. In the western *gubernii* this meant relying to a considerable extent on the Polish petty *szlachta*, who had no interest in implementing the political aims of the Russian state in this area and who compiled and interpreted the *lustracje* in a manner detrimental to the peasantry.[38]

Even if Kiselev's ministry had aimed at rapid social change in the western *gubernii*, it lacked the resources to bring it about. For example, it considered education important but did very little about it. In 1845 there were only 3,644 children in the elementary schools of the ministry in the western *gubernii* in a state peasant population of almost a half million.[39] On the whole, the activities of officials employed by Kiselev's ministry had very little impact on the manner in which the local state peasants viewed the world, organized their lives, and cultivated the soil. As a result, they remained for the most part economically and socially dependent on the local Polish *szlachta*. They also often found themselves at the mercy of incompetent and dishonest minor officials and of new state regulations they did not understand. Kiselev's reform, therefore, may very well have done more to produce peasant complaints and organized resistance to the implementation of official policies than it did to gain support for the government of the Orthodox "Russian" peasants of this area.

It was even more difficult for the Russian government to improve the lot of the Belorussian and Ukrainian serfs who lived on the private estates of Polish landowners in Belorussia, Lithuania, and the Right-Bank Ukraine. As much as Russian officials wanted to weaken the Polish landowners in this region, they had no intention of introducing radical social reforms likely to cause unrest among the local serfs. They were, however, willing to consider moderate reforms based on the inventories (*inwentarze*) of obligations of serfs living on privately

---

[38] Ibid., 2: 574-78; Koniukhova, *Gosudarstvennaia derevnia*, pp. 68-85, 144-57, 210-31; Neupokoev, *Krest'ianskii vopros*, pp. 208-50; *Istoricheskoe obozrenie piatidesiatiletnei deiatel'nosti Ministerstva gosudarstvennykh imushchestv*, 1: 34-35, 46-48.

[39] *Istoricheskoe obozrenie*, vol. 2, sec. 1, pp. 49-58; sec. 2, pp. 89-90.

owned lands that had been used in the former Polish-Lithuanian Commonwealth since the sixteenth century. These *inwentarze* were similar to the *lustracje* for peasants on lands owned by the state prior to the partition of Poland.

In 1840 the question of peasant reform in the western *gubernii* to be based on the verification and enforcement of inventories of peasant obligations, was brought before the Western Committee. This committee, together with the Ministries of the Interior and State Domains, worked out the principles of an inventory reform during the following four-year period. In April 1844 provincial committees were formed. Each provincial committee consisted of the civil governor as chairman, four Russian officials, and five landowners representing the local *szlachta*. On April 15, 1844, Nicholas I approved the rules that regulated the compilation and confirmation of inventories on private estates throughout the western *gubernii*. The government, however, encountered resistance to the inventory reform on the part of both peasants and landowners. Governor-General Bibikov decided that the only way to deal with landowner resistance and to gain the confidence of the peasants was to guarantee their continued use of the lands assigned to them in the inventories and to oblige the landowners to prepare new inventories in conformity with norms prescribed by rules confirmed by Nicholas I on December 29, 1848. Although these rules were extended to Lithuania and Belorussia when Bibikov became minister of the interior in 1852, it was only in the Right-Bank Ukraine that they were applied systematically and, to some extent, enforced.[40]

The government's attempt to introduce and enforce new inventory regulations perhaps accomplished even less than did its other special measures in the former Polish provinces during the period 1831-1855. These other measures, it will be recalled, fell far short of transforming

[40] Russia, Ministerstvo vnutrennikh del, Zemskii otdel, *Inventarnye polozheniia zapadnykh gubernii* (St. Petersburg: Kommissiia dlia sostavleniia polozhenii o krest'ianakh, 1859), pp. 1-63, *prilozheniia*: pp. 53-59, 190-211; A. K. Koshik, "Inventarnaia reforma 1847-1848 gg. i krest'ianskoe dvizhenie na provoberezhnoi Ukraine," in Kievskii gosudarstvennyi universitet, *Istoricheskii sbornik* (1949, no. 2), pp. 97-122; Kh. P. Strods, "Sostavlenie obiazatel'nykh inventarei v pomeshchich'ikh imeniiakh Latgalii v 40-50-kh godakh XIX veka i znachenie ikh kak istoricheskogo istochnika," *Istochnikovedcheskie problemy istorii narodov Pribaltiki* (Riga: "Zinātne," 1970), pp. 213-28; N. N. Ulashchik, "Vvedenie obiazatel'nikh inventarei v Belorussii i Litve," *Ezhegodnik po agrarnoi istorii vostochnoi Evropy 1958 g.* (Tallinn: Akademiia Nauk Estonskoi SSR, 1959), pp. 256-77; Ulashchik, "Inventari pomeshchich'ikh imenii zapadnoi Belorussii i Litvy 40-kh godov XIX veka," *Problemy istochnikovedeniia* 10 (1962): 85-103; V. I. Semevskii, *Krest'ianskii vopros v Rossii v XVIII i pervoi polovine*, 2 vols. (St. Petersburg: "Obshchestvennaia Pol'za," 1888), 2: 483-513.

the *szlachta*, serfs, and state peasants of the western *gubernii* into peaceful, loyal, and dependable subjects of the Russian tsar. As regards the Belorussian, Latvian, Lithuanian, and Ukrainian serfs living on private estates in the western *gubernii*, their economic position was not significantly improved by the inventory reform. The government was not in a position to carry out the reform without the assistance of local *szlachta* society, which, in last analysis, looked with disfavor upon any attempt to regulate its relations with the serf population. But the very attempt of the government to regulate these relations suggested to the peasants that there were limits to the landowners' power. Russian gendarme officials thought that there was a connection between the inventories and social unrest in the area. Whether or not they were correct, it is clear that the serfs in the western *gubernii* often reacted with overt antagonism to the efforts of marshals of the nobility, civil governors, and other representatives of the government and the nobility to verify and enforce the inventories. The Belorussian, Lithuanian, and Right-Bank Ukrainian countrysides were among the areas of the empire where social unrest reached a degree of maximum intensity during the 1840s, 1850s, and early 1860s. In 1848, for example, 201 cases of serious peasant unrest occurred in the western *gubernii*, or more than half of such cases for the whole Russian Empire during that year.[41]

State-peasant reform had similar results, especially among the Lithuanian state peasants in Kowno *guberniia*. In 1863-1864 a considerable number of them voluntarily joined the ranks of the Polish insurgents in a common struggle against Russia.[42] Both the state-peasant and the inventory reforms were too limited in scope, too paternalistic in application, and too bureaucratic in execution to produce significant and immediate results for the purposes of official Russian policy in the western *gubernii*. Yet, these reforms were important if for no other reason than that they offered young Russian officials working

[41] Koshik, "Inventarnaia reforma 1847-1848 gg. i krest'ianskoe dvizhenie na pravoberezhnoi Ukraine," p. 106-22; Ulashchik, "Vvedenie obiazatel'nykh inventarei v Belorussii i Litve," pp. 262, 275-77; *Krest'ianskoe dvizhenie v Rossii v 1826-1849 gg.: Sbornik dokumentov* (Moscow: Sotsekgiz, 1961), pp. 426-31, 554-58, 609-30; G. M. Deich, "Inventarnye pravila," *Sovetskaia istoricheskaia entsiklopediia*, 5 (Moscow: "Sovetskaia Entsiklopediia," 1964): 828; Druzhinin, *Gosudarstvennye krest'iane*, 1: 511, 530; Smirnov, *Vosstanie 1863 goda v Litve i Belorussii*, pp. 141-57.

[42] Koniukhova, *Gosudarstvennaia derevnia*, pp. 230-31; V. I. Neupokoev, "Kontrreforma v gosudarstvennoi derevne Litvy (1857-1862)," in *Revoliutsionnaia situatsiia v Rossii v 1859-1861 gg.* (Moscow: "Nauka," 1970), p. 56. However, as Neupokoev points out, Murav'ev's counterreforms of 1857-1862 played an important role in turning Lithuanian state peasants against Russia.

for the Ministries of Interior and State Domains an opportunity to acquire knowledge and expertise concerning the peasants and the social and economic problems of the western borderlands of the empire.

In the first years of the reign of Alexander II, the emperor and his principal advisers, fearing peasant unrest and needing to concentrate on the central task of reform, pursued a generally conciliatory policy in the borderlands. Only in the Right-Bank Ukraine, Belorussia, and Lithuania did the Russian government then continue to follow the more or less Russificatory policies of Nicholas I. To be sure, the government and Russian publicists of those days considered Belorussians and Ukrainians to be Russians. Although certain concessions were then made to the wishes of this area's dominant Polish minority, Russian remained the official language of its schools and local administration. Its courts and municipal and *guberniia* institutions continued to operate as part of the general legal-administrative system established by Catherine II's Provincial Reform of 1775. In the early 1860s Russian officials saw no reason not to proceed with plans to extend Russian agrarian, judicial, educational, and other reforms to the western *gubernii*.

Problems of social control and security, however, soon persuaded the Russian authorities that they could not realistically insist on complete uniformity and standardization in extending reform to the western borderlands. Thus, in 1863 the terms of the Emancipation Edict of 1861 in the nine western *gubernii* were altered. In January of that year the Polish revolutionary government in Lithuania had promised the peasants land; on March 1, 1863, in an obvious attempt to isolate the Polish insurrectionists, the Russian government confirmed the peasants of Wilno, Grodno, and Kowno *gubernii* and of Latgale in the possession of all the land they had cultivated before the emancipation. By November 1863 the revised inventory had been introduced throughout the western *gubernii*, making available to the peasants several million desiatins of additional land and fixing peasant obligations at a level that was considerably lower than elsewhere in the empire. These new arrangements did not, however, mark any radical break with the past, for the new reforms of 1863 were still based on the old Polish *lustracje* and *inwentarze*. The major change was that Russians imported from other parts of the empire now replaced the Polish *szlachta* as the local arbitrators who interpreted the inventories and decided the extent of the peasants' obligations and how much land they were to receive. But the large estates of the Polish landowners, the separate peasant household (as contrasted with the repartitional type of commune in the Great-Russian areas of the em-

138

pire), and landless or poor peasants remained characteristic features of the life of the countryside in the western *gubernii*.[43]

Russian distrust of local society also contributed to keeping these *gubernii* apart from the rest of the empire. The decision not to introduce zemstvos into this area until the twentieth century (and then only in six of nine *gubernii*) is perhaps the best illustration of this point. Zemstvos were not introduced simply because the Russian authorities feared that the Polish landowners would dominate them. Elsewhere in the empire zemstvos encouraged local elements to engage in socially useful activities, especially the building of rural elementary schools. The absence of zemstvos in the western *gubernii* and the insistence on Russian as the language of instruction in rural schools effectively discouraged both peasants and landowners from taking the initiative in developing education locally. As a result, the literacy rate of army recruits put these *gubernii* in the company of the most backward of the fifty provinces of European Russia.[44] The area was well served by railroads in the second part of the nineteenth century, and its Polish large landowners and a minority of peasant proprietors (the so-called kulaks) prospered. The majority of the local Belorussian, Latvian, Lithuanian, and Ukrainian peasants remained, on the other hand, landless or at least socially and economically backward, poor, and cut off from the main currents of Russian life. The rural elementary school represented one possible way to change this situation, but the Russian government did not have the financial and human resources to promote education to any significant extent in this area, while local society tended to view suspiciously Russian-language schools funded and controlled by outsiders.

The punitive and severe measures introduced by M. N. Murav'ev, the "hangman of Wilno," and his successors during and following the Polish insurrection of 1863-1864 weakened the position of the Polish element in this area. This is not surprising, for its Polish minority was too small (probably about ten percent of the total population) to serve in the long run as the basis for a successful struggle against both the Russian state and the emerging national movements among the Belorussians, Lithuanians, and Ukrainians. In 1830-1831 as well as in

[43] R. F. Leslie, *Reform and Insurrection in Russian Poland 1856-1863* (1963; reprint ed., Westport, Conn.: Greenwood Press, 1969), pp. 226-27; Jerzy Ochmański, *Historia Litwy* (Wrocław: Ossolineum, 1967), pp. 180-82; P. A. Zaionchkovskii, *Provedenie v zhizn' krest'ianskoi reformy 1861 g.* (Moscow: Sotsekgiz, 1958), pp. 365-422.

[44] Ochmański, *Historia Litwy*, pp. 183-85; *Istoriia Belorusskoi SSR*, 1: 420-21; A. G. Rashin, *Naselenie Rossii za 100 let (1811-1913 gg.): Statisticheskie ocherki* (Moscow: Gosstatizdat, 1956), pp. 305-6.

1863-1864 the ethnic composition of the population of the western *gubernii* complicated for the Poles the task of organizing an anti-tsarist insurrection.

In 1863-1864 the Poles were the most successful in obtaining support for their cause among some 1.4 million Lithuanians, who then constituted about 13 percent of the population of the western *gubernii*. In contrast to the Lithuanians, the more than four million Right-Bank Ukrainians (38 percent of the population) gave very little support to the Polish insurrection; indeed, a large number of Ukrainians used the rebellion as a pretext to take their own action against Polish landowners. On the other hand, Polish influence was somewhat stronger among some 2.6 million Belorussians (about one-fourth the population of these *gubernii*), especially in the western and partly Catholic areas of Belorussia. Konstanty Kalinowski, the author of *Muzhytskaia prauda* and today—despite his Polish-*szlachta* origin—a Belorussian national hero, did manage to attract a number of Belorussian supporters for the insurrection in western Belorussia; Ludwik Zwierzdowski, on the other hand, ran into the resistance of the local Orthodox population when, in the spring of 1863, he tried to organize a peasant uprising in Eastern Belorussia.[45] Of all the nationalities of the western *gubernii*, with the exception of the Latvians in Latgale (whose "national awakening" began toward the end of the nineteenth century), the Belorussians were the least successful in organizing their own national movement.

Although it shared some of the weaknesses of the Belorussian movement, the Ukrainian national movement greatly benefited from the decentralization and relaxation of political controls early in the reign of Alexander II. The Ukrainian cultural renaissance began in the latter part of the eighteenth century. Under Nicholas I Russian universities at Kharkov and Kiev introduced young Ukrainians to romantic nationalism and stimulated their interest in Ukrainian ethnography, folklore, and language. A setback for the Ukrainian national revival was the arrest, imprisonment and exile in 1847 of V. M. Bilozers'kyi, M. I. Kostomarov, P. A. Kulish, Taras Shevchenko, and others associated with the Brotherhood of St. Cyril and Methodius. Amnestied by Alexander II, they resumed Ukrainian literary, scholarly, and journalistic activities in St. Petersburg in the late 1850s. Their example and influence helped to give birth to Ukrainian cultural

[45] Smirnov, *Vosstanie 1863 goda*, pp. 85-100, 201-9, 219-28, 341-45; P. N. Batiushkov (ed.), *Atlas narodonaseleniia zapadno-russkogo kraia po ispovedaniiam* (St. Petersburg, 1863).

societies in Poltava, Chernigov, Kharkov, Kiev, and elsewhere. Ukrainian elementary schools for children and Sunday schools for adults were organized, Ukrainian belles-lettres and scholarship were fostered and textbooks for schools published, and Ukrainian culture in the form of theatrical performances, concerts, and lectures were promoted wherever possible. The Russian authorities, however, soon curtailed Ukrainian cultural and educational activities, and between 1863 and 1905 the government systematically suppressed the Ukrainian language and culture in schools and public life.[46] This policy of suppression and the illiteracy and social and economic backwardness of the Ukrainian peasantry impeded Ukrainian national development. But a beginning had been made, especially during the 1850s and early 1860s. In the long run, the existence of the second-to-the-largest Slavic people could not be denied.

Of all the emerging peasant peoples of the western *gubernii*, the Lithuanians were the most successful in laying the foundations for a viable national movement. Lithuanian national leaders came chiefly from the families of well-to-do peasants in Samogitia and trans-Niemen Lithuania (Užnemunė). In western Samogitia near the Prussian and Kurland borders, middle and certain state peasants had profited from favorable market conditions or the reforms introduced by Kiselev. In Lithuania south of the Niemen, a number of peasants, who had been emancipated in 1807 together with the Polish serfs of the Duchy of Warsaw, had sizable holdings. Prosperous peasants in Samogitia, Užnemunė, and elsewhere in Lithuania sent at least one son to school to prepare for the priesthood.[47] Not all of these sons turned out to be priests, for many of them did not enter the Church but became moderate or radical members of the secular Lithuanian national movement. The initial stage of the Lithuanian national movement was, however, dominated by the Church.

The bishop of Samogitia between 1850 and 1875, Motiejus Valančius, was the son of a local peasant. A student at Wilno University before the insurrection of 1830-1831, he and other Lithuanians came

---

[46] Pelech, "Toward a Historical Sociology," pp. 48-245; D. Doroshenko, *A Survey of Ukrainian History*, ed. O. W. Gerus (Winnepeg: Humeniuk Publications Foundation, 1975), pp. 525-27, 535-44; *Istoriia Ukrainskoi SSR*, 2 vols. (Kiev: "Naukova Dumka," 1969), 1: 402-8, 472-75; E. S. Shabliovskii, "N. I. Kostomarov v gody revoliutsionnoi situatsii (1859-1861 gg.)," *Revoliutsionnaia situatsiia v Rossii v 1859-1861 gg.: 1970* (Moscow: Akademiia Nauk, 1970), pp. 101-23.

[47] Koniukhova, *Gosudarstvennaia derevnia*, pp. 172-76, 202-8; S. A. Suziedelis, "The Lithuanian Peasantry of Trans-Niemen Lithuania, 1807-1864: A Study of Social, Economic and Cultural Change" (University of Kansas Ph.D. dissertation, 1977).

into contact in Wilno with Poles interested in the language, culture, and history of Lithuania. In the decades following the closing of Wilno University hundreds of historical, ethnographic, and popular religious works were published in Lithuanian. Bishop Valančius himself was a talented writer who wrote ethnographic tales and other didactic works widely read among the peasants. His influential treatise of 1858 on temperance appeared in some 40,000 copies. Between 1858 and 1864 the temperance society sponsored by Valančius attracted 83.3 percent of the Catholics in Kowno *guberniia*. Equally important, he continued efforts of his predecessors to promote education, increasing the number of church schools in Samogitia and improving their administration and the supervision of teachers. Being a social conservative who did not approve of revolution, Valančius strongly criticized peasant involvement in the insurrection of 1863-1864; and in 1864 he offered to cooperate with tsarist officials in seeing to it that a prominent place would be given to instruction in Russian in Catholic schools as long as Lithuanian would also be taught. Soon, however, in reaction to the closing of Lithuanian church schools and to the ban on the publication of Lithuanian books not printed in a new, especially adapted Cyrillic alphabet, he began to organize a system of undergound Lithuanian elementary schools and the smuggling into Russia of Lithuanian books and anti-Russian pamphlets printed in Latin letters. He became a formidable opponent of Russification. The struggle he and the Roman Catholic clergy led against the Cyrillic alphabet and the Russification of education politicized the peasants, making them more aware of their cultural and national identity as Lithuanians than they had ever been before.[48]

The Poles were the one major nationality in the western *gubernii* which declined in relative importance during the second part of the nineteenth century. The punitive and discriminatory measures of the Russian government after 1863 wiped out the limited gains they had made during the period 1855-1863. In Belorussia the Poles were not only displaced by Russian administrators, priests, and schoolteachers but also by Russian nobles as the owners of the greater proportion of manorial lands, especially in the two eastern *gubernii* of Mohylew and Witebsk. In the Right-Bank Ukraine, the Polish economic position

---

[48] Suziedelis, "The Lithuanian Peasantry," pp. 451-74, 498-501; K. J. Čeginskas, "Die Russifizierung und ihre Folgen in Litauen unter zaristischer Herrschaft," *Commentationes Balticae* 6/7 (1959): 6, 121-34; *Iz istorii shkoly Belorussii i Litvy*, ed. V. Z. Smirnov, Izvestiia Akademii Pedagogicheskikh Nauk RSFSR, no. 131 (Moscow: "Prosveshcheniia," 1964), pp. 194-215; Jerzy Ochmański, *Litewski ruch narodowo-kulturalny w XIX wieku* (Białystok: PWN, 1965), pp. 78-117.

was somewhat stronger, but the enmity between Poles and the Ukrainian nationalist intelligentsia and emancipated peasantry augured ill for the future of the Poles in three southwestern *gubernii* of Kiev, Podolia, and Volhynia. Even in the two Lithuanian *gubernii* of Kowno and Wilno, where Poles retained control of about three-fourths of manorial land as late as 1904, the dominance of Polish civilization and culture locally was increasingly challenged by an independent Lithuanian church hierarchy, the Lithuanian nationalist movement, social unrest among landless peasants, and the growing economic power of the Lithuanian middle and well-to-do peasants. Yet, though their relative numbers declined, the Poles in the western *gubernii* remained a sufficiently vital social and economic force locally to continue to trouble tsarist officialdom even into the twentieth century.[49]

The Poles of the Congress Kingdom were even more of a problem for Russian officialdom. Here, as in the western part of Austrian Galicia and in Prussian Upper Silesia and Poznania, they constituted a clear majority of the local population. In these provinces would-be national leaders bent on transforming the old *szlachta* democracy into a modern Polish nation did not, as they did in Eastern Galicia, Belorussia, Lithuania, and the Right-Bank Ukraine, have to compete with new national movements produced by economic and social change. In dealing with ethnically Polish areas, the Austrians, Prussians, and Russians all found it difficult to meet the needs and satisfy the desires of their Polish subjects without risking what seemed to be the vital interests of the modern state.

By 1870 Austria had become Austria-Hungary, with special provisions for a Galicia dominated by Polish *szlachta* and aristocrats, while Prussia by then had almost completed the unification of a Germany that was to attempt the full integration of Poles into the national, social, and political structure of the German Empire. Meanwhile, Russia vacillated considerably in her Polish policy. Between 1831 and 1870 the milestones of Russian policy in Congress Poland were the Organic Statute of 1832, Paskevich's military dictatorship, the era of Great Reforms, Wielopolski's and Konstantin Nikolaevich's brief experiment with Polish autonomy and self-rule, and the beginnings of Russification under N. A. Miliutin, F.W.R. von Berg, and D. A. Tolstoi.

---

[49] *Istoricheskii obzor deiatel'nosti Komiteta ministrov*, vol. 3, pt. 1, pp. 159-227; vol. 4, pp. 213-23; Piotr S. Wandycz, *The Lands of Partitioned Poland, 1795-1918* (Seattle: University of Washington Press, 1974), pp. 239-54; Leon Wasilewski, *Litwa i Białoruś* (Cracow: "Książka," [1912]), pp. 78-117; S. M. Sambuk, *Politika tsarizma v Belorussii vo vtoroi polovine XIX veka* (Minsk: "Nauka i Tekhnika," 1980), pp. 103-10.

CHAPTER 8

CONGRESS POLAND

BETWEEN 1815 AND 1830 Congress Poland enjoyed a greater degree of autonomy than any other Russian borderland. All Polish citizens were equal before the law and were assured basic personal and civil rights. Like Finland, the Kingdom of Poland was allowed to retain its own laws and institutions of self-government, which operated under the general supervision of the Russian ruler but independently of the control of the Russian Senate and ministries in St. Petersburg. Unlike the Swedo-Finns, however, the Poles of the kingdom had a parliament and a constitution that guaranteed their laws, special rights, and national institutions.

The Organic Statute of February 14, 1832, which significantly modified the administrative, political, and legal order introduced in 1815, clearly reflected the ambivalence of Russian policy in Congress Poland. The manifesto that accompanied the Organic Statute referred to Poland as an "indivisible part of the empire" and proclaimed that henceforth the Poles "constituted with the Russians a nation united in concord and fraternity."[1] But Nicholas I and his advisers considered it premature to proceed rapidly with the full integration of Poland into the administrative and legal system that prevailed elsewhere in the empire. One important consideration was the possible adverse reaction of the European powers to such integration on the basis of international agreements concerning Poland made at Vienna in 1815.[2] Nicholas I and his government firmly rejected the right of any foreign power to intervene in the internal affairs of the Russian Empire, but radical revision of the rule of law that had existed in Poland before 1830 was avoided in the Organic Statute, which reaffirmed the principle of equality before the law, the essentially Polish character of Congress Poland's internal administrative and legal system, and most of the personal and civil rights and freedoms granted in the Constitutional Charter of 1815. In addition, the Polish minister state secretary in St. Petersburg continued to countersign laws and orders and

---

[1] Winiarksi, *Les institutions politiques en Pologne*, p. 114.

[2] A. P. Shcherbatov, *General-Fel'dmarshal Kniaz' Paskevich: Ego zhizn' i deiatel'-nost'*, 7 vols. (St. Petersburg: V. A. Berezovskii, 1888-1904), 5: 12.

to serve as an intermediary between the emperor and the Russian authorities in Congress Poland. But no provision was made in the Organic Statute for the continued existence of the Sejm, and Article 20 abolished the separate Polish army that until then had spared the Polish youth from serving in the Russian army for twenty-five years. Article 31, by specifying that new law projects could be considered only in relation to the empire's existing legislation and must be reviewed by a new Department for Polish Affairs attached to the Russian State Council in St. Petersburg, narrowly limited the role of the Polish State Council in preparing new laws for Congress Poland.[3]

Over a period of twenty-five years extraordinary military and civil powers in Congress Poland were concentrated in the hands of Prince Field Marshal I. F. Paskevich. In 1831 he became viceroy and commander of the Russian army in Poland and headed the Polish provisional government. Beginning in 1832 he chaired the Polish State and Administrative Councils in Warsaw and the Department for Polish Affairs of the Russian State Council in St. Petersburg. Internally, marshal law had been declared in 1831 and was not formally terminated until 1856; it was enforced by the presence of a Russian army of occupation in Poland throughout this period. In addition, in 1832 the Third Section's Corps of Gendarmes was extended to Poland, where it was subordinated to Paskevich's personal chancery and army command. During the next several decades some seven hundred gendarmes watched over Polish society, reporting on anti-government sentiment and conspiracies and arresting hundreds of Poles for various political crimes.[4]

Paskevich, who was Nicholas I's trusted personal agent in Congress Poland, ruled with a firm hand. He dealt severely with those who had been involved in the insurrection of 1830-1831. By 1832 about ten percent of the property of the landowning *szlachta* in Congress Poland had been confiscated. Tens of thousands of former Polish soldiers and officers, although officially amnestied, were, after returning to Russia from Austria and Prussia, incorporated into the Russian army

[3] The Russian text of the Organic Statute has been republished in *Konstitutsionnaia khartiia 1815 goda i nekotorye drugie akty*, pp. 121-36. Cf. *Dziennik praw*, 14 (1832): 160-249; PSZ, 2nd ser., 7: 83-90, no. 5,165, February 14, 1832; Winiarski, *Les Institutions politiques en Pologne*, pp. 116-17; Reinke, *Ocherk*, pp. 85-86.

[4] Amburger, *Geschichte der Behördenorganisation*, pp. 426-34. The best account in English concerning the activities of the Third Section in Poland under Paskevich is an unpublished paper presented by Jacob Kipp at the 1976 meeting of the Midwest Slavic Conference in Chicago: "The Paskevich System and the Corps of Gendarmes: Some Observations on the Search for Order in the Polish Kingdom."

and sent to the Caucasus and Siberia.[5] As viceroy and chairman of the Administrative Council, Paskevich saw to it that only Russians were appointed to the position of Warsaw chief of police and that between 1832 and 1850 Russians headed the branch of the Polish administration that controlled police, ecclesiastical, and educational affairs—namely, the Commission for Internal and Ecclesiastical Affairs and Public Education. The directors of the remaining two Commissions of Justice and Finance were Poles. Since Paskevich introduced the use of Russian in the Administrative Council and in his own chancery, non-Russian-speaking Polish commission directors and members of the Administrative Council were obliged to communicate in French with their Russian colleagues. Questions discussed in the Administrative Council were to be decided by a majority vote, but whenever the viceroy disagreed with a majority decision he could usually have his way by referring the matter to the Polish king, that is, Nicholas I. The other principal organ of central government of Congress Poland, the State Council, was even less independent of Paskevich's control than the Administrative Council, for the viceroy not only chaired and appointed the members of the State Council but he also could review its recommendations concerning new law projects as chairman of the Department for Polish Affairs of the Russian State Council in St. Petersburg. The Warsaw State Council, in effect, became more and more superfluous. It was abolished in 1841.[6]

Paskevich opposed the full and immediate integration of Congress Poland into the general administrative structure of the Russian Empire. He had little respect for the formalism and red tape of the Russian *chinovnik* and believed that the very size of the empire prevented the central ministries in St. Petersburg from being well informed about the affairs of the provinces. Not the slow-moving Russian bureaucracy, he argued, but an "exclusive power" that stood outside the law was required to deal with the special problems of Russia's borderlands.[7] However, he shared the view of Nicholas I and his centralizing advisers that Poland had to be brought into a closer union

---

[5] Winiarski, *Les institutions politiques en Pologne*, pp. 113-16; N. Reinke, *Ocherk*, pp. 85-86; Z. Lenskii, "Pol'skoe vosstanie 1863 g.," *Istoriia Rossii v XIX veke* (St. Petersburg: A. I. Granat, n.d.), 3: 268-71; *Historia Polski*, ed. T. Manteuffel (Warsaw: PWN, 1959), vol. 2, pt. 3, pp. 5-7; S. Kieniewicz, *Historia Polski 1795-1918* (Warsaw: PWN, 1968), pp. 114-15.

[6] Amburger, *Geschichte der Behördenorganisation*, pp. 431-33; Reinke, *Ocherk*, pp. 83, 88-91; Winiarski, *Les institutions politiques en Pologne*, pp. 115-18.

[7] Shcherbatov, *General-Fel'dmarshal Kniaz' Paskevich*, 5: 12-13, 390-92.

with Russia, and in 1851 he expressed satisfaction that since the Polish insurrection of 1830-1831 "the administration of the Kingdom of Poland had been brought into a more proper position that approximates as much as possible the order of general administration in the empire."[8]

When Paskevich wrote to Nicholas I in 1847 about the perils of too rapid administrative centralization and the need for an "exclusive power" in the borderlands, he apparently had L. A. Perovskii especially in mind. Perovskii, the minister of the interior between 1841 and 1852, strongly recommended the rapid introduction of Russian institutions into the western borderlands.[9] The full integration of these borderlands would have, of course, strengthened the hold of the Ministry of the Interior and its agents over police and municipal institutions and provincial administration. Paskevich had good reason to question the ability of the agents of the Ministry of the Interior to function effectively in Congress Poland. He did not and could not, however, object to Nicholas I's general policy of administrative centralism; as long as his special position as Russian viceroy in Warsaw was respected, he cooperated with St. Petersburg officials in introducing a number of standardizing reforms into Congress Poland. Thus, in 1837 the eight Polish województwa were replaced by five Russian-style gubernii, the subdivisions of which were no longer referred to after 1842 as obwody and powiaty but thenceforth as uezdy and okrugi. A Warsaw School Region under the Russian Ministry of Education was organized in 1839, and in 1841 the Ninth and Tenth Departments of the Russian Senate replaced the Polish State Council in Warsaw. In 1846 Congress Poland's road and transportation system came under the jurisdiction of the Russian Main Administration for Communications. In 1848 the Russian system of weights and measures was introduced into Poland. In 1850 the customs frontier between the Kingdom of Poland and the rest of the empire was abolished, and in the following year the Polish postal service was brought under central Russian control. Finally, in 1852 Polish censorship regulations were brought into line with those current in Russia.[10]

[8] "Raport namestnika Tsarstva Pol'skogo ego Imperatorskomu Velichestvu," SIRIO, 98 (1895): 592.

[9] [L. A. Perovskii], "O neobkhodimosti vvesti v vsekh guberniiakh i oblastiakh Imperii russkie organicheskie zakony," CHTENIIA, 1865 (July-September), bk. 3, pt. 5 (Smes'), pp. 182-83.

[10] PSZ, 2nd ser., 7: 109, no. 5,192, February 27, 1832; ibid., 12: 293, no. 10,203, May 3, 1837; ibid., 14: 886, no. 12,908, November 20, 1839; ibid., 16: 522-24, no. 14,852, September 6, 1841; ibid., 20: 65-66 (appendix), no. 18,136a, August 9, 1844;

Viceroy Paskevich, then, did not oppose in principle the introduction of Russian laws and institutions into Poland. When he did oppose policies advocated by St. Petersburg officials, he usually did so for practical reasons based on a healthy skepticism about the effectiveness of their routine and bureaucratic methods in the borderlands. He was, however, only the equal but not the superior of the heads of ministries and other high officials in St. Petersburg. Despite his good relations with Nicholas I, he did not necessarily win all his battles with the bureaucrats in St. Petersburg.

In the first part of the 1830s, for example, he opposed proposed legislation that aimed at transforming the Polish *szlachta* into a reasonable facsimile of the Russian *dvorianstvo*. Under Paskevich, the *szlachta* had few real powers and functions, for everyone in Poland was equal before the law and no assemblages of the nobility, where they might have exerted some influence over local affairs, were convened. Paskevich saw no reason to change this state of affairs, and he feared that a most unwelcome rebirth of the *szlachta* as a powerful social force could result from granting them certain of the privileges of the Russian *dvorianstvo*. But Paskevich was overruled, apparently because of difficulties arising out of integrating Polish officers into the Russian army and Russians into state service in Poland. There were, therefore, good bureaucratic reasons for uniformity. An *ukaz* of June 25, 1836, established new norms for noble status in Congress Poland that were, in many respects, based on the model of the Russian *dvorianstvo*. This new social category had, however, little attraction for the *szlachta*, who—apart from about 25,000 out of perhaps 300,000 members of this former social class—showed little interest in having their noble status confirmed by the Russian state.[11]

There were also, on the other hand, instances of fairly close cooperation between Paskevich and ministers in St. Petersburg. For example, after the formation of the Warsaw School Region and the placing of education in Congress Poland under the administration of the Russian Ministry of Education, S. S. Uvarov seems to have always made it a point to obtain Paskevich's approval for policies and measures to be carried out in Poland. In 1839 Paskevich conferred with Uvarov in St. Petersburg about the need to counter the intrigues of

---

ibid., 21: 462-63, no. 20,669, December 5, 1846; ibid., 23: 53, no. 21,907, January 20, 1848; ibid., 25: 14, no. 24,533, October 13, 1850; ibid., 26: 75-76, 167-68, nos. 24,853, 25,000, January 20 and March 4, 1851; ibid., 27: 264, no. 26,155, April 10, 1852.

[11] Jerzy Jedlicki, "Geneza wtórnego szlachectwa w Królestwie Polskim," in *Wiek XIX: Prace ofiarowane Stefani Kieniewiczowi w 60 rocznice urodzin* (Warsaw: PWN, 1967), pp. 195-210; Łepkowski, *Polska-nardoziny nowoczesnego narodu*, pp. 144-45; *Dziennik praw*, 19 (1836): 186-289.

emissaries from abroad in Polish schools, to improve supervision over the activities and education of gymnasium students, and to prepare young Poles for further study in Russian universities.[12] Poles had to be sent to Russian universities above all because the closing of Warsaw University in 1831 had made it extremely difficult to train legal specialists for service in the judicial system, which was still entirely Polish in law, language, and organization. Here the Ministry of Education proved to be of great assistance to Paskevich by sending Russian teachers to Poland and by establishing chairs in the civil, criminal, and administrative law of the Kingdom of Poland at the Universities of Moscow and St. Petersburg.[13]

Paskevich and Uvarov were also in agreement about the importance of the Russian language in Congress Poland. To help young Poles learn Russian, not only the Russian language but also Polish and Russian history, statistics, and geography were taught in Russian in a number of Polish secondary schools by the mid-1840s.[14] In his ten-year report of 1843, however, Uvarov argued that it was premature to make a mastery of Russian obligatory for students in the schools of Congress Poland, as had already been done in the schools of the western and Baltic provinces; in Poland he wanted to use gentle persuasion and to win gradually the confidence of the Polish youth in the government and its respect for Russian education.[15] But such optimism about the prospects of Russian education in Poland was perhaps more characteristic of the flowery rhetoric of Uvarov's official reports than of the actual policy he pursued in Poland, where the same system of bureaucratic supervision, strict discipline, high tuition, and class restrictions on admission to secondary schools prevailed as elsewhere in the empire. Meanwhile, the youth of Congress Poland and the apparent degree of its involvement in secret political activities were viewed with great concern by the Russian authorities, as is illustrated by their decision of 1846 to prohibit anyone born in the western *gubernii* from studying in the schools of the Warsaw School Region.[16]

[12] Shcherbatov, *Paskevich*, 5: 200-201.

[13] Ibid., p. 201; Reinke, *Ocherk*, p. 77; Jan Kucharzewski, *Epoka Paszkiewiczowska: Losy oświaty* (Warsaw-Cracow: Gebethner i Wolff, 1914), pp. 624-28.

[14] Russia, Ministerstvo narodnogo prosveshcheniia, *Obshchii otchet predstavlennyi ego Imperatorskomu Velichestvu po Ministerstvu narodnogo prosveshcheniia za 1845 god* (St. Petersburg: Imperatorskaia Akademiia Nauk, 1846), pp. 67, 107.

[15] S. S. Uvarov, *Desiatiletie Ministerstva narodnogo prosveshcheniia, 1833-1843 gg.* (St. Petersburg: Tipografiia Imperatorskoi Akademii Nauk, 1864), p. 69.

[16] Kieniewicz, *Historia Polski*, pp. 116, 211-12; *Historia Polski*, ed. Manteuffel, vol. 2, pt. 3, pp. 8, 183; Rozhdestvenskii, *Istoricheskii obzor*, p. 317; Shcherbatov, *Paskevich*, 5: 201-2.

Russian school policy in Poland impeded the development of education during the period 1830-1855. This was particularly true of secondary schools, whose students declined in number from 9,833 in 1829 to 6,156 in 1848. The number of students in elementary schools did approximately double to 64,613 during the same period, but dropped to 52,256 in 1855 as a result of the repressive conduct of educational policy by Paskevich and the new curator of the Warsaw School Region after 1851, P. A. Mukhanov. The imposition of Russian norms and standards on the administration of Polish schools could, of course, hardly be expected to stimulate the modernization and development of education, for even as late as 1869 the proportion of young people in school was four times lower in the central *gubernii* of Russia than in Congress Poland.[17] But Paskevich and Russian educational bureaucrats in St. Petersburg seem to have been more interested in social control then than they were in social modernization and development.

Paskevich also cooperated with officials in St. Petersburg with regard to the interests of the Orthodox Church in the Congress Kingdom, where 216,000 Uniates and 100,000 Orthodox believers lived at the beginning of the 1830s out of a total population of approximately four million. In the latter part of the 1820s Orthodox believers living in Poland were placed under the Russian Holy Synod and the Volhynian eparchy. Paskevich tried to place Orthodox landowners on lands confiscated from Polish *szlachta* who had been found guilty of treason during 1830-1831, but he managed this only with limited success. In 1836 Russian laws concerning mixed marriages between Orthodox and members of other churches were extended to Congress Poland, regulating such marriages according to the rules of the Orthodox Church. In 1840 a separate Orthodox eparchy was established in Warsaw to minister to the needs of Orthodox Christians, and possibly also to those of the Uniates living in the Congress Kingdom. The Uniates were concentrated in the Chełm region in the southeastern corner of the kingdom. Paskevich worked throughout the thirties to persuade their hierarchy to install iconostases and "tsar's doors" (*tsarskie vrata*) in Uniate churches and otherwise to conform to Orthodox practices. Paskevich, however, soon encountered resistance to his efforts to prepare the Chełm Uniates for eventual reunion with Orthodoxy. Finding no influential person in the Uniate hierarchy willing to cooperate with the Russian authorities and realizing that Rome still

[17] Łepkowski, *Polska-narodziny nowoczesnego narodu*, pp. 261-62; *Historia Polski*, ed. Manteuffel, vol. 2, pt. 3, pp. 183, 395.

exercised a greater force of attraction for the Uniate clergy than did the Holy Synod, Paskevich and Nicholas I did not seriously try to force the Chełm Uniates to unite with Orthodoxy.[18]

Paskevich and St. Petersburg bureaucrats did not even have a serious quarrel on the subject of the relationship of Polish law and courts to Russian law and judicial authorities. Perhaps he had no objections because he was dealing not with bureaucrats working for a powerful ministry, but with the Russian Senate and the Second Section of His Imperial Majesty's Own Chancery. The Ninth and Tenth Departments of the Russian Ruling Senate were organized in Warsaw during 1841-1842 on the basis of detailed proposals prepared by Paskevich. Beginning in 1842 the Ninth and Tenth Departments served as the highest courts for civil and criminal cases in Congress Poland. The General Assembly of the two departments took over a good part of the functions of the former Polish State Council, which was dissolved in 1841. They worked under the overall supervision of the director of the Commission for Justice in Warsaw, who was a Pole and therefore familiar with the local legal system; the Russian viceroy presided whenever the two departments met together as a general assembly. At the same time, the Warsaw departments were an integral part of the Russian Senate, which assured the proper subordination of Congress Poland's legal system to the central authorities in St. Petersburg.[19]

In 1833 a Codification Commission for the Laws of Congress Poland was organized within the Second Section of His Imperial Majesty's Own Chancery. Although the Second Section aimed at bringing local laws everywhere into conformity with the general laws of the empire, it wished to avoid undue haste in imposing Russian legal norms on the inhabitants of the western borderlands. With regard to Congress Poland, the Second Section relied heavily on the expert advice of such competent Polish jurists as Ignacy Turkułł, Cyprian Zaborowski, and Romuald Hube. The head of the Second Section, D. N. Bludov, always informed Paskevich in advance about legislative projects that concerned Congress Poland in any way. The materials systematically collected and edited by the Codification Commission for the Laws of Congress Poland never received official sanction as the basis for legal

[18] Reinke, Ocherk, pp. 81-82; Shcherbatov, Paskevich, 5: 22-23, 123-24, 195-96, 216-17, 220-21.

[19] Reinke, Ocherk, p. 71; Amburger, Geschichte der Behördenorganisation Russlands, pp. 427, 433; Istoriia pravitel'stvuiushchego Senata za dvesti let, 3: 337-55; PSZ, 2nd ser., 16: 522-24, no. 14,852, September 6, 1841; ibid., 17: 214-29, no. 15,428, March 26, 1842.

order in the kingdom, but they did subsequently prove to be useful for the purposes of would-be Russifiers during the 1870s. However, one small part of the Codification Commissions's work, namely a new criminal code, was introduced in 1848 throughout Congress Poland, mainly because Nicholas I and Paskevich were interested in achieving as great a degree of uniformity as possible in the imposition of legal penalties for the commission of criminal acts. After 1848, for example, legislation making the conversion of Orthodox Christians to other religions a criminal offense was also enforced in Congress Poland.[20]

In the last analysis, neither Paskevich's form of "exclusive power" in Warsaw nor the centralizing policy of the St. Petersburg ministries had a particularly profound influence on the lives of the inhabitants of the Kingdom of Poland and on the conduct of its internal financial, judicial, and governmental affairs. Russians controlled the police and army and ran the Administrative Council and several other important offices in Warsaw, but the judges in the courts and the local policemen, officials, and teachers were all Poles who conducted their daily affairs in Polish and according to Polish laws and precedents. A few courses taught in Russian in Polish secondary schools, several hundred Russian Orthodox landowners who had received confiscated Polish estates,[21] and a handful of former *szlachta* who allowed themselves to be integrated into the ranks of the Russian service *dvorianstvo* had relatively little impact on what remained essentially a Polish world. Even the Ninth and Tenth Departments of the Russian Ruling Senate seem to have been Russian in name only, for Poles, as the only ones with the requisite knowledge of Polish law, had to be appointed as senators in Warsaw, and it was only in 1872 that Russian was introduced as the official language of the Warsaw Departments of the Senate.[22] During the reign of Nicholas I the Polish directors of the Commissions of Justice and Finance were routinely made members of the Russian Senate, as were also certain Polish legal specialists (for example, Romuald Hube) and the Polish minister state secretaries in

---

[20] P. M. Maikov, *Vtoroe otdelenie sobstvennoi ego imperatorskogo velichestva kantseliarii 1826-1882: Istoricheskii ocherk* (St. Petersburg: I. N. Skorokhodov, 1909), pp. 222-24, 312-16; R. Staël von Holstein, "Die Kodifizierung des baltischen Provinzialrechts," BM 52 (1901): 275-78, 353-58; Władysław Sobociński, "Z dziejów prac kodyfikacyjnych dla Królestwa Polskiego i Rosji: Romuald Hube wobec kwestii chłopskiej," in *Wiek XIX: Prace ofiarowane Stefanowi Kieniewiczowi w 60 rocznice urodzin*, pp. 175-77; Reinke, *Ocherk*, pp. 164-65; Ludwik Kulczycki, *Królestwo Polskie, 1815-1914* (Cracow: Nakładem Centralnego Biura Wydawnictw, 1916), p. 35.

[21] Reinke, *Ocherk*, p. 80; Shcherbatov, *Paskevich*, 5: 139-40.

[22] Reinke, *Ocherk*, p. 166.

St. Petersburg.[23] Furthermore, business and decisions pertaining to Poland continued to pass through the hands of the Polish minister state secretary in St. Petersburg. No Pole who occupied this position ever succeeded in influencing Nicholas I and his advisers in the manner of Robert Rehbinder and Alexander Armfelt, the two Finnish minister state secretaries. Yet, the mere presence of a Polish minister state secretary in the Russian capital symbolized the continued existence within Russia of a separate Polish borderland that in no way constituted, to quote the Organic Statute, "a nation united [with Russia] in concord and fraternity."

If Paskevich's police and military regime failed to unite Poles and Russians in "concord and fraternity," it did succeed in maintaining order. For several decades his gendarmes and soldiers in the Kingdom of Poland arrested, interrogated, imprisoned, and sent to Siberia thousands of Poles involved in revolutionary activities. In 1846 and 1848 a revolution did not spread to Russian Poland, probably because of Paskevich's system of strict controls over Polish society and the presence of hundreds of thousands of Russian troops in the kingdom and in the western *gubernii*. In 1849 Paskevich commanded the Russian army that suppressed the Hungarian Revolution. He also supported those who, following the discovery of the Ukrainian Cyril and Methodius Society, criticized Minister of Education Uvarov's relative leniency in dealing with the press and society.[24] The resignation of Uvarov in 1849 marked the beginning in Russia of a period of petty censorship and of other restrictions and repressive measures that aimed (as did also Paskevich's regime in Warsaw) at keeping society under control and avoiding a revolution.

The external pacification of Poland by Paskevich's gendarmes and soldiers turned out, however, to be no long-term solution of Russia's Polish problem. The outcome of the Crimean War tended to discredit not only the bureaucratic formalism of St. Petersburg officialdom that Paskevich had criticized but also the heavy-handed police regime he had established in Poland. This regime, as one Russian observer wrote in the early 1860s,

[23] Amburger, *Geschichte der Behördenorganisation*, pp. 433-34; "Spisok senatorov," *Istoriia Pravitel'stvuiushchego senata za dvesti let*, 5: 111-61.

[24] Janusz Berghausen, *Ruch patriotyczny w Królestwie Polskim 1833-1850* (Warsaw: PWN, 1974), pp. 29-31, 102-4, 184-86, 274-81, 301-13; Georges Luciani, *Le livre de la genèse du peuple ukrainien* (Paris: Institut d'Etudes Slaves, 1956), pp. 61-63, 70-85; A. S. Nifontov, *Rossiia v 1848 g.* (Moscow: Uchpedgiz, 1949), pp. 210-11, 244-49, 269-97; W. Bruce Lincoln, *Nicholas I: Emperor and Autocrat of All the Russians* (Bloomington-London: Indiana University Press, 1978), pp. 295-302, 309-23.

. . . rejects any thought of legality . . . and has as its objective the creation of an external pacification, does not bring into existence any proper, lawful government. With the passage of time it creates more evil than good for it stirs up in the whole country a hatred towards the government, which lives on from generation to generation. It causes disrespect towards it [the government]. Even beyond that it destroys the very instruments upon which the government most depends—law, respect for law and order.[25]

At the beginning of Alexander II's reign both reform-minded officials in the central government and officially tolerated liberal, Slavophile, and conservative journalists favored a conciliatory but cautious policy in Poland. The new viceroy, M. D. Gorchakov, generally preferred to rely on cooperation with conservative and more affluent elements among the Poles rather than on the police methods of Paskevich in pursuing the objectives of Russian policy. Alexander II was then, at a time when preparations for basic reform in the central Russian parts of the empire began in earnest, inclined to accept the policy recommendations of his viceroy in Warsaw. In 1856 and 1857 Alexander, therefore, amnestied Polish political offenders, approved the opening of a Medical-Surgical Academy in Warsaw, and permitted the establishment of an Agricultural Society, which soon became an all-important forum for discussion by the nobility of social and economic reforms in the Polish countryside. But the Russian emperor, especially when he visited Warsaw in May 1856, cautioned the Poles not to have daydreams (*"point de rêveries, point de rêveries"*). He pointedly reminded a group of assembled *szlachta* and clergy representatives that religion was the moral basis of society and that it was their duty to teach their countrymen that "the happiness of Poland consists in her complete union with the peoples of my empire."[26]

The decision of the Russian authorities to allow the Agricultural Society, which consisted of several thousand progressive Polish landowners, to discuss agrarian reform was an important one. It meant that they did not intend to introduce Russian peasant reforms into the Congress Kingdom; it meant that they made a distinction between it and the western *gubernii*; and it meant that in the kingdom social and

[25] Gosudarstvennaia Publichnaia Biblioteka im. Saltykova-Shchedrina, f. 208 (A. V. Golovnin), delo 37/38, "Zapiska neizvestnogo o deiatel'nosti Vel. K. Konstantina Nikolavevicha v kachestve namestnika v Pol'she (sentiabr' 1863 g.)," as cited and translated by Kipp, "The Paskevich System and the Corps of Gendarmes," p. 18.

[26] N. V. Berg, *Zapiski N. V. Berga o pol'skikh zagovorakh i vosstaniiakh 1831-1862* (Moscow: "Russkii Arkhiv," 1873), pp. 145-49.

economic reform was to be prepared and carried out in cooperation with the organized leadership of the local nobility.

The granting of land ownership to the peasants (*uwłaszczenie*) and the commutation of compulsory labor to rent payments were two basic problems of agricultural reform in Congress Poland. Polish peasants had struggled for *uwłaszczenie* and against compulsory labor ever since they had become legally free in 1807. After the November Insurrection of 1830 both the Polish democratic Left and the Russian government had given considerable attention to the situation of the peasant in Congress Poland, because they saw a possible ally in him. Many progressive landowners interested in more efficient production shifted their estates to wage labor during the first part of the nineteenth century; but the democratic Left found little support among the landowning nobility for the granting of ownership of land to the Polish peasants.[27] The Russian government, for its part, was constrained in both the Kingdom of Poland and the western *gubernii* from making use of the peasants as allies against the Polish *szlachta* because of its dependence on the landowning nobility as the main pillar of social order in pre-reform Russia. Nevertheless, Nicholas I felt obliged to experiment cautiously with legislation to improve the lot of the peasants throughout the "Polish" lands of the empire.

In the Kingdom of Poland the Russian government tried to create better conditions for peasants living on state lands, which included about one-fourth of the kingdom's land, or 1.12 million acres. On the approximately 40 percent of this land that had been given to some two hundred Russian nobles as entailed estates, the obligations of the peasants were gradually converted from compulsory labor to rent payments after the mid-1830s. In the forties and fifties these measures were extended to peasants on other state lands, assuring them the use (though not ownership) of the land they cultivated at reasonable rents and under conditions more favorable than those of state peasants in Russia. In 1846, after the Polish peasant uprising in neighboring Galicia, the Russian authorities, on the initiative of Nicholas I himself, also introduced measures to protect the interests of the majority of Polish peasants living on private estates, who, if they were cultivators of at least three *morgi* (4.14 acres) of soil, could no longer be evicted from their holdings as long as they continued to perform their duties. The government elaborated the procedures for handling cases of conflict with landowners and for commuting compulsory labor into rent

---

[27] Stefan Kieniewicz, *The Emancipation of the Polish Peasantry* (Chicago-London: University of Chicago Press, 1969), pp. 73-74, 96-112, 145-53; Shcherbatov, *Paskevich*, 5: 139-42.

payments.[28] These regulations did somewhat strengthen the position of the peasant in the Polish countryside, and they represented the point of departure for further discussion of peasant reform at the end of the fifties and the beginning of the sixties.

The 1857 Charter of the Polish Agricultural Society permitted progressive landowners to meet annually in order to discuss the improvement of farming techniques. In 1859 the Russian government authorized the Society to widen the scope of its discussions to include the preparation of reform legislation aiming at the abolition of agricultural labor services in Congress Poland.[29] At that time St. Petersburg officialdom was seriously considering measures to decentralize administration and to develop local self-government throughout the empire. Accordingly, not only Polish landowners but also privileged nobles and townsmen in the Baltic provinces and Finland were allowed to discuss reform of local society. In Congress Poland, in contrast to the Baltic provinces and Finland, such discussions were accompanied by a rapidly worsening political situation.

The first serious clashes between the Russian authorities and the Poles occurred during 1861. In Warsaw patriotic manifestations had taken place as early as 1858 on such occasions as the funeral of a widow of a general who had died defending Warsaw in 1831, or the anniversaries of battles or other events of importance in the national history of Poland. Around the 1860s the so-called Reds began work to increase the political activity of the Warsaw population in order to impress on the Russians the need for further reforms and to oblige the Polish Agricultural Society to act speedily in finding a solution to Poland's agrarian crisis. The émigré democratic Left, to be sure, had insisted on far-reaching agrarian reforms and justice for the Polish peasant since the 1830s. So did the radicals in Warsaw during the early 1860s, among whom were many Polish students who had attended universities and other specialized institutions in the interior of the empire, where they often came under the influence of the incipient Russian revolutionary movement. Whether abroad or in Russia, all Poles interested in organizing insurrection against Russia realized that they had little chance for success unless they offered land to the peasants on terms acceptable to the peasants themselves.[30]

[28] Kieniewicz, *Emancipation*, pp. 97-98, 149-49, 256-58.

[29] Zbigniew Stankiewicz, *Dzieje wielkości i upadku Aleksandra Wielopolskiego* (Warsaw: Wiedza Powszechna, 1967), pp. 105-8.

[30] Wandycz, *The Lands of Partitioned Poland*, pp. 118-19, 159-62, 172; S. Kieniewicz, *Les chances de l'insurrection polonaise de 1863*. Académie Polonaise des Sciences, Centre Scientifique à Paris, Conférences, no. 99 (Warsaw: PWN, 1973), pp. 5-6; Smirnov, *Vosstanie 1863 goda v Litve i Belorussii*, pp. 53-73, 85-100.

Both St. Petersburg officials and leaders of Russian public opinion responded rather hesitantly to the very serious and developing revolutionary situation in the Polish borderlands of the empire. Alexander II's first reaction was to use force to restore order, especially in the western *gubernii*. In Warsaw, however, his viceroy, M. D. Gorchakov, advised taking advantage of the fears of the "majority of the upper and middle classes" about the possible consequences of the activities of the "wild (*burnye*) demagogues."[31] In St. Petersburg the Warsaw viceroy's recommended policy of cautious concessions to the wishes of moderate elements in Congress Poland was supported by new reform-minded ministers brought into the government in 1861: Minister of War D. A. Miliutin, Minister of Finance M. Kh. Reutern, Minister of Education A. V. Golovnin, and Minister of the Interior P. A. Valuev. Valuev, in particular, opposed all attempts to return to the police methods of Paskevich in Congress Poland. The tsar's own brother, Konstantin Nikolaevich, advocated support for the initiative of Polish moderates in reforming local society as the best way to end the agitation of the Reds in the Kingdom of Poland. Equally important, A. M. Gorchakov, the influential minister of foreign affairs from 1856 to 1882 and the cousin of the Russian viceroy in Warsaw, maintained that the Polish policy of Nicholas I and Paskevich had been detrimental to Russian state interests; he argued that every effort should be made to avoid taking measures in Poland that would unnecessarily irritate the Polonophile Parisian press and endanger Franco-Russian diplomatic cooperation in Europe.[32]

In 1861 and 1862 the reform and modification of Paskevich's system in Poland resulted largely from the initiative and tenacity of Margrave Aleksander Wielopolski, a leading advocate of "organic work" (that is, working legally to advance cultural and social progress among Poles living in Austria, Prussia, and Russia). A hardheaded pragmatist, Wielopolski wanted a separate administration, education, and social and economic progress for Congress Poland, but he insisted on the necessity of maintaining order and cooperating with Russia. Being the only

---

[31] *Korespondencja namestników Królestwa Polskiego z 1861 roku*, ed. S. Kieniewicz and I. Miller (Wrocław-Warsaw: Ossolineum-PWN, 1964), pp. 13-14, 18.

[32] Irena Koberdowa, *Wielki książę Konstanty w Warszawie 1862-1863* (Warsaw: PWN, 1962), pp. 22-30; Jacob W. Kipp, "The Genesis of Reform: The Grand Duke Konstantin Nikolaevich and the *Konstantinovtsy* in the Epoch of the Great Reforms, 1850-1865" (Pennsylvania State University Ph.D. dissertation, 1970); V. G. Revunenkov, *Pol'skoe vosstanie 1863 g. i evropeiskaia diplomatiia* (Leningrad: Izdatel'stvo Leningradskogo Universiteta, 1957), pp. 27-34, 77-78, 87-90; P. A. Valuev, *Dnevnik P. A. Valueva ministra vnutrennikh del*, ed. P. A. Zaionchkovskii, 2 vols. (Moscow: Akademiia Nauk, 1961), 1: 165-66.

prominent Pole upon whom the Russians then could rely, he managed to persuade the Russian government to agree to reforms that at least partially restored to the Kingdom of Poland the autonomous position within the empire that it had lost since 1831: a restored Polish State Council replaced the dissolved General Assembly of the Warsaw departments of the Russian Senate; Wielopolski became the head of a separate Polish educational system as director of a reorganized Commission of Education and Religious Cult; local self-government was reestablished in towns and on the levels of the district and *guberniia*; Wielopolski's proposal for emancipation of the Jews was approved; and peasant labor services were converted to rents.[33] These reforms represented a notable concession on the part of the Russian government; but they satisfied neither the Reds, who demanded a more basic reform of the kingdom's political and social structure, nor the peasants, who wanted a firm guarantee of their permanent possession of the land they cultivated and of their traditional rights to use manorial woods and pastures (servitudes).

At the end of 1861 and early in 1862 Wielopolski's reforms were called into question by new political demonstrations and the declaration of marshal law by the Russian authorities in Warsaw. In May 1862, however, Alexander II confirmed Wielopolski as the head of the civil government in Congress Poland and appointed Konstantin Nikolaevich as Russian viceroy in Warsaw. Konstantin Nikolaevich arrived in Warsaw in June 1862, instructed by Alexander II to keep in mind as his most important goal the reestablishment of political order on the basis of reforms that had just been granted to the Poles. Russian interests were always to come first, and Konstantin was to make clear to the Poles that no new concessions would be made and that, especially, there would be no constitution or Polish national army. Alexander warned Konstantin about certain elements of the Catholic clergy who sought to use religion for political purposes. He was to act circumspectly but firmly and to demonstrate to Margrave Alexander Wielopolski, the head of the reformed Polish internal administration, that now he, Konstantin Nikolaevich, was in charge of Poland.[34]

---

[33] Stankiewicz, *Dzieje wielkości i upadku Alesandra Wielopolskiego*, pp. 164-72, 195-208; Krzysztof Groniowski, *Uwłaszczenie chłopów w Polsce: Geneza-realizacja-skutki* (Warsaw: Wiedza Powszechna, 1976), pp. 128-31; Kieniewicz, *Emancipation*, pp. 157-60; I. M. Roseveare, "From Reform to Rebellion: A. Wielopolski and the Polish Question, 1861-1863," *Canadian Slavic Studies* 3 (1969): 263-85.

[34] Alexander II to Konstantin Nikolaevich, June 18/30, 1862, "Perepiska Imperatora Aleksandra II-go s Velikim Kniazem Konstantinom Nikolaevichem za vremia prebyvaniia ego v dolzhnosti namestnika Tsarstva Pol'skogo v 1862-1863 gg.," *Dela i dni* 1 (1920): 123-35.

Konstantin Nikolaevich retained his position as Russian viceroy in Warsaw for more than eight months after the Polish National Central Committee began its insurrection against Russia on January 10/22, 1863. As long as the tsar's brother remained in Warsaw the Russian government hesitated to end Congress Poland's separate existence within the empire. It had acted more resolutely in suppressing the insurrection in the western *gubernii*. In the Wilno *general-gubernatorstvo* M. N. Murav'ev was given dictatorial powers as early as April 1863. The Russian nobility, the liberal press, and the greater part of educated society rallied in support of Murav'ev's "energetic measures." Murav'ev, a very unpopular figure who had once been considered an enemy of progress and justice for the peasants, was suddenly transformed into a sort of national hero—especially in the pages of M. N. Katkov's *Moskovskie vedomosti (Moscow News)*. Even such liberal bureaucrats and Slavophile or liberal intellectuals as D. A. and N. A. Miliutin, Iu. F. Samarin, I. S. Aksakov, A. I. Koshelev, and K. D. Kavelin now affirmed the necessity of military dictatorship in Wilno. Moreover, whatever disagreements they had among themselves concerning questions of Russian internal policy, they united in warm praise of Murav'ev's program to improve the economic position of the local "Russian" (that is, Belorussian or Ukrainian) peasants through agrarian reform.[35]

The big question in the late spring and summer of 1863 was whether or not the policies followed by Murav'ev in Wilno would be extended to the Kingdom of Poland. In Warsaw Grand Duke Konstantin Nikolaevich continued to support a Russian policy based on preserving some degree of local autonomy and cooperation with the educated and property-owning elements that until then had dominated Polish society. The grand duke's defense of a civilian government run principally by Poles became increasingly unpopular among Russians as the Polish underground proceeded to organize a National government (*Rząd Narodowy*) that challenged the authority of Russia even in a Warsaw that was full of Russian soldiers and policemen. Meanwhile, high officials in St. Petersburg, who were disturbed by Konstantin's failure

---

[35] Smirnov, *Vosstanie 1863 goda v Litve i Belorussii*, pp. 304-7; Samarin, *Sochineniia*, 1: 310-16, 344-50; Anatole Leroy-Beaulieu, *Un homme d'état russe (Nicolas Milutine) d'après sa correspondance inédite: Etude sur la Russie et la Pologne pendant la règne d'Alexandre II (1855-1872)* (Paris: Hachette, 1884), pp. 200-209; M. N. Katkov, editorials of March 14 (no. 58), June 12 (no. 128), July 15 (no. 155), August 3 and 22 (nos. 170 and 184), September 28 (no. 211), and October 11 (no. 221), 1863, *Sobranie peredovykh statei Moskovskikh vedomostei: 1863 god* (Moscow: V. V. Chicherin, 1897), pp. 117-18, 301-3, 378-82, 428-32, 473-76, 568-70, 594-96.

to crush the Polish underground, allowed Katkov's *Moscow News* to publish reports describing the chaos in the Kingdom of Poland and criticizing the Polish civilian government that continued to exist in Warsaw with the blessings of Konstantin Nikolaevich. The grand duke was not attacked directly, but the *Moscow News* press coverage focused attention on what seemed to be the ineptitude of the conduct of Russian policy in Warsaw, in this way strengthening the hand of those in the government who advised Alexander II to alter this policy. In mid-August, Konstantin Nikolaevich was summoned to Tsarskoe Selo to discuss the affairs of Congress Poland with his brother. For the last time the grand duke had an opportunity to defend the principle of Polish civilian rule in Warsaw. Then he returned to the Polish capital, handed over the viceroyalty to General Friedrich Wilhelm Rembert von Berg, and, on August 27, departed for western Europe.[36]

General von Berg was a Baltic German who had served Russia for fifty years, including twelve years under Paskevich in Warsaw and five years as Russian governor-general in Helsingfors. As Konstantin Nikolaevich's successor in Warsaw he followed Murav'ev's example in establishing a military dictatorship and relying on public executions and punitive measures and on soldiers, policemen, and gendarmes to pacify Poland and to restore civil order.[37] The Russian authorities, however, also had to do something to win over the Polish peasants to the side of the government, since one of the first acts of the Polish Provisional National Government had been to give the peasants the land they cultivated and to guarantee their "servitude" rights. Since the Russian government wanted to assure peasant loyalty, it was obliged to uphold these peasant gains and to proceed with the program of agrarian reform in Congress Poland. Obviously, General von Berg, a Livland nobleman and *Rittergut* owner who felt a natural sympathy for fellow landowners elsewhere in the borderlands of the empire, was not the man to carry out an ambitious program of social reform in Poland. Instead, this task was entrusted to N. A. Miliutin, who had been one of the principal architects of peasant reform in Russia between 1855 and 1861.

[36] Koberdowa, *Wielki książe Konstanty w Warszawie*, pp. 232-44; N. V. Berg, *Zapiski N. V. Berg o pol'skikh zagovorakh i vosstaniiakh 1831-1864*, 4 vols. (Poznan: Tipografiia Krashevskogo, 1883-1884), 3: 135-38, 159, 183, 252, 296-303.

[37] N. V. Berg, *Zapiski*, 3: 137-38, 157, 303-11; DBL, p. 50; *Le Feldmaréchal Comte Berg, Namiestnik dans le Royaume de Pologne: Notice biographique publiée à l'occasion du jubilé de 60 ans de service* (Warsaw: J. Unger, 1872), pp. 1-16; Leslie, *Reform and Insurrection in Russian Poland 1856-1865*, pp. 234-35.

Alexander II selected Miliutin to reform Congress Poland's social and political structure because he knew that the latter was a hard-working bureaucrat and statist who sympathized neither with the Polish *szlachta* nor with other landowning aristocrats, whatever their nationality. In the late 1850s and at the beginning of the 1860s he, together with a number of other officials and intellectual leaders with a Slavophile or moderately liberal orientation, favored encouraging the peasants to play a more independent role in local affairs so that the government would have a broader base of social support. In 1862 Miliutin had grave reservations about the Polish policy formulated by Wielopolski and Konstantin Nikolaevich. In August 1863 he welcomed Alexander II's assurance that Russia had broken with the "Polish aristocracy" and would henceforth seek to "lift up the people and to seek from it support." After he had had an opportunity to consult with his friends Iurii Samarin and Prince V. A. Cherkasskii, who shared his views on Poland and peasant reform, Miliutin accepted the task of reforming Polish society and encouraging a broader base of social support for Russia.[38]

In October 1863 Miliutin, together with Cherkasskii, Samarin, and Senator V. A. Arcimowicz (Artsimovich), all traveling in a military convoy, conducted an inspection of the Polish countryside. Among the members of Miliutin's inspection team, only Arcimowicz, a Russian official of Polish origin, spoke Polish and had more than a superficial knowledge of the conditions of Polish life and society. Miliutin, Cherkasskii, and Samarin, however, had been actively involved in the preparation of the emancipation statutes of February 19, 1861, in Russia. The "enlightened" Russian bureaucrat Miliutin and the liberal Russian landowners Cherkasskii and Samarin, therefore, knew what questions to ask and what to look for in their encounters with Polish peasants in the fall of 1863. The report they submitted to Alexander II in November 1863, which Samarin wrote, showed an awareness of the complexity of the Polish agrarian question and a sensitivity to what the Polish peasants wanted and what they considered to be their rights. If Russia would help to defend these rights, Miliutin and his friends suggested, the Polish peasants could possibly be made the allies of Russia in Congress Poland. It was extremely important to win the

---

[38] I. I. Kostiushko, *Krest'ianskaia reforma 1864 goda v Tsarstve Pol'skom* (Moscow: Akademiia Nauk, 1962), p. 79; Leroy-Beaulieu, *Un homme d'etat russe*, pp. 128-98; W. Bruce Lincoln, *Nikolai Miliutin: An Enlightened Russian Bureaucrat* (Newtonville, Mass.: Oriental Research Partners, 1977), pp. 78-81; *Russification in the Baltic Provinces and Finland, 1855-1914*, ed. Thaden, p. 26; P. A. Valuev, *Dnevnik P A Valueva ministra vnutrennikh del*, 1: 166.

support of the Polish peasants for Russia, for, as Samarin argued both in the report and in an article he published in September 1863 in Aksakov's newspaper *Den' (Day)*, the peasant was the key not only to Russia's "political dominion over Poland" but also to the "very future of the Polish people."[39]

Working rapidly, Miliutin and his associates presented to Alexander II as early as December 21, 1863, a fairly detailed plan for Russian action in Poland. The Polish peasants were to become full owners of the land they cultivated with their "servitude" rights guaranteed and without payment to the state or landowners. Reorganized institutions of self-government were to be provided to enable the Polish peasants to liberate themselves from the influence of the landowning *szlachta*. At the same time, an *"organic transformation* [Miliutin's italics] of Polish civil society" was needed. For Russia to conform to practices then current in Europe, Polish institutions had to be in *"full and unconditional agreement"* with the *"institutions of the other parts of the empire"* (Miliutin's italics).[40] Local administration in the Kingdom of Poland was to be brought into direct contact with the central government; its police institutions, the administration of state lands, town and provincial administration, and court system were to be thoroughly reformed; its system of public education was to be reorganized to exclude from Polish schools "influences hostile to both legal authority and social order"; and the religious freedom of its non-Catholics had to be protected, especially the "Greco-Uniate Church" that had been so "oppressed and humiliated by the arrogant Latin clergy." Local, educated Poles, Miliutin pointed out in his memorandum of December 21, 1863, could not be depended on to carry out such fundamental reforms. Russians, therefore, had to be enlisted for service in Poland, especially those who had experience as arbitrators in the Great-Russian countryside during the years immediately following the emancipation of the serfs on February 19, 1861. To coordinate the activities of Russian agents serving in Poland, Miliutin suggested the creation of a Constituent Committee, which would supervise the implemen-

---

[39] "Poezdka po nekotorym mestnostiam Tsarstva Pol'skogo v oktiabre 1863 goda," in N. A. Miliutin (ed.), *Issledovaniia v Tsarstve Pol'skom po vysochaishemu poveleniiu, proizvedennye pod rukovodsvom Senatora, Stats-sekretaria Miliutina*, 6 vols. (St. Petersburg: n.p., 1863-1866), 1: 22. The report is also available in Samarin, *Sochineniia*, 1: 346-84. For Samarin's article of September 1863 ("Sovrenennyi ob"em pol'skogo voprosa"), see *Sochineniia*, 1: 319-43.

[40] "Vypiski iz vsepoddanneishei dokladnoi zapiski Senatora Miliutin, ot 21 dekabria 1863 g., o polozhenii Tsarstva Pol'skogo," *Issledovaniia v Tsarstve Pol'skom*, 1: 9.

tation of new peasant statutes and then "perhaps be charged with working out many other organic questions."[41]

A good part of Miliutin's program for transforming Polish society had been carried out by November 1866, when a stroke disabled him and forced him to retire from Russian state service. Four *ukazy* of February 19, 1864, the third anniversary of the emancipation of the Russian serfs, completed the *uwłaszczenie* of the Polish peasants on terms that compared favorably with the emancipation settlement in not only the Great Russian but also in the western *gubernii* of the empire; and peasant institutions of self-government were freed from the tutelage of the landowning *szlachta* (only, however, to be replaced by that of Russian *chinovniki* and policemen). Beginning in 1864 a Constituent Committee in Warsaw and Russian peasant commissions and commissioners for peasant affairs in the provinces saw to it that the four *ukazy* were carried out in accordance with the views of the government, settled disputes between peasants and landowners, and supervised the new institutions of rural local government. Furthermore, in Congress Poland between the beginning of 1864 and the end of 1866 the school system was reorganized in order to exclude *szlachta* and clerical influences from education, and to provide non-Polish minorities (more than one-fourth of Congress Poland's population), especially the Ukrainian-speaking Uniates, with schools in their own languages or Russian. The majority of Roman Catholic monasteries and convents were closed, church lands were secularized, and the clergy and Church hierarchy were subordinated to the Roman Catholic College and to the Main Administration for the Ecclesiastical Affairs of the Foreign Confessions in St. Petersburg. On December 19, 1866, one month after Miliutin's stroke, the "*ukaz* on the new organization of *guberniia* and *uezd* administration in the Kingdom of Poland" divided Russian Poland into ten *gubernii*, each of which was thenceforth to be administered according to the same rules and procedures regulating *guberniia* administration elsewhere in the empire. Three months later, on March 28, 1867, it was decreed that the governmental commissions in Warsaw that had administered local affairs since 1815 were to be abolished in order to facilitate "the full merger [*sliianie*] of this part of our state" with the rest of the empire.[42]

[41] *Issledovaniia*, pp. 6-8, 10-12.

[42] Lincoln, *Nikolai Miliutin*, pp. 85-100; Stanley J. Zyzniewski, "Russian Policy in the Congress Kingdom of Poland, 1863-81" (Harvard University Ph.D. dissertation), pp. 58-169; Leroy-Beaulieu, *Un homme d'état russe*, pp. 230-320; Kieniewicz, *Emancipation*, pp. 170-86, 259-62; Kostiushkov, *Krest'ianskaia reforma 1864 goda v Tsarstve*

N. A. Miliutin, like his friends Prince Cherkasskii and Iurii Samarin, favored cultural autonomy and opposed a policy of Russification in Poland. As Miliutin wrote in 1864:

> What concerns finally the question of the Russian language, it is obviously necessary to renounce firmly artificial measures to Russify the Poles in the kingdom. For that we do not have sufficient means. Besides experience has shown that an excellent knowledge of the Russian language—and even with full external Russification—often conceals an irreconcilable hatred for Russia. It is necessary to repeat: no external knowledge artificially inculcated can bring the Polish upper classes [*sosloviia*] any closer to Russia.[43]

But Miliutin's hatred (which Valuev once described as "bilious") of the Polish clergy, *szlachta*, and intelligentsia during the years immediately following the January Insurrection of 1863 led him to undertake a radical transformation of Polish society without the participation of its own intellectual leaders. These he hoped to replace with select Russians who shared his own vision of the future of the Polish people. The trouble was that few of the Russians who enlisted for service in Poland proved capable of distinguishing between administrative and cultural Russification; Miliutin's own closest friends and associates did make this distinction, but they were few in number and only served in Poland for several years. Needing a large number of Russians in Poland to carry out his ambitious projects, he was obliged to rely on the assistance of the Russian police and military apparatus in Poland controlled by Viceroy Berg. This reliance on Berg's agents tended to associate the implementation of Miliutin's program with the sort of "artificial" police, military, and administrative methods that

---

Pol'skom, pp. 121-466; Krzysztof Groniowski, *Realizacja reformy uwłaszczeniowej 1864 r.* (Warsaw: PWN, 1963); "O Nalozhenii i vzyskanii denezhnykh strafov s dukhovnykh lits," Wojewódzkie Archiwum Państwowe w Lublinie, Kanceliaria Gubernatora Lubelskiego, 1867, no. 72; *Vsepoddanneishii otchet o deistviiakh upravleniia generalpolitseimeistra v Tsarstve Pol'skom*, 2 vols. (Warsaw: V Tipografii Voenno-Politseiskogo Upravleniia, 1865-1866), 1: 3, 39-86, 151-61; 2: 1-16, 19-58, 96-105, 119-47; *O khode krest'ianskogo dela v Tsarstve Pol'skom* (St. Petersburg: Voennaia Tipografiia, 1864), pp. 1-2, 20-22; Russia, Komitet po delam Tsarstva Pol'skogo, *Sbornik pravitel'stvennykh rasporiazhenii po uchreditel'nomu komitetu v Tsarstve Pol'skom*, 7 vols (Warsaw: Tipografiia Upravlenii Varshavskogo Zhandarmskogo Okruga, 1867-1871), 3: 280-347; 4: 21-22; 5: 27; Amburger, *Geschichte der Behördenorganisation Russlands*, pp. 176, 182-83, 429-34; Reinke, *Ocherk*, pp. 111-30, 138-42, 148-51, 155-57, 163-70.

[43] "Obshchaia ob"iasnitel'naia zapiska ob ustroistve uchebnoi chasti v Tsarstvom Pol'skom," *Issledovaniia v Tsarstve Pol'skom*, 4: 19.

Miliutin and his supporters had identified with what they considered the unsuccessful conduct of Russian policy in Poland at the time of Paskevich and Nicholas I.[44]

Berg's soldiers and policemen introduced in Congress Poland the first completely Russian administration linking central authorities in Warsaw not only with *uezd* and *guberniia* officialdom but also with the Polish, Lithuanian, and Ukrainian-Uniate countryside. The increasing use of Russian in the administration of Miliutin's reforms as well as everyday government in Poland argued for the rapid expansion of Russian instruction in Polish schools, which was undertaken not by Ia. A. Solov'ev, Miliutin's candidate for the position of director of the Commission Education in Warsaw, but by Viceroy Berg's candidate, Friedrich Witte, a Lutheran Kurlander with a doctorate in jurisprudence from Dorpat University. Despite his origins and religion, Witte was an old-fashioned *chinovnik* who zealously, but somewhat mechanically, promoted Russian language and culture in Polish schools, first as director of the Commission of Education from 1866-1867 and then, after the abolition of the commission in 1867, as curator of the Warsaw School Region between 1867 and 1879. In the latter position he worked energetically under the direction of Minister of Education D. A. Tolstoi, an anti-Catholic, anti-Polish bureaucrat trained in the school of Nicholas I, to Russify all levels of education in Poland.[45]

Neither Miliutin's attempted "organic transformation" of Polish society nor Russification achieved the purposes of the Russian government in Poland. In 1864 Miliutin had seen the improvement of material conditions among the Polish peasants and the establishment of institutions of rural self-government and elementary schools independent of the control of the *szlachta* and Catholic clergy as highly significant changes on which "the entire future direction of the Polish nation may depend."[46] There can be little question that the peasant

---

[44] Valuev, *Dnevnik*, 2: 21; Krzysztof Groniowski, "Walka Milutina z Bergiem (spór o reorganizacje Królestwa Polskiego po roku (1863)," *Kwartalnik historyczny* 49 (1962): 891-906; "O russkom iazyke v Tsarstve Pol'skom," *Varshavskii dnevnik*, 1867, no. 188 (August 29), pp. 763-64; ibid., 1867, no. 189 (September 1), pp. 769-70; Zyzniewski, "Russian Policy in the Congress Kingdom of Poland," pp. 112-15, 170-81; A. I. Koshelev, *Zapiski* (1884; reprint ed., Newtonville, Mass.: Oriental Research Partners, 1976), pp. 142-184, 213-32.

[45] *Varshavskii dnevnik*, 1867, pp. 763-64, 769-70; Koshelev, *Zapiski*, p. 148; DBL, p. 873; D. A. Tolstoi, *Rechi i stat'i* (St. Petersburg: V. S. Balashev, 1876), pp. 12-15, 65; *Tsirkuliary po upravleniiu Varshavskogo uchebnogo okruga za 1867 g.* (Warsaw: Varshavskii Uchebnyi Okrug, 1867), pp. 28-35, 74.

[46] "Obshchaia ob"iastnitel'naia zapiska ob ustroistve uchebnoi chasti v Tsarstve Pol'skom," *Issledovaniia v Tsarstve Pol'skom*, 4: 16.

reforms introduced by Russia did benefit the Polish peasantry. This was, however, as Miliutin realized, only a first step, for peasant self-government in Poland could only produce the results desired by Russia if the Polish peasants would take some initiative themselves in financing education and improving agriculture. Unfortunately, the Polish peasant, because he was generally illiterate and lacked the requisite knowledge and experience, could not do very much to promote social and economic progress unassisted by the local intelligentsia and clergy. Miliutin and those who followed him, however, deliberately isolated the Polish intelligentsia from the peasants and took the clergy out of the school classroom. Furthermore, Russian interference in the Polish peasants' institutions of so-called self-government, and the gradual Russification of these institutions as well as of rural elementary schools during the 1870s, led to general apathy among the Polish peasants. Both Russification and measures against the Catholic church alienated the Polish peasant from the government rather than winning him over to the side of Russia, as Miliutin and Samarin hoped would happen when they journeyed through the Polish countryside in October 1863.[47]

The educated strata of the Polish population also do not seem to have been brought significantly closer to Russia by the policies pursued by the government after 1864. Russian officials, to be sure, repeatedly denied any attention to Russify in the sense of forcibly transforming them into Russians. Instruction in Russian for Poles, they said, had as its primary objective the training of good subjects of the tsar and uniting them with the Russian center of the empire.[48] Yet, there seems to be little question that learning Russian well did not substantially alter the educated Poles' attitude toward Russia; their "external Russification," to use Miliutin's words, often concealed an "irreconcilable hatred of Russia." Furthermore, Congress Poland continued to have a sizable professional intelligentsia that spoke, wrote, and thought in Polish. Even after the Polish universities at Warsaw and Wilno closed following the insurrection of 1830-1831, Poles still received professional training in Polish in specialized secondary schools, at the universities of Kraków and Lwów, or at the Medical-Surgical

---

[47] Kieniewicz, *Emancipation*, pp. 184-87; Zyzniewski, "Russian Policy in the Congress Kingdom," pp. 98-99, 217; A. A. Kornilov, "Reforma 19 fevralia 1864 goda v Tsarstve Pol'skom," in *Velikaia reforma: Russkoe obshchestvo i krest'ianskii vopros*, ed. A. K. Dzhivelov, S. P. Mel'gunov, and V. I. Picheta, 5 vols. (Moscow: I. D. Sytin, 1911), 5: 307-8.

[48] Tolstoi, *Rechi i stat'i*, pp. 14-15; *Svod vysochaishikh otmetok po vsepoddanneishim otchetam za 1896 g. general-gubernatorov, gubernatorov i gradonachal'nikov* (St. Petersburg: Gosudarstvennaia Tipografiia, 1898), pp. 34-38.

Academy (after 1857) and at the *Szkoła Główna* (1862-1869). In the 1860s there were some 15,000 Polish-trained doctors, pharmacists, technicians, engineers, officials, schoolteachers, and other professionally trained people in Congress Poland.[49] Their ranks were considerably augmented during the ensuing decades by further urbanization and economic expansion in Congress Poland. Their relative strength and continued identification with Polish culture and nationality almost assured the failure of Russification during the 1880s and 1890s. Congress Poland remained an essentially Polish world in which Russians could only feel uncomfortable as outsiders and strangers.[50]

Yet Russian military, police, and punitive measures, Miliutin's reforms, Russification, and administrative merger with the rest of the empire seemed to achieve at least one important objective of the Russian government in Poland: legal order was maintained without serious challenges by the Poles during the remainder of the nineteenth century. This objective was achieved by resorting to forms of military and police action and bureaucratic centralization resembling those employed by Paskevich and Nicholas I a generation earlier. Now, however, because of the gradual expansion of secondary and higher education and because of the internal reforms of the 1860s and 1870s, the Russian civil and military-police bureaucracies were in a better position than ever before to assure the strict control, policing, and regulation of educated society in both the Russian center and the borderlands of the empire. The crisis in Poland, it is important to note, coincided with the appearance of a Russian revolutionary intelligentsia that challenged the authority of the government and traditional society in Russia. It was this fatal coincidence of internal crisis in the Russian center and Polish borderlands of the empire that brought to power in St. Petersburg a new generation of officials who profoundly distrusted all autonomous social and political forces in Russia and who believed that her salvation could come only from firm authority and resolute action from above by the government.

The two Polish crises of 1830-1831 and 1863-1864 almost unavoidably had to have some effect on Russia's remaining privileged borderlands: Finland and the Baltic provinces. Finland, to be sure, suc-

---

[49] Ryszarda Czepulis-Rastenis, *"Klassa umysłowa": Inteligencja Królestwa Polskiego 1832-1862* (Warsaw: "Książka i Wiedza," 1973), pp. 123-25, 210-48; Czepulis-Rastenis, "Inteligencja," in *Przemiany społeczne w Królestwie Polskim 1815-1864*, ed. Witold Kula and Janina Leskiewiczowa (Wrocław: Ossolineum, 1979), pp. 337-41.

[50] A good illustration of this point is the defensive tone of the nationalistic chronicler of the history of the Russians in Warsaw: A. A. Sidorov, *Russkie i russkaia zhizn' v Varshave* (2nd ed.; Warsaw: V Tipografii Gubernskogo Upravleniia, 1901), p. 184.

ceeded in preserving her internal autonomy throughout the period 1830-1870; yet, even in Finland certain issues that remained unresolved during the reigns of Nicholas I and Alexander II contributed to an uncertain future for Finland's special position within the empire. The Baltic provinces, which were directly subordinated to the authority of officials in St. Petersburg, could not escape so easily the effects of the reassessments of Russian borderland policy and the intensified bureaucratic centralization that followed both insurrections in Poland. But the proverbial loyalty of the Baltic Germans to the tsar, and the internal development of Baltic society that was markedly different from that of the rest of the empire, prevented, as will be discussed in the following chapter, nationalistic and centralizing leaders of Russian society and officialdom from fully integrating the Baltic borderlands into the general social, cultural, and even administrative structure of the empire.

CHAPTER 9

THE BALTIC PROVINCES

Both Nicholas I and Alexander II confirmed the special rights and privileges of the Baltic towns and nobility. Nicholas I indicated his high opinion of the Baltic nobility early in his reign by replacing the willful Paulucci with General Karl Magnus von der Pahlen, a former Estland *Landrat* who occupied the position of Baltic governor-general from 1830 to 1845.[1] Nicholas, however, did not exempt the Baltic provinces from his general policy of administrative centralization, and by the early 1840s projects drafted by his officials for legal, educational, religious, peasant, and municipal reform in the Baltic provinces had greatly alarmed the *Ritterschaften* and the spiritual leaders or intellectuals associated with the Lutheran Church, Baltic secondary schools, and Dorpat University. During the 1840s, when L. A. Perovskii served as minister of the interior, interference in local Baltic affairs reached a high point, especially while E. A. Golovin was Baltic governor-general between 1845 and 1848.

Nicholas had no intention of unnecessarily alarming the Baltic nobles. On February 28, 1846, he tried to reassure them concerning his intentions by receiving personally a delegation of Livland nobles headed by former *Landmarschall* Alexander von Oettingen and *Landrat* Reinhold Samson von Himmelstiern. Beginning in German and continuing in French, the emperor told the Livland delegation that the rights and privileges of the Baltic nobility remained under "the protection of the law, under my protection." He commented in some detail concerning the codification of law, conditions among Baltic peasants, and the relations between the Orthodox and Lutheran churches, apparently wishing to suggest to the members of the Livland delegation that the Russian government had acted with care and restraint in dealing with matters affecting their interests. But he reminded them that for 130 years they have been Russians, not Germans, even though they call themselves Estlanders, Kurlanders, and Livlanders. Many of them had been his own "true servants." They were of knightly origin and he wanted them continue to be *chevalliers*

[1] DBL, pp. 572-73.

according to their rights and institutions; however, he urged them, "soyez aussi des Russes de coeur et d'âme."[2]

In 1867 Alexander II, in addressing the representatives of the Baltic estates at Riga, echoed his father's words (but now in Russian rather than in French or German) in asking them to become an integral part of the "Russian family" and to cooperate with him and his officials in carrying out "the measures and reforms which I consider necessary and useful."[3] By the mid-1860s Alexander II's officials had begun working energetically on a program of Baltic reform that aimed at increasing the use of the Russian language in Baltic schools and administrative offices, defending the interests of the Orthodox Church in the Riga eparchy, and bringing Baltic court and municipal institutions into a greater degree of conformity with those of the rest of the empire.

Efforts to integrate the Baltic region with the rest of the empire had, however, been relaxed and even virtually suspended during the preceding period of almost twenty years, beginning in 1848 with the appointment of Prince A. A. Suvorov as Baltic governor-general. Suvorov, a cosmopolitan Germanophile who had attended school in German Switzerland and then studied at the Universities of Paris and Göttingen, usually could be counted on to defend the point of view of the Baltic Germans in their disputes with the central ministries. The Baltic Germans benefited as well from policies of administrative decentralization and local-government reform favored by the tsar's influential advisers during the decade immediately following the Crimean War. It was especially during this decade that the *Ritterschaften* and other privileged Germans succeeded in delaying the introduction of Russian reforms into the Baltic provinces and in proceeding with local peasant and educational reform in a manner that defined even more sharply than before the separate identity of the Baltic provinces within the Russian Empire. At the same time, native intellectual leaders emerged who laid the foundations for the viable Estonian and Latvian national movements that appeared later in the nineteenth century.

Legal and court reform was of central importance for the integration of the borderlands into the general political, social, and administrative

---

[2] Woldemar von Bock (ed.), "R.J.L. Samson's Bericht über die Audienz der livländischen Deputation beim Kaiser Nikolaus am 28. Februar a. St. (aus des Verfassers handschriftlich hinterlassenem Tagebuche: 'Mein Aufenthalt in St. Petersburg im Jahr 1846')," in *Livländische Beiträge zur Verbreitung gründlicher Kunde von der protestantischen Landeskirche und dem Rechte und von ihrem Kampf um Geistesfreiheit*, vol. 2, no. 2, pp. 110-15, 118-19.

[3] Tobien, *Die Livländische Ritterschaft*, 1: 183.

structure of the empire. As was pointed out in chapter seven, such integration became possible in Russia only after the Second Section had completed its work early in the 1830s on the collection and systematization of Russian law, but the codification of local laws in the Caucasus, Poland, Finland, and the Baltic provinces was a necessary first step before such integration could be realized. All legal specialists working on local codes were instructed to model their collections after the Russian *Svod zakonov* and to modify local laws that conflicted in any way with Russian fundamental law. *Landrat* Reinhold Samson von Himmelstiern, who was assigned to the Second Section in 1829 to take charge of work on the Baltic code, received the same instructions. He differed, however, from the legal experts who worked on the other local codes (for example, Danilowicz, Turkułł, Zaborowski, and Hube) in that he was not only a university-trained (Leipzig, 1796-1798) and experienced jurist but also an elected officer of the Livland *Landratskollegium*, the executive organ that carried out the directives of the Livland Diet. Samson and other representatives of the Baltic *Ritterschaften* involved in the codification of the Baltic law were, then, no mere legal specialists employed by the Russian state, for they were in a position to speak with a voice of authority in defending the interests and prerogatives of their native provinces.[4]

The Baltic *Ritterschaften* had tried for centuries to persuade their Polish, Swedish, and Russian rulers to approve the codification of their local laws. Such codification, they believed, would provide a firm legal basis for Baltic rights and privileges and existing social order. Russian officials, on the other hand, attached importance to bringing local laws into conformity with the general laws of the empire, but they did not agree among themselves about how and when the convergence of Russian and local law was to occur in each individual borderland area. A centralizing administrator such as Minister of the Interior Perovskii viewed the provincial law codes primarily as materials to be used for the establishment of a system of laws, legal norms, and procedures that could be applied uniformly throughout the empire. M. A. Balugianskii, D. N. Bludov, D. V. Dashkov, and M. M. Speranskii, who directed the work in the Second Section, would seem to have preferred to publish a collection of Baltic laws as an appendix to the Russian *Svod zakonov*; but being more flexible on the subject of administrative and legal centralization than was Perovskii, they did not strongly object when Nicholas I decided at the end

---

[4] Maikov, *Vtoroe otdelenie sobstevennoi ego imperatorskogo velichestva kantseliarii 1826-1882*, pp. 222-24, 312-29; Staël von Holstein, "Die Kodifizirung des baltischen Provinzialrechts," pp. 276-80, 305-16; DBL, p. 667.

of the 1830s to approve and publish a separate Baltic code. Between 1840 and 1845 final corrections were made and details taken care of, including the extension to the members of the Estland and Livland *Ritterschaften* the exclusive right (which their Kurland brothers already possessed) to own manorial land (*Rittergüter*). In 1845 appeared the first two volumes of the *Provinzialrecht* on administrative law and the rights and privileges of the Baltic estates. A third volume on civil law was published in 1865.[5]

If publication of the first two volumes of the Baltic code in 1845 represented a victory for privileged Baltic Germans, it was a limited one. It provided, for example, no protection against certain provisions of the Law for the Evangelical-Lutheran Church in Russia of December 28, 1832, which authorized removal from office of pastors who officiated at mixed marriages between Orthodox and Lutheran believers, baptized children from such marriages, or allowed Orthodox Christians to take part in the divine services and sacraments of the Evangelical-Lutheran Church. These provisions were reinforced by including them in the new Russian criminal code of 1845 that was also published in the Baltic provinces.[6] In the 1860s, early 1870s, and, again, in the 1880s and 1890s the overwhelming majority of Baltic pastors was indicted, prosecuted, or punished on the basis of Russian criminal law, though for reasons that then were not considered criminal in most other European countries.

A more immediate threat to Baltic German special rights and privileges were the plans for educational reform outlined by S. S. Uvarov during the 1830s. In reporting to Nicholas I in 1835 that the new curator of the Dorpat School Region, Gustav Craffström, would reside in Dorpat, he informed the emperor that he would introduce at Dorpat the general University Statute of 1835. Although he then noted the need to proceed cautiously and to study the Baltic situation carefully, in the following year he proposed fairly far-reaching measures to reform Baltic education. These included the placing of secondary schools in the Dorpat School District directly under the control of

---

[5] Schmidt, *Rechtsgeschichte*, pp. 146-48, 175-79, 242-51; Staël von Holstein, "Die Kodifizirung des baltischen Provinzialrechts," pp. 313-16, 322-58; [Perovskii], "O neobkhodimosti vvesti v vsekh guberniiakh i oblastiakh Imperii russkie organicheskie zakony," CHTENIIA, 1865, bk. 3 (July-September), pt. 5, p. 184; A. E. Nol'de, *Ocherki po istorii kodifikatsii*, vol. 2: *Kodifikatsiia mestnykh zakonov pribaltiiskikh gubernii* (St. Petersburg: Senatskaia Tipografiia, 1914), pp. 355-419, 655-56.

[6] Schmidt, *Rechtsgeschichte*, p. 284; Gert Kroeger, "Die evangelisch-lutherische Landeskirche und das griechisch-orthodoxe Staatskirchentum in den Ostseeprovinzen 1840-1918," in *Baltische Kirchengeschichte*, ed. Reinhard Wittram (Göttingen: Vandenhoeck & Ruprecht, 1956), pp. 177-78.

Curator Craffström, the use of more Russian in Baltic schools, and the appointment of Russians to fill teaching and administrative vacancies in secondary schools as well as at Dorpat University. Obtaining Nicholas I's approval of these measures, Uvarov instructed Craffström to make knowledge of Russian a requirement for admission at the University of Dorpat by no later than 1841. On January 20, 1837, the general School District Statute of June 25, 1835, was applied to the Baltic provinces, ending the role of Dorpat University professors in secondary school administration. Secondary schools now came directly under the administrative direction of Curator Craffström. In May 1837 Uvarov filled the vacant post of the director of the Mitau Gymnasium with a Russian, and in a report of June 1838, which Nicholas I also approved, he announced his intention of giving a preference to Russians in filling future teacher vacancies and of introducing instruction in the Russian language at the gymnasium.[7]

Uvarov only partly succeeded in carrying out his proposed measures. He expanded and improved Russian-language instruction in Baltic schools. Native Russian-language teachers were assigned to Baltic secondary schools, among whom were a number of dedicated and well-prepared language specialists who published useful dictionaries and textbooks and other teaching aids for Baltic gymnasia and *uezd* schools. Special attention was paid to the preparation of additional Russian-language teachers at the teachers' seminary in Dorpat, and Russian elementary schools were established in Dorpat, Jakobstadt, and Mitau. A Ministry of Education circular of January 1837 instructed all Baltic *uezd* schools to teach at least four hours of the Russian language and two hours of Russian history and geography a week. Competency in Russian came to be required for obtaining academic degrees at Dorpat University, and by the mid-1840s all students matriculating there were required to pass a rigorous entrance examination in Russian.[8] But Uvarov soon encountered Baltic German resistance to his measures for the reform of education in the Baltic

[7] [Alexander Buchholtz], *Fünfzig Jahre russischer Verwaltung in den baltischen Provinzen* (Leipzig: Duncker & Humblot, 1883), pp. 21-25; Uvarov, *Desiatiletie Ministerstva narodnogo prosveshcheniia*, pp. 48-49, 56-57; E. V. Petukhov, *Imperatorskii tur'evskii universitet za sto let ego sushchestvovaniia (1802-1902)*, 1: 353-56; 421-28; [S. N. Shafranov], *Istoricheskii obzor mer pravitel'stva dlia usileniia v ostzeiskom krae sposobov k izucheniiu russkogo iazyka* (St. Petersburg: I. Ogrizko, 1863), p. 14.

[8] S. G. Isakov, *Russkii iazyk i literatura v uchebnykh zavedeniiakh Estonii XVIII-XIX stoletii*, 2 vols. (Tartu: Tartuskii Gosudarstvennyi Universitet, 1973), 1: 91-92, 106-7, 139-41; Rozhdestvenskii, *Istoricheskii obzor deiatel'nosti Ministerstva narodnogo prosveshcheniia*, pp. 323-24; P. Maikov, "Vvedenie russkogo iazyka v ostzeiskikh guberniiakh," *Russkaia starina* 130 (April 1907): 60.

provinces, especially after details concerning his plans had been leaked to the German-language press in Russia and abroad. The adverse publicity proved to be somewhat embarrassing for him, and he was obliged to shelve the Russification of the administration and instructional staff of Baltic schools. As for Dorpat University, it remained a thoroughly German institution. Several Russians who were added to its faculty during the 1830s and 1840s taught in German, though the Baltic German who lectured on Russian law, Ewald Tobien, did lecture in Russian. In 1848 Uvarov, in response to criticism concerning the low level of Russian proficiency in Baltic schools, opposed "further measures of compulsion," arguing that they would do more "harm than good" and that much progress had already been made in the "development of the Russian language in the Baltic region."[9]

With regard to Baltic elementary schools, Uvarov was obliged to trim his sails even sooner. In 1837, when the administration of Baltic schools was removed from Dorpat University and placed in the hands of the Dorpat School District curator, Uvarov tried to bring the Lutheran elementary schools directly under the control of his ministry. The Livland, Estland, and Kurland *Ritterschaften* quickly united in opposing administration of these schools by the Ministry of Education. They emphasized the religious nature of elementary education in the Baltic provinces and the role of the Lutheran clergy and the local nobility in seeing to it that the peasants acquired basic skills in reading, arithmetic, and religious instruction in preparation for confirmation. Even Craffström pointed to the many practical difficulties he would have in trying to supervise and in applying Russian regulations to the education of Lutheran Estonian and Latvian peasants. In consideration of these difficulties and of the insistence of the Baltic nobility on having a Lutheran and religious education for the Estonian and Latvian peasants, the Russian Committee of Ministers decided in 1838 that all Baltic rural elementary schools were to be organized and administered independently of the Ministry of Education and according to the model provided by Livland's church school system.[10] Nominally, this system functioned under the general guidance and direction of the Main Administration for the Ecclesiastical Affairs of the Foreign Confessions, an agency of the Ministry of the Interior. But

[9] [Buchholtz], *Fünfzig Jahre*, pp. 25-42; Petukhov, *Imperatorskii iur'evskii universitet*, 1: 427-36; Ewald Tobien, "Vvedenie v istoriiu russkogo prava: Pervaia lektsiia na russkom iazyke v Derptskom Universite 30 iunia 1844 g.," *Zhurnal Ministerstva narodnogo prosveshcheniia* (1845, no. 10), pp. 65-80; Rozhdestvenskii, *Istoricheskii obzor*, p. 324.

[10] Speer, *Das Bauernschulwesen im Gouvernement Estland*, pp. 135-40.

neither the main administration nor the ministry ever exercised effective control over of what went on in the rural schools of the Baltic provinces.

It was during the 1840s, when bureaucratic centralizer Perovskii served as minister of the interior, that the German landowners and clergy began to take seriously the task of carrying out the stipulations of earlier legislation calling for obligatory peasant schooling and literacy in the Baltic provinces. Especially important, the *Ritterschaften* and clergy then organized seminaries to train Estonian and Latvian teachers at Dorpat and Walk in Livland, Kuda in Estland, and Irmlau in Kurland. Schools gradually replaced domestic instruction as a means of teaching reading skills in preparation for confirmation. Supported financially by the local nobility and the peasants, these schools were the point of departure for the Lutheran rural school system in the Baltic provinces that would teach reading, arithmetic, and religion to the majority of Estonian and Latvian children by the 1870s.[11] They were educated in schools watched over by German landowners and clergy and supported by the resources of local society. The Russian Ministry of the Interior had, of course, the right to supervise Baltic rural schools and the activities of the Lutheran Church. In Perovskii's time, however, the Ministry of Interior showed little evidence of exercising this right. Indeed, Perovskii and his colleagues in the Russian government were scarcely in a position to do much about elementary education anywhere in the empire. Accordingly, short of closing the Lutheran schools, there was little they could do about the emergence of a rural school system in the Baltic provinces that set the Estonian and Latvian peasants more and more apart from their social peers elsewhere in the empire.

The somewhat less than three hundred Lutheran pastors of the Baltic provinces were closely associated with the local nobility by virtue of their German nationality, education, economic and social standing, and involvement in local government and school administration on the lowest level of the parish. Since the time of Peter the Great the *Ritterschaften* had considered recognition of the Augsburg Confession and the special position of the Evangelical-Lutheran *Landeskirchen* in the Baltic provinces to be among the most important rights and privileges granted to them by the rulers of Russia. They certainly realized that the pastors and the Lutheran Church provided a useful instrument for the molding of the peasants into God-fearing

[11] Ibid., pp. 158-61, 198-200, 227-28, 257-64; Tobien, *Die Livländische Ritterschaft*, 1: 242; *Ocherki istorii shkoly i pedagogicheskoi mysli narodov SSSR*, p. 473.

Christians who accepted the authority of their German landowners as part of the natural order of things in this world. Until the mass conversions to Orthodoxy of the 1840s the religious authority of the Lutheran Church was unchallenged in the Estonian and Latvian countryside.[12]

During the period 1830-1870, however, the influence of the Lutheran Church on the lives of the Estonian and Latvian peasants gradually declined. The Law for the Evangelical-Lutheran Church in Russia of December 28, 1832, was an important landmark, for it placed the Lutheran *Landeskirchen* of the Baltic provinces directly under the supervision of a bureaucratic organ located in St. Petersburg, the General Consistory for the Evangelical-Lutheran Church in Russia. Until then the Lutheran consistories in the Baltic provinces had operated under the general supervision of the Justice College for Livland and Estland Affairs and, after 1818, the Main Administration for the Ecclesiastical Affairs of the Foreign Confessions, which allowed the Baltic consistories and *Ritterschaften* to run local church affairs with a minimum of interference on the part of the central authorities. Until 1832 the Baltic clergy and nobility successfully resisted the efforts of St. Petersburg officials responsible for the administration of the foreign confessions to create a centralized direction for Russia's Lutherans similar to the Roman Catholic Ecclesiastical College that had existed since 1801.[13]

The law of December 28, 1832, also defined more precisely the relationship of the Evangelical-Lutheran Church to the Russian state church. The Russian government then refused to give the Lutherans in the Baltic provinces the same special rights in mixed marriages with Orthodox Christians that Lutherans enjoyed in Finland, where since 1812 the father's religion determined the church to which the children of such mixed couples belonged as long as they resided in the Grand Duchy. In the Baltic provinces the law of 1832 called for the enforcement of Russian religious legislation concerning mixed marriages, obliging parents to commit themselves in writing to baptize their children and to raise them as Orthodox Christians. Furthermore, as has already been mentioned, Lutheran pastors who did not observe the special rights the Orthodox Church enjoyed in the

[12] Wilhelm Lenz, "Zur Verfassung- und Sozialgeschichte der baltischen evangelisch-lutherischen Kirche 1710-1914," in Wittram (ed.), *Baltische Kirchengeschichte*, pp. 110-29.

[13] R. Staël von Holstein, "Zur Geschichte des Kirchengesetzes vom Jahre 1832," BM 52 (1901): 128-76.

Russian Empire were faced with the prospect of possibly being prosecuted under the pertinent paragraphs of the Russian criminal code.[14]

In 1836 an Orthodox bishopric was established in Riga and a seminary for Orthodox priests opened in Pskov, located near the eastern border of Livland. The Russian government then pursued a general policy of promoting Orthodoxy throughout the empire and of founding bishoprics in such hitherto neglected areas as Congress Poland, Kamchatka, and Russian America. In Riga the Russian authorities initially seemed to have been mainly interested in increasing their influence over the well-established Russian Old-Believer community and in ministering to the religious needs of the growing number of Russian Orthodox merchants in the Baltic provinces and of Baltic German families that had become Orthodox through marriage.[15] They did not pay much attention to the Estonian and Latvian peasants until 1841, when a large number of them suddenly and unexpectedly requested to be accepted into the Orthodox Church and established direct contact with Russian Bishop Irinarkh in Riga. These peasant requests were rejected and social unrest in the countryside was suppressed, but in the ensuing four-year period the Russian government reassessed its policy with regard to the conversion of Estonians and Latvians to Orthodoxy. Beginning in the school year 1842-1843, for example, Latvian and Estonian language instruction was introduced at the Orthodox seminary in Pskov, and Estonian and Latvian translations of an Orthodox prayer book and catechism were published in Dorpat in 1843.[16]

In 1841 Baltic Governor-General Pahlen, Minister of the Interior A. G. Stroganov, and influential Third Section Chief Alexander von Benckendorff had all opposed the conversion of Baltic peasants to Orthodoxy. These peasants, on the basis of rumors whose origins have never been adequately explained, then believed that the tsar had promised them land in the warm south if they accepted Orthodoxy. However naive these peasants may seem to have been, they were also, in their own way, clearly trying to defend their self-interests. In

---

[14] Woldemar von Bock, "Memorial von 1857 betreffend die rechtliche Lage der protestantischen Kirche in den deutschen Ostseeprovinzen," *Livländische Beiträge*, vol. 1, pt. 2, pp. 153-54; Kroeger, "Die evangelisch-lutherische Landeskirche und das griechisch-orthodoxe Staatskirchentum in den Ostseeprovinzen 1840-1918," in *Baltische Kirchengeschichte*, pp. 177-80

[15] Kroeger, "Die evangelisch-lutherische Landeskirche," p. 182; [Buchholtz], *Fünfzig Jahre*, pp. 42-43.

[16] Hans Kruus, *Talurahva käärimine Lõuna-Eestis XIX sajandi 40-ndail aastail* (Tartu: Eesti Kirjanduse Kirjastus, 1930), pp. 46-166, 175.

numerous petitions they presented at the time, they protested, in effect, against the terms of the emancipation settlement earlier in the nineteenth century that left them at the mercy of short-term leases, uncontrolled corvée obligations, and the overwhelming social, economic, and political power of the landowners. Their lot then seemed all the more intolerable following the crop failures of 1838-1840 and the famine of 1841. Riga Bishop Irinarkh helped to strengthen their hopes for assistance from the tsar by receiving them sympathetically and taking their names if they expressed a wish to become Orthodox believers. In August 1841, however, Nicholas I forbade Irinarkh to accept any additional petitions from Estonian and Latvian peasants, and in October he was removed from his post.[17]

Within the Russian government such influential figures as Uvarov and N. A. Protasov, the chief procurator of the Holy Synod, saw no reason not to accept Estonians and Latvians into the Orthodox Church. In October 1841 L. A. Perovskii became minister of the interior; he also supported a more active defense of the interests of Orthodoxy in the Baltic provinces. When Benckendorff died in September 1844, what Iurii Samarin sarcastically described as the Ministry of Baltic (*ostzeiskie*) Affairs in St. Petersburg lost a good measure of the powerful influence it had had until then on Nicholas I's Baltic policy. In 1845 new Third Section Chief A. F. Orlov joined forces with Protasov, and they persuaded Nicholas I to replace Pahlen with General E. A. Golovin as governor-general in Riga. In this way a major obstacle in the way of bringing Estonians and Latvians into the Orthodox Church was removed from the scene. The new governor-general received instructions not to permit anyone to obstruct the conversion of Estonians and Latvians to Orthodoxy but, at the same time, to do nothing in violation of the special rights and privileges the rulers of Russia had granted to the Baltic provinces. Both Golovin and Riga Bishop Filaret were told that conversion to Orthodoxy had to be based not on material rewards and incentives but on religious conviction alone.[18]

Approximately 100,000 Estonians and Latvians of a total population

[17] Ibid.; Samarin, *Sochineniia*, 10: 455-622; I. Ia. Steprane, *Krest'ianskoe dvizhenie v Lifliandii v 40-kh godakh XIX veka* (Riga: Candidate-dissertation *avtoreferat*, Academy of Sciences of the Latvian SSR, 1966), pp. 9-10, 15-19.

[18] Kruus, *Talurahva käärimine Lõuna-Eestis*, pp. 175-82; Samarin, *Sochineniia*, 10: 432-63; E. A. Golovin, "Vsepoddanneishii otchet po upravleniiu Baltiiskim kraem s maia 1845 po fevral' 1848 goda," CHTENIIA, 1871, bk. 2 (April-June), pt. 5, p. 99; *Sbornik materialov i statei po istorii Pribaltiiskogo kraia*, 4 vols. (Riga: A. I. Lipinskii, 1876-1882), 4: 465.

of 775,000 in Livland, or about 13 percent of the total population of that province, converted to Orthodoxy between 1845 and 1848. Renewal of Estonian and Latvian interest in the Orthodox Church began in Riga, even before Pahlen was replaced by Golovin. The decision of the Russian authorities early in 1845 to allow a small number of Herrnhuters to enter the Orthodox Church suggested to peasants outside Riga that their acceptance of Orthodoxy might gain for them Russian support—again at a time of crop failure and famine in the Baltic provinces—for the improvement of their economic and legal position vis-à-vis the local German landowners. For several years tens of thousands of these peasants refused to believe reiterated official statements informing them that no material benefit would result from conversion to Orthodoxy. Governor-General Golovin welcomed Estonian and Latvian interest in Orthodoxy, but he considered it his responsibility to point out to his superiors that the Russian government and Orthodox Church lacked the resources to accommodate a large number of new converts and that the mass conversion of Estonian and Latvian peasants could only alarm the local German clergy and nobles. Nicholas I, however, continued to insist until as late as 1848 that the Estonians and Latvians should not be denied the right to become Orthodox believers. For, as he told the delegation of Livland nobles he received in February 1846, he could not allow that a "Lutheran who wishes to convert to Orthodoxy out of genuine religious conviction should be prevented from doing so." He realized that the straitened circumstances of the Livland peasants might have something to do with their attraction to Orthodoxy, and, to assure that conversion would be based on religious conviction, decreed a six-month waiting period as a condition for final acceptance into the Orthodox Church. He reminded the Livland delegation, however, that the German Lutheran pastors often seemed alien to their Estonian and Latvian parishioners because of their close personal and social ties with the landowning nobility. In Finland, Lutheran country pastors had quite a different relationship to their parishioners, and there was "not a single example of a Finnish peasant who had ever been converted to the Greek-Russian Church."[19] Be this as it may, it is to

[19] Kruus, *Talurahva käärimine Lõuna-Eestis*, pp. 165-263; N. A. Leisman, *Sud'ba pravoslaviia v Lifliandii s 40-kh do 80-kh godov XIX stoletiia* (Riga: G. Gempel', 1908), pp. 60-64, 71; Kabuzan, *Narodonaselenie Rossii v XVIII-pervoi polovine XIX v.*, p. 162; Horst Garve, *Konfession und Nationalität: Ein Beitrag zum Verhältnis von Kirche und Gesellschaft in Livland im 19. Jahrhundert*, Wissenschaftliche Beiträge zur Geschichte und Landeskunde Ostmitteleuropas, no. 110 (Marburg: J. G. Herder-Institut, 1978), pp. 60-68; E. A. Golovin, "Mnenie i rasporiazheniia pribaltiiskogo general-gubernatora

be noted that by 1849 the Estonian and Latvian peasants had become convinced that conversion would bring them no material benefits and, consequently, they lost their interest in the Orthodox Church.

The Lutheran Church's loss of so many of its Estonian and Latvian members shook the very foundations of traditional Baltic society. Even with the first indications of the Estonians' and Latvians' interest in Orthodoxy at the beginning of the 1840s, Iurii Samarin wrote more than a century ago, it was "impossible not to understand that the conversion to Orthodoxy of the common people would cut to the very root the exclusive domination of the Baltic privileged strata and bring about in the entire region such a basic change that its consequences would be incalculable."[20] To be sure, the entire peasant population did not become Orthodox, but the total spiritual domination of Lutheranism over the Latvians and Estonians had been broken.

The Baltic nobility and clergy made surprisingly little fuss officially about the conversion movement during the years 1845-1848. There was of course hardly any basis for official protest, because it was obvious that the handful of Orthodox priests then in Livland could not have set into motion tens of thousands of Estonian and Latvian peasants. Yet, as is documented by the proceedings of the Lutheran synods and by letters, memoranda, and entries into diaries written during these years, there is no mistaking that the conversions gave rise to deeply felt concern among the Livland clergy and nobility about the possible consequences of the foothold that Orthodoxy had gained in Livland for the future of Baltic German society.

As details of Uvarov's plans for Baltic education came out into the open, it became apparent that Baltic leaders had been equally troubled a few years earlier. In 1839, following the publication of one of Uvarov's reports to Nicholas I in the Augsburg *Allgemeine Zeitung*, the acting *Landmarschall* of Livland, Karl von Bruiningk, formally protested in a petition presented to Nicholas I against Uvarov's alleged violation of the educational and language rights of the Livland nobility and clergy. This petition registered the concern of the Livlanders, however, in a fairly circumspect manner. Others attacked Uvarov more directly, especially Friedrich Parrot, one of the founders of Dorpat University, and Karl Ulmann, the rector at Dorpat during 1839-1841. They both stressed the importance for Russia of preserving the Lutheran religion and the Germanic character of education in the

Golovina po delam prisoedineniia Liuterov v Lifliandii k pravoslaviiu," *Sbornik materialov i statei po istorii Pribaltiiskogo kraia*, 4: 576-91; Bock (ed.), "R.J.L. Samson's Bericht" in *Livländische Beiträge*, vol. 2, pt. 2, pp. 112-15.

[20] Samarin, *Sochineniia*, 10: 566.

Baltic provinces in view of their importance as an intermediary for European enlightenment and knowledge in Russia.[21]

An even more basic formulation of Baltic provincial ideology soon followed with the anonymous publication in 1841 of Otto Mueller's *Die livländischen Landesprivilegien und deren Confirmation.* Mueller, a future mayor of Riga and delegate of the Riga Council to the Livland Diet, treated Livland privileges as not only the rights of separate estates, but as the result of a gradual historical and organic development of Germanic law in the Baltic provinces. He condemned administrative centralization as a form of harmful despotism; he saw in the historical privileges and institutions of self-goverment the basis of legal order and the well-being of Livland, which had, he believed, stood in a contractual relationship to Russia since the time of Peter the Great. As did Carl Schirren and other defenders of Baltic autonomy a generation later, Mueller argued that it would be a violation of Livland rights to reform or alter that province's rights and privileges unilaterally and arbitrarily without the consent of both contracting parties.[22]

A few years later a competing Russian Baltic ideology was formulated by Iurii Samarin, then a young Ministry of the Interior official assigned to a special commission charged with the working out of a new system of municipal government for Riga. Minister of the Interior Perovskii had recommended as early as 1841 that Riga's special rights be abolished and replaced by Russian municipal laws and institutions, and in 1845 he established the commission to which Samarin had been assigned. Between 1845 and 1848 this commission, which was headed by Adolf Stackelberg and A. V. Khanykov, collected a mass of materials concerning Riga's legal, political, and economic institutions, including a detailed and lengthy history of Riga prepared by Samarin and based on archival sources: *The Social Order of the Town of Riga: Studies of the Investigation Commission Named by the Ministry of the Interior, 1845-1848.* At the request of Governor-General Suvorov in 1848, the Stackelberg-Khanykov Commission was dissolved and its recommendations were not carried out.[23] Its work,

[21] [Buchholtz], *Fünfzig Jahre*, pp. 30-55; Gert von Pistohlkors, *Ritterschaftliche Reformpolitik zwischen Russifizierung und Revolution*, Göttinger Bausteine zur Geschichtswissenschaft, no. 48 (Göttingen: Musterschmidt, 1978), pp. 62-67, 70-79, 100-102; Garve, *Konfession und Nationalität*, pp. 60-68.

[22] Pistohlkors, *Ritterschaftliche Reformpolitik*, pp. 114-21; Garve, *Konfession und Nationalität*, pp. 82-84.

[23] [Buchholtz], *Fünfzig Jahre*, pp. 78-80, 179-80; B. E. Nol'de, *Iurii Samarin i ego vremia* (Paris: Imprimerie de Navarre, 1926), pp. 37-43; [Perovskii], "O neobkhodi-

however, provided useful background materials for other Ministry of the Interior officials who would, in 1877, extend the Russian Municipal Reform of 1870 to the Baltic provinces. Working for the commission also helped to make one of tsarist Russia's most renowned and effective publicists an expert on Baltic affairs.

The first coherent exposition of a Russian view of the Baltic question was contained in Samarin's unpublished "Letters from Riga" of 1848. They were read or communicated to a fairly wide circle of friends, acquaintances, and officials in St. Petersburg and Moscow during the second part of 1848 and early in 1849. In his "Letters from Riga" Samarin contemptuously relegated the privileges of the Baltic nobles and guilds to the Middle Ages, arguing that they were not in keeping with the historical development of the modern world. The Russian state, he emphasized, had a right and responsibility to improve conditions among Estonian and Latvian peasants, to allow these peasants to leave the church of their German conquerors and become Orthodox Christians, and to defend the rights of many Russians living in the Baltic provinces who had been disenfranchised by the laws of the German towns and *Ritterschaften*. He saw no reason to permit privileged local Germans to reject reforms proposed by the Russian government on the grounds that such reforms were contrary to the historical privileges of the Baltic nobility and towns.[24] The author of "Letters from Riga," however, had not been trained only in Perovskii's and Uvarov's school of administrative centralization, for he was also a historian and a brilliant writer. He was particularly dangerous to the Baltic Germans because he so persuasively stated views widely held by Russian officials and religious leaders about the need to subordinate local Baltic rights to what they perceived to be the general welfare of the empire.

Baltic German leaders always made it a point to keep informed about everything said and done in the Russian capital that was likely to affect the interests of their three provinces. They were, therefore, quite aware that in the early and mid-1840s high-ranking Russian officials tended to blame the religious and social disturbances in the

mosti vvesti v vsekh guberniiakh i oblastiakh Imperii russkie organicheskie zakony," CHTENIIA, 1865, bk. 3 (July-September), pt. 5, p. 184; [Samarin], *Obshchestvennoe ustroistvo goroda Rigi: Issledovaniia Revizionnoi Kommisii naznachennoi Ministerstvom vnutrennikh del* (St. Petersburg: Tipografiia Ministerstva Vnutrennikh Del, 1852), republished with minor editorial changes in vol. 7 of Samarin's *Sochineniia*.

[24] Samarin, "Pis'ma iz Rigi," *Sochineniia*, 7: 3-160. Cf. E. C. Thaden, *Conservative Nationalism in Nineteenth-Century Russia* (Seattle: University of Washington Press, 1964), pp. 133-34, 136.

Livland countryside on the poor economic situation of the Estonian and Latvian peasants. This was also the view of Nicholas I, who bluntly told representatives of the Livland nobility in 1846 that the peasant legislation of 1819 had not produced the beneficial results anticipated by Alexander I. Iurii Samarin, prior to being assigned to the municipal government commission in Riga, worked five months in St. Petersburg for the Ministry of the Interior on Baltic agrarian questions. In 1845, 1846, and 1848 another young official employed by that same ministry, future Minister of Education A. V. Golovnin, prepared four long reports that detailed how Baltic Germans had conquered and exploited the Estonian and Latvian peasants over the centuries and how they had used agrarian legislation during the nineteenth century to serve their own interests, usually to the detriment of the Estonians and Latvians. Fortunately for the Baltic Germans, Minister of the Interior Perovskii, who previously had served in the Ministry of the Court and Appanages, was extremely conservative in all that pertained to the peasants of the Russian Empire. Most important of all, he often opposed the projects proposed by Minister of State Domains P. D. Kiselev, the principal advocate within the government of applying to the Baltic provinces special legislation that had already been introduced into the western *gubernii* to regulate landowner-peasant relations.[25]

In Livland consideration of agrarian reform began immediately following the religious and peasant unrest of the summer of 1841 in the Deliberating Assembly of the Diet (*delibierender Adelskonvent*) and in a circle of nobles led by Hamilcar Baron von Fölkersahm. There was no agreement on the subject of agrarian reform among the Livland nobles. Fölkersahm's group wanted to separate peasant land (*Bauernland*) from the manors of the nobility, to make it possible for peasants to purchase land, and to move rapidly in the direction of replacing the corvée with money rents. Conservatives in the Livland nobility, on the other hand, feared that any basic changes in the existing economic and social arrangements in the Baltic provinces would undermine the position of the nobility. They, therefore, emphasized

[25] [Perovskii], "O neobkhodimosti," CHTENIIA, 1865, bk. 3, pt. 5, p. 184; A. V. Golovnin, "Kratkii istoricheskii ocherk otnoshenii lifliandskikh krest'ian k pomeshchikam so vremeni pokoreniia kraia germanskimi vykhodtsami do nashikh vremen," Manuscript Section, Saltykov-Shchedrin Public Library, Leningrad, f. 208, no. 7, fol. 68; Golovnin, "I. O volnenii lifliandskikh krest'ian 1841 g., II. O sobytiiakh v Lifliandii v 1845 g., III. O polozhenii krest'ian v sobstvenno-russkikh guberniiakh i v Lifliandii," ibid., no. 6; Tobien, *Die Agrargesetzgebung*, 2: 91-93, 98-101, 109-11, 118-20, 139-44, 331-32, 428-520; Samarin, *Sochineniia*, 10: 439-40.

the need to maintain patriarchal order in the countryside and to reinforce the privileged position of the corporations of the nobility. In February 1842 the *Landtag* gave qualified approval to Fölkersahm's approach to agrarian reform, apparently because Third Section Chief Benckendorff and Baltic Governor-General Pahlen had led them to believe that the emperor favored such reform. But when conservative leaders of the Livland nobility joined the so-called St. Petersburg Commission that had been founded in the first part of 1842 to discuss proposals for Baltic agrarian reform, they quickly discovered that Emperor Nicholas and his principal advisers were extremely reluctant to move forward with proposals of peasant reform. Armed with this knowledge, they easily persuaded the Livland Diet at its next meeting in December to reverse itself and to reject Fölkersahm's ideas on reserving *Bauernland* for the exclusive use of the peasants. But the St. Petersburg Commission, which became the permanent Baltic Committee in 1846, continued to meet, and the renewal of peasant and religious unrest in Livland during 1845 and 1846 once again called attention to the urgency of peasant reform in the Baltic provinces. At the same time, the existence of Fölkersahm's reform party in Livland offered the government an opportunity to experiment, as Alexander I had done at the beginning of the century, with reform projects that were still politically unfeasible in the Russian provinces of the empire. But ample precautions were taken to assure the protection of the interests of the Baltic nobility by including among the twelve original members of the Baltic Committee nine men who were of Baltic German origin. Three of them were elected by the Livland Diet; two, namely Samson von Himmelstiern and Fölkersahm, were Livland *Landräte* and experts on Baltic peasant affairs who had been appointed to the committee by the Russian government at the recommendation of Governor-General Golovin. Only three of seven government members of the Baltic Committee were not matriculated Baltic noblemen: Minister of the Interior Perovskii, his assistant I. G. Seniavin, and Minister of State Domains Kiselev.[26]

The final peasant legislation for the Baltic provinces, which Alex-

---

[26] Pistohlkors, *Ritterschaftliche Reformpolitik*, pp. 74-114; idem, "Juhan Kahk's Interpretation of Feudal Agrarian Economy in Estonia and Northern Livonia, 1825-1850: A Review Article," *Journal of Baltic Studies* 9 (1978): 367-74; Tobien, *Die Agrargesetzgebung*, 2: 48-65, 89-141; R. Staël von Holstein, *Baron Hamilkar von Fölkersahm* (Riga: W. F. Häcker, 1907), pp. 13-63; Juhan Kahk, *Murrangulised neljakümnendad* (Tallinn: "Eesti Raamat," 1978), pp. 72-166; A. V. Golovnin, "Obshchii vzgliad na istoriiu lifliandskikh krest'ian," Manuscript Section, Saltykov-Shchedrin Library, f. 208, no. 6, fols. 114-15; Golovnin, "Kratkii istoricheskii," ibid., no. 7, fols. 3-4.

ander II approved for Estland in 1856, for Livland in 1860, and for Kurland in 1863, was based on ideas and principles developed by Fölkersahm and his supporters during the 1840s in interaction with the Russian government and his conservative opponents in the Livland Diet. Despite their differences, Fölkersahm's group and the conservatives both gave first priority to defending the special rights and prerogatives of the Baltic nobility and to maintaining its monopoly of economic and political control of the Estonian and Latvian countryside. The resolutions accepted by the Livland Diet in 1847 represented a compromise between Fölkersahm and his opponents. Fölkersahm and his supporters no longer insisted on the rapid abolition of the corvée, while his opponents made concessions on the questions of separating peasant from manorial land and peasant ownership. The compromise reached in 1847 also took into consideration the views of the Russian government, which relied on the legal and agricultural expertise of the Baltic nobles, and allowed them to draft all basic projects for agricultural reform; but the Russian government reserved for itself the final right of review. On July 9, 1849, partly because Perovskii prevailed over Kiselev, Nicholas I approved the 1847 resolutions of the Livland Diet in the form of a temporary law to be tried out over the six-year period 1849-1855. Following the European Revolution of 1848, these were years of extreme caution in Russia with regard to all aspects of peasant-landowner relations, enabling the Baltic nobles to delay the introduction of money rents and to attempt the revision of the temporary law of 1849. At the beginning of the reign of Alexander II, however, discussion of the terms of the emancipation of the Russian serfs, which limited the freedom of action of landowners much more than what Fölkersahm had proposed, made it clear that it was in the interest of the Baltic corporations of the nobility to settle for a separate Baltic peasant reform along the lines of the 1849 temporary law for Livland. Baltic agrarian legislation approved between 1856 and 1863 confirmed for the Estonian and Latvian peasants the right to buy land (*Bauernland*), but on terms determined not by Russian officials but by local market conditions and the Baltic German nobles.[27] This meant that the patterns of property ownership, social organization, and agricultural production in the Baltic countryside

---

[27] Steprane, *Krest'ianskoe dvizhenie v Lifliandii v 40-kh godakh XIX veka*, p. 23; Pistohlkors, *Ritterschaftliche Reformpolitik*, pp. 110-12; Tobien, *Die Agrargesetzgebung*, 2: 166-240; Juhan Kahk, "On the Agrarian Policy in the Baltic Provinces in the 1840s (An Attempt at an Analytic Approach to Political Development)," in *Studia Historica in Honorem Hans Kruus*, ed. J. Kahk and A. Vassar, pp. 326-27, 329-30, 336-39; Staël von Holstein, *Baron Hamilkar von Fölkersahm*, p. 105.

continued to differ markedly from those of other parts of the empire. During the last half century of tsarist history, this, more than perhaps anything else, was the principal foundation upon which the separate identity of the Baltic provinces rested.

The leaving of Baltic peasant reform in the hands of the Baltic German nobles themselves, whether in the Baltic Committee or the provincial diets, illustrated a tendency during the last decade of Nicholas I's reign to relax centralizing pressures in certain parts of the empire. This relaxation would seem to have begun in the Caucasus, where attempts during the thirties and forties to rule this region with Russian officials according to standard Russian laws and procedures had produced not only administrative confusion but also open resistance to Russian authority. From 1844 to 1854 a newly appointed viceroy, M. S. Vorontsov, reestablished traditional territorial units in the Caucasus, respected Georgian, Armenian, and Moslem laws, and gave responsible positions to native Caucasian officials in an effort to win the confidence and cooperation of the local nobility.[28] Even in the western *gubernii* Minister of Education Uvarov inclined during the 1840s toward a flexible policy in the use of Polish teachers in secondary schools; the need to take into consideration the sensibilities of the Baltic German nobility, clergy, and intellectuals also obliged him to modify his program for increasing the use of Russian in Baltic school administration and instruction. Baltic Governor-General Golovin recommended a more flexible religious policy than that pursued by Perovskii and the Holy Synod. Perovskii himself supported the Fölkersahm proposals approved by the Livland Diet in 1847 against the objections of Kiselev.

In February 1848 Prince Aleksandr Suvorov became Baltic governor-general. Golovin was replaced for two reasons: because local Germans, no doubt to a large extent without justification, associated his name with conversion to Orthodoxy and the unpopular Stackelberg-Khanykov Commission, and because Emperor Nicholas had decided that only a conciliatory policy, not measures of compulsion, would be the most effective means to bring the local inhabitants of the Baltic provinces closer to the rest of Russia. As governor-general, Suvorov, certainly with the approval of Nicholas I, carefully cultivated the good will and friendship of the Baltic German nobility and townsmen. When he arrived in the Baltic provinces in March 1848, he insisted on speaking

[28] Laurens Hamilton Rhinelander, Jr., "Viceroy Vorontsov's Administration of the Caucasus," *Kennan Institute for Advanced Russian Studies, Occasional Papers*, no. 98; Rhinelander, "The Incorporation of the Caucusus into the Russian Empire: The Case of Georgia, 1801-1854" (Columbia University Ph.D. dissertation, 1971).

German with local officials, even when they were willing to try Russian. In Riga, according to Samarin in a letter to M. P. Pogodin of April 1848, he even scolded Orthodox priests for their excessive proselytism and commented to a bystander: "Ce sacré *Pravoslavie* [Orthodoxy], on l'a employé ici pour faire toutes sortes de cochonneries."[29] In dealing directly with Bishop Filaret, Suvorov was deferential but firmly requested that Orthodox priests and monks no longer accept petitions from Estonian and Latvian peasants concerning their grievances against Baltic German officials, pastors, and landowners, for these concerned only the Russian secular authorities. Filaret, who felt that Suvorov was preventing him from defending the interests of Orthodox Estonians and Latvians, protested in vain to the Holy Synod and was transferred to Kharkov by the end of 1848. Meanwhile, Suvorov learned how unpopular the municipal reforms proposed by the Stackelberg-Khanykov Commission were among privileged Riga townsmen. He probably also saw in the commission's projects a challenge to his own authority as governor-general. In January 1849 he was in St. Petersburg, where he attended special meetings of the Baltic Committee on Riga municipal reform. Here he criticized the Stackelberg-Khanykov Commission's recommendations in detail and managed to have them referred for further examination to a new commission in Riga to be chaired by himself as Baltic governor-general. As a result, work on Baltic municipal reform was virtually suspended until after Suvorov left the Baltic provinces in 1861.[30]

Iurii Samarin was the principal Baltic expert representing the Ministry of the Interior at the January 1849 meetings of the Baltic Committee. By this time a fairly large number of individuals in Moscow and St. Petersburg knew about Samarin's "Letters from Riga," including Minister of the Interior Perovskii, and Minister of State Domains Kiselev. If Samarin believed that the letters would help Perovskii and Kiselev to win battles over the Baltic question, he was very much mistaken because Nicholas I strongly disapproved of public discussion of any aspect of state policy. Suvorov, whose policy and actions Samarin had criticized in the presence of a number of persons in the

[29] Samarin, *Sochineniia*, 7: xcii, 12: 260-61; Samarin to P. A. Valuev, November 1848, Manuscript Section, Institute of Russian Literature, Academy of Sciences, USSR, Leningrad, f. 559, op. 57, fols. 1-3.

[30] I. Listovskii, "Filaret Arkhiepiskop Chernigovskii," *Russkii arkhiv* 25 (1887), pt. 3, pp. 214-38; [Buchholtz], *Fünfzig Jahre*, pp. 175-81; "Ein pseudonymer Brief des Staatsraths Chanykov an den Fürsten Suworow vom Jahre 1848," BM 43 (1896): 73-87; Thaden, "The Russian Government," in *Russification*, p. 51; Samarin, *Sochineniia*, 7: lix-lxxii.

second part of 1848, formally accused Samarin of having violated his oath as a Russian official through unauthorized revelation of confidential information to which only he was privy as a specialist employed by the government. Samarin was arrested in March 1849, kept in the Peter-and-Paul Fortress for twelve days, and then personally interrogated by Nicholas I. The emperor upbraided him for having stirred up trouble among Germans and Russians and for having attacked German families that had served Russia loyally and provided her with up to 150 generals. In turning public opinion against the government, Nicholas suggested, Samarin was really preparing a repetition of the Decembrist uprising of 1825, however good his intentions might have been. But Nicholas treated Samarin more generously than he did Dostoevskii a month later. Samarin was not subjected to additional punishment; he was told to continue serving, "as you have sworn to do, faithfully and truthfully, but do not attack the government."[31] This advice also applied to others who still might have wished to oppose the new orientation of the government's policy in the Baltic provinces.

Being predicated on good relations and cooperation with the *Ritterschaften* and patricians of Riga and discouraging interference in local Baltic affairs by the central ministries in St. Petersburg, this new policy orientation lessened the government's influence over areas of social, economic, and religious activity to which Nicholas I continued to attach considerable importance. What happened to Baltic peasant reform between 1847 and 1860 is one illustration of this point. During this period Nicholas I, Alexander II, Golovin, Suvorov, Perovskii, and S. S. Lanskoi (minister of the interior, 1855-1861) all ended up supporting the projects and proposals prepared and presented by the Baltic *Ritterschaften* and the Baltic Committee rather than those drafted by such critics of Baltic peasant conditions and agricultural legislation as Ministers of State Domains Kiselev and M. N. Murav'ev. To be sure, no one then seems to have been fully aware of the extent to which the peasant legislation prepared by Fölkersahm's group in the 1840s and, finally, approved as law in 1860 would be instrumental in setting the Baltic provinces apart socially and economically from the rest of the empire. By 1860, however, it was clear to Baltic German nobles that their interests would probably be adversely affected by the introduction of Russian agrarian legislation into the Baltic prov-

---

[31] Samarin, *Sochineniia*, 7: lxiv-c, 637-38; 12: 258-65, 334-37; Samarin to D. N. Sverbeev, November 1848, Manuscript Section, Lenin Public Library, Moscow, f. 265, karton 52, ed. khr. 11, fols. 1-16.

inces, and at least some Russians realized that it was hardly prudent to approve special peasant legislation for the Baltic region shortly before the promulgation of peasant statutes for the Russian provinces of the empire.[32]

Two other examples of the government's declining influence over the internal development of the Baltic provinces pertained to the use of the Russian language in schools and in the bureaucracy and to the relative position of the Orthodox Church in Baltic society. With regard to the obligatory use of Russian as the business language for government offices in the Baltic provinces, this was first suggested by Perovskii and Golovin in 1847 and then approved by the Committee of Ministers and confirmed as law by Nicholas I in January 1850. Suvorov, however, persuaded the government to introduce the obligatory use of Russian gradually and in four stages, for he wanted to avoid serious disruption of government work in the Baltic provinces, especially on the *uezd* level, where few officials had an adequate knowledge of Russian. After January 1, 1858, only officials competent in Russian were to be appointed to new positions in state offices in the Baltic provinces. By the end of 1858 Suvorov and Finnish Governor-General Berg, the future viceroy of Poland, induced Alexander II to postpone indefinitely the carrying out of the language law of 1850. In 1867 another Baltic governor-general, P. P. Al'bedinskii, complained that it was above all because of Suvorov's inactivity that so little progress had been made in increasing the official use of Russian in the Baltic provinces, commenting that during the preceding seventeen years posts "filled by officials knowing the Russian language had been for the greater part filled by those not knowing it at all."[33]

The measures introduced by Nicholas I to improve and expand the instruction of Russian in Baltic secondary schools remained in effect throughout the 1850s, but they were not vigorously enforced. Russian teachers were isolated figures in Baltic German schools, and moral and group pressure was put on them to give students "no. 1" (*ochen' khorosho*) grades on their Russian examinations, even when not deserved, so that they could advance to the next class, graduate, and

[32] Tobien, *Die Agrargesetzgebung*, 2: 172-89, 224-28, 235-37; Thaden, "The Russian Government," p. 37.

[33] Tobien, *Die Livländische Ritterschaft*, 1: 360; [Alexander Buchholtz], *Deutschprotestantische Kämpfe in den baltischen Provinzen Russlands*, pp. 299-307; PSZ, 2nd ser., 25, 1st sec., pp. 5-6, no. 23,796, January 3, 1850; P. P. Al'bedinskii, "Vsepoddanneishii otchet po voprosu ob ispolnenii zakona 3 ian. 1850 g. o vvedenii russkogo deloproizvodstva v Pribaltiiskikh guberniiakh," Central State Historical Archive, Leningrad, f. 1016, op. 1, d. 968, fols. 79-83.

then move on to Dorpat University. To make matters worse, local school administrators did not give a very high priority to the Russian language and did not offer in their schools a sufficient number of hours of Russian instruction to enable students to acquire the level of proficiency in Russian then formally required by law. Neither Suvorov, his successor Wilhelm Lieven, nor Georg von Bradke, who became curator of the Dorpat School Region in 1854, took measures to remedy this situation. Indeed, in 1862 Bradke, in response to a petition of Baltic secondary-school teachers, approved new rules that reduced the passing grade in Russian to "no. 2," or simply *khorosho*. This action officially sanctioned the relaxation of efforts to improve a system of Russian language instruction that was unacceptable to Russian teachers in the Dorpat School Region for use in educational institutions supported by the Russian state.[34]

Governors-General Suvorov and Lieven were also lax in promoting the interests of the Orthodox Church in the Baltic provinces. The 100,000 Estonians and Latvian converts were organized into 72 parishes in 1848, increasing to 150 by 1870. An Orthodox ecclesiastical seminary opened its doors in Riga in 1847, and in 1850 rules were issued for newly founded Orthodox schools, of which there were 107 parish and 252 auxiliary schools with 9,500 pupils by 1870. All this, to have been done properly, required generous monetary and strong administrative support. The Holy Synod, unfortunately, was not then in a position to obtain the additional funds needed to build churches and schools that could compete with those already well established by the Lutherans in the Baltic provinces. Locally, the German landowners generally refused to contribute either their time or money to the support of the activities of the Orthodox Church, and they controlled the local administration upon which the Russian government had to depend in order to carry out its policies. Both Suvorov and Lieven usually took the side of the privileged Germans in their disputes with the Orthodox clergy in the Baltic provinces. This meant that the Orthodox clergy was in a disadvantageous position in trying to promote the interests of their church and parishioners, about one-fourth of whom became disenchanted with Orthodoxy by the 1860s and made every effort to return to the Lutheran Church of their ancestors.[35]

[34] [S. N. Shafranov], *Istoricheskii obzor mer dlia usilenii v ostzeiskom kraiu sposobov k izucheniiu russkogo iazyka*, pp. 29-30, 33-36, 47-58.

[35] Samarin, *Sochineniia*, 9: 112-22, 157-58; M. Stoliarov, "Pravoslavnye shkoly v Pribaltiiskom krae," *Zhurnal Ministerstva narodnogo prosveshcheniia*, 1895, October, pp. 19-37; "Uchrezhdenie rizhskoi dukhovnoi seminarii," *Sbornik materialov i statei po*

Nicholas I died midpoint in Suvorov's governor-generalship. Since 1848 Nicholas' Baltic policy had been conciliatory toward the *Ritterschaften* but, as elsewhere in the empire, repressive toward the press, censorship, and intellectual life in general. Such measures as limiting enrollment at Dorpat University, temporarily closing bookstores in Dorpat and Riga, and harassing and exiling a handful of *Literaten* did not have a particularly adverse effect on the interests of the Baltic nobility. Indeed, these measures probably helped the conservative wing in the corporations of the Baltic nobility to win political battles in their respective diets. Thus, in 1851 the Livland nobility did not reelect Fölkersahm as *Landmarschall*, and replaced him with a political opponent, Gustav von Nolcken, who worked to dismantle the temporary agrarian legislation approved in 1849 and to retain patriarchal relationships in the Livland countryside. Nolcken's group in the Livland Diet achieved a partial victory in 1856 by passing in the *Landtag* new resolutions that substantially altered the legislation the Russian government had provisionally approved in 1849. This victory, however, was short-lived, for the discussion of peasant and other reforms in Russia strengthened the position of Fölkersahm's followers (Fölkersahm died in 1856), who, in 1857, once again took over control of the Livland Diet.[36]

The relaxation of censorship at that time helped to give birth to a reform-minded political press in the Baltic provinces. Although a Baltic liberal and reform movement never fully developed, a new generation of journalists trained in law or philosophy at Dorpat and German universities and writing for the newly founded *Baltische Monatsschrift* and *Revaler Zeitung* and the revitalized *Rigaer Zeitung* revealed to a broad spectrum of Baltic Germans what was then going on in Russia and Europe. These young journalists brought home to their readers the lesson that they could not, if they wished to avoid assimilation, afford to lag behind in the era of Great Reforms in Russia.[37]

The liberal journalists in the Baltic provinces who advocated agrar-

istorii Pribaltiiskogo kraia, 4: 592-98; "O povinnostiakh i daniakh pravoslavnykh v pol'zu liuteranskoi tserkvi v Lifliandii," ibid., pp. 598-617; Leisman, *Sud'ba pravoslaviia v Lifliandii s 40-kh do 80-kh godov stoletiia*, p. 111.

[36] [Buchholtz], *Fünfzig Jahre*, pp. 203-35; DBL, p. 550; Tobien, *Agrargesetzgebung*, pp. 214-40.

[37] Reinhard Wittram, *Liberalismus baltischer Literaten: Zur Entstehung der baltischen politischen Presse* (Riga: G. Löffler, 1931), pp. 11-13, 39, 62-70, 85-98; Wittram, *Meinungskämpfe im baltischen Deutschtum während der Reformepoche des 19. Jahrhunderts* (Riga: E. Bruhns, 1934), pp. 14-17, 25-26; Pistohlkors, *Ritterschaftliche Reformpolitik*, pp. 110-14; "Lifländische Korrespondenz," BM 6 (1862): 372, 586.

ian, judicial, constitutional, political, and social reform at the beginning of the 1860s were usually *Literaten*. One notable contributor to the *Baltische Monatsschrift*, Woldemar von Bock, was a Livland nobleman. In 1862 he brought the liberal reform program before the Livland Diet; however, the Livland nobles were unwilling to share any of their special political and economic advantages other than to relinquish their exclusive right to own manorial land. Otherwise, they limited their reform efforts to minimal modification of the Livland *Bauernverordnung* of 1860 in favor of the peasantry and to discussion of possible changes in the antiquated Baltic judicial system. But discussion of judicial reform among the *Ritterschaften* and towns produced no concrete results, for the Baltic nobles could not bring themselves to accept a unified judicial system for all three provinces. The Russian government disapproved of such a unified system as well. As P. A. Valuev told Livland Marshal of the Nobility Paul Lieven in 1864, even friends of the Baltic Germans in St. Petersburg condemned all efforts of the provinces "to join together in a special administrative group isolated from the empire."[38]

It is important to note that the government allowed the Baltic diets and the Baltic Committee to prepare the principal legislative projects complementing the peasant laws of 1856, 1860, and 1863 for Estland, Livland, and Kurland. This was no small concession in view of the circumstances of the 1860s: renewed unrest in the Baltic countryside; Estonian and Latvian petitions to introduce into the Baltic provinces the Russian peasant statutes of February 19, 1861; anti-Baltic-German agitation in the Moscow Slavophile and nationalistic press; and the projects of bureaucratic centralizers in St. Petersburg. All this put considerable pressure on the government to take out of the hands of the German landowners such matters as the passport regulations controlling the eastward migration of Estonian and Latvian peasants, abolition of the corvée and of corporal punishment, and peasant self-government.

The government did see to it that the law of 1866 on peasant self-government in the Baltic provinces forbade direct landowner interference in the affairs of the peasant rural community, but on the whole the matriculated Baltic nobles succeeded remarkably well in retaining their dominant position in the countryside. In the latter part of the nineteenth century agricultural capitalism based on well-organized

[38] R. Staël von Holstein, *Fürst Paul Lieven als Landmarschall von Livland* (Riga: W. F. Häcker, 1906), pp. 86-177; Staël von Holstein, "Materialien zu einer Geschichte des livländischen Landesstaates im neunzehnten Jahrhundert" (Welding Collection, Bremen), 5: 234-35, 288-306, 349-51, 353-454.

manorial and peasant-proprietor production and on the growing market for agricultural products in the Russian Empire flourished in the Baltic provinces. By the beginning of the twentieth century Baltic German publicists liked to contrast the achievements and productivity of Baltic agriculture with the chronic problems of the Russian peasant and agricultural economy. The other side of the coin, however, was that the so-called Fölkersahm reforms ignored the economic, social, and political interests of the overwhelming majority of the Estonian and Latvian peasantry, namely, the landless laborers in the countryside.[39]

Russian officials in St. Petersburg hesitated, however, to allow local control by Baltic nobles and townsmen of other aspects of reform activity. At the beginning of the 1860s they viewed the Baltic provinces differently than they did Congress Poland, where they had begun to extend their authority only during the preceding two decades, while they had been intervening directly in Baltic internal affairs since the eighteenth century. Thus, an influential figure such as Grand Duke Konstantin Nikolaevich had been willing to associate his own name and reputation with a separate, Polish internal administration for Congress Poland; but he was among the most consistent advocates of general Russian reforms for the Baltic provinces. The critical examination of current Baltic problems and the reform projects of the Baltic liberals began as early as 1861-1862 in organs controlled by Konstantin Nicholaevich's naval ministry, namely the *Morskoi sbornik* and the *Kronshtadtskii vestnik*. But Alexander II had confirmed Baltic privileges in 1856, and kept a Russian defender of these privileges, Prince Suvorov, in his post as governor-general until 1861, replacing him then with a Baltic German, Wilhelm Baron von Lieven. The role played by Suvorov and Lieven until the end of 1864 in defending the viewpoint and reform projects or legislation that originated with privileged Baltic Germans was greatly facilitated by the tendency in official circles in the late 1850s and at the beginning of the 1860s to favor decentralization of government and to encourage local initiative in social and economic affairs. In 1864, for example, Lieven was able to obtain approval for representatives of the *Ritterschaften* and towns to

---

[39] Thaden, "The Russian Government," pp. 38-42, 71; Tobien, *Agrargesetzgebung*, 2: 241-301. The problem of the Baltic landless laborers has been analyzed by Adolf Agthe, *Ursprung und Lage der Landarbeiter in Livland*, Ergänzungsheft, no. 29, Zeitschrift für die gesamte Staatswissenschaften (Tübingen: H. Laupp, 1909). On the organization of agricultural production in the Baltic provinces at the beginning of the twentieth century, see Schlingensiepen, *Der Strukturwandel des baltischen Adels in der Zeit vor dem Ersten Weltkrieg.*

meet as a central judicial commission that was to submit a proposal for Baltic judicial reform to the governor-general by November 1, 1865. Yet in 1862, Alexander II, at the time that he approved the basic principles for the reform of courts in the empire, had announced that the principles of Russian judicial reform would apply to "all regions governed under special institutions." Any proposals for a separate judicial reform for the three Baltic provinces that the Baltic central judicial commission might have proposed clearly would not have been in keeping with Alexander II's announcement. However, there was never a direct confrontation between the central judicial commission and St. Petersburg officials because attacks in the Moscovite press soon made Lieven's position untenable in Riga and because nothing concrete resulted from the labors of the commission.[40]

At the beginning of 1865 a new Baltic governor-general, P. A. Shuvalov, a native Russian and the future chief of the Third Section and ambassador to England, arrived in Riga. The decision in the latter part of 1864 to replace Lieven with Shuvalov marked an important turning point. After this change, further reforms in the Baltic provinces were no longer made by the Baltic nobility and townsmen in consultation with the Russian government, but by Russian officials in St. Petersburg in consultation with representatives of Baltic society. By this time Poland had been pacified and the major Russian reforms (other than military) for the interior of the empire had been promulgated. Those in high posts in St. Petersburg seemed to have agreed that Russian reforms, with due allowances made for local conditions and circumstances, were to be extended to the empire's borderlands. When and to what extent this would be done obviously depended on a number of considerations. As regards the Baltic provinces, Shuvalov did not advocate full merger with the empire. He belonged to the so-called "German" party that preferred to base Russian policy in the borderlands on cooperation with the landowning nobility, and he wanted to introduce Russian reforms gradually, with due consideration given to the material interests of the privileged elements of local society. Resistance to any reform decided upon by the Russian authorities was not to be tolerated, however. Or, as Minister of the Interior Valuev, another high official usually identified with the "German" party, bluntly

[40] S. G. Isakov, *Ostzeiskii vopros v russkoi pechati 1860-kh godov*, Turku Riikliku Ülikool, Toimetised, no. 107 (Tartu: Riikliku Ülikool, 1961), pp. 14-16; V. V. Ivanov, "Korrespondentsiia iz portov," *Morskoi sbornik*, vol. 56, no. 11 (November 1861), pp. 57-59; vol. 57, no. 1 (January 1862), p. 64, no. 2 (February 1862), p. 154; Tobien, *Die Livländische Ritterschaft*, 1: 92-93, 107-8, 489-91; Thaden, "The Russian Government," pp. 34-35, 42-43.

told Livland Marshal of the Nobility Paul Lieven in 1864: "The special interests of the provinces must . . . converge with those of the empire."[41]

Alexander II reinforced Valuev's confidential words to Lieven three years later, when, on June 15, 1867, he asked representatives of the four Baltic corporations of the nobility in Riga to cooperate with his officials in carrying out measures that he considered "necessary and useful." Two weeks earlier, on June 1, 1867, Alexander had confirmed a decision of the Committee of Ministers to enforce the language law of 1850 that had made Russian the obligatory business language of all state authorities in the Baltic provinces. This time Russian officialdom acted rapidly and purposefully, and by January 1, 1870, Russian had been officially introduced as the business language of all branches of the central government in the Baltic provinces, including the military, excise, customs, assay, and post offices, the Riga Office of the State Bank, and the administration of Dorpat University and Baltic secondary schools.[42] The all-encompassing character of the government's measures to establish Russian as the official language of state authorities in the Baltic provinces, the rapidity with which it carried out these measures between 1867 and 1870, and the firmness with which it disregarded protesting petitions all made it clear to Baltic Germans that the rights and privileges confirmed by Russian emperors since 1710 could no longer be relied upon as a dependable foundation for the special position of their provinces within the Russian Empire.

Alexander III was to be the first Russian ruler who refused to confirm Baltic rights and privileges. These rights and privileges, however, had lost much of their previous meaning once Alexander II and his advisers overcame their hesitations about introducing into the Baltic provinces reforms they considered necessary but knew would be unacceptable to the local privileged Germans, whose response was almost immediate. Such polemical Baltic-German works as Woldemar von Bock's *Livländische Beiträge* (1867) and Carl Schirren's *Livländische Antwort an Herrn Juri Samarin* (1869) challenged Russia's right to enforce the empire's religious laws and to introduce centralizing or Russifying reforms in the Baltic provinces. These men insisted, as Otto Mueller had done before them, on the contractual nature of the religious, linguistic, and self-government rights that had been granted

[41] Thaden, "The Russian Government," pp. 25-26, 34, 36, 38; Staël von Holstein, "Materialien zu einer Geschichte des livländischen Landesstaates," 5: 306.

[42] PSZ, 2nd ser., 25, 1st sec., pp. 845-46, no. 44,651, June 1, 1867; Michael H. Haltzel, "The Baltic Germans," in *Russification*, pp. 139-40; Thaden, "The Russian Government," ibid., p. 47; Rozhdestvenskii, *Istoricheskii obzor*, p. 578.

to the Baltic estates in 1710 and confirmed by Russian rulers beginning with Peter I. The best documented and argued Russian attempt to refute this defense of Baltic historical rights and privileges was contained in the volumes of *The Borderlands of Russia* (*Okrainy Rossii*) published by Iurii Samarin between 1868 and 1876. Although Samarin was in no way a spokesman for official Russia, few Russians disagreed with him that Russian interests must take precedence over local Baltic concerns and that only those Baltic rights and privileges that were compatible with the general welfare of the empire should be retained. Baltic German publicists who questioned this proposition publicly had to do so from abroad. Between 1866 and 1869 the leading champions of Baltic separate identity, Woldemar von Bock, Julius Eckardt, and Carl Schirren, were obliged to leave Russia and to relocate in Germany.[43]

After 1870 the exploitation of long-standing connections held by prominent members of the *Ritterschaften* in the government and in Russian conservative, landowning circles was certainly the most dependable way through which to work for preservation of the Baltic provinces' separate identity within the empire. Thanks to these connections and to the political skills of outstanding marshals of the nobility, *Landräte*, and other Baltic leaders, zemstvos were never introduced into the Baltic provinces, the introduction of Russian courts and schools was delayed until the end of the eighties, important concessions in the area of religious policy were obtained on several occasions, and the local institutions of the four *Ritterschaften* continued to exist until 1917. These concessions were based not on historic rights and privileges but on the natural alliance between the Baltic nobility and large landowners and hereditary nobles in Russia, who dominated, even into the twentieth century, Russian politics and government to a degree unknown in any other major European country.

Perhaps most important of all the concessions made to privileged Baltic Germans was the decision of Alexander II and his advisers not to proceed immediately with the Russification of Baltic schools. Between 1863 and 1870 Ministers of Education Golovnin and Tolstoi saw to it that existing programs for the teaching of Russian in the Baltic provinces were thoroughly studied. Unsatisfied with the progress that had been made, they recommended a number of measures to expand and improve instruction in Russian in Baltic schools. Both Golovnin

---

[43] Haltzel, "The Baltic Germans," pp. 124-33; Carl Schirren, *Livländische Antwort an Herrn Juri Samarin* (1869; reprint ed., Hannover-Döhren: Harro von Hirschheydt, 1971); Thaden, "Samarin's *Okrainy Rossii* and Official Policy in the Baltic Provinces," *Russian Review* 33 (1974): 405-15.

and Tolstoi repeated Uvarov's earlier recommendation of subordinating the Lutheran elementary schools to the direct control of the Ministry of Education. In the second part of the 1860s, Baltic Governor-General P. P. Al'bedinskii and Dorpat School Region Curator Alexander Keyserling cooperated with Golovnin and Tolstoi in improving Russian language instruction in Baltic schools, but they insisted on retaining the Germanic character of education at Dorpat University and in the secondary schools. Plans to bring the Estonian and Latvian elementary schools under the Ministry of Education were frustrated by the refusal of Baltic nobles to continue financial support for these schools unless they remained under the direction of the Lutheran clergy and local representatives of the four corporations of the nobility. There can be little question that had Minister of Education Tolstoi had his way, the government would have moved forward with the Russification of elementary schools in the Baltic provinces at about the same pace that it did in Congress Poland. He did not, however, seem to have been able to find a good answer to the argument that the Russian government still lacked the resources to fund elementary education among the Estonians and Latvians and that it was therefore not prudent to subordinate the Lutheran rural schools to the control of the Ministry of Education and risk the withdrawal of financial support from the German landowners.[44]

Around 1870 a majority of school-age Estonians and Latvians received at least several years of elementary instruction in their own native languages. The postponement of educational Russification until the end of the 1880s gave Estonians and Latvians another two decades to continue long-term efforts to spread literacy and raise the cultural level of their two peoples. It was at this time that the first Estonian and Latvian song festivals were held and literary and cultural societies were organized. Because the Baltic peasant self-government law of 1866 opened to Estonians and Latvians new areas of activity free of German-landowner control, they demonstrated greater willingness than before to contribute to the support of local schools. In Estland, for example, the number of children attending Lutheran elementary schools doubled between 1866 and 1869, and by 1875 75 percent of all school-age children in Estland attended village schools. As a result, almost

[44] Isakov, *Russkii iazyk i literatura v uchebnykh zavedeniiakh Estonii XVIII-XIX stoletii*, 2: 3-22; Rozhdestvenskii, *Istoricheskii obzor*, pp. 471-75, 576-81; Speer, *Das Bauernschulwesen im Gouvernement Estland*, pp. 298-311; [Shafranov], *Istoricheskii obzor mer pravitel'stva* (1863); [Krišjānis Valdemārs], *Ob uchebnykh zavedeniiakh Pribaltiiskogo kraia v otnoshenii k russkomu iazyku*, tr from German (St. Petersburg: F. S. Sushchinskii, 1866); Samarin, *Sochineniia*, 9: 208-9.

all Estonians and Latvians born during the 1850s and 1860s were literate by the time they became adults. During the period 1874-1883, 95 percent of the Estland and Livland and 60 percent of the Kurland peasants and townsmen recruited into the Russian army were literate, compared with 25 percent for the empire as a whole.[45]

Baltic rural elementary schools, of course, needed teachers. School-teachers, together with successful peasant-proprietors who acquired land as a result of the agrarian laws of 1856, 1860, and 1863, provided the principal initial social base for the emerging Estonian and Latvian national movements. Independent Estonian and Latvian newspapers, which emerged during the relaxed censorship early in the reign of Alexander II, found a steadily expanding audience among predominantly literate Estonian and Latvian peasants and townsmen. By the time the government undertook to Russify the entire instructional program of Dorpat University and of all Baltic elementary and secondary schools, the Estonians and Latvians already had at least an elementary education in their own languages as well as their own national organizations and cultural institutions. By this time they were very much aware of their own national identity; their cultural and social development had advanced too far to be reversed by the policy of cultural Russification introduced by Alexander III and K. P. Pobedonostsev during the 1880s.[46]

Neither Baltic German leaders nor Russian officials anticipated or welcomed the emergence of Estonians and Latvians as self-sufficient cultural and national communities. Germans and Russians usually agreed that Estonians and Latvians, being small peasant peoples without a historical past, were not intended for independent cultural and political development. It was assumed that sooner or later the socially mobile elements among the Estonians and Latvians had to be either Germanized or Russified.[47] Russians were reasonably certain that, in the long run, they would manage to assimilate these elements, assuming of course the prevalence of Russian as a language of administration and, eventually, in the schools and public life of the Baltic provinces.

[45] Speer, *Das Bauernschulwesen*, pp. 256-57, 264-68, 391; Andrejs Plakans, "The Spread of Literacy Among the Latvians" (unpublished paper, presented at the Sixth Conference of Baltic Studies, May 1978, Toronto); Toivo U. Raun, "The Development of Estonian Literacy in the 18th and 19th Centuries," *Journal of Baltic Studies* 10 (1979): 115-26; A. G. Rashin, *Naselenie Rossii za 100 let (1811-1913 gg.): Statisticheskii ocherk*, pp. 304-5.

[46] Cf. the essays on the Latvians and Estonians by Plakans and Raun in *Russification in the Baltic Provinces and Finland*.

[47] Isakov, *Ostzeiskii vopros*, pp. 148, 172-73, 178-80; Wittram, *Liberalismus baltischer Literaten*, pp. 49-50, 83-84, 99-100.

The Estonians and Latvians did not in any way seem to pose a threat to Russia: they were much smaller peoples than the Ukrainians and Belorussians (the total population of Estland, Livland, and Kurland ca. 1860 was only a little more than 1.6 million); they seemed powerfully attracted to Russia, for a large part of them had converted to Orthodoxy and had petitioned for the introduction of Russian zemstvos, courts, and peasant legislation until the 1880s; and there was no omnipotent church hierarchy that could be accused, as was the Roman Catholic hierarchy in Lithuania and Poland, of conspiring with the enemies of Russia. The measures Russia introduced in the Baltic provinces aimed, therefore, at weakening the position of the Germans in local life rather than that of the Estonians and Latvians, who steadily developed their respective national cultures and societies during the Russo-German political battles of the 1860s, 1870s, and 1880s. By the time Estonians and Latvians began to demand separate national, cultural, and even political rights for themselves, it was too late for the Russians to use effectively in the Baltic provinces measures of national repression similar to what they had tried earlier in the Ukraine, Belorussia, and Lithuania.

The Finns, across the Gulf of Finland from Estland, also developed nationally and culturally during the nineteenth century. They had several advantages over the Estonians and Latvians to the south. Living in the Grand Duchy of Finland and administered locally apart from the rest of the empire, they were not subject to recruitment into the Russian army and had little direct contact with Russian officialdom as such. They had never been serfs and the social and national cleavages that separated them from their Swedish-speaking officials and nobles had never been as great as in the Baltic provinces and in the lands dominated by the Polish *szlachta*. Indeed, a significant proportion of the Swedish-speaking educated elite identified itself with the Finnish language and culture and provided a first generation of leaders for the Finnish national movement. Swedish-speaking officials, in their turn, performed an important service to the Finnish cause by using the same sort of connections the Baltic German nobles had in the Russian capital to preserve Finland's separate identity and rights and privileges, enabling Finland to make her own decisions about her internal political, cultural, and economic development. The absence of serious internal social and religious unrest in Finland gave Russian outsiders few occasions and pretexts for interfering in Finnish affairs. On the contrary, until the 1890s Russia's representatives in Finland usually supported the efforts of Finnish officialdom to preserve and even to further develop the internal autonomy of the Finnish Grand

Duchy. As will be discussed in the following chapter, these efforts were particularly successful during the period 1830-1870. Alexander II and his advisers, however, stopped short of granting the Finns the constitutional guarantees they had sought ever since Alexander I promulgated the Constitutional Charter for Congress Poland in 1815.

CHAPTER 10

FINLAND

$\mathbf{F}$INNS FAMILIAR with the attitudes of Russian officialdom toward the borderlands were pessimistic about the future of Finnish autonomy within the empire. To protect Finnish interests they had tried to obtain an explicit, written guarantee of Finland's special rights and privileges similar to the Polish Constitutional Charter of 1815; but Alexander I, after initial hesitations, decided against granting the Finns a constitution. In 1826 A. A. Zakrevskii's success in persuading Nicholas I to abolish the Committee for Finnish Affairs left executive and legislative power in Finland concentrated in the hands of the governor-general. A Finnish Diet might have served as a counterpoise to the governor-general's power, but neither Alexander I nor Nicholas I chose to reconvene the Diet. The State Secretariat for Finnish Affairs, which replaced the Committee, functioned only as the emperor's Finnish chancery; it had no legislative or formal advisory functions and could only comment officially on matters channeled through it if asked to do so by the emperor.

Yet it was during the period 1830-1870 that the Finns consolidated their position within the empire by developing internally as a nation. To be sure, they especially moved forward with their own programs of liberal reform during the era of Great Reforms in Russia; but even under Nicholas I Russian officialdom approved in Finland notable departures from norms observed elsewhere in the empire. Finland's special position within the empire during the reign of Nicholas I depended to a large extent on the agreement of the emperor and Governor-General A. S. Menshikov that there was no reason to break with Alexander I's precedent of ruling Finland independently of the Russian ministries in St. Petersburg. There was little danger that centralizing bureaucrats such as Perovskii and Uvarov would extend their influence to Finland, as long as a figure with Menshikov's standing and connections in St. Petersburg represented Russian authority in the Grand Duchy and insisted on its administrative separation from the rest of the empire. The sword of Damocles that hung over the Finns' heads was that at any time Menshikov could be replaced by a new governor-general who favored the integration of Finland with the rest of the empire and who would cooperate with the bureaucratic centralizers in St. Petersburg. Or, as Minister State Secretary Alexander Armfelt wrote in 1851:

> We live at a critical moment, at a time when it is a question of that amalgamation, that centralization, which is supposed to extend to the entire empire. If until now Finland has remained extraneous to the question, it is only the prince [i.e. Menshikov] whom we have to thank for this, the prudent way he has governed us and the way that he, although a Russian, has understood how to speak in favor of our cause and to support our interests. But this will never be the same way with his successor.[1]

Because it was unlikely that a new governor-general in Helsingfors would be equally supportive of Finnish interests, Armfelt considered it essential to revive the Committee for Finnish Affairs, which his father, Gustav Mauritz, had created in 1811 and Zakrevskii had abolished in 1826. The principal purpose of the revived Committee, as seen by Armfelt, was to provide an institutionalized means for the Finns to present their views to the emperor before decisions were made concerning questions of vital importance for Finland. Armfelt, however, had to wait until 1857 before his idea was finally approved by Alexander II. Meanwhile, he and his predecessor Rehbinder had to rely on their own skills as courtiers and on their expert knowledge of Finnish affairs to prevent any governor-general from using his extensive executive and administrative powers to the detriment of Finland.[2]

During the period 1831-1855 Rehbinder and Armfelt, in cooperation with leaders of the Senate in Helsingfors, succeeded in influencing Governor-General Menshikov to defend Finland's interest on most important issues. Menshikov did so because he identified Finland with his own authority and because he saw Finnish interests as usually being compatible with those of Russia. He seldom found time to appear personally in Finland, since he resided in St. Petersburg and occupied himself mainly with naval affairs and with the other matters Nicholas I referred to him as one of his most trusted lieutenants. In St. Petersburg Menshikov maintained his own private Finnish chancery headed by a special assistant, K. I. Fisher. Fisher, however, concentrated more on naval and other internal Russian affairs than on Finland and never found the time to study Finnish problems system-

---

[1] Carl von Bonsdorff, "Ministerstatssekretarenen Greve Alexander Armfelts memoarer," *Historisk tidskrift för Finland* 14 (1929): 93.

[2] Ibid., pp. 93-97; Hans Hirn, *Alexander Armfelt*, 2: 268-302.

atically. The Finns generally distrusted him, calling him Mr. Meddler (*Monsieur touche-à-tout*), but he seldom did Finland any particular harm. On occasion, he even helped the Finns to bring Menshikov around to their point of view on matters affecting the interests of both Finland and the empire. In Helsingfors, Menshikov was represented by his adjunct, Alexander Amatus Thesleff, who, from 1833 to 1847, presided over the Senate and occupied the position of vice chancellor of Helsingfors University (the chancellor being the heir apparent). General Thesleff, a Swedo-Finn from Viborg who had worked his way up through the ranks in the Russian army, was a fairly ineffective figure. Very good-natured but not very well educated, Thesleff was not taken too seriously by anyone and had relatively little influence on Finnish affairs.[3]

To govern Finland well and to promote the welfare of the emperor's Finnish subjects effectively, Menshikov very much depended on the assistance of such figures as Alexander Armfelt in the State Secretariat for Finnish Affairs and Lars Gabriel von Haartman in the Finnish Senate. Armfelt's influence grew gradually over the years. He had an extraordinarily large number of friends and acquaintances, thanks to his charm and winning personality as well as to a varied and long career. After he had completed law studies at Åbo University in 1814, he served in the army in Russia and Finland (where he was an adjutant of Steinheil and Zakrevskii), and then continued with assignments as director of the Bank of Finland (1827-1832), Rehbinder's assistant in St. Petersburg (1832-1841), and minister state secretary (1841-1876). As long as Menshikov lived, the Finnish minister state secretary was clearly subordinated to the governor-general. Armfelt's relations with Menshikov, however, were cordial, and his family had been on good terms with the Menshikovs since the 1790s. These good relations were instrumental in preventing the centralizing St. Petersburg officials from imposing their will on Finland in the 1840s. After Menshikov died the revival of the Committee for Finnish Affairs enabled Armfelt to achieve at least parity with and sometimes even superiority over the governor-general in battles concerning the shaping of Finnish policy.[4]

As influential as Armfelt became after 1855, under Nicholas I he

[3] M. M. Borodkin, *Istoriia Finliandii: Vremia Nikolaia I*, pp. 160-72, 515-22; Hirn, *Alexander Armfelt*, 2: 62-67. K. I. Fisher's interesting but not always reliable memoirs were published in 1908: "Zapiski Senatora K. I. Fishera," *Istoricheskii vestnik* 111 (1908): 43-70, 438-60, 796-818; 112 (1908): 58-78, 426-65, 825-45; 113 (1908): 50-70, 426-47, 792-821; 114 (1908): 45-73, 422-48, 848-60.

[4] Hirn, *Alexander Armfelt*, vols. 1 and 2; *Finsk biografisk handbok*, ed. Tor Carpelan (Helsinki: G. W. Edlunds Förlag, 1903), pp. 110-11.

was clearly eclipsed as a Finnish leader by Lars Gabriel von Haart-man. As did Armfelt, Haartman belonged to the same social class of Swedo-Finnish nobles who first served the Swedish kings and then the Russian emperors as soldiers and officials. Haartman, however, was not born into this class, but married into it. He did come from a distinguished academic family that had produced a number of physi-cians and professors of medicine, but he chose to study law at Åbo and, in 1808, entered the Russian civil service. Between 1808 and 1830 he served in the Russian Ministry of Foreign Affairs, the Com-mittee for Finnish Affairs, and the State Secretariat for Finnish Af-fairs. In St. Petersburg he met the two women he successively mar-ried, both maids of honor at the Imperial Court and daughters of Count Carl Erik Mannerheim, the despotic vice chairman (the chair-man being always nominally the governor-general) and driving force in the Finnish Senate between 1822 and 1826. Haartman returned to Finland in 1830 to serve briefly in the Senate and then, between 1831 and 1840, as governor in Åbo. During the 1830s the Russian author-ities called upon him on a number of occasions to chair committees on foreign trade, taxation, and monetary reform. In 1840 he rejoined the Senate, becoming vice chairman of the Financial Department in 1841. In this position he served in the same despotic tradition as such predecessors as Anders Henrik Falk (1828-1833) and his father-in-law, C. E. Mannerheim. He remained in this position from 1841 to 1858, becoming a very respected but feared person among his contempo-raries. A Russian observer, K. I. Fisher, described him, perhaps with some exaggeration, as a financial Colbert, a political Machiavelli, and a Sixtus V in willpower.[5]

Beginning in the 1830s Haartman sent to Menshikov from Åbo fairly regular, confidential reports concerning Finland. Menshikov's support and his own energy and expertise in many areas of financial policy enabled Haartman to carry out a number of projects that he consid-ered useful for Finland. Haartman was an old-fashioned economist who believed in financial stability, gradual economic expansion, and a slow and deliberate development of trade and industry. He was, however, somewhat less conservative and cautious than Minister of Finance E. F. Kankrin in Russia, for he did believe in making bank loans available for purposes of industrial expansion. In general, he tried to encourage economic activity in Finland by equalizing and simplifying taxes on land, establishing an agricultural institute in Mus-

---

[5] *Finsk biografisk handbok*, pp. 575-76, 851-61, 1436-39; Fisher, "Zapiski Senatora K. I. Fishera," *Istoricheskii vestnik* 113: 62.

tiala and technical high schools in Helsingfors, Åbo, and Vasa, and finding financial support for digging the Saima Canal, which, exiting to the Gulf of Finland at Viborg, opened to the outside world the vast lake region of the central part of the country. Even before he took charge of the Senate's Financial Department, Haartman chaired a committee to reform Finland's monetary system. The implementation of this committee's recommendation at the beginning of the 1840s stabilized the Finnish monetary system by bringing it into conformity with the Russian silver-ruble reform of 1839. In conjunction with this reform the modest operations of the Bank of Finland were somewhat expanded so that it could issue bank notes in larger denominations and retire Swedish paper money that was still in circulation in Finland throughout the 1830s. The monetary reform, therefore, tended to bring Finland closer to Russia and separate her from Sweden, which was in accord with the wishes of both Haartman and Menshikov.[6]

Haartman's customs policy, on the other hand, tended to separate Finland from Russia. The high tariffs Kankrin had set on imports into Russia had adversely affected Finnish trade. The prices for Finnish consumers rose, smuggling activities increased in the extensive skerries off the coast of Finland, and customs revenue declined. Haartman brought to Menshikov's attention the various problems caused for Finland by Kankrin's high tariffs, emphasizing that geography and Finland's economic conditions dictated a lowering of customs duties on imports. Through Menshikov, Nicholas I was persuaded to permit Haartman to lower tariff rates for Finnish imports, but Haartman was instructed to keep this secret and to try to improve the administration of the Finnish customs service. In 1841 Haartman secretly enforced tariffs that were lower for Finland than elsewhere in Russia, and during the remainder of the 1840s he reorganized the customs administration, improved the guard service in the skerries, and appreciably increased customs revenue. In 1850, however, the abolition of the customs frontier between Congress Poland and Russia suggested to Nicholas I that the customs administration of Finland should also be integrated with that of the rest of the empire. Haartman, Menshikov, and K. I. Fisher, who became assistant state secretary for Finnish affairs in 1851, all tried to persuade Nicholas I to change his mind, pointing out that Finland's long coastline and the small scale of her industrial and commercial enterprises had to be taken into consider-

[6] Borodkin, *Istoriia . . . Nikolaia I*, pp. 201-10, 221-55; *Finsk biografisk handbok*, pp. 853-58; M. G. Schybergson, *Finlands politiska historia 1809-1919* (Helsinki: Söderström & Co., 1923), pp. 104-8.

ation. They warned that rapid and total merger of the Finnish customs administration with that of the empire might cause friction and even disturb what had been a most harmonious relationship between Finland and Russia. Nicholas I did not accept these arguments, but he did agree to implement the projected unification of the two customs systems gradually. War on the Black Sea and in the Crimea, however, intervened, and the matter was dropped until the end of the 1880s. The customs frontier between Finland and the rest of the empire was never abolished.[7]

Nicholas I's reluctance to retain the Russo-Finnish customs frontier demonstrated his continued interest in bringing Finland closer to the rest of the empire. As in the Baltic provinces, however, he expected his officials to respect the rights and privileges of the local estates that both he and his brother, Alexander I, had confirmed at the beginning of their respective reigns. This recognition of the special position in the empire of German- and Swedish-speaking elites limited the freedom of action of Russian officials concerned with the affairs of the Baltic provinces and Finland. In Finland their hands were further tied by the denial to the central Russian ministries of the right to intervene in Finnish internal affairs and the inapplicability of many Russian norms or reforms to Finnish conditions. There was, for example, no reason to organize in Helsingfors a committee similar to that of Khanykov, for Helsingfors was only about one-fourth the size of Riga in the 1840s and had few Russian residents and little contact with or commercial importance for Russia. Russian norms or reforms were no more applicable to the problems of Finnish peasant society. Although poor and subject to crop failures and occasional famine, Finnish peasants were free, had the right to own property, and enjoyed some rights of self-government. The one region of major peasant unrest in Finland in the first part of the nineteenth century was Old Finland, where the gift of Crown lands to Russians and others who had served the state reduced many peasants to a condition resembling that of Russian serfs.[8]

In Old Finland some 100,000 Finnish-speaking peasants, many of whom were Greek Orthodox in religion, lived on so-called donated lands. These peasants, because of the special rights in Old Finland

---

[7] Borodkin, *Istoriia . . . Nikolaia I*, pp. 216-20; Fisher, "Zapiski Senatora K. I. Fishera," *Istoricheskii vestnik* 113: 792-95; Schybergson, *Finlands politiska historia*, pp. 103-4; Thaden (ed.), *Russification*, p. 79.

[8] Peter Scheibert, "Die Anfänge des Finnischen Staatswerden unter Alexander I," *Jahrbücher für osteuropäische Geschichte*, o.s. 4 (1939): 421-23; Borodkin, *Istoriia . . . Nikolaia I*, pp. 266-95; Schybergson, *Finlands politiska historia*, pp. 94-95.

enjoyed by landowners to whom the Russian state had given land, were inadequately protected against eviction from the farmsteads they occupied and against other forms of arbitrary treatment on the part of the landowners. Clearly, a Russian reformer like Kiselev had little to offer to peasants in Old Finland (or anywhere else in Finland); but what these peasants needed were the same rights and protection under law enjoyed by peasants elsewhere in Finland. The problems both Orthodox and Lutheran Finnish-speaking peasants had with landowners in Old Finland seem to explain at least partly why Orthodoxy and the myth of the benevolent tsar had very little attraction for Finnish peasants. No mass conversions to Orthodoxy occurred in Finland. Given this situation, it was obviously futile for the Russian state to try to promote the interests of the Orthodox Church in Finland in the same manner that it had in the western *gubernii* and the Baltic provinces; it did insist (in 1827) that Orthodox Christians could no longer be barred from military and civil service in Finland. Generally speaking, the Russian authorities viewed the Finnish Lutheran Church in a favorable light and heavily relied on it to maintain social order in the Finnish countryside.[9]

Nicholas I and his advisers acted with somewhat less hesitation in their efforts to promote the Russian language in Finland and to prepare for the eventual adaptation of Finnish laws to a single legal system for the entire empire. But, as will be discussed below, Finnish resistance to codification plans for Finland persuaded Russian officials to postpone the integration of Finland into the general legal system of the empire. On the subject of the Russian language, there was general agreement among Finnish and Russian leaders that the Finns needed to learn Russian. Many of them did so during the first decades of Russian rule. Yet, by mid-century the majority of educated Finns, including those serving the emperor in the Finnish Senate, knew very little, if any, Russian.

Increasing the knowledge of Russian in Finland depended largely on Russian-language instruction in Finnish secondary schools and at Helsingfors University. The Russian Ministry of Education did not control school administration and educational policy in Finland. Emperor Nicholas I, Menshikov, Rehbinder, and Armfelt, however, all gave high priority to the teaching of Russian in Finnish schools and attentively followed the work of Finnish committees concerned with

[9] Hirn, *Alexander Armfelt*, 2: 219-27, 259-67; Borodkin, *Istoriia . . . Nikolaia I*, pp. 548-49; Alfons Takolander, *Erik Gabriel Melartin*, 2 vols. (Ekenäs: Ekenäs Tryckeri Aktiebolag, 1926-1927), 1: 78-83, 290-95.

reform of Finland's secondary schools. At the beginning of the 1840s a uniform secondary school system was established for Finland, providing for Swedish as the language of instruction (replacing German in Old Finland), Finnish as part of the school curriculum, and an increased number of hours of Russian instruction. In 1841 Iakov Karlovich Grot, an eminent authority on Russian literature and philology as well as Finnish and Scandinavian languages and literatures, was appointed full professor at Helsingfors University. Grot and a second Russian teacher on the associate-professor level had the responsibility of not only teaching Russian but also of verifying the Russian-language competence of students at the university and Finnish secondary schools. Unlike in the Baltic provinces, however, in Finland the regulations governing examinations and proficiency in Russian were written by the native officials. Only students intending to go into state service were obliged to demonstrate proficiency in Russian, while those in theology, the humanities, education, and medicine were not. At Helsingfors University, Grot experienced the same sort of moral and psychological pressures to be lenient in evaluating examinations that was experienced by Russian-language teachers in the Baltic provinces. When he did try to impose higher standards, he was boycotted by students, and the windows of his apartment were broken. Early in 1852 Grot, who had become discouraged about the obstacles standing in the way of effective Russian language instruction in Finland, proposed to K. I. Fisher (since 1851 assistant state secretary for Finnish affairs in addition to his previous duties as Menshikov's assistant) that control over the teaching of Russian in Finland be placed in the hands of the Russian governor-general. In the early fifties, however, Russian officials were much more reluctant than they had been during the thirties and forties to interfere in the internal affairs of the privileged elites of the western borderlands, as Prince Suvorov demonstrated with his nonenforcement of the language law of 1850 in the Baltic provinces. In Finland, Fisher did not act on Grot's proposal. At the end of 1852 Grot returned to Russia.[10]

During the twelve years he spent in Finland, Grot forged close ties of friendship that linked himself and Russia with Finnish cultural leaders such as Elias Lönnrot, the compiler of the *Kalevala*, and Johan Ludvig Runeberg, Finland's greatest national poet in the Swedish

[10] Hirn, *Alexander Armfelt*, 2: 174-79; Takolander, *Erik Gabriel Melartin*, 2: 161; Borodkin, *Istoriia . . . Nikolaia I*, pp. 445-51, 572-86; Ia. K. Grot, *Perepiska Ia. K. Grota s P. A. Pletnevym*, ed. K. Ia. Grot, 3 vols. (St. Petersburg: Tipografiia Ministerstva Putei Soobshcheniia, 1896), 2: 43-45, 600-601, 626-27, 640-42, 648, 691-692, 695-96, 699; 3: 190-91, 566-68.

language. He could not, however, do very much about motivating Finns to learn Russian. As long as the majority of gymnasium and university students were not obliged to master Russian and as long as even those who prepared for careers in the Finnish state service knew that they would probably never have any need to use it (for Swedish and Finnish were the only languages used internally in Finland), learning Russian served no practical purpose and could only be considered superfluous as far as most Finns were concerned.[11] It was therefore not surprising that during the period 1830-1870 the Russian language made even less progress in Finland than it did in the Baltic provinces.

Nicholas I's officials also achieved minimal results in preparing Finland for the eventual adaptation of her laws to a uniform legal system for the entire empire. In Finland, as elsewhere in the borderlands, such adaptation could not take place without the availability to Russian officials of simplified and systematized collections of local laws in the native language and in Russian translation. Work on such a collection of Finnish laws had begun under Alexander I; but it only moved forward with any purposeful direction after 1835, when the Russian *Svod zakonov* went into effect as the source of law and as the official guide for Russian law courts and administrative offices. After 1826 the Second Section of His Imperial Majesty's Own Chancery directed all work on both the Russian *Svod zakonov* and the various collections of local laws. The Second Section, like other branches of Nicholas I's personal bureaucracy, operated independently of the Russian Senate, State Council, and central ministries. With respect to Finland, nothing prevented the Second Section from dealing directly with the Senate, committees, and officials in Helsingfors. As a practical matter, it kept Menshikov and the Finnish minister state secretary in St. Petersburg informed about all important decisions and developments concerning the codification of Finnish laws; but it did not consider Finland to be very much different from other borderland areas and instructed the Finnish Codification Commission organized in Helsingfors in 1835 to follow the model of the *Svod zakonov* in collecting and systematizing local Finnish laws.[12]

At first Carl Johan Walleen, the chairman of the Finnish Codification Commission, seems to have assumed that the work of his com-

[11] Grot, *Perepiska*, 2: 878; 3: 190-91, 567-68; Eino Karhu, *Finliandskaia literatura i Rossiia 1800-1850* (Tallinn: Estonskoe Gosudarstvennoe Izdatel'stvo, 1962), pp. 113-96.

[12] Maikov, *Vtoroe otdelenie sobstvennoi ego imperatorskogo velichestva kantseliarii 1826-1882*, pp. 223-24; Osmo Jussila, "Finnland in der Gesetzkodifikation zur Zeit Nikolajs I.," *Jahrbücher für Geschichte Osteuropas*, n.s. 20 (1972): 26-30.

mission offered an opportunity to define more satisfactorily Finland's legal position within the empire. The final draft of the project that he sent to Second Section Chief Bludov in 1841, therefore, contained an initial section on Fundamental Laws (*osnovnye zakony*), which defined Finland's relationship to her ruler and Russia and the nature of her internal government essentially on the basis of two Swedish constitutional documents: the Form of Government of 1772 and the Union and Security Act of 1789. Walleen, a member of G. M. Armfelt's Committee for Finnish Affairs between 1811 and 1820, had been one of the Finnish statesmen who had tried to persuade Alexander I to grant Finland a written constitution and a diet that would meet at regular intervals. As was mentioned in Chapter 5, Alexander I never agreed to a written Finnish constitution, and in 1842 Bludov advised Nicholas I to eliminate the section on Fundamental Laws from Walleen's project because many of the matters included in it did not properly belong in a local code. Bludov also feared that this part of Walleen's project might hinder the "final equalization (*uravnoveshenie*) of the mutual relations between the inhabitants of the empire and those of the Grand Duchy of Finland." Nicholas I followed Bludov's recommendation to exclude the Fundamental Laws section from Walleen's codification project.[13]

In the early forties Menshikov learned that a number of leading Finns in the Senate and at Helsingfors University were concerned about Bludov's codification plans for Finland. Personally, Menshikov had nothing against bringing Finnish laws into a greater degree of conformity with those of the empire, but he wanted to avoid upsetting the Finns unnecessarily and prevailed upon Bludov and Nicholas I to make certain modifications in the procedures for codifying Finnish laws. These modifications, however, did not satisfy the Finnish Revision Committee founded at the end of 1842 to review the Walleen commission's codification project. Criticizing the commission's procedures, the Revision Committee especially objected to the manner in which the Swedish Code of 1734 (that is, the collection of laws then still in effect in Finland) had been reworked and altered. It warned that the proposed changes in the Code of 1734 would cause uneasiness and apprehension among Finns, who had come to consider this law a "highly valued inheritance from their forefathers" and the "most irrevocable safeguard of their civil rights." Accordingly, the commit-

---

[13] Jussila, "Finnland," pp. 32-39; Jussila, *Suomen perustuslait*, pp. 101-2, 105-19, 157-60, 194-206, 254-60; D. N. Bludov, "Neskol'ko zamechanii na Proekt Svoda osnovnykh zakonov Finliandii," in Jussila, *Suomen perustuslait*, p. 261.

tee requested that the Code remain intact and that it not be changed in any way by further work on the codification of Finnish laws. This recommendation was reinforced by separate opinions prepared by law professors Wilhelm Gabriel Lagus and Johan Jakob Nordström of Helsingfors University. Their former student Johan Philip Palmén was secretary of the Revision Committee and played a leading role in its deliberations.[14]

Once Menshikov was reminded by Alexander Armfelt how important Russia's respect for Finnish law and traditions had been in making Finland's union with Russia popular, he sided with the Revision Committee and persuaded Nicholas I to leave the Code of 1734 unaffected by the codification work of Walleen and the Second Section. The codification of Finnish laws was, therefore, to concentrate on compiling a separate and complementary collection of enactments issued since 1734. Nicholas's decision, which was made in 1847 for obviously political reasons, delayed completion of the work on Finnish codification. Further delays occurred at the beginning of Alexander II's reign.[15] Unlike in the Baltic provinces, Finland's laws were never codified according to procedures prescribed by the Second Section of His Imperial Majesty's Own Chancery.

In 1915 Palmén's son described the dropping of the Second Section's projected codification of Finnish laws as "an indisputable victory for the Finnish people." Recently, Finnish historian Osmo Jussila has disputed this interpretation, pointing out that codification in the terms outlined by Bludov in the 1840s did not threaten Finnish rights and privileges and that the subsequent consolidation of Finland's special position within the empire resulted not from frustrating Bludov's codification plans but from the reforms of Alexander II.[16] As valid and well argued as Jussila's point is, he seems to underestimate the importance of the constitution that Alexander I supposedly granted to Finland at the beginning of the nineteenth century as a unifying patriotic ideology and as a definition of objectives in the subsequent Finnish battle, especially during Alexander II's reign, to expand and secure their country's internal autonomy. The repressive measures introduced in Finland during the last years of Nicholas I's reign, as

[14] Jussila, "Finnland," pp. 37-39; Jussila, *Suomen perustuslait*, pp. 204-7; Maikov, *Vtoroe otdelenie*, pp. 325-29; E. G. Palmén, *Till hundraårsminnet af Johan Philip Palmén 1811-1911*, 2 vols. in 4 pts. (Helsinki: F. Tilgman, 1915-1917), 2: 127-34; *Finsk biografisk handbok*, pp. 1269, 1581-82, 2315-17.

[15] Jussila, "Finnland," pp. 39-40; Jussila, *Suomen perustuslait*, pp. 207-11; Palmén, *Till hundraårsminnet*, 2: 134-39.

[16] Palmén, *Till hundraårsminnet*, 2: 139; Jussila, "Finnland," pp. 40-41.

well as the knowledge of well-informed Finns about the recommendations made by Minister of the Interior Perovskii before the State Council in December 1846 to introduce Russian laws, institutions, and language into borderlands,[17] must have made victory in this battle seem to be a matter of vital importance for the future of Finland. In this struggle the Swedish Code of 1734, the Form of Government of 1772, the Union and Security Act of 1789, and Alexander I's promises of 1809 had much the same meaning for the Finns as did the capitulations of 1710 and the Treaty of Nystad of 1721 for the Baltic Germans. In both cases the myth of contractually secured rights provided ideological justification for either resisting Russificatory pressures or for reinforcing local autonomy in anticipation of what might happen in an uncertain future.

The struggle during the second part of the nineteenth century to expand and further develop Finnish autonomy was conducted mainly by a new generation of Swedish-speaking liberals and Fennomans. These new political leaders could not, however, have accomplished what they did without the efforts during the preceding half century of such courtiers and old-regime officials as Gustav Mauritz and Alexander Armfelt, Robert Henrik Rehbinder, and Lars Gabriel von Haartman to base Finland's relationship with Russia on eighteenth-century Swedish laws and constitutional enactments, to create and develop institutions of internal administration, and, generally, to defend the interests of Finland. During Nicholas I's reign Finnish intellectuals tended to distrust the aristocrats who controlled the Senate in Helsingfors and the State Secretariat in St. Petersburg, whom they associated with political oppression, indifference to Finnish nationalism, and the subordination of Finland to Russia. However, as much as the Swedish- and French-speaking upper-class Finns serving in the Finnish Senate and State Secretariat believed in the necessity of bringing Finland closer to Russia and of discouraging any signs of independent thought likely to disturb Nicholas I and Menshikov, they were loyal to Finland and unwilling to accept the sort of heavy-handed administrative Russification proposed by Perovskii at the end of 1846. Four years later, in 1851, Armfelt wrote the words about centralization and amalgamation that were quoted at the beginning of this chapter. However compliant he might have seemed at the beginning of

[17] Bruno Lesch, "Greve Leo Perovskij och Finland," *Historisk tidskrift för Finland* 30 (1945): 1-19. Perovskii's report to the State Council was translated into Swedish and widely known among Finnish officials: "Underdånigt betänkande angående nödvandigheten att införa ryska rikets grundlager i alla Ryssland underlydande provinser," Finnish National Archives, Poliitisia asiakirjoja, no. 73.

his career, from the late 1840s and on he gradually unfolded as an extremely adept and effective defender of the special position of Finland within the Russian Empire.

The achievements of the new generation of Finnish leaders during the second part of the nineteenth century often departed from the internal national, social, and economic developments of Finnish society that had taken place before the reign of Alexander II. Exemption from service in the Russian army and from the financial burdens of the empire's military expenditures, and the social, institutional, and partial economic separation of Finland, a country whose population was free and to a large extent literate, from a backward Russia was one necessary condition for this development. The conservative and prudent men who then ran Finnish affairs sympathized with modern nationalism and intellectual dissent no more than did Russian officials; but they refrained from taking unnecessarily severe measures to curtail the activities of Fennomans who set out to build a modern Finnish nation on the foundation of the language and culture of the majority of its inhabitants. The sound fiscal policies, improvement of internal communications, and promotion of commerce, technical education, and practical instruction for artisans during the first part of the nineteenth century helped provide the building blocks for Finland's expanding economy in the second part of the century. Economic and urban growth before 1850 was not dramatic, but a 49 percent increase in population between 1815 and 1850 (1,096,000 in 1815, 1,637,000 in 1850) produced new economic opportunities for the Finnish middle class. The basic social structure of society changed very little, and only five to six percent of the population lived in towns in mid-century. Finland's largest city, Helsingfors, then still had only 21,000 inhabitants, but this number had increased from 5,000 in 1812 when Helsingfors became the country's capital.[18]

Three representative intellectual leaders of the new Finnish elite that appeared in the first half of the nineteenth century and dominated Finnish society and political affairs in the second part of the century were Elias Lönnrot, Johan Ludvig Runeberg, and Johan Vilhelm Snellman. All three came from modest homes and from the thin social stratum of Finnish, Swedish, and foreign origin that for centuries had provided Finland with artisans, merchants, schoolteachers,

---

[18] Juhani Paasivirta, *Finland and Europe: International Crises in the Period of Autonomy 1808-1914*, tr. A. F. and S. R. Upton and ed. D. G. Kirby (Minneapolis: University of Minnesota Press, 1981), pp. 72-79; B. R. Mitchell, *European Historical Statistics 1750-1970* (abridged ed.; New York: Columbia University Press, 1978), pp. 4, 13; Schybergson, *Finlands politiska historia*, p. 67.

minor officials, and seamen. The fathers of Runeberg and Snellman were sea captains from the west coast of Finland, while Lönnrot's father was a village tailor from the northern Finnish-speaking part of Nyland (Uusimaa) province.[19] In the fall of 1822 Lönnrot, Runeberg, and Snellman matriculated at the University of Åbo, where, to one degree or another, they came under the influence of the so-called Åbo Romanticists.

Between 1817 and 1823 the Åbo Romanticists actively published in the journals *Aura* and *Mnemosyne* and the newspaper *Åbo Morgonblad*. They wrote patriotic verse and articles advocating the study of the Finnish language, the collection of Finnish folk poetry and songs, and the development of a Finnish national culture and literature. Although currents of romantic nationalism in Germany and Sweden influenced the ideas expressed by these romanticists, they were remarkable for the extent to which they, educated Swedo-Finns, identified themselves with the language and future of Finnish-speaking peasants. They went so far, as did Johan Gabriel Linsén in 1819, to urge the Swedish-speaking upper class to accept Finnish as an official language in courts and public offices and to master it as a written language that could be used as an instrument to guide and educate the lower orders of society.[20] After the most prominent representative of the Åbo Romanticists, Adolf Ivar Arwidsson, had been dismissed from the university in 1822 and emigrated to Sweden in 1823, restrictive measures introduced by the Finnish authorities tended to discourage bold speculation in print. Several of the Åbo Romanticists continued as professors at Åbo/Helsingfors University, however, where they were in a position to pass on their ideas to the younger generation.

Lönnrot and Runeberg were able to realize some of the cultural goals of the Åbo Romanticists by publishing folk poetry or literature that not only compared favorably with that of other countries but also reflected the life of Finnish-speaking peasants as well as the creative potential of Finnish popular culture. Lönnrot was the first person to make effective use of the rich store of traditional Finnish songs in Finnish and Russian Karelia and, in his *Kalevala*, to arrange songs collected from all parts of Finland into a systematic whole. Lönnrot

[19] *Finsk biografisk handbok*, pp. 1402-12, 1843-57, 2001-10.
[20] Jaako Ahokas, *A History of Finnish Literature* (Bloomington: Indiana University Press, 1973), pp. 35-38; Schybergson, *Finlands politiska historia*, pp. 77-82; D. G. Kirby, *Finland and Russia 1808-1920: From Autonomy to Independence* (New York: Barnes & Noble, 1976), pp. 36-37; E. G. Palmén, *L'oeuvre demi-séculaire de la société de litterature finnoise et le mouvement nationale en Finlande de 1831 à 1881* (Helsinki: Société de Litterature Finnoise, 1882), pp. 12-13.

was a charter member of the Finnish Literary Society (*Suomalaisen Kirjallisuuden Seura*), which was founded in 1831 and which subsidized Lönnrot's expeditions and the publication of his major works. He himself probably contributed more than any other individual to carrying out a principal goal of the Society: "to propagate more exact knowledge about the fatherland and its history, to cultivate the Finnish language, and to bring forth in this language a literature for the educated classes as well as for the people."[21]

Although the introduction to the statutes of the Finnish Literary Society asserted that a "national literature is not possible without a national language," the first and perhaps greatest Finnish national poet, Runeberg, wrote in Swedish. He had, however, learned Finnish and was able to observe and study the life of Finnish-speaking peasants during the year and a half he spent between 1823 and 1825 as a tutor in central Finland. It was especially in the moving patriotic poem *Fänrik Ståls sägner* (*The Tales of Ensign Stål*) that Runeberg extolled the moral qualities of Finnish peasants and depicted the heroism of those who vowed during the war with Russia in 1808 that their "native earth" would never "be wrested bloodless by the hand of tyrants from her sons' possession." This poem was introduced by the song "Our Land" (*Vårt Land*), which was published separately at the beginning of 1848 and eventually became Finland's national anthem.[22]

Both the *Kalevala* and *Fänrik Ståls sägner* aroused the attention of the academic youth and of middle-class intellectuals who had been dissatisfied with the smug, small world of Finnish officialdom and of the academic establishment. Or, as one contemporary, Zachris Topelius, commented:

> The generation that experienced in its youth the *Kalevala* and *Fänrik Stål* witnessed a turning point in the life of the Finnish people, one which will not recur for centuries. These two works could only be born out of the ripening times, only when the past had fulfilled its mission and something new was beginning. Only then, not sooner or later, could "Our Land" come to be a folk

---

[21] Ahokas, *A History of Finnish Literature*, pp. 70-72; *The Kalevala or Poems of Kaleva District*, ed. Francis P. Magoun, Jr. (Cambridge: Harvard University Press, 1963), pp. 342-56; Palmén, *L'oeuvre demi-séculaire*, p. 24. For an interesting discussion of how generations of Finns used the *Kalevala* to further their political purposes and national aspirations, see William A. Wilson, *Folklore and Nationalism in Modern Finland* (Bloomington: Indiana University Press, 1976).

[22] Ahokas, *A History of Finnish Literature*, pp. 41-46; Estlander, *Elva årtionden ur Finlands historia*, 1: 150-80; Johan Ludvig Runeberg, *The Tales of Ensign Stål*, tr. Charles W. Stork (Princeton: Princeton University Press, 1938), p. 89.

song. The fatherland as a conscious idea is a result of a development over a long period of time, but the *Kalevala* was its inspiration (*ursprungsord*) and *Fänrik Stål* its standard-bearer.[23]

The "fatherland as a conscious idea" was a particularly important
goal for Hegelian philosopher and publicist Johan Vilhelm Snellman.
Snellman published his most important philosophical work, *Lären om
staten (The Theory of the State)* in Stockholm in 1842. In it he systematically discussed the responsibilities and relationship of the individual to the family, society, nation, and state. The state and nation
were the principal instruments for the realization of spiritual freedom
in history. A central task for the individual was to try to identify himself with the historical process through patriotism, or the love of his
own people's language, country, customs, laws, and institutions. A
precondition for patriotism, according to Snellman, was the existence
of a national spirit that had gradually evolved over the centuries as a
particular and unique form of human culture. Patriotism was a dy-
namic force that "gave impetus to the development of a nationality
and maintained it as a definite form of universal human civilization
(*bildningen*)." The national spirit was also, in Snellman's view, realized through the individual's aspiration for moral freedom, by which
he apparently meant that the individual had the responsibility of acting according to rationally determined laws of ethical conduct and to
serve the national community with which he identified himself.[24]

Between 1844 and 1846 Snellman published in Kuopio the Swedish-language newspaper *Saima*. Newspapers in Finland during the
1830s and 1840s generally offered their readers little more than official
announcements, anecdotes, and, at best, literary criticism. Snellman,
who had honed his verbal and critical skills as a journalist and independent scholar in Sweden and Germany between 1839 and 1842,
provocatively discussed a wide range of economic, social, and cultural
topics, including industry, trade, criminal law, the state of the Finnish
press, literature, charity, foreign affairs, the plight of dispossessed
farmers, school reform, and university policy. As the father of the
Fennoman movement, he of course used his organ to propagate his
own views on the Finnish language and on the moral responsibility of
the educated minority to participate in the struggle to arouse the
Finnish people to consciousness of its own nationality. A prerequisite

[23] Zachris Topelius, *Anteckninger från det Helsingfors som gått*, ed. Torsten Stenby
(2nd ed.; Helsinki: Hufvudstadsbladets Förlag, 1969), p. 79.
[24] Johan Vilhelm Snellman, *Läran om staten* (Stockholm: Zacharias Haeggström, 1842),
pp. 8-17, 302-5, 444-48.

for such self-awareness was the national literature that Finland still did not have. Echoing the early Åbo Romanticists more than Hegel, Snellman insisted that a Finnish national literature had to be in the Finnish language. To make this possible, Finnish had to become the language of the school and public life in Finland. And, in 1845, he told Finland's younger generation, in Swedish, that "each Swedish word used by you from now on is relatively wasted for Finnish literature, or the glory of the Finnish name and yourselves; only the mother tongue will give what you write and your name a place in the world."[25]

At the end of 1846 Governor-General Menshikov suppressed *Saima*. Earlier that year Snellman had tweaked the noses of the Finnish and Russian authorities by reprinting and cautiously commenting on information from the Finnish-language newspaper *Kanava* concerning the plight of former farmers in Viborg province who had been somehow reduced to the status of beggars. The issue was a sensitive one because it touched upon government social and economic policy toward Finnish peasants living on former Crown lands that had been given to Finnish and Russian nobles. Following the suppression of *Saima*, the outbreak of revolution in Western Europe in 1848 made the control of the press seem all the more important to Menshikov. He chaired the special committee Nicholas I then established to study ways to improve the administration of censorship throughout the empire and, especially, to prevent the dissemination of harmful ideas among the common people. In 1850 Menshikov arranged to have forbidden in Finland the appearance of all Finnish-language newspapers and publications other than those intended exclusively for "religious edification and economic utility." Menshikov issued no similar prohibition for Swedish-language publications, apparently because they were intended for the upper and middle, not the lower, classes and because they were easier to control (there was no shortage of Swedish-reading censors). Students at Helsingfors University, however, represented one element among Swedish-speaking Finns that worried Russian and Finnish officials at the time. They therefore introduced a number of measures at the beginning of the 1850s to make it easier for the authorities to control Helsingfors students and to protect them from allegedly harmful influences. These measures included obligatory uniforms, the abolition of fraternities and philosophy courses, the

[25] Ibid., pp. 310-21; Thiodolf Rein, *Johan Vilhelm Snellman*, 2 vols. (2nd ed.; Helsinki: Otava, 1904), 1: 411-18, 444-50; L. V. Suni, *Ocherk obshchestvenno-politicheskogo razvitiia Finliandii 50-70e gody XIX v.* (Leningrad: "Nauka," 1979), pp. 117-18; John H. Wuorinen, *Nationalism in Modern Finland* (New York: Columbia University Press, 1931), p. 89.

limitation of university autonomy, and the appointment of proctors to monitor the students.[26]

The Finnish policy pursued by Menshikov and Nicholas I after 1846, it should be emphasized, aimed not at administrative centralization but at social control and the insulation of the lower orders of Finnish society from outside influences considered harmful by the Russian authorities. The recommendations Minister of the Interior Perovskii made before the State Council in December 1846 to extend Russian law, language, and institutions to the empire's borderlands was, in effect, rejected by Nicholas I, for during the last decade of his reign he based his policy in the western borderlands, especially in the Baltic provinces and Finland, on accommodation with the privileged strata of local society. In Finland, for example, he followed the advice of Menshikov, deciding to support the Finnish view of codification at the very time that Perovskii made his report before the State Council; and at the beginning of the 1850s he did not carry out plans for the unification of the Finnish and Russian customs services.

Neither Finnish nor Russian officials necessarily had anything against the Finnish language as such. Snellman's *Saima* had been suppressed not because of its championing the Finnish language but because of the serious consideration its editor gave to issues the authorities preferred not to have discussed. A number of Finnish officials were interested in strengthening the position of the Finnish language in Finland, as were many Russians who saw in it a means of separating Finland from Sweden. The desirability of filling vacancies in the church, elementary schools, courts, and administrative offices in the Finnish-speaking part of the country with candidates who had a good command of the Finnish language was officially affirmed at the beginning of the 1850s. At the same time, a professorship in Finnish was established at Helsingfors University, its first appointee being the distinguished Finno-Ugric scholar, M. A. Castrén. Elias Lönnrot became the second professor of Finnish at the university upon the premature death of Castrén in 1852.[27]

During the Crimean War the overwhelming majority of Finns remained loyal to Russia, even though a strong undercurrent of Russophobia was also apparent in Finland throughout the 1850s. In the

[26] Rein, *Johan Vilhelm Snellman*, 1: 514-25; Schybergson, *Finlands politiska historia*, pp. 108-15; Rolf Lagerborg, *Friherre Casimer von Kothen (1807-80) enligt aktstycken och brev*, Bidrag till kännedom af Finlands Natur och Folk utgifna af Finska Vetenskaps-Sociététen, no. 97 (Helsinki: n.p., 1953), pp. 58-72; Scheibert, "Finland zur Zeit Kaiser Nikolaus I.," *Jahrbücher für Geschichte Osteuropas*, o.s. 5 (1940): 172-81.

[27] Schybergson, *Finlands politiska historia*, pp. 108-14, 123, 125.

summers of 1854 and 1855 the British naval squadrons that appeared in the Baltic destroyed or seized a good part of the Finnish merchant fleet, attacked various points on the Finnish coast, destroyed Uleå-borg (Oulu) and Brahestad (Raahe), occupied the Åland Islands, and bombarded the Sveaborg fortress outside Helsingfors. The English attack at Gamla Karleby (Kokkola) was thrown back by a combined force of Russian soldiers and Finnish peasants and townsmen. During the war 70,000 Russian soldiers were stationed in Finland and 10,000 Finns mobilized in militia battalions. To inform the Finns about the war and the British threat to Finland, censorship was relaxed, first for Swedish- and then Finnish-language newspapers. Menshikov's measures of 1850 against the Finnish-language press still remained in effect. In March 1854, however, they were modified when Finland's two major Finnish-language newspapers, the *Suometar* in Helsingfors and the *Oulun Wiiko-Sanomat* in Uleåborg, were permitted to publish news about the international situation. The dissemination of information about the British raids and the joint Finnish-Russian defense effort helped to turn the Finns against the British and bring them closer to Russia. In 1856 both Alexander II and Governor-General F.W.R. von Berg expressed their satisfaction about Finnish loyalty during the war.[28]

Finns, however, considering themselves part of Western Europe, had never wanted to be absorbed by autocratic Russia. Close cultural ties with Sweden had been maintained throughout the first part of the nineteenth century. Finnish émigrés in Sweden, especially Arwidsson and Israel Hwasser, had kept alive, at a time of repressive censorship in Finland, discussion of a separate development for Finland based on eighteenth-century Swedish political and legal order and Finnish popular culture. Many Finns (for example, Snellman) spent time in Sweden and returned home with impressions from a freer and more open society; and Swedish newspapers and publications seem to have always been available to Finns who wanted to read them. At the time of the Crimean War, contacts with Sweden carried to Finland the currents of Scandinavianism that called for Sweden's joining the anti-Russian coalition of powers and for the liberation of Finland from Russia and her return to Sweden within a Scandinavian union. Such a possible outcome of the Crimean War met with some sympathetic response among Helsingfors students, who had very much resented Finland's isolation from Europe since 1848. These students, however, represented but a small minority among educated Finns,

[28] Ibid., pp. 147-55; Paasivirta, *Finland and Europe*, pp. 88-92, 96-100, 107-8.

who generally saw the future of their country in terms of a social and cultural development different from that of both Sweden and Russia. Scandinavianism probably never had much of a chance of becoming a dominant political and intellectual movement among them, but the Russian authorities continued to react nervously to all signs of Scandinavianist sentiment in Finland.[29]

One obvious alternative to Scandinavianism was a program of internal reform undertaken by the Finns themselves as loyal subjects of Alexander II. On September 8/20, 1856, Frans Ludvig Schauman, a professor of theology and the future bishop of Borgå, boldly outlined such a program in a speech at Helsingfors University in connection with Alexander II's coronation in Moscow. Expressing gratitude to Alexander for the love he had demonstrated toward "your Finnish people," Schauman affirmed that the Finns would remain true to their oath of working "unremittingly for Finland's welfare and happiness." First of all, according to Schauman, the Finnish people aspired to achieve an "independent, national development"—that is, the development of its culture, literature, material well-being, Christian way of life, and "own laws and social institutions." Although never a Fennoman, Schauman, like Snellman, held that acceptance of Finnish as a language of culture and education was a condition for Finland's further progress as a nation. In a common endeavor to promote such progress, he emphasized, neither Alexander nor the Finnish people wanted to do anything that did not conform to Finland's laws and constitution, a most important provision of which was that the people, through its representatives from the four Estates, had the right to consider and give advice concerning Finnish internal affairs in Diets convened by the ruler. Schauman, who had an interest in constitutional law because of his own research and lectures on church law, described for Alexander in some detail the scope of the Diet's activities and functions, as well as its relationship to the sovereign power based on the Swedish Form of Government of 1772 and Union and Security Act of 1789. Alexander's reconvening the Diet after a lapse of fifty years would, Schauman suggested, pave the way for the discussion and implementation of measures to promote the development of industry, agriculture, commerce, the merchant marine, education, culture, and the welfare of the Finnish people. "Our prayers for you

[29] Estlander, *Elva årtionden ur Finlands historia*, 1: 254-55, 267-68; Kirby, *Finland and Russia*, pp. 42-51; Lolo Krusius Ahrenberg, *Der Durchbruch des Nationalismus und Liberalismus im politischen Leben Finnlands 1856-1863*, Annales Academiae Scientiarum Fennicae, no. 33 (Helsinki: Druckerei-A.G. der Finnischen Literaturgesellschaft, 1934), pp. 29-41, 64-65.

[Alexander II]," Schauman concluded, "rise up to God who is the King of all kings and the Lord of all lords, the Father of all fathers in heaven and on earth, and your name shall be blessed from generation to generation by all true citizens of Finland."[30]

Seven years after Schauman's speech Alexander II summoned the first Finnish Diet since Alexander I appeared before the assembled Finnish Estates at Borgå in 1809. In 1856 Schauman's boldness in presuming to speak for the Finnish people had greatly irritated Alexander II, who had Schauman reprimanded through Armfelt and university authorities in Helsingfors. At the time Schauman delivered his speech, his attempt to formulate Finnish goals and objectives was premature, since neither the Finnish and Russian authorities nor most educated Finns, who had just experienced thirty years of paternalistic rule under Nicholas I, were accustomed to thinking in terms of having representatives of the four Estates participate actively in the shaping of Finland's future. At the beginning of Alexander II's reign, however, attitudes regarding internal reform changed rapidly among both Russians and Finns. A new and ambitious governor-general, F.W.R. von Berg, vigorously promoted economic reforms and, as a Livland nobleman, favored the convocation of a Finnish Diet. At the same time, such Finns as Armfelt, Snellman, Fabian Langenskiöld, and Johan Philip Palmén worked to reassure Russians about the loyalty and dependability of Finns and to direct the attention of their Finnish compatriots to essential tasks of internal cultural, economic, and political reform.

In the years immediately following the Crimean War, the Russian authorities displayed considerably less hesitation and nervousness in dealing with the issues of internal reform in Finland than they did in Congress Poland, the western *gubernii*, and the Baltic provinces. As early as March 1856, while visiting Helsingfors, Alexander II asked the Finnish Senate to prepare for him proposals regarding the extension and promotion of trade, maritime commerce, and industry; the linkup of the interior of the country with the outside world through the construction of railways and new canals; the organization of schools for rural communities; and the increase of salaries of lower officials. Governor-General Berg, an extraordinarily able individual and the future Russian viceroy in Warsaw, not only supported the Finns in promoting their economic development and in building Finland's first railway between Helsingfors and Tavastehus (Hämeenlinna), but he

[30] Frans Ludvig Schauman, *Tal och uppsatser rörande statsrättliga förhållanden i Finland* (Porvoo: G. L. Söderströms Förlag, 1876), pp. 1-22.

also helped them to revive the Diet and to retain the customs frontier with Russia on terms favorable to Finland. Berg, however, became increasingly unpopular among Finns because of his use of censorship powers to control the press and, especially, to forbid all discussion of the Diet question in newspapers and journals. He alienated university students, professors, and liberal leaders by unnecessarily linking them with Scandinavianism, whose danger he very much exaggerated. In addition, old-fashioned, Swedish-speaking bureaucrats disliked him because of his support for the increased use of Finnish as an official language. Like other high-ranking Russian officials, Berg viewed the language question in Finland mainly as a means of weakening the influence of Sweden; he did not believe Finnish had a future as a language of civilization and culture.[31]

Finnish State Secretary Alexander Armfelt understood the importance of Berg's efforts to promote economic progress in Finland and to support various Finnish reform projects. But Berg's active involvement in the internal affairs of Finland could only make Armfelt feel uneasy, for he had always feared the possible consequences of concentrating too much power in the hands of the governor-general. In 1857 he finally succeeded in persuading Alexander II to revive the Committee for Finnish Affairs, an advisory body for all matters referred to it by the emperor. It consisted of a chairman, the minister state secretary, his assistant, one person appointed by the tsar, and two Finns chosen jointly by the Finnish Senate and governor-general. Inasmuch as K. I. Fisher, a Russian, was replaced as assistant minister state secretary in 1857 by Armfelt's personal friend and fellow Finnish courtier Knut Emil Stjernvall-Walleen, only the single member of the Committee for Finnish Affairs appointed by the tsar was likely to be a Russian. Finns, therefore, clearly dominated the revived committee. During the decades that followed it strengthened the position of the minister state secretary vis-à-vis the governor-general in Helsingfors and often proved useful in defending Finnish interests in St. Petersburg.[32]

To keep well informed, Armfelt maintained a network of personal friends and regular correspondents in Finland who reported to him about the activities in the Finnish Senate, Helsingfors University, the provincial bureaucracy, and Finnish society in general. Added to his

---

[31] M. M. Borodkin, *Istoriia Finliandii: Vremia Imperatora Aleksandra II* (St. Petersburg: Gosudarstvennaia Tipografiia, 1908), pp. 24-31, 37-49, 64-77, 91-114; Krusius-Ahrenberg, *Der Durchbruch des Nationalismus und Liberalismus im politischen Leben Finnlands*, pp. 60-80, 301-11.

[32] Borodkin, *Istoriia . . . Aleksandra II*, pp. 49-52; Krusius-Ahrenberg, *Der Durchbruch*, pp. 129-45.

list of correspondents during the period immediately following the Crimean War was the once controversial Johan Vilhelm Snellman, who in 1856 became Professor of Ethics and Scientific System (the word philosophy was still taboo) at Helsingfors University and editor of the newspaper *Litteraturblad*. Both Armfelt and Governor-General Berg found Snellman a useful ally in combatting the influence of Scandinavianism in Finland and in educating the general reading public and students in the spirit of moral responsibility as citizens of Finland and Russia. In 1857 and 1858 Snellman largely succeeded in discrediting Scandinavianism and Swedophile liberalism by sharply criticizing Finnish exiles in Sweden who presumed to speak for Finland as well as those Finns who remained at home and sent misleading information about Finland to Swedish newspapers. At the same time, he became increasingly involved in various issues of economic and state policy, resulting eventually, in 1863, in his becoming part of Finnish officialdom as a senator. Although personally always more interested in advancing the Finnish language than in legal and constitutional matters, here too Snellman made at least a modest contribution to enlightening the public by commenting in detail in the *Litteraturblad* on the publications of the legal scholar Johan Philip Palmén.[33]

Palmén, a law professor at Helsingfors University since 1844 and dean of the law faculty from 1853 until he was appointed senator in 1867, had served as secretary of the Finnish Revision Committee of 1843 and had been mainly responsible for this committee's critical review of the codification work undertaken by Walleen and Bludov. Governor-General Berg's prohibition of discussion in the press of the Diet question in no way hindered Palmén's activities as a legal scholar. During these years he trained a new generation of legal scholars competent in all areas of Finnish constitutional law and published textbooks and scholarly studies that provided detailed discussion of the eighteenth-century Swedish legislation defining the powers and functions of the Finnish Diet. Palmén's most important publication during these years was his *Basic Laws of the Grand Duchy of Finland Together with the Pertinent Acts of State* of 1861. This edition and the handbook on the Diet prepared in 1863 by Palmén's younger colleague, Professor Johan Vilhelm Rosenberg, were the two principal reference works used by the politically inexperienced members of the Diet that was reconvened by Alexander II after a hiatus of fifty-four years.[34]

[33] Rein, *Johan Vilhelm Snellman*, 2: 1-416.
[34] Palmén, *Till hundraårsminnet af Johan Philip Palmén*, 2: 132-38, 313-97, 1167, 1171-72; Schybergson, *Finlands politiska historia*, pp. 174-75.

The specialized publications of Palmén and other legal scholars, discussion of these publications by journalists, and lectures on law and history at Helsingfors University served to inform a fairly broad public about the significance of the Borgå Diet of 1809 and about eighteenth-century Swedish constitutional precedents for representation by the Estates in Finland. Berg, who was quite aware of the growing importance of the Diet question for Finns, soon came to the conclusion that he would not obtain Finnish support for his own ambitious program of social and economic reform without some kind of consultation with the four Finnish Estates. In 1859, on Berg's advice, Alexander II made a first step in this direction by instructing the Finnish Senate to prepare a list of urgent legal and economic questions that "according to the fundamental laws could not receive a final resolution by administrative action alone." The emperor's instructions did not refer directly to summoning the Diet, but it was clear to both Berg and the Senate that the list of urgent questions lying outside the Senate's own sphere of administrative activity was intended for consideration by a Finnish Diet.[35]

On March 29/April 10, 1861, Alexander II announced his intention to form a special committee to prepare proposals for presentation to the Finnish Estates. The committee was to consist of twelve representatives of each of the four Estates. But Alexander II did not mention when the Finnish Diet would meet. Concern about social and political unrest resulting from the developing crisis in Poland and the emancipation of the Russian serfs made Alexander and his advisers uncertain about the direction of Russian borderland policy. They hesitated to commit themselves unequivocally to the principle of holding a Diet in Helsingfors in the near future. They feared that such a commitment would encourage Russian constitutionalists to expect a similar elective assembly for the Russian provinces of the empire and that Poles in the Kingdom of Poland would demand the revival of the Polish Sejm. Meanwhile, in Finland the postponement of the meeting of the Diet and the ambiguous manner in which the emperor had announced the 48-member committee gave rise to fears that this committee was intended as a surrogate for the Diet. Replacing the Diet with a 48-member committee representing the Estates was, in the opinion of Finnish leaders in Helsingfors, a violation of the fundamental laws of Finland. In order to protest against and to preclude such a possibility, they organized on April 22/May 4 some three or

[35] Krusius-Ahrenberg, *Der Durchbruch*, pp. 155-61; Jussila, *Suomen perustuslait*, pp. 216-20.

four hundred people in the first political demonstration in the history of Helsingfors. As remarkable as this demonstration was for the Finland of the mid-century, it was a restrained and moderate expression of Finnish dissatisfaction. The Finns did not imitate the Reds in Warsaw or the Russian revolutionary movement in challenging directly the authority of the Russian government. The events in Helsingfors, however, provided Armfelt with an occasion to obtain the assurance from Alexander II that the 48-member committee would act constitutionally and refer questions that "can only be resolved according to the fundamental laws" to the Diet and emperor. The replacement of the unpopular Berg with General P. I. Rokasovskii at the end of 1861 and the beginning of the 48-member committee's work on preparing proposals for the Diet in January 1862 soon restored political peace to Helsingfors.[36]

In June 1863 Alexander II announced his decision to convene the Finnish Diet in the fall of that same year. In January rebellion had broken out in Poland, but Grand Duke Konstantin Nikolaevich still served as the Russian viceroy in Warsaw, and Baltic-German Wilhelm Lieven remained Russian governor-general in Riga. Alexander and his advisers continued to hesitate to extend Murav'ev's repressive regime in Wilno to Congress Poland. As long as they did, foreign policy remained for them a very important consideration in their conduct of borderland affairs. During the spring and summer of 1863 the British and French tried to intervene diplomatically and limit Russian freedom of action in Poland. Although the Russians rejected the right of the powers to intervene on behalf of the Poles, they viewed the raising of this issue as a serious threat to the security of the empire's western frontiers. This threat, as well as the prolonged resistance to the Russian pacification of Poland, made the loyalty and cooperation of non-Polish elements in the western borderlands extremely important for Russian policy makers. Such loyalty and cooperation depended on at least partial recognition by Russia of Baltic German and Finnish claims to their legitimate rights and aspirations. The friendship of Finland, a land located in the immediate neighborhood of St. Petersburg, was, of course, essential for Russia in the event of an Anglo-French military intervention. Furthermore, a satisfied Finland would provide a welcome refutation of allegations in the increasingly

[36] Estlander, *Elva årtionden ur Finlands historia*, 1: 269-75; Schybergson, *Finlands politiska historia*, pp. 164-69; Krusius-Ahrenberg, *Der Durchbruch*, pp. 215-347; Borodkin, *Istoriia . . . Aleksandra II*, pp. 78-79, 122-29; Starr, *Decentralization and Self-Government in Russia*, pp. 262-71; V. V. Garmiza, *Podgotovka zemskoi reformy 1864 goda* (Moscow: Izdatel'stvo Moskovskogo Universiteta, 1957), pp. 51-82.

Russophobe Western press about the repressive nature of Russian policy in the borderlands of the empire.[37]

In July 1863 Alexander II appointed Snellman as chief of the Finance Department of the Finnish Senate. Up to the time he became senator and laid down his pen as journalist and editor of the *Litteraturblad*, Snellman continued to condemn various unrealistic and anti-Russian schemes of Finnish Scandinavianists and of exiles living in Sweden. He especially criticized articles appearing during the spring of 1863 in the *Helsingfors Dagblad* that advocated a Finnish flag for ships owned by Finns and a policy of neutrality in the event of a war between the Western powers and Russia over the Polish question. This apparent loyalty to Russia of Snellman and his Fennomans made them the natural allies of the Russian authorities in their efforts to develop for Russia a position of strength inside Finland. The Russian authorities then rewarded Snellman and his Fennomans for their loyalty to the empire by promising to make Finnish equal to Swedish (which remained, however, Finland's official language) in the courtroom and state offices by no later than 1883. During the 1860s Russian officials continued to see no particular danger for the empire in the promotion of the Finnish language and culture, for they viewed Finnish as a peasant language that could never compete seriously with Swedish and Russian as a language of higher culture and civilization. The development of Finnish, they believed, would produce a decline in the use of Swedish and weaken the Swedish element in Finland that still maintained close ties with Sweden. Later, such Russian officials as Governors-General F. L. Heiden and N. I. Bobrikov even optimistically viewed the Finnicization of Finland as a means of Russifying the educated strata of the Finnish population; they assumed that with the decline of Swedish, an increasing number of educated Finns would accept Russian as a language of culture because of the decline in the use of Swedish. In the 1860s, however, no serious attention was given to such plans for Russification in Finland. On the contrary, Alexander and his advisers even permitted the elimination of one of two professorships in the Russian language at Helsingfors University and the abolition in Finnish schools of all obligatory Russian-language courses and examinations. Neither Alexander II nor Finnish Minister State Secretary Armfelt approved of these measures; but they did not want to sacrifice Russia's popularity among Finns for

[37] Paasivirta, *Finland and Europe*, pp. 120-21, 129-32; V. G. Revunenkov, *Pol'skoe vosstanie 1863 g. i evropeiskaia diplomatiia* (Leningrad: Izdatel'stvo Leningradskogo Universiteta, 1957), pp. 200-355.

the sake of forcing reluctant Finnish school children and university students to learn the Russian language.[38]

In September 1863 Alexander II appeared personally in Helsingfors and opened the Finnish Diet. This institution, which met at regular intervals after 1863, made close cooperation with the Russian emperor and his advisers a political necessity for all realistic Finnish leaders. At first the four Finnish Estates (Knights and Nobility, Clergy, Burghers, and Peasants), which represented about 30 percent of the population of Finland, met and voted separately and did not have the right of legislative initiative. The usual pattern for Finnish legislation was preparation and study in the Senate and/or Finnish State Secretariat, acceptance, alteration, or rejection by the emperor, and then presentation to the Diet for approval. As long as the emperor remained well disposed, this system worked to the benefit of the Finns. In the Diets of 1863 and 1867, for example, the Finnish Estates found themselves in a position to discuss and approve important measures that freed rural local government and schools from the control of the Lutheran Church, assured peasants living on donated lands in Viborg province the same property rights that their social peers enjoyed elsewhere in Finland, brought the distillation of spirits in Finland under the control of the government, liberalized and expanded the Finnish banking system, provided funding for the establishment of a national educational system and for the construction of railways linking Helsingfors with Tammerfors and St. Petersburg, and reformed the Finnish monetary system.[39]

Of all these measures, the Finnish monetary reform was perhaps the most remarkable. It established a separate currency based on silver for Finland, with a monetary unit named the mark (*markka*) divided into a hundred pennies. The Finns first proposed a separate monetary system at the end of the 1850s because of the adverse effect of fluctuations in the value of the Russian ruble on the Finnish economy. Both A. M. Kniazhevich, Russian minister of finance from 1858 to 1862, and Rokasovskii, first as a member of the Committee for

[38] Rein, *Johan Vilhelm Snellman*, 2: 244-47, 381-440; Krusius-Ahrenberg, *Der Durchbruch*, pp. 365-403; idem, " 'Dagbladsseparatismen' år 1863 och den begynnande panslavismen," *Historiska och litteraturhistoriska studier* 30 (Skrifter utgivna av Svenska Litteratursällskapet i Finland, no. 346; Helsinki, 1954): 183-87; Osmo Jussila, "Förfinskning och förryskning: Språkmanifestet år 1900 och dess bakgrund," *Historisk tidskrift för Finland* 65 (1980): 1-17; Paasivirta, *Finland and Europe*, pp. 130-31; Borodkin, *Istoriia . . . Aleksandra II*, pp. 63-66, 243-500.

[39] Schybergson, *Finlands politiska historia*, pp. 173-78, 189-204; Estlander, *Elva årtionden*, 1: 288-305; Borodkin, *Istoriia . . . Aleksandra II*, pp. 147-315.

Finnish Affairs in St. Petersberg and then as governor-general in Helsingfors, opposed such a separate monetary system for Finland, which they considered to be contrary to the interest of the empire. The tsar's brother and Polish Viceroy Konstantin Nikolaevich and the new minister of finance after 1862, the Baltic German and liberal economist Michael von Reutern, on the other hand, favored the reform. Its approval in principle in 1862 was in accord with Russia's general policy at that time in both Finland and Poland. In August 1863, when it seemed that generosity in Finland would serve the interests of Russian foreign policy in Europe, Alexander II agreed to carry out the Finnish monetary reform once the details securing its financing had been worked out. These were arranged during the next several years, thanks to the efforts of the Finnish Diet and Senate, and on November 2/13, 1865, Alexander II promulgated the reform. This, as well as other reforms approved by the Diet, encouraged a distinctive economic and cultural development in Finland that differed appreciably from that in other parts of the empire during the second half of the nineteenth century.[40]

Finland, however, could not remain entirely unaffected by the return to bureaucratic centralism in Russia following the Polish insurrection of January 1863. In general, the Russian press gave favorable coverage to the 1863 Diet and other events in Finland. Muscovite journalist M. N. Katkov, however, considered it his patriotic duty to place Finland in the general category of dangerous borderland "separatism" when the *Helsingfors Dagblad* proposed Finnish neutrality in the event of a European war and when the Knights and Nobility Estate excluded from its membership several "foreign" noblemen who were Finns but in active Russian service. In 1865, the St. Petersburg liberal newspaper *Golos*, in commenting on the promulgation of the Finnish monetary reform, expressed similar concern about Finland's pursuit of her own interests even though she was an integral part of the Russian Empire.[41] Even more serious, growing Russian uneasiness about what was going on in the western borderlands prevented Finnish political leaders from obtaining Russian approval of a new Form of Government that would have regulated Finno-Russian relations in a manner highly favorable to Finland.

[40] Hugo E. Pipping, *Myntreformen år 1865* (Helsinki: Centraltryckeri, 1928), pp. 18-48, 66-76, 86-103, 116-40, 302-37.

[41] Keijo Korhonen, *Autonomous Finland in the Political Thought of Nineteenth Century Russia*, Annales Universitatis Turkuensis, ser. B, no. 105 (Turku: Turun Yliopisto, 1967), pp. 56-65, 75-76; Krusius-Ahrenberg, " 'Dagbladsseparatismen' år 1863 och den begynnande panslavismen," pp. 170-214.

Before he became governor-general, Rokasovskii, as a member of the Committee for Finnish Affairs, had expressed reservations about the proposed Finnish monetary reform, but between 1861 and 1864 he did not make it a point to oppose the establishment of a separate Finnish monetary system. During the first three years he served as governor-general he found himself to be a popular figure inside Finland and had a very good working relationship with Armfelt, Stjernvall-Walleen, Snellman, and Johan Mauritz Nordenstam, the influential vice chairman of the Finnish Senate. Rokasovskii, although aware of attacks against Finnish "separatism" in the Russian press, then argued that it was in Russia's interest to summon periodic Diets and to govern Finland legally in conformity with Finnish custom and law. Toward the end of 1864, however, he learned that two committees created by Alexander II in December 1863 to prepare a new Form of Government Act and a Senate reform proposed to remove the Russian governor-general from the Finnish Senate and to formulate Finnish fundamental laws in a manner that seemed to be detrimental to the empire. Seeing in the Finns' plans a personal attack against himself, Rokasovskii accused them of trying to obtain a constitution for the Finnish Grand Duchy and to limit the "Sovereign Power" (*Verkhovnaia Vlast'*) and the authority of the emperor's principal representative in Helsingfors, the governor-general. In May 1865 he even warned Alexander II about the activities of a "radical party" in Finland aiming at separating the Grand Duchy from the rest of the empire. He continued energetically and persistently to criticize the projects of the two Finnish committees and of the Senate and State Secretariat throughout 1865 and into 1866.[42]

Rokasovskii's intransigence of 1865-1866 made his position untenable as governor-general in Helsingfors. He was replaced by General N. V. Adlerberg in May 1866, but before then he managed to convince Alexander II that acceptance of the Finns' Senate and Form of Government projects would be detrimental to the interests of the empire. As a result, the Senate was not reformed and the Finns, once again, failed to gain unequivocal Russian recognition of Finland's au-

[42] Pipping, *Myntreformen år 1865*, pp. 63-64, 310-12; Borodkin, *Istoriia . . . Aleksandra II*, pp. 186-87, 220-23, 254-60, 507-46; Krusius-Ahrenberg, "Från grundlagskommitté till lantdagsordning." *Historiska och litteraturhistoriska studier* 20 (Skrifter utgivna av Svenska Litteratursällskapet i Finland, no. 298; Helsinki, 1944): 250-358; Robert Schweitzer, *Autonomie und Autokratie: Die Stellung des Grossfürstentums Finnland im russischen Reich in der zweiten Hälfte des 19. Jahrhunderts (1863-1899)*, Marburger Abhandlungen zur Geschichte und Kultur Osteuropas, no. 19 (Giessen: Wilhelm Schmitz, 1978), pp. 52-60.

tonomy on the basis of the fundamental laws of eighteenth-century Sweden.

The Finns did, however, manage to salvage one part of their work on a new Finnish Form of Government, namely, the Diet Statutes Alexander II approved in 1869. In addition to outlining detailed rules and regulations for the Finnish Diet, these statutes provided for meetings of the Diet every fifth year and specified that Finnish "fundamental laws" could only be enacted or altered through the common action of the ruler and all four Estates—two concessions obtained from a reluctant Alexander above all as a result of the efforts of Governor-General Adlerberg. These concessions unquestionably strengthened the autonomous position of the Grand Duchy within the empire, but Finnish autonomy continued to be based not on legally binding guarantees but on a sort of gentlemen's agreement.

Alexander Armfelt once compared the Finnish constitution to the illegal relationship of a married man: "Everyone knows about it, everyone tolerates it; the less it is talked about the happier the contracting parties will live with each other."[43] As long as Armfelt, his successor Stjernvall-Walleen, and Alexander II lived and as long as N. V. Adlerberg remained governor-general in Helsingfors, both Finnish and Russian publicists were discouraged from discussing publicly alleged Finnish separatism and constitutionalism. This changed after the retirements of Stjernvall-Walleen and Adlerberg and the assassination of Alexander II.

During the 1860s, as Robert Schweitzer has convincingly shown, Finland obtained from Alexander II neither a constitution nor a desired formal, legal regulation of her relationship with Russia. Until 1899, the Russian autocrat did not consider it necessary to alter the form of Finnish autonomy, but he clearly reserved for himself the right to do so should this be required by the vital interests of the empire. In Helsingfors, the governor-general, whose powers the Finns failed to limit during the 1860s, continued to represent the emperor and to head the Finnish internal administration.[44]

[43] Jac. [Johan Jakob] Ahrenberg, *Människor som jag känt: Personliga minnen* (Helsinki: Söderström, 1904), pp. 151-52.

[44] Krusius-Ahrenberg, "Från grundlagskommitté till lantdagsordning," pp. 359-433; Schweitzer, *Autonomie und Autokratie*, pp. 60-74, 98-101, 369; Borodkin, *Istoriia . . . Aleksandra II*, pp. 277-85, 288-92.

CONCLUSION

Russia's rulers during the period 1710-1870 seem to have been in essential agreement that the special rights and privileges of borderland elites could only be permitted as long as they were compatible with the interests and general welfare of the empire. Catherine II even tried to impose Russian norms on privileged local society in the western borderlands. Her son Paul and grandson Alexander restored borderland privileges but intended to limit this restoration to certain local administrative and social activities. Alexander I, as has been pointed out in the introduction to Part Two, added a qualifying clause to the routine confirmation of Livland and Estland rights and privileges, "insofar as they are in agreement with the general decrees and laws of our state." His brother, Nicholas I, pursued a policy of administrative and even cultural Russification in the western *gubernii*, Congress Poland, and the Baltic provinces. This policy was somewhat relaxed toward the end of the 1840s and during the first part of Alexander II's reign, but resumed more energetically than ever before following the Polish insurrection of 1863-1864.

It was not easy to bring the western borderlands closer to the rest of the empire. Among the complicated problems, special circumstances, and centrifugal forces that impeded administrative centralization and the homogenization of the peoples of the empire were the following:

1. The personal and arbitrary power of the tsar was not excercised consistently in support of the policies of centralizing officials in St. Petersburg but also in defense of the special privileges, rights, and interests of the borderlands.

2. Because Peter the Great and many of his successors held up the laws, institutions, and the social and political organization of the western borderlands as models for the rest of the empire to imitate, Russian centralizers often found it difficult to justify the imposition of the empire's norms on these borderlands.

3. Problems connected with the preservation of social order in a vast old-regime, multinational empire in which serfdom existed until 1861 tended to make Russia's rulers dependent locally on

231

the cooperation of the western borderlands' dominant German, Polish, and Swedish elites.

4. During wars with Sweden, Turkey, and France, foreign-policy considerations led to the granting of concessions and new rights to the privileged elites of the western borderlands, making it all the more difficult for St. Petersburg officials to achieve a greater degree of uniformity and centralization in administering the affairs of the empire.

5. Beginning in the 1820s and 1830s the growing incompatibility of Russian and Polish objectives in the western *gubernii* and Congress Poland led to conflicts that strained the empire's human and financial resources to the utmost.

6. Religion, partly because of the policies pursued by the Russian state, turned out to be a divisive rather than a unifying force in the western borderlands.

7. In the latter part of the eighteenth and early in the nineteenth century German, Polish, and Swedish elites began to use forces of social change and modernization to develop local particularism; it was only toward the very end of the period treated in this study that certain Russian intellectuals and officials understood that the same forces could be used to bring about the integration of the western borderlands into the general social, economic, and political structure of the empire.

The personal and arbitrary power of the tsar was not consistently exercised in support of the policies of centralizing officials in St. Petersburg, for the tsar often listened to the advice of those who criticized these policies. If only such courtiers from the borderlands as Adam Czartoryski, Alexander von Benckendorff, and Gustav and Alexander Armfelt had opposed the policies of St. Petersburg centralizers, the latter may have had their way more often than they actually did. Far more formidable and influential critics of their policies were the governors-general and viceroys in Helsingfors, Riga, and Warsaw. Such governors-general and viceroys, who were the personal agents of the Russian autocrat in the borderlands, possessed rank and status equivalent to the ministers' in St. Petersburg. They were inclined to defend jealously the full extent of their local authority and to view suspiciously even the most legitimate efforts of St. Petersburg ministers to make their influence felt in the borderlands. In Riga such Baltic governors-general as Filippo Paulucci, Karl Magnus von der Pahlen, Prince A. A. Suvorov, and Wilhelm Baron Lieven blocked the implementation in the Baltic provinces of a number of projects favored by St. Petersburg centralizers; and they assisted local German elites to obtain approval for programs of educational, peasant, and legal reform that often conflicted with reforms under consideration for the empire as a whole. In Helsingfors the Finns could not have achieved the degree of autonomy they did by 1870 without the support of Governors-General A. S. Menshikov, F.W.R. von Berg, and N. V. Adlerberg. In Warsaw Viceroys M. D. Gorchakov and Konstantin Nikolaevich were largely responsible for overcoming Alexander II's misgivings about going ahead with a conciliatory policy in Congress Poland at the end of the 1850s and at the beginning of the 1860s; and the "exclusive power" exercised by I. F. Paskevich, certainly no friend of the Poles, served for an entire generation to keep Congress Poland apart, as a separate Polish world, from the rest of Russia. Even in the western *gubernii*, where the Russians followed a Russificatory policy after 1831, the arbitrary power of governors-general hardly encouraged the orderly extension of the bureaucratic authority of the central ministers to this region.

The fact that Peter the Great and many of his successors admired the laws, schools, and political and social institutions of the western borderlands also slowed the progress of bureaucratic centralization. Since Peter's time the rulers of Russia had been trying to reshape society and government in Russia in the image of the old-regime, Swedish and central-European *Polizeistaat* of the seventeenth and eighteenth centuries. German, Polish, and Swedish elites of the western borderlands were well prepared for the role of intermediaries between Russia and Europe, for they had been comparatively well educated and had gained administrative experience and expertise in institutions of self-government that closely resembled those of Sweden and central and western Europe. Indeed, in the Baltic provinces, Congress Poland, and Finland, European forms of political and social organization already existed within the Russian Empire. Peter the Great, Alexander I, and even Catherine II, therefore, looked to these borderlands for ideas and inspiration in undertaking to reform Russia's internal administration. Was it, then, wise to proceed so rapidly in imposing Russian political and social norms on these borderlands? Did not Russia's laws first have to be codified, her courts and institutions of self-government reformed, her educational system expanded and improved, and—above all—her serfs emancipated?

Russian political leaders were equally deterred from pursuing a consequential centralizing policy in the western borderlands by the importance of German, Polish, and Swedish elites in maintaining political and social order. These elites had centuries of experience in controlling local peasants within a traditional framework of custom, laws, and social and political institutions. They also had a sufficient knowledge of local languages to communicate with their peasants. For a long time Russia remained dependent on German, Polish, and Swedish elites to run the local administration and economy, because until the second part of the nineteenth century there were few Russians with the expertise and knowledge of requisite languages to serve competently and effectively in the western borderlands.

At the same time, in the Baltic and "Polish" provinces the traditional elites depended on Russian military power to restore order in times of social tension and crises. In the Baltic provinces a number of widespread peasant disturbances were quelled during the eighteenth and nineteenth centuries by bringing in Russian troops. In the "Polish" borderlands, the Russian army protected Polish landowners from the fury of Ukrainian serfs and *haidamak* insurgents even before Russia acquired the Right-Bank Ukraine in the Third Partition of Poland. In the nineteenth century the Russian government and Polish landowners, despite the Polish insurrection of 1830-1831, continued to be aware of the common interests they shared in preserving social order in the countryside. Thus, the Russian authorities proceeded with extreme caution in experimenting with legislation to improve conditions among the peasantry of the western *gubernii* and Congress Poland. What reforms the Russian government did introduce before 1863 were generally carried out locally by Polish landowners and minor officials and administrators. Only after the Great Reforms had begun in Russia and after the insurrection of 1863-1864 had been crushed did Russians feel confident enough to use their own imported agents to impose Russian norms on local society in Congress Poland and the western *gubernii*.

In Finland, too, high priority was given to maintaining social order. However, during the first part of the nineteenth century, peasant unrest presented a serious problem only in Old Finland. Here peasants living on land that had been given to Russians and others by Russia during the eighteenth century had to wait until the 1860s to obtain the same rights and legal protection enjoyed by peasants elsewhere in Finland. However insignificant social unrest was in Finland before the 1850s, the Finnish and Russian official servants of Alexander I and Nicholas I were determined to do what they could to protect peasants and a handful of townsmen from Swedish nationalism and liberalism and from various other new teachings originating in western Europe. This point is perhaps best illustrated by the petty harassment of Adolf Ivar Arwidsson in the 1820s and of Johan Vilhelm

Snellman in the 1840s. Finnish officials were particularly interested in preserving the appearance of social tranquility and stability in Finland. By adroitly associating this tranquility and stability with the Russian rulers' respect for Finnish laws and institutions, Finnish leaders helped frustrate on more than one occasion the plans of certain centralizing St. Petersburg officials for Finland.

Foreign policy was another consideration in following a conciliatory policy in the western borderlands, which became part of Russia between 1710 and 1815 after wars with Sweden, Turkey, Poland, and France. The cooperation of German, Polish, and Swedish elites was essential for the conduct of Russian foreign policy in Europe throughout the period examined in this study. These elites, once their traditional rights had been recognized, helped Russia maintain her control over newly conquered areas and defend her interests as a great power. The Baltic Germans cooperated after 1710 with Russia in defeating Sweden in the Great Northern War. They were involved, as diplomats, administrators, and soldiers, in the extension of Russia's sphere of influence and control into Poland and northern Germany. Within the Polish-Lithuanian Commonwealth many Polish magnates and *szlachta* believed that their interests coincided with those of Russia, and they worked together with the Russians both before and after the three partitions of Poland. During the Napoleonic Wars, despite the faith many Poles had in Napoleon, the support for Russia among Polish magnates and landowning *szlachta* was sufficiently strong to justify a constitutional regime under the auspices of Russia in Congress Poland. Meanwhile, in 1809, Alexander I had assured the cooperation of the Swedo-Finnish Estates in consolidating Russian rule in newly conquered Finland by confirming their traditional rights and privileges and by granting them a degree of provincial autonomy they had never enjoyed as part of Sweden.

In the nineteenth century, ministers of foreign affairs in St. Petersburg were reassured by Finnish and Baltic German loyalty to Russia. They knew that revanchist and Russophobe sentiment still existed in Sweden, but whatever danger that sentiment posed for Russia was rendered insignificant by the Finns' decision to try to work out their future within the framework of the Russian Empire. Baltic Germans not only backed Russian policy in Poland but participated actively in the pacification of that country in 1830-1831 and 1863-1864. Russians particularly appreciated Baltic German and Finnish loyalty and Prussian diplomatic support during the Polish insurrection of 1863-1864, when Britain and France showed some inclination to interfere in the affairs of Congress Poland. It is to be noted that Alexander II personally opened the Finnish Diet in Helsingfors in September 1863, shortly after he had decided to replace Konstantin Nikolaevich with General F.W.R. von Berg as viceroy in Warsaw and to entrust the administration of Polish reform to the Polonophobe, N. A. Miliutin. At the same time, Wilhelm Baron von Lieven remained in Riga as Baltic governor-general until the end of 1864, when Emperor Alexander replaced him with P. A. Shuvalov. The latter brought to Riga a new program of Russian reform, but he firmly opposed hasty measures likely to affect adversely the interest of the privileged elements of local Baltic society. One reason these elements were then treated so considerately was the generally pro-Prussian and pro-German orientation of Russian foreign policy, which continued even after the unification of Germany and—despite vociferous criticism of this orientation in the Russian press—into the first years of the reign of Alexander III.

The Polish question complicated the conduct of Russian state policy both externally and internally. Externally, it offered opportunities to other powers to try to interfere in Polish-Russian relations and tended to make Russia dependent on Prussia in Europe. Internally, the incompatibility of Russian and Polish interests, which became apparent even before the insurrection of 1830-1831, persuaded the Russians to embark on a policy of Russification and repression, especially in the western *gubernii*, but they still lacked the human and financial resources to carry out this policy successfully. The Russified schools of the western *gubernii* and Paskevich's regimentation of education in Congress Poland simply failed to transform perhaps a million former *szlachta* in a borderland of approximately 600,000 square kilometers into loyal subjects of the Russian tsar. At the same time, various experiments with social, religious, and peasant reform, especially in the western *gubernii*, would seem to have exacerbated social and religious tensions among Belorussians, Lithuanians, Poles, and Ukrainians without substantially lessening the dependence of the Russian government on the landowning Polish nobility as its principal partner in maintaining social and political order in Russian lands that were once part of the Polish-Lithuanian Commonwealth.

In Congress Poland following the January Insurrection of 1863, F.W.R. von Berg, like Paskevich before him, relied mainly on soldiers, gendarmes, and policemen to carry out the purposes of Russian Polish policies. N. A. Miliutin, whom Alexander II had charged with reform of Poland's countryside and political and social structure, disliked Berg and sharply criticized the police methods Paskevich had employed in Poland between 1831 and 1855. Yet, Miliutin's own plans for the "organic transformation" of Polish society without the cooperation of the Polish nobility, clergy, and intelligentsia would seem to have been little more than fantasy. In the long run, the Polish peasant could not be relied upon as the ally of the tsar, because there was no way for the socially backward rural population of Poland to interact positively with officials imported from Russia who neither spoke Polish nor felt comfortable with Poles. Unable to obtain effective support from the peasantry and having rejected the option of support from conservative elements in the clergy, *szlachta*, and professional intelligentsia, Miliutin could not avoid dependency on the military and police apparatus of Viceroy Berg to carry out his projects. By the time of his incapacitating stroke in 1866, Miliutin had little to offer aside from administrative centralization, police regulation, and other bureaucratic solutions to the problems Russia faced in Congress Poland. That the intelligent and able Miliutin had been forced into this impasse is perhaps not all that surprising, for he was a Russian bureaucrat who had served a long apprenticeship in the Ministry of the Interior under Nicholas I and L. A. Perovskii during the 1840s and early 1850s.

The importance official Russia attached to the defense of the interests of the Orthodox Church in the conduct of policy in the western borderlands (except for Finland) is noteworthy. At a time of growing secularism and religious toleration elsewhere in Europe, Russian policy makers gradually reverted to the religious policy advocated in the eighteenth century by such anti-Polish and anti-Catholic Ukrainian churchmen as Georgii Konisskii, Mel'khidsidek, and Viktor Sadkovskii. Catherine II's identification with this policy was sporadic and, it would seem, politically motivated. By the time of Nicholas I, however, Russian historians and officials associated with the Holy Synod and the Main Administration for the Ecclesiastical Affairs of the Foreign Confessions had formulated a fairly coherent ideological justification and fashioned the bureaucratic and legal tools for the Orthodox Church's work of reunion and conversion in the western *gubernii*, Congress Poland, and the Baltic provinces. As late as 1875 the reunion with Orthodoxy of the Uniates of the Chełm district in Congress Poland was proclaimed. A system of penalties and official harassment kept these Ukrainian-speaking peasants in the Orthodox Church until the promulgation of religious tolerance in 1905, when from 100,000 to 200,000 of them converted to Roman Catholicism. The Chełm area was detached from Congress Poland and made a separate Russian *guberniia* in 1912; today, although there is still a small Ukrainian-speaking minority, it is a region of Poland.[1]

---

[1] "O nalozhenii i vzyskanii denezhnykh shtrafov s dukhovnykh lits," Wojewódzkie

Conclusion

Russian religious policy was similarly counterproductive in the Baltic provinces. In the 1840s the support given by certain high-ranking government and Church officials to peasants in Livland who sought social and economic justice through acceptance of Orthodoxy did strengthen the position of the Orthodox Church; but the overwhelming majority of Estonians and Latvians remained Lutherans, and the conversion movement was accompanied by prolonged and widespread unrest among Livland peasants, undermining the very foundations of social and political stability in that province. Beginning in 1848 and continuing until the 1860s, Governors-General Suvorov and Lieven curtailed the activities of Orthodox priests and officials in Livland. At the same time, the Russian authorities were ill-prepared to take care of the religious needs of so many new converts, a large part of whom soon pressed to revert to the Lutheranism of their ancestors, which was prohibited by Russian law. The ensuing cases of individual psychological suffering and proceedings against Lutheran pastors could only alienate many Estonians and Latvians, fan the flames of Russophobia among Baltic Germans, and give Russia a reputation for religious obscurantism and persecution in Europe and North America.

In the western *gubernii* Russian religious policy would seem to have done much to reinforce resentments and antipathies that the Catholic population of the western part of this area had long felt for Russians and the Eastern Orthodox Church. The support given by many Lithuanian and Catholic Belorussian peasants to the Polish insurrection of 1863-1864 is one illustration of this point. Russian religious policy was, to be sure, more successful among Belorussian and Ukrainian Orthodox Christians, who generally took no part in the activities of Polish insurrectionists or even assisted the Russian authorities in suppressing them. The resulting Russification of private landownership and the strengthening of the position of the Orthodox Church was not, however, an unmitigated blessing, for until the 1860s the Catholic Church and the Polish nobility played at least a modest role in promoting educational and economic progress in areas populated by Belorussian and Ukrainian peasants.

Archiwum Państwove w Lublinie, Kancelaria Gubernatora Lubelskiego, 1867, no. 72; "O vysylke Greko-uniatskikh sviashchenennikov, ustranennykh ot prikhodskikh dolzhnostei v drugie mesta," ibid., 1874, nos. 20, 93, and 272, 1875, no. 100; Józef Tomczyk (ed.), *Wojewódzkie archiwum państwowe w Lublinie: Przewodnik po zespole akt Kanceliarii gubernatora lubelskiego z lat 1866-1917* (Warsaw: Naczelna Dyrekcja Archiwów Państwowych, 1966), pp. xxii-xxiv, 9, 33-36, 94-95, 100-102; Edward Chmielewski, *The Polish Question in the Russian State Duma* (Knoxville: University of Tennessee Press, 1970), pp. 111-37.

Conclusion

After 1830, and especially after 1863-1864, such initiative was discouraged by the Russian authorities, who were more interested in social control than in promoting social and economic progress in this area. Thus, following the January Insurrection of 1863, their fear of Polish influence delayed the introduction of zemstvos into the western *gubernii* until 1910 (and then in only six of nine *gubernii*). In all *gubernii* of this area with a preponderance of Russian landowners and an Orthodox population of more than 70 percent (Kiev, Minsk, Mohylew, Podolia, and Volhynia), the proportion of literates in the general population in 1897 was less than 18.1 percent, placing these *gubernii* in the company of Bessarabia and of socially underdeveloped areas in the Left-Bank Ukraine and eastern European Russia.[2] Illiterate Belorussian and Ukrainian peasants usually did not know Russian, the communication tool necessary to establish contact with the Russian nation to which they supposedly belonged.

The importance of the borderland elites' ability to use economic and social change to achieve their respective local purposes needs to be emphasized. Before the 1870s Russian authorities were much less successful in harnessing the forces of economic and social change to unify the empire. The predecessors of Alexander II seldom fully appreciated the possibilities that education and economic and social modernization offered as a means of strengthening the ties that linked the borderlands with the rest of the empire. The borderland elites, on the other hand, had been predisposed to accept the necessity of at least a minimal social and economic reform by their participation and involvement in the affairs of the Polish-Lithuanian Commonwealth, the Duchy of Warsaw, eighteenth-century Sweden, or the Baltic corporations of the nobility and by the university studies many of them had pursued at Åbo, Kraków, and Wilno or in Germany. In the first third of the nineteenth century the more advanced parts of the western borderlands were a generation or two ahead of the empire's Russian provinces in providing educational facilities for the nobility and townsmen; and by 1870 elementary education had progressed in Finland and the Baltic provinces to the point that virtual universal literacy among Estonians, Finns, and Latvians could be achieved within a single generation. By 1820 peasants were legally free in the Baltic provinces, Congress Poland, and Finland, while the emancipation of the Russian serfs did not occur until 1861. Literacy,

---

[2] Rashin, *Naselenie Rossii za 100 let*, pp. 308-9; Ochmański, *Historia Litwy*, p. 184; *Iz istorii shkoly Belorussii i Litvy*, ed. V. Z. Smirnov, pp. 68-71; Batiushkov, *Atlas narodonaseleniia zapadnorusskogo kraia po ispovedovaniiam.*

free peasants, and various locally initiated legal, social, and economic reforms reinforced patterns of property ownership, social organization, and agricultural production that differed markedly from those of the Russian provinces of the empire. It was above all this separate socioeconomic development that made it so difficult for would-be Russifiers of the second part of the nineteenth century to carry out their programs in the Baltic provinces, Congress Poland, and Finland.

In the western *gubernii*, despite separate peasant households and the lack of repartitional tenure, patterns of educational, social, and economic development conformed more closely to those of the empire's Russian provinces. Russian officials always made a distinction between this area and the other western borderlands, whose inhabitants were expected to learn Russian and become loyal subjects of the tsar but not, necessarily, to abandon Roman Catholicism or Protestantism or their Estonian, Finnish, German, Latvian, or Swedish nationality. In the western *gubernii*, on the other hand, Belorussians and Ukrainians were considered to be Russians who had been forcibly detached by the Polish *szlachta* and Catholic and Uniate clergy from the Russian nation to which they rightfully belonged.

Only western *gubernii* where at least 30 percent of the population was Catholic (Grodno, Kowno, Wilno, and Witebsk) could boast of a literacy rate higher than the average for European Russia (22.9 percent). Kowno *guberniia*, where 75 percent of the landowners were Poles and 83 percent of the population Catholic, had a literacy rate of 42 percent, which, apart from the Baltic provinces and Finland, was exceeded in European Russia only by that of St. Petersburg *guberniia* (55 percent). Yet in 1897 no more than 6.8 percent of Kowno school-age children attended the hated official schools, compared to the average of 42 percent for all fifty-two provinces of European Russia.[3] In other words, it would seem that the relatively high rate of literacy in Kowno *guberniia* was a result of successful resistance to Russification and of the efforts of Lithuanian intellectual leaders and of the Roman Catholic clergy to educate and form the values of the younger generation in accordance with the traditions and needs of local society.

These various frustrations and dilemmas of Russian policy in the western borderlands were unmistakably reflected in the polemics and debates over Russian nationality policy during the 1860s. Following the emancipation of the Russian serfs and the Polish insurrection of 1863-1864, Russian conservative-nationalist, liberal, and Slavophile

---

[3] Rashin, *Naselenie Rossii za 100 let*, pp. 308-9; Ochmański, *Historia Litwy*, p. 184; Smirnov, *Iz istorii*, pp. 68-71; Batiushkov, *Atlas*.

journalists and intellectuals wanted the government to pursue a consequential policy that would defend the interests of the Russian national state and integrate the western borderlands organically into the general political, economic, and social structure of the empire. They emphatically rejected Polish aspirations to rule over Orthodox Russians (namely, Belorussians and Ukrainians) in the western *gubernii* as well as the arguments of German and Finnish publicists that held Russia to be morally and contractually bound to recognition of rights and privileges gained since 1710. M. N. Katkov and Iurii Samarin warned that such rights and privileges could become exceedingly dangerous for Russia if combined with Finnish "separatism" and the Germanization of the Estonians and Latvians (a danger, incidentally, that they clearly exaggerated) in the Baltic provinces. In addition, Katkov and Samarin noted with alarm the growing German nationalism in the Baltic provinces at a time of Prussian military victories and national consolidation within the German Confederation.

Among the critics of official Russian policy in the western borderlands, Iurii Samarin above all understood some of the weaknesses of Russian social and economic policy in this region. He wanted the government to remedy the defects of borderland social and economic policy by vigorously promoting the social and economic interests of the Belorussian, Estonian, Latvian, and Ukrainian peasants living in the western *gubernii*, Congress Poland, and the Baltic provinces. Such a policy, he believed, would win the mass of the local population for Russia and weaken the position of traditional elites still unwilling to unify with the rest of Russia.[4] The rural population of the western borderlands, however, was seen by Samarin from above and through the eyes of a Russian landowner, though an enlightened one, to be sure. Thus, he overestimated the attraction of Orthodoxy for Latvians and Estonians and would seem to have detected in them little potential for developing their own national cultures. He viewed the peasants of Belorussia and the Ukraine with similar condescension. When he was in Congress Poland in 1863 in the company of N. A. Miliutin, he no doubt displayed considerable expertise concerning economic and social conditions among Polish peasants, but his hatred of what he called "Polonism" blinded him to the latent significance of Roman Catholicism and the Polish nationality for these peasants. But he knew very little about Lithuanians and Finns. He did not welcome the con-

---

[4] E. C. Thaden, "Samarin's *Okrainy Rossii* and Official Policy in the Baltic Provinces," *Russian Review* 33 (1974): 405-13; Thaden, *Conservative Nationalism in Nineteenth-Century Russia*, pp. 133-37.

solidation of Finnish autonomy during the 1860s and did not devote himself seriously to that question.

St. Petersburg officials of the 1860s shared many of the concerns of Russian nationalistic journalists and intellectuals about the empire's western borderlands. Thus, such influential officials as D. A. Tolstoi and the brothers D. A. and N. A. Miliutin could usually be counted on to support measures aiming at extending the Russian Great Reforms to the borderlands, pacifying Poland, favoring "Russian," Orthodox or even Polish peasants at the expense of non-Russian landowners, and, generally speaking, defending what they considered Russian national interests. Such other equally influential officials as P. A. Shuvalov and P. A. Valuev favored a more cautious and moderate policy in uniting the peoples of this area with the rest of Russia, for they did not want to risk total alienation of the traditional borderland elites in an empire in which public order continued to be so dependent on the social and economic predominance of the landowning nobility in the countryside. In the 1860s the proponents of moderation and consideration for the social and material interests of traditional elites still prevailed in the formulation of Russian policy for the western borderlands; later, a more ambitious policy of cultural Russification, at least for a short time, was to follow. Finland, in many ways, remained a special case, but, as was pointed out at the end of Chapter 10, the Russian tsar reserved for himself the right to alter the form of Finnish autonomy if this were required by what he considered the vital interests of Russia.

In last analysis, the traditional societies and separate institutions and special rights and privileges of Russia's western borderlands represented an obvious anachronism in nineteenth-century Europe. Ironically, at the very time Russians began to aspire to build a modern nation-state, new national elites emerged in these borderlands. More and more of these new elites came to demand separate national and cultural rights for themselves, while the older German, Swedish, and even Polish elites still played a prominent role in the local economy, society, and cultural establishment. It proved difficult for tsarist Russia to undo the work of the centuries that had shaped the institutions, customs, cultures, and social values and structures of the empire's western borderlands. The interests of these borderlands often did not converge with those of the rest of the empire; in 1870 there was, in certain important respects, more diversity than there had been 160 years before.

GLOSSARY OF
PLACE AND TERRITORIAL NAMES

Listed are the English, German, Polish, or Swedish place and territorial names most frequently used in the text. For additional information concerning foreign terms, administrative and territorial units, institutions, and offices, see my glossary in *Russification in the Baltic Provinces and Finland, 1855-1914.*

Åbo (Sw.); Turku (Fin.)
Åland Islands (Sw.); Ahvenanmaa (Fin.)
Białystok (Pol.); Belostok (Rus.); Belastok (Belor.)
Borgå (Sw.); Porvoo (Fin.)
Bracław (Pol.); Bratslav (Rus. and Ukr.)
Brahestad (Sw.); Raahe (Fin.)
Chełm (Pol.); Kholm (Rus. and Ukr.)
Czehryń (Pol.); Chigirin (Rus.); Chyhyryn (Ukr.)
Dorpat (Ger.); Tartu (Est.)
Estland (Ger.); Eestimaa (Est.)
Helsingfors (Sw.); Helsinki (Fin.)
Iziasław (Pol.); Iziaslav (Rus. and Ukr.)
Kowno (Pol.); Kovno (Rus.); Kaunas (Lith.)
Krzemieniec (Pol.); Kremenets (Rus.); Kremianets (Ukr.)
Kuda (Ger.); Kuuda (Est.)
Kurland (Ger.); Kurzeme (Lat.)
Left-Bank and Right-Bank Ukraine (Eng.): Beginning in the second part of the seventeenth century, the Dnieper River separated the Polish Right-Bank Ukraine from the Russian Left-Bank Ukraine. The city of Kiev on the right bank and the Zaporozhian region within the bend of the Dnieper were, however, included in the Russian part of the partitioned Ukraine. In the nineteenth century Kiev was reunited with the Right-Bank Ukraine, where Polish influence remained strong until after the insurrection of 1863-1864.
Livland (Ger.); Vidzeme (Lat.); Liivimaa (Est.)
Lwów (Pol.); L'vov (Rus.); L'viv (Ukr.); Lemberg (Ger.)
Mitau (Ger.); Jelgava (Lat.)
Mohylew (Pol.); Mogilev (Rus.); Magileu (Belor.); Mohyliv (Ukr.)

Nyland (Sw.); Uusimaa (Fin.)
Nystad (Sw.); Uusikaupunki (Fin.)
Ösel (Ger.); Saaremaa (Est.)
Pernau (Ger.); Pärnu (Est.)
Podolia (Eng.); Podole (Pol.); Podillia (Ukr.); Podoliia (Rus.)
Połock (Pol.); Polotsk (Rus.); Polatsk (Belor.)
Reval (Ger.); Tallinn (Est.); Revel' (Rus.)
Słuck (Pol.); Slutsk (Belor. and Rus.)
Sveaborg (Sw.); Suomenlinna (Fin.)
Tammerfors (Sw.); Tampere (Fin.)
Tavastehus (Sw.); Hämeenlinna (Fin.)
Uleåborg (Sw.); Oulu (Fin.)
Viborg (Sw.); Viipuri (Fin.); Vyborg (Rus.)
Volhynia (Eng.); Wołyń (Pol.); Volyn' (Rus. and Ukr.)
Walk (Ger.); Valga (Est.); Valka (Lat.)
Wenden (Ger.); Cēsis (Lat.)
Wilno (Pol.); Vil'na (Rus.); Vilnius (Lith.)

BIBLIOGRAPHY

ARCHIVES

Bremen, Germany.
    Universitätsbibliothek. Welding collection.
Helsinki, Finland.
    Valtionarkisto. Poliitisia asiakirjoja.
Leningrad, USSR.
    Gosudarstvennaia publichnaia biblioteka im. M. E. Saltykova-
    Shchedrina, f. 208 (A. V. Golovnin).
    Institut russkoi literatury Akademii nauk SSSR. f. 265 (I. V.
    Gurko). f. 559 (P. A. Valuev).
    Tsentral'nyi gosudarstvennyi istoricheskii arkhiv SSSR. f. 1016
    (Von der Pahlen family collection).
Lublin, Poland.
    Wojewódzkie Archiwum Państwowe w Lublinie, Kanceliaria Gu-
    bernatora Lubelskiego, 1867.
Moscow, USSR.
    Gosudarstvennaia publichnaia biblioteka im. V. I. Lenina. f. 26
    (Samarin family collection).

BOOKS AND ARTICLES

Ahokas, Jaako. *A History of Finnish Literature.* Bloomington: Indiana University Press, 1973.

Allen, W.E.D. *The Ukraine: A History.* 2nd ed. New York: Russell & Russell, 1963.

Amburger, Erik. *Geschichte der Behördenorganisation Russlands von Peter dem Grossen bis 1917.* Leiden: E. J. Brill, 1966.

Ammann, Albert M. *Abriss der ostslawischen Kirchengeschichte.* Vienna: Verlag Herder, 1950.

Armstrong, John A. "Mobilized Diaspora in Tsarist Russia: The Case of the Baltic Germans." In *Soviet Nationality Politics and Practices.* Ed. J. R. Azrael, pp. 63-104. New York: Praeger, 1978.

Askenazy, Szymon. *Rosya-Polska 1815-1830.* Lwów: H. Altenberg, 1907.

Bantysh-Kamenskii, N. N. *Istoricheskoe izvestie o voznikshei v Pol'she Unii.* 2nd ed. Vilnius: A. Syrkin, 1866.

Batiushkov, P. N., ed. *Atlas narodonaseleniia zapadnorusskogo kraia po ispovedovaniiam sostavlen pri Ministerstve vnutrennikh del v Kantsteliarii zavedyvaiushchego ustroistvom Pravoslavnykh tserkvei zapadnykh gubernii.* St. Petersburg: n.p., 1864.

―――. *Belorussiia i Litva: Istoricheskaia sud'ba severo-zapadnogo kraia.* St. Petersburg: "Obshchestvennaia Pol'za," 1890.

―――. *Podoliia: Istoricheskoe opisanie.* St. Petersburg: "Obshchest-vennaia Pol'za," 1891.

Beauvois, Daniel. *Lumières et société en Europe de l'Est: L'Université de Vilna et les écoles polonaises de l'Empire russe (1804-1832).* 2 vols. Lille: Atelier Reproduction des Thèses Université de Lille III, 1977.

Berendts, E. N. *Lektsii po administrativnomu pravu Velikogo Kniazhestva Finliandii.* Vol. 2: *Glavnye organy upravlenii v Finliandii.* St. Petersburg: R. Golike, A. Vil'borg, 1903.

Berg, N. V. *Zapiski N. V. Berga o pol'skikh zagovorakh i vosstaniiakh 1831-1862.* Moscow: "Russkii Arkhiv," 1873.

―――. *Zapiski N. V. Berg o pol'skikh zagovorakh i vosstaniiakh 1831-1864.* 4 vols. Poznań: Tipografiia Krashevskogo, 1883-1884.

Berghausen, Janusz. *Ruch patriotyczny w Królestwie Polskim 1833-1850.* Warsaw: PWN, 1974.

Berkis, Alexander V. *The History of the Duchy of Courland (1561-1795).* Towson, Maryland: P. M. Harrod, 1969.

Bienemann, Friedrich. *Die Statthalterschaft in Liv- und Estland (1783-1796): Ein Capitel aus der Regierungspraxis Katharinas II.* Leipzig: Duncker und Humblot, 1886.

Blackwell, William L. "Alexander I and Poland: The Foundations of His Polish Policy and Its Repercussions on Russia, 1801-1825." Princeton University Ph.D. dissertation, 1959.

Blinov, Iv. *Gubernatory: Istoriko-iuridicheskii ocherk.* St. Petersburg: E. L. Pentkovskii, 1905.

Blum, Karl Ludwig. *Ein russischer Staatsmann: Des Grafen Jakob Johann Sievers Denkwürdigkeiten zur Geschichte Russlands.* 4 vols. Leipzig-Heidelberg: C. F. Winter'sche Verlagsbuchhandlung, 1857-58.

Bock, Woldemar von, ed. *Livländische Beiträge: Zur Verbreitung gründlicher Kunde von der protestantischen Landeskirche und dem deutschen Landesstaate in den Ostseeprovinzen Russlands, von ihrem guten Rechte und von ihrem Kampf um Gewissens-*

freiheit. 3 vols. Berlin: Stilke & van Muyden, 1867-1868; Leipzig: Duncker & Humblot, 1869-1871.

Bonsdorff, Carl von. *Gustav Mauritz Armfelt: Levnadsskildring.* 4 vols. Skrifter utgivna av Svenska Litteratursällskapet i Finland, nos. 212, 223, 231, 245. Helsinki: Mercators Tryckeri, 1930-1934.

————. *Opinioner och stämningar i Finland 1808-1814.* Skrifter utgivna av Svenska Litteratursällskapet i Finland, no. 141. Helsinki: Tidnings- och Tryckeri-Aktienbolagets Tryckeri, 1918.

————. *Staatsmän och dignitärer: Interiörer ur ämbetsmannavärlden i Finland vid ryska tidens början.* Skrifter utgivna av Svenska Litteratursällskapet i Finland, no. 159. Helsinki: Tidnings- och Tryckeri-Aktienbologets Tryckeri, 1921.

Borodkin, M. M. *Istoriia Finliandii: Vremia Elizavety Petrovny.* St. Petersburg: Gosudarstvennaia Tipografiia, 1910.

————. *Istoriia Finliandii: Vremia Imperatora Aleksandra I.* St. Petersburg: Gosudarstvennaia Tipografiia, 1909.

————. *Istoriia Finliandii: Vremia Aleksandra II.* Petrograd: Gosudarstvennaia Tipografiia, 1908.

————. *Istoriia Finliandii: Vremia Imperatora Nikolaia I.* St. Petersburg: Gosudarstvennaia Tipografiia, 1915.

Bortnowski, Władysław. *Powstanie listopadowe w oczach Rosjan.* Uniwersytet Łódzki, Prace Instytutu Historycznego, no. 10. Warsaw: Wykonanno w Zakładzie Graficznim Politechniki Warszawskiej, 1964.

[Buchholtz, Alexander]. *Deutsch-protestantische Kämpfe in den Baltischen Provinzen Russlands.* Leipzig: Duncker & Humblot, 1888.

————. *Fünfzig Jahre russischer Verwaltung in den baltischen Provinzen Russlands.* Leipzig: Duncker & Humblot, 1883.

Čeginskas, K. J. "Die Russifizierung und ihre Folgen in Litauen unter zaristischer Herrschaft." *Commentationes Balticae* 6/7 (1959): 87-138.

Chechulin, N. D., ed. *Nakaz Imperatritsy Ekateriny II, dannyi Kommissii o sochinenii proekta novogo ulozheniia.* Pamiatniki russkogo zakonodatel'stva 1649-1832 gg., izdavaemye Imperatorskoi Akademiei Nauk, no. 2. St. Petersburg: Imperatorskaia Akademiia Nauk, 1907.

Czartoryski, A. J. *Mémoires du Prince Adam Czartoryski et correspondance avec l'Empereur Alexandre 1er.* 2 vols. Paris: Librairie Plon, 1887.

Czepulis-Rastenis, Ryszarda. *"Klassa umysłowa": Inteligencja Królestwa Polskiego 1832-1862.* Warsaw: "Książka i Wiedza," 1973.

Deutschbaltisches biographisches Lexikon 1710-1960. Begun by Olaf Welding and edited by Wilhelm Lenz with the assistance of Erik Amburger and Georg Krusenstjern. Cologne: Böhlau, 1970.

Donnert, Erich. *Johann Georg Eisen (1717-1779): Ein Vorkämpfer der Bauernbefreiung in Russland*. Leipzig: Koehler & Amelang, 1978.

Doroshenko, Dmytro. *A Survey of Ukrainian History*. Ed. O. W. Gerus. Rev. ed., Winnipeg: Humeniuk Publications Foundation, 1975.

Druzhinin, N. M. *Gosudarstvennye krest'iane i reforma P. D. Kiseleva*. 2 vols. Moscow-Leningrad: Akademiia Nauk, 1946-1958.

Dukes, Paul. *Catherine the Great and the Russian Nobility: A Study Based on the Materials of the Legislative Commission of 1767*. Cambridge, England: At the University Press, 1967.

Dziennik praw. 71 vols. Warsaw: W Drukarni Rządowej, 1815-1871.

Eckardt, Julius. *Bürgerthum und Büreaukratie*. Leipzig: Duncker & Humblot, 1870.

——. *Livland im achtzehnten Jahrhundert: Umrisse zu einer livländischen Geschichte*. Leipzig: Duncker & Humblot, 1876.

Elias, Otto-Heinrich. *Reval in der Reformpolitik Katharinas II.* Quellen und Studien zur baltischen Geschichte, no. 3. Bonn-Bad Godesberg: Verlag Wissenschaftliches Archiv, 1978.

——. "Zur Lage der undeutschen Bevölkerung im Riga des 18. Jahrhunderts." *Jahrbücher für Geschichte Osteuropas*, n.s. 14 (1966): 481-84.

Estlander, Bernhard. *Elva årtionden ur Finlands historia*. 5 vols. Helsinki: Söderström, 1929-1930.

Fabre, Jean. *Stanislas-Auguste Poniatowski et l'Europe des lumières*. Paris: "Les Belles Lettres," 1952.

Garve, Horst. *Konfession und Nationalität: Ein Beitrag zum Verhältnis von Kirche und Gesellschaft in Livland im 19. Jahrhundert*. Wissenschaftliche Beiträge zur Geschichte und Landeskunde Ostmitteleuropas, no. 110. Marburg: J. G. Herder-Institut, 1978.

Golobutskii, V. A. *Zaporozhskoe kazachestvo*. Kiev: Gospolitizdat, 1957.

Groniowski, Krzysztof. *Realizacja reformy uwłaszczeniowej 1864 r.* Warsaw: PWN, 1963.

——. *Uwłaszczenie chłopów w Polsce: Geneza-realizacja-skutki*. Warsaw: Wiedza Powszechna, 1976.

——. "Walka Milutina z Bergiem (spór o reorganizacje Królestwa Polskiego po roku (1863)." *Kwartalnik historyczny* 49 (1962): 891-906.

Grot, Ia. K. *Perepiska Ia. K. Grota s P. A. Pletnevym.* Ed. K. Ia. Grot. 3 vols. St. Petersburg: Tipografiia Ministerstva Putei Soobshcheniia, 1896.

Haltzel, Michael. *Der Abbau der deutschen ständischen Selbstverwaltung in den Ostseeprovinzen Russlands 1855-1905.* Marburger Ostforschungen, no. 37. Marburg: J. G. Herder-Institut, 1977.

Hirn, Hans. *Alexander Armfelt.* 2 vols. Skrifter utgivna av Svenska Litteratursällskapet in Finland, nos. 267, 315. Helsinki: Mercators Tryckeri, 1938-1948.

History of Poland. Ed. A. Gieysztor, S. Kieniewicz, et al. Warsaw: PWN, 1968.

Hoensch, Jorg K. *Sozialverfassung und politische Reform: Polen im vorrevolutionären Zeitalter.* Cologne-Vienna: Böhlau Verlag, 1973.

Isakov, S. G. *Ostzeiskii vopros v russkoi pechati 1860-kh godov.* Turku Riikliku Ülikool, Toimetised, no. 107. Tartu: Riikliku Ülikool, 1961.

———. *Russkii iazyk i literatura v uchebnykh zavedeniiakh Estonii XVIII-XIX stoletii.* 2 vols. Tartu: Tartuskii Gosudarstvennyi Universitet, 1973.

Istoriia Belorusskoi SSR. Ed. L. S. Abetsedarskii et al. 2 vols. Minsk: Akademiia Nauk Belorusskoi SSR, 1961.

Istoriia Estonskoi SSR. Ed. A. Vassar and G. Naan. 3 vols. Tallinn: Estonskoe Gosudarstvennoe Izdatel'stvo, 1961-1974.

Istoriia Latviiskoi SSR. Ed. A. A. Drīzulis. 2nd ed. Riga: "Zinātne," 1971.

Istoriia Pravitel'stvuiushchego senata za dvesti let 1711-1911 gg. Ed. A. N. Filippov et al. 5 vols. St. Petersburg: Senatskaia Tipografiia, 1911.

Istoriia Ukrainskoi SSR. Ed. K. K. Dubina et al. 2 vols. Kiev: "Naukova Dumka," 1969.

Iz istorii shkoly Belorussii i Litvy. Ed. V. Z. Smirnov. Izvestiia Akademii Pedagogicheskikh Nauk RSFSR, no. 131. Moscow: "Prosveshcheniia," 1964.

Jannau, H. J. *Geschichte der Sklaverey, und Charakter der Bauern in Lief- und Ehstland: Ein Beytrag zur Verbesserung der Leibeigenschaft.* Riga: n.p., 1786.

Jobert, Ambroise. *La Commission d'Education Nationale en Pologne (1773-1794).* Paris: Droz, 1941.

Jones, Robert E. *The Emancipation of the Russian Nobility.* Princeton, N.J.: Princeton University Press, 1973.

Jungar, Sune. *Finländare i Ryssland: Utflyttningan till Ryssland 1809-1917.* Turku: Åbo Akademi, 1971.

Jussila, Osmo. *Suomen perustuslait venäläisten ja suomalaisten tulkintojen mukaan 1808-1863.* Historiallisia Tutkimuksia Julkaissut, no. 77. Helsinki: Suomen Historiallinen Seura, 1969.

Jutikkala, Eino (with Kauko Perinen). *A History of Finland.* Tr. Paul Sjöblom. London: Thames and Hudson, 1962.

Kabuzan, V. M. *Narodonaselenie Rossii v XVIII-pervoi polovine XIX veke.* Moscow: Akademiia Nauk SSSR, 1963.

Kahk, Juhan. *Die Krise der feudalen Landwirtschaft in Estland (Das zweite Viertel des 19. Jahrhunderts).* Tallinn: "Eesti Raamat," 1969.

————. *Krest'ianskoe dvizhenie i krest'ianskii vopros v Estonii v kontse XVIII i v pervoi chetverti XIX veka.* Tallinn: Akademiia Nauk Estonskoi SSR, 1962.

————. *Murrangulised neljakümnendad.* Tallinn: "Eesti Raamat," 1978.

Käiväräinen (Kiaiviariainen), I. I. *Mezhdurnarodnye otnosheniia na severe Evropy v nachale XIX veka i prisoedinenie Finliandii k Rossii v 1809 godu.* Petrozavodsk: Karel'skoe Knizhnoe Izdatel'stvo, 1965.

Kaplan, Herbert H. *The First Partition of Poland.* New York and London: Columbia University Press, 1962.

Karpachev, A. M., and P. G. Kozlovskii. "Dinamika chislennosti naseleniia Belorussii vo vtoroi polovine XVII-XVIII v." In *Ezhegodnik po agrarnoi istorii vostochnoi Evropy 1968 g.* Ed. Iu. V. Bromlei et al., pp. 81-94. Leningrad: "Nauka," 1972.

Kharuzin, M. N., ed. *Ukazatel' khronologicheskii i sistematicheskii zakonov dlia Pribalitiiskikh gubernii s 1704 g. po 1888 g.* Tallinn: Estliandskaia Gubernskaia Tipografiia, 1888.

Kieniewicz, Stefan. *The Emancipation of the Polish Peasantry.* Chicago: University of Chicago Press, 1969.

Kiprianovich, G. Ia. *Istoricheskii ocherk pravoslaviia, katolichestva i Unii v Belorussii i Litve.* 2nd ed. Vilnius: I. Bliumovich, 1899.

Klochkov, M. V. *Ocherki pravitel'stvennoi deiatel'nosti vremeni Pavla I.* Petrograd: Senatskaia Tipografiia, 1916.

Koberdowa, Irena. *Wielki książe Konstanty w Warszawie 1862-1863.* Warsaw: PWN, 1962.

Kohut, Zenon E. "Myths Old and New: The *Haidamak* Movement and the Koliivshchyna (1768) in Recent Historiography." *Harvard Ukrainian Studies* 1 (1977, no. 3): 359-78.

————. "The Abolition of Ukrainian Autonomy (1763-1786): A Case Study of the Integration of a Non-Russian Area into the Empire." University of Pennsylvania Ph.D. dissertation, 1975.

Koialovich, M. O. *Istoriia vossoedineniia zapadnorusskikh Uniatov starykh vremen.* St. Petersburg: Vtoroe Otdelenie Sobstvennoi E.I.V. Kantseliarii, 1873.

Koniukhova, T. A. *Gosudarstvennaia derevnia Litvy i reforma P. D. Kiseleva.* Moscow: Izdatel'stvo Moskovskogo Universiteta, 1975.

Konstitutsionnaia khartiia 1815 goda i nekotorye drugie akty byv-shego Tsarstva Pol'skogo (1814-1881). Biblioteka Okrain Rossii, no. 5. St. Petersburg: A. S. Suvorin, 1907.

Korelin, A. P. *Dvorianstvo v poreformennoi Rossii 1861-1904 gg.: Sostav, chislennost', korporativnaia organizatsiia.* Moscow: "Nauka," 1979.

Korhonen, Keijo. *Autonomous Finland in the Political Thought of Nineteenth Century Russia.* Annales Universitatis Turkuensis, ser. B, no. 105. Turku: Turun Yliopisto, 1967.

————. *Suomen asian komitea: Suomen korkeimman hallinnon järjestelyt ja toteuttaminen vuosina 1811-1826.* Historiallisia Tutkimuksia, no. 65. Helsinki: Suomen Historiallinen Seura, 1963.

Korzon, Tadeusz. *Wewnętrzne dzieje Polski za Stanisława Augusta (1764-1794): Badania Historyczne ze Stanowiska ekonomicznego i administracyjnego.* 6 vols. 2nd ed. Cracow-Warsaw: T. Parocki, 1897-1898.

Koshik, A. K. "Inventarnaia reforma 1847-1848 gg. i krest'ianskoe dvizhenie na provoberezhnoi Ukraine." In Kievskii gosudarstvennyi universitet, *Istoricheskii sbornik* (1949, no. 2), pp. 97-122.

Kostiushkov, I. I. *Krest'ianskaia reforma 1864 goda v Tsarstve Pol'skom.* Moscow: Akademiia Nauk, 1962.

Kropotov, D. A. *Zhizn' grafa M. N. Murav'eva v sviazi s sobytiiami ego vremeni i do naznacheniia ego gubernatorom v Grodno.* St. Petersburg: V. Bezobrazov, 1874.

Krusius-Ahrenberg, Lolo. " 'Dagbladsseparatismen' år 1863 och den begynnande panslavismen." *Historiska och litteraturhistoriska studier* 30 (Skrifter utgivna av Svenska Litteratursällskapet i Finland, no. 346; Helsinki, 1954): 170-214.

————. *Der Durchbruch des Nationalismus und Liberalismus im politischen Leben Finnlands 1856-1863.* Annales Academiae Scientiarum Fennicae, no. 33. Helsinki: Druckerei-A.G. der Finnischen Literaturgesellschaft, 1934.

Krusius-Ahrenberg, Lolo. "Från grundlagskommitté till lantdagsordning." *Historiska och litteraturhistoriska studier*, 20 (Skrifter utgivna av Svenska Litteratursällskapet i Finland, no. 298; Helsinki, 1944): 219-433.

Kruus, Hans. *Talurahva käärimine Lōuna-Eestis XIX sajandi 40-ndail aastail*. Tartu: Eesti Kirjanduse Kirjastus, 1930.

Sbornik materialov i statei po istorii Pribaltiiskogo kraia. 4 vols. Riga: A. I. Lipinskii, 1876-1882.

Kucharzewski, Jan. *Epoka Paszkiewiczowska: Losy oświaty*. Warsaw-Cracow: Gebethner i Wolff, 1914.

Kutrzeba, Stanisław. *Historya ustroju Polski w zarysie*. 4 vols. Lwów-Warsaw: Bernard Poloniecki, 1905-1920.

Lehtonen, U. L. *Die polnischen Provinzen Russlands unter Katharina II. in den Jahren 1772-1782*. Tr. G. Schmidt. Berlin: Georg Reimer, 1907.

Lenchyk, Wasyl. *The Eastern Catholic Church and Czar Nicholas I*. Rome-New York: Ukrainian Catholic University Press, 1966.

Lenz, Wilhelm. *Der baltische Literatenstand*. Wissenschaftliche Beiträge zur Geschichte und Landeskunde Ost-Mitteleuropas, no. 7. Marburg: n.p., 1953.

Lepkowski, Tadeusz. *Polska-narodziny nowoczesnego narodu 1764-1870*. Warsaw: PWN, 1970.

Leroy-Beaulieu, Anatole. *Un homme d'état russe (Nicolas Milutine) d'après sa correspondance inédite: Etude sur la Russie et la Pologne pendant la règne d'Alexandre II (1855-1872)*. Paris: Hachette, 1884.

Lesch, Bruno. "Greve Leo Perovskij och Finland." *Historisk tidskrift för Finland* 30 (1945): 1-19.

Likowski, Edward. *Dzieje Kościoła unickiego na Litwie i Rusi*. 2 vols. 2nd ed. Warsaw: Gebethner i Wolff, 1906.

Lillja, Alexis A. *Arsenijj Andrejevitj Zakrevskij*. Helsinki: Mercators Tryckeri, 1948.

Lincoln, W. Bruce. *Nikolai Miliutin: An Enlightenend Russian Bureaucrat*. Newtonville, Mass.: Oriental Research Partners, 1977.

Łojek, Jerzy. *Misja Debolego w Petersburgu w latach 1787-1792*. Wrocław: Ossolineum, 1962.

―――. *Przed Konstytucje Trzeciego Maja*. Warsaw: Pax, 1977.

―――. *Upadek Konstytucji 3 Maja*. Wrocław: Ossolineum, 1976.

Lord, Robert H. *The Second Partition of Poland: A Study in Diplomatic History*. Cambridge: Harvard University Press, 1915.

Łubieńska, Cecylia. *Sprawa dysydencka 1764-1766*. Cracow-Warsaw: W. L. Anczyc, 1911.

Luciani, Georges. *Le livre de la genèse du peuple ukrainien.* Paris: Institut d'Etudes Slaves, 1956.

Madariaga, Isabel de. *Russia in the Age of Catherine the Great.* New Haven and London: Yale University Press, 1981.

Maikov, P. M. *Vtoroe otdelenie sobstvennoi ego imperatorskogo velichestva kantseliarii 1826-1882: Istoricheskii ocherk.* St. Petersburg: I. N. Skorokhodov, 1909.

Markina, V. A. *Krest'iane pravoberezhnoi Ukrainy Konets XVII- 60-e gody XVIII st.* Kiev: Izdatel'stvo Kievskogo Universiteta, 1971.

Meleshko, V. I. *Ocherki agrarnoi istorii vostochnoi Belorussii (vtoraia polovina XVII-XVIII v.).* Minsk: "Nauka i Tekhnika," 1975.

Merkel, Garlieb. *Die Letten, vorzüglich in Liefland, am Ende des philosophischen Jahrhunderts: Ein Beitrag zur Völker- und Menschenkunde.* Leipzig: Heinrich Graff, 1797.

Miliutin, N. A., ed. *Issledovaniia v Tsarstve Pol'skom po vysochaishemu poveleniiu, proizvedennye pod rukovodsvom Senatora, Statssekretaria Miliutina.* 6 vols. St. Petersburg: n.p., 1863-1866.

Mizia, Tadeusz. *O Komisji Educacji Narodowej.* Warsaw: PWN, 1972.

Mościcki, Henryk. *Dzieje porozbiorowe Litwy i Rusi 1772-1800.* Vilnius: J. Zawadzki, [1913].

Mykhailyna, P. V. *Mista Ukrainy v period feodalizmu.* Chernivtsi: Chernivets'kyi Derzhavnyi Universytet, 1971.

Neupokoev, V. I. *Krest'ianskii vopros v Litve vo vtoroi treti XIX veka.* Moscow: "Nauka," 1976.

Neuschäffer, Hubertus. *Katharina II. und die baltischen Provinzen.* Beitrage zur baltischen Geschichte, no. 2. Hannover: Hirschheydt, 1975.

Nifontov, A. S. *Rossiia v 1848 g.* Moscow: Uchpedgiz, 1949.

Nol'de, A. E. *Ocherki po istorii kodifikatsii mestnykh grazhdanskikh zakonov pri grafe Speranskim.* 2 vols. St. Petersburg: Senatskaia Tipografiia, 1906-1914.

Nol'de, B. E. *Ocherki russkogo gosudarstvennogo prava.* St. Petersburg: "Pravda," 1911.

O'Brien, C. Bickford. *Muscovy and the Ukraine: From the Pereiaslav Agreement to the Truce of Andrusovo, 1654-1667.* Berkeley and Los Angeles: University of California Press, 1963.

Obushenkova, L. A. *Korolevstvo Pol'skoe v 1815-1830 gg.: Ekonomicheskoe i sotsial'noe razvitie.* Moscow: "Nauka," 1979.

Ocherki istorii shkoly i pedagogicheskoi mysli narodov SSSR XVIII v.-pervaia polovina XIX v. Ed. M. F. Shabaeva. Moscow: "Pedagogika," 1973.

Ocherki istorii SSSR. Period feodalizma: Rossiia vo vtoroi polovine XVIII v. Ed. A. I. Baranovich, B. B. Kafengauz, et al. Moscow: Akademiia Nauk, 1956.

Ochmański, Jerzy. *Historia Litwy.* Wrocław: Ossolineum, 1967.

——. *Litewski ruch narodowo-kulturalny w XIX wieku.* Białystok: PWN, 1965.

Paasivirta, Juhani. *Finland and Europe: International Crises in the Period of Autonomy 1808-1914.* Tr. A. F. and S. R. Upton, and ed. D. G. Kirby. Minneapolis: University of Minnesota Press, 1981.

Palmén, E. G. *L'oeuvre demi-séculaire de la société de litterature finnoise et le mouvement nationale en Finlande de 1831 à 1881.* Helsinki: Société de Litterature Finnoise, 1882.

——. *Till hundraårsminnet af Johan Philip Palmén 1811-1911.* 2 vols. Helsinki: F. Tilgman, 1915-1917.

Pelech, Orest. "Toward a Historical Sociology of the Ukrainian Ideologues in the Russian Empire of the 1830's and 1840's." Princeton University Ph.D. dissertation, 1976.

Pelenski, Jaroslaw. "The Haidamak Insurrections and the Old Regimes in Eastern Europe." In *The American and European Revolutions, 1776-1848: Sociopolitical and Ideological Aspects.* Ed. J. Pelenski, pp. 228-47. Iowa City: University of Iowa Press, 1980.

Peterson, Claes. *Peter the Great's Administrative and Judicial Reforms: Swedish Antecedents and the Process of Reception.* Skrifter utgivna av Institutet för Rättshistorisk Forskning, series 1; Rättshistorisk Bibliotek, no. 29. Stockholm: A.-B. Nordiska Bokhandeln, 1979.

Petukhov, E. V. *Imperatorskii iure'evskii, byvshii derptskii universitet za sto let ego sushchestvovaniia (1802-1902).* 2 vols. Tartu: K. Mattisen, 1902; St. Petersburg: Senatskaia Tipografiia, 1906.

Pipping, Hugo E. *Myntreformen år 1865.* Helsinki: Centraltryckeri, 1928.

Pistohlkors, Gert von. *Ritterschaftliche Reformpolitik zwischen Russifizierung und Revolution.* Göttinger Bausteine zur Geschichtswissenschaft, no. 48. Göttingen: Musterschmidt, 1978.

Pokrovskii, S. P. *Ministerskaia vlast' v Rossii: Istoriko-iuridicheskoe issledovanie.* Iaroslav: Tipografiia Gubernskogo Pravleniia, 1906.

Poland and Ukraine: Past and Present. Ed. Peter J. Potichnyj. Edmonton-Toronto: The Canadian Institute of Ukrainian Studies, 1980.

Predtechenskii, A. V. *Ocherki obshchestvenno-politicheskoi istorii Rossii v pervoi chetverti XIX veka.* Moscow-Leningrad: Akademiia Nauk SSSR, 1957.

Problemy istoricheskoi demografii SSSR: Sbornik statei. Ed. R. N. Pullat. Tallinn: Akademiia Nauk Estonskoi SSR, 1977.

Raeff, Marc. "The Well-ordered Police State and the Development of Modernity in Seventeenth- and Eighteenth-Century Europe: An Attempt at a Comparative Approach." *American Historical Review* 80 (1975): 1221-44.

Ragsdale, Hugh, ed. *Paul I: A Reassessment of His Life and Reign.* UCIS Series in Russian and East European Studies, no. 2. Pittsburgh: University Center for International Studies, 1979.

Rashin, A. G. *Naselenie Rossii za 100 let (1811-1913 gg.): Statisticheskie ocherki.* Moscow: Gosstatizdat, 1956.

Rein, Thiodolf. *Johan Vilhelm Snellman.* 2 vols. 2nd ed. Helsinki: Otava, 1904.

Reinke, N. *Ocherk zakonodatel'stva Tsarstva Pol'skogo (1807-1881 g.).* St. Petersburg: Senatskaia Tipografiia, 1902.

Rhinelander, Laurens Hamilton. "The Incorporation of the Caucusus into the Russian Empire: The Case of Georgia, 1801-1854." Columbia University Ph.D. dissertation, 1971.

Roberts, Michael. *The Swedish Imperial Experience.* London-New York-Melbourne: Cambridge University Press, 1979.

Rozhdestvenskii S. V., ed. *Istoricheskii obzor deiatel'nosti Ministerstva narodnogo prosveshcheniia 1802-1902.* St. Petersburg: Gosudarstvennaia Tipografiia, 1902.

Russia, Komitet ministrov. *Istoricheskii obzor deiatel'nosti Komiteta ministrov.* Ed. S. M. Seredonin. 4 vols. St. Petersburg: Gosudarstvennaia Tipografiia, 1902.

Sacke, Georg. "Livländische Politik Katharinas II." *Quellen und Forschungen zur baltischen Geschichte* 5 (1944): 26-72.

Samarin, Iu. F. *Sochineniia.* Vols. 1-10, 12 published. Moscow: A. I. Mamontov, 1877-1911.

Sambuk, S. M. *Politika tsarizma v Belorussii vo vtoroi polovine XIX veka.* Minsk: "Nauka i Tekhnika," 1980.

Sbornik materialov dlia istorii prosveshcheniia v Rossii izvlechennykh iz arkhiva Ministerstva narodnogo prosveshcheniia. 4 vols. St. Petersburg: "Obshchestvennaia Pol'za," 1893-1902.

Sbornik statei po istorii prava posviashchennyi M. F. Vladimirskomu-Budanovu. Ed. M. N. Iasinskii. Kiev: S. V. Kul'zhenko, 1904.

Schauman, Frans Ludvig. *Tal och uppsatser rörende statsrättliga förhållanden i Finland.* Porvoo: G. L. Söderströms Förlag, 1876.

Scheibert, Peter. *Volk und Staat in Finnland in der ersten Hälfte des vorigen Jahrhunderts.* Breslau: P. Plischke, 1941.

Schirren, Carl. *Livländische Antwort an Herrn Juri Samarin.* 1869; reprint ed., Hannover-Döhren: Harro von Hirschheydt, 1971.

Schmidt, Oswald, *Rechtsgeschichte Liv-, Est- und Curlands.* Ed. E. von Rottbeck. 1894; reprint ed., Hannover-Döhren: Hirschheydt, 1968.

Schweitzer, Robert. *Autonomie und Autokratie: Die Stellung des Grossfürstentums Finnland im russischen Reich in der zweiten Hälfte des 19. Jahrhunderts (1863-1899).* Marburger Abhandlungen zur Geschichte und Kultur Osteuropas, no. 19. Giessen: Wilhelm Schmitz, 1978.

Schybergson, M. G. *Finlands politiska historia 1809-1919.* Helsinki: Söderström & Co., 1923.

Semashko, Iosif. *Zapiski Iosifa Mitropolita Litovskogo.* 4 vols. St. Petersburg: Imperatorskaia Akademiia Nauk, 1883.

Semevskii, V. I. *Krest'ianskii vopros v Rossii v XVIII i pervoi polovine.* 2 vols. St. Petersburg: "Obshchestvennaia Pol'za," 1888.

Serczyk, Władysław. "The Commonwealth and the Cossacks in the First Quarter of the Seventeenth Century." *Harvard Ukrainian Studies* 2 (1978): 73-93.

———. *Hajdamacy.* Cracow: Wydawnictwo Literackie, 1972.

[Shafranov, S. N.]. *Istoricheskii obzor mer pravitel'stva dlia usileniia v ostzeiskom krae sposobov k izucheniiu russkogo iazyka.* St. Petersburg: I. Ogrizko, 1863.

Shcherbatov, A. P. *General-Fel'dmarshal Kniaz' Paskevich: Ego zhizn' i deiatel'nost'.* 7 vols. St. Petersburg: V. A. Berezovskii, 1888-1904.

Snellman, Johan Vilhelm. *Läran om staten.* Stockholm: Zacharias Haeggström, 1842.

Solov'ev, S. M. *Istoriia Rossii.* 15 vols. Moscow: Sotsekizdat, 1959-1966.

———. *Geschichte des Falles von Polen.* Tr. J. Spörer. Gotha: E. F. Thienemann, 1865.

Speer, Helmut. *Das Bauernschulwesen im Gouvernement Estland von Ende des achtzehnten Jahrhunderts bis zur Russifizierung.* Tartu: J. G. Krüger, 1936.

Staël von Holstein, Baron R. "Die Kodifizierung des baltischen Provinzialrechts." BM 52 (1901): 185-208, 249-80, 305-58.

————. "Zur Geschichte der livländischen Privilegien." BM 51 (1901): 1-30, 81-98.

Starr, S. Frederick. *Decentralization and Self-Government in Russia 1830-1870.* Princeton: Princeton University Press, 1972.

Staszyński, Edward. *Polityka oświata cartu w Królestwie Polskim.* Warsaw: Państwowe Zakłady Wydawnictw, 1968.

Stone, Daniel. *Polish Politics and National Reform 1775-1788.* Boulder: East European Quarterly, 1976.

Studia historica in honorem Hans Kruus. Ed. J. Kahk and A. Vassar. Tallinn: Eesti Teaduste Akadeemia Ajaloo Institut, 1971.

Subtelny, Orest. *The Mazepists: Ukrainian Separatism in the Early Eighteenth Century.* Boulder: East European Monographs, 1981.

Suni, L. V. *Ocherk obshchestvenno-politicheskogo razvitiia Finliandii 50-70e gody XIX v.* Leningrad: "Nauka," 1979.

Suziedelis, S. A. "The Lithuanian Peasantry of Trans-Niemen Lithuania, 1807-1864: A Study of Social, Economic and Cultural Change." University of Kansas Ph.D. dissertation, 1977.

Tabiś, Jan. *Polacy na Uniwersytecie Kijowskim 1834-1863.* Cracow: Wydawnictwo Literackie, 1974.

Takolander, Alfons. *Erik Gabriel Melartin.* 2 vols. Ekenäs: Ekenäs Tryckeri Aktiebolag, 1926-1927.

Taranovskii, F. "Politicheskaia doktrina v Nakaze Imperatorsitsy Ekateriny II." In *Sbornik statei po istorii prava posviashchennyi M. F. Vladimirskomu-Budanovu.* Ed. M. N. Iasinskii. Kiev: S. V. Kul'zhenko, 1904.

Thackeray, Frank W. *Antecedents of Revolution: Alexander I and the Polish Kingdom, 1815-1825.* Boulder: East European Monographs, 1980.

Thaden, Edward C., ed. *Russification in the Baltic Provinces and Finland, 1855-1914.* Princeton: Princeton University Press, 1981.

Tobien, Alexander von. *Die Agrargesetzgebung Livlands im 19. Jahrhundert.* 2 vols. Berlin: Puttkammer & Mühlbrecht, 1899; Riga: G. Löffler, 1911.

————. *Die Livländische Ritterschaft in ihrem Verhältnis zum Zarismus und russischen Nationalismus.* 2 vols. Riga: G. Löffler, 1925; Berlin: Walter deGruyter, 1930.

Tolstoi, D. A. *Romanism in Russia: An Historical Survey.* Tr. Mrs. M'Kibbin. 2 vols. 1874; reprint ed., New York: AMS Press, 1971.

Tommila, Päiviö. *La Finlande dans la politique européene en 1809-1815.* Studia Historica, no. 3. Helsinki: Suomen Historiallinen Seura, 1962.

Truchim, Stefan. *Współpraca polski-rosyjska nad organizacją szkolnictwa rosyjskiego w paczątkach XIX wieku*. Łodź: Ossolineum, 1969.

Ulashchik, N. N. *Predposylki krest'ianskoi reformy 1861 g. v zapadnoi Belorussii*. Moscow: "Nauka," 1965.

Uustalu, Evald. *The History of the Estonian People*. London: Boreas, 1952.

Uvarov, S. S. *Desiatiletie Ministerstva narodnogo prosveshcheniia, 1833-1843 gg*. St. Petersburg: Tipografiia Imperatorskoi Akademii Nauk, 1864.

Valuev, P. A. *Dnevnik P. A. Valueva ministra vnutrennikh del*. Ed. P. A. Zaionchkovskii. 2 vols. Moscow: Akademiia Nauk, 1961.

Vernadsky, George V. *La charte constitutionnelle de l'Empire russe de l'an 1820*. Paris: Librairie du Recueil Sirey, 1933.

Villebois, Arthur von. "Die Landvolksschulen." In *Baltische Bürgerkunde: Versuch einer gemeinverständlichen Darstellung der Grundlagen des politischen und sozialen Lebens in den Ostseeprovinzen Russlands*. Ed. Carl von Schilling and Burchard von Schrenck, pp. 240-55. Riga: G. Löffler, 1980.

Wandycz, Piotr S. *The Lands of Partitioned Poland, 1795-1918*. Seattle: University of Washington Press, 1974.

Wasilewski, Leon. *Litwa i Białoruś*. Cracow: "Książka," [1912].

Wedel, Hasso von. *Die Estländische Ritterschaft vornehmlich zwischen 1710 und 1783: Das erste Jahrhundert russischer Herrschaft*. Osteuropäische Forschungen, no. 18. Königsberg-Berlin: Ost-Europa-Verlag, 1935.

Wihksninsch, N. *Die Aufklärung und die Agrarfrage in Livland*. Riga: Verlag Walters und Rapa, 1933.

Winiarski, Bohdan. *Les institutions politiques en Pologne au XIXe siècle*. Paris: Picart, 1924.

Wittram, Reinhard. *Baltische Geschichte 1180-1918: Die Ostseelande Livland, Estland, Kurland*. Munich: Oldenbourg, 1954.

————, ed. *Baltische Kirchengeschichte*. Göttingen: Vandenhoeck & Ruprecht, 1956.

————. *Liberalismus baltischer Literaten: Zur Entstehung der baltischen politischen Presse*. Riga: G. Löffler, 1931.

————. *Meinungskämpfe im baltischen Deutschtum während der Reformepoche des 19. Jahrhunderts*. Riga: E. Bruhns, 1934.

————. *Peter I Czar und Kaiser: Zur Geschichte Peter des Grossen in seiner Zeit*. 2 vols. Göttingen: Vandenhoeck & Ruprecht, 1964.

Wójcik, Zbigniew. *Traktat andruszowski 1667 roku i jego geneza*. Warsaw: PWN, 1959.

Bibliography

Woliński, Janusz. *Polska i kościół prawosławny: Zarys historyczny.* Lwów: Ossolineum, 1936.

Wuorinen, John H. *Nationalism in Modern Finland.* New York: Columbia University Press, 1931.

Yaney, George. *The Systematization of Russian Government: Social Evolution in the Domestic Administration of Imperial Russia 1711-1905.* Urbana-London-Chicago: University of Illinois Press, 1973.

Zaionchkovskii, P. A. *Provedenie v zhizn' krest'ianskoi reformy 1861 g.* Moscow: Sotsekgiz, 1958.

Zatko, J. J. "The Organization of the Catholic Church in Russia, 1772-1784." *Slavonic and East European Review* 43 (1965): 303-13.

Zutis, Ia. Ia. *Ostzeiskii vopros v XVIII veke.* Riga: Knigoizdatel'stvo, 1946.

―――. *Politika tsarizma v Pribaltike v pervoi polovine XVIII v.* Moscow: Gosudarstvennoe sotsial'no-ekonomicheskoe Izdatel'stvo, 1937.

Zyzniewski, Stanley J. "Russian Policy in the Congress Kingdom of Poland, 1863-81." Harvard University Ph.D. dissertation, 1956.

INDEX

Index

Index

Left-Bank Ukraine, 8, 9-10, 17, 18, 24, 35

Legislative Commission (1767), 19; and agrarian reform, 22; and Baltic provinces, 20; and Ukraine, 20

Lelewel, Joachim, 79

Łepkowski, Tadeusz, 79

"Letters from Riga" (Samarin), 182, 187

Levashov, V. V., 125

liberals: in Baltic provinces, 191-92; Swedish-speaking in Finland, 212

liberum veto: in Poland-Lithuania, 3, 34, 48; abolition of, 49

Lieven, Karl von, 111

Lieven, Paul von, 195; as Livland *Landmarschall*, 192

Lieven, Wilhelm von, 194, 236; and decentralization in Baltic provinces, 232-33; as governor-general in Riga, 193-94, 225; and judicial reform, 193-94; and Orthodox Church, 190, 238; and Russian language in Baltic schools, 190

Linsén, Johan Gabriel, 214

Lintsevskii, Gervasii. *See* Gervasii Lintsevskii, Bishop of Pereiaslav

literacy: in Baltic provinces, 7, 111; in Belorussia, 239; in Congress Poland, 166; Estonian, 197-98, 239; in Finland, 82, 213, 239; in Kowno *guberniia*, 240; Latvian, 197-98, 239; Lithuanian, 240; in Russia, 111; Swedish state and, 82; Ukrainian, 239; in western *gubernii*, 139, 239, 240

Literaten, 21, 23, 98, 112, 191, 192. *See also* literati

literati, 11

Literaturblad (Snellman), 223, 226

Lithuania: education in, 240; political and social repression in, 77; population of, 53n; question of reunion with Poland, 77; Uniates in, 52-53

Lithuanian peasants: and Roman Catholic Church, 141-42; and Polish insurrection of 1863-64, 137, 238

Lithuanians: and Cyrillic alphabet, 142; population in western *gubernii*, 140

Lithuanian Statute, 35, 44, 54; abolition of, 123, 125-26

Little Russia. *See* Left-Bank Ukraine

Little Russian College, 24

Little Russian Hetmanate: abolition of, 24. *See also* hetmanate

Livland: area and population of, 5; local government in, 6, 99-100, 103; political crisis of 1803 in, 101

Livland Diet, 6; and agrarian reform, 22-23, 101, 104, 105, 183-85, 191; and Fölkersahm reform, 183-84; regulations of, 15; Riga representatives in, 15

Livländische Antwort an Herrn Juri Samarin (Schirren), 195

Livländische Beiträge (Bock), 195

livländischen Landesprivilegien und deren Confirmation, Die (Mueller), 181

Livland Land Survey Commission, 107

Livland Regional Inspection Commissions, 105-106, 107

Livland *Ritterschaft*, 97; and agrarian reform, 183-86; composition of, 15; register of 1747, 15; and Fölkersahm, 191, and Paulucci, 103

Livland statute of 1804, 105

local government: Alexander I and, 60-61; in areas annexed in 1793-1795, 51; in Baltic provinces, 6, 7, 9, 13-14, 15, 30, 109; Catherine II and, 23; in Congress Poland, 144, 152; in Estland, 6; in Finland, 88; in Kurland, 96-97; in Left-Bank Ukraine, 9-10; in Livland, 6, 99-100, 103; Nicholas I and, 177-78; non-Russian elites and, 80; Paul I and, 60; in Poland-Lithuania, 34; reform in Russia, 25-26; in Riga, 100; in Sweden, 6-7; Swedish influence on Baltic, 7; Troshchinskii and, 99; in western *gubernii*, 66-67, 68, 124. *See also* rural self-government

Loewis of Menar, Friedrich von, 102, 103, 104

Lönnrot, Elias: and Åbo Romanticists, 214; background of, 213-14; and Finnish Literary Society, 214-15; at Helsingfors University, 218; *Kalevala*, 208, 214, 215, 216

Lower Land Courts, 27, 28, 102

Lower *Rasprava*, 27

lustracje, 133-34, 135, 138

Lutheran Church: and Baltic conversion

Index

Roman Catholic Church (*cont.*)
of, 46, 67; in Eastern Belorussia and
Latgale, 47n; and education in Kowno
guberniia, 240; and education in western *gubernii*, 238; and literacy in
western *gubernii*, 142, 240; in Lithuania, 52-53; and Lithuanian national
movement, 141-42; in Poland-Lithuania, 33, 36; punitive measures
against, 131
Roman Catholic Ecclesiastical College,
67-68; Uniate Department of, 131
Rosenberg, Andreas von, 70
Rosenberg, Johan Vilhelm, 223
Rostworowski, E., 48
Rozhdestvenskii, S. V., 110-11
Rumiantsev, P. A., 18, 24, 25
Runeberg, Johan Ludvig: and Åbo Romanticists, 214; background of, 213-14;
Fänrik Ståls sägner, 215; and Grot,
208; "Our Land," 215
rural self-government: in Baltic provinces, 7, 109, 192; in Congress Poland,
163; in Russia, 118
Russian landowners: in Eastern Belorussia, 45; in western *gubernii*, 142-43,
238
Russian language: in Baltic provinces,
28, 173-74, 189-90, 195; in Congress
Poland, 146, 149, 152, 164, 166; at
Dorpat University, 173-74, 195; in
Eastern Belorussia, 45; in Finland, 89,
207-208, 209, 226-27; in Old Finland,
83; in western *gubernii*, 138, 139
Russian officialdom: and agrarian reform
in western *gubernii*, 137-38; and Baltic
agrarian reform, 16, 104, 105-106, 107;
and Baltic provinces, 110-11, 111-12,
194, 195, 199; and borderland policy,
119-20; and Committee for Finnish Affairs, 91; in Congress Poland, 146,
152-53; and education in Congress Poland, 150; and Estonian and Latvian
nationalism, 198-99; and Finland, 91-
92, 217-18, 221-22, 226; and Livland
Landräte, 99-100; and office of governor-general, 102-103; and Paulucci,
102-103; and Polish policy of Alexander I, 75; and Polish schools of
Right-Bank Ukraine, 70; and Russian

language in Baltic provinces, 195; and
Scandinavianism, 220; and social control in western *gubernii*, 239; in western *gubernii*, 138; and *szlachta*, 33-34,
123-24
Russian public opinion: and Baltic question, 192, 194, 241; criticism of
pro-German foreign policy, 236; and
Finland, 228, 229, 241; and Polish
question, 241
Russian schools: in western *gubernii*,
128-29
Russian Senate: Warsaw departments of
(ninth and tenth), 151, 152, 158
Russian teachers: in Baltic provinces, 173
Russification: in Baltic provinces, 198; in
Congress Poland, 80, 164-65; in Eastern Belorussia, 45; in Finland, 226; in
western borderlands, 242; in western
gubernii, 80, 124, 236
Russophobia: among Baltic Germans,
238; in Finland, 218; in Sweden, 235;
in Western press in 1863, 225-26
Russo-Turkish War of 1768-1774, 41
Ruthenian language: in Poland-Lithuania, 30

Sadkovskii, Viktor. *See* Viktor Sadkovskii, Archbishop of Minsk, Iziasław,
and Bracław
Saima: published by Snellman, 216;
suppression of, 217, 218
Saima Canal, 205
St. Cyril and Methodius, Brotherhood
of, 140, 153
St. Petersburg Committee for the Investigation of Livland Affairs, 105, 106,
107
St. Petersburg *guberniia*: literacy in, 240
St. Vladimir University. *See* Kiev University
Salza, Alexander von, 104
Samarin, Iu. F., 119, 166, 178; and Baltic provinces, 180, 187, 196; *Borderlands of Russia*, 196; on emancipation
in Baltic provinces, 183; on emancipation in Russia, 161; and Governor-
General Suvorov, 187-88; "Letters
from Riga," 182, 187; and Murav'ev,
159; and Nicholas I, 187-88; and Or-

274

LIBRARY OF CONGRESS CATALOGING IN PUBLICATION DATA

Thaden, Edward C.
  Russia's western borderlands, 1710-1870.

  Bibliography: p.
  Includes index.
  1. Soviet Union—Politics and government—1689-1800. 2. Soviet Union—Politics and government—19th century. 3. Nationalism—Europe, Eastern. 4. Europe, Eastern—Politics and government. I. Thaden, Marianna Forster. II. Title.
DK62.9.T47   1985   947   84-13300
ISBN 0-691-05420-7 (alk. paper)

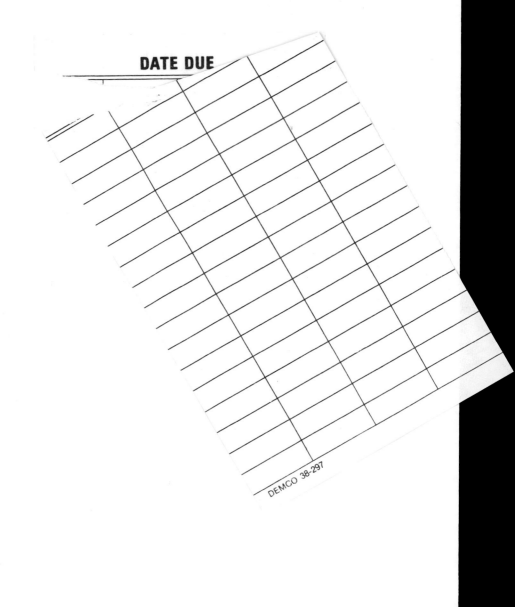

DATE DUE

DEMCO 38-297